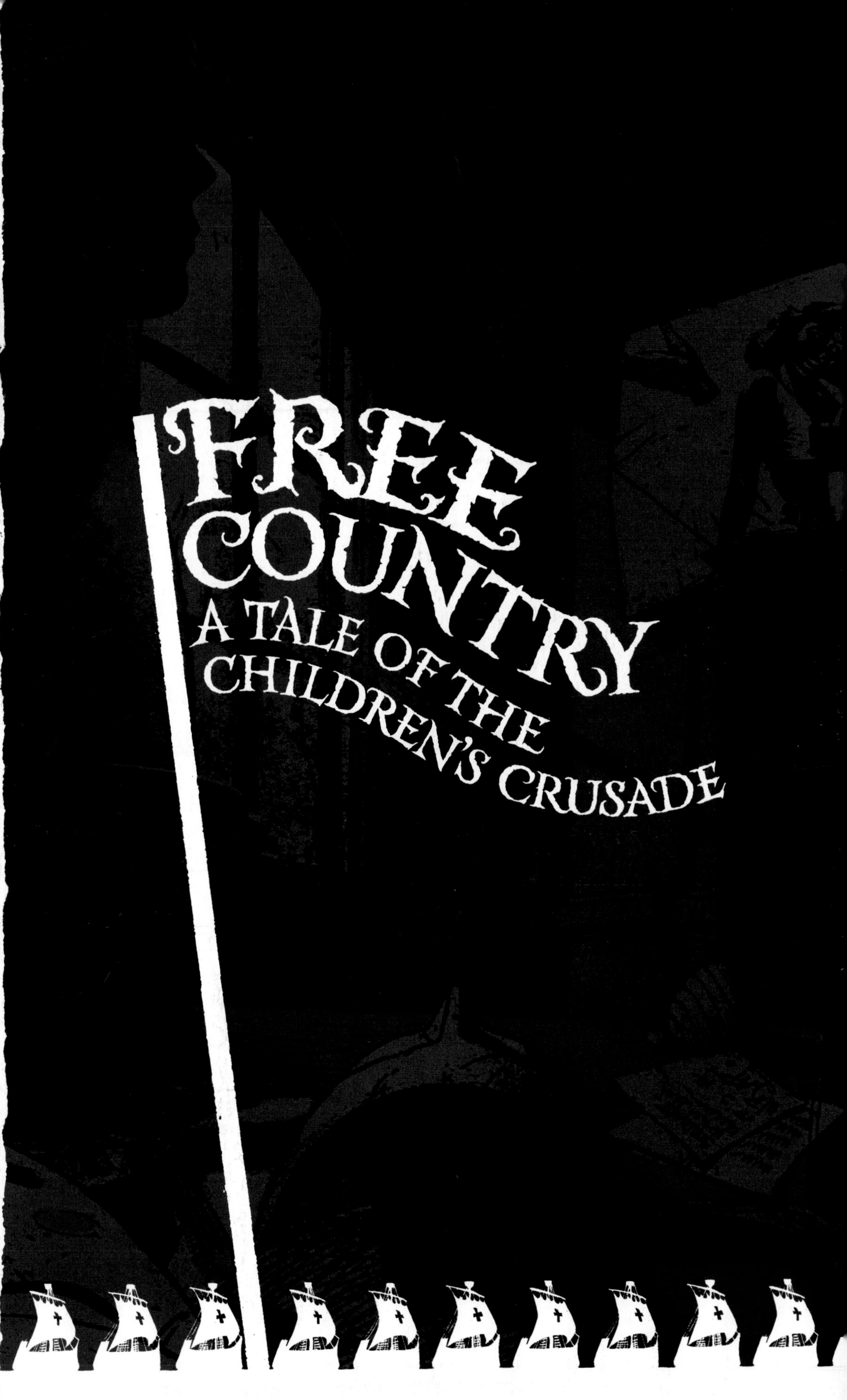
FREE COUNTRY
A TALE OF THE CHILDREN'S CRUSADE

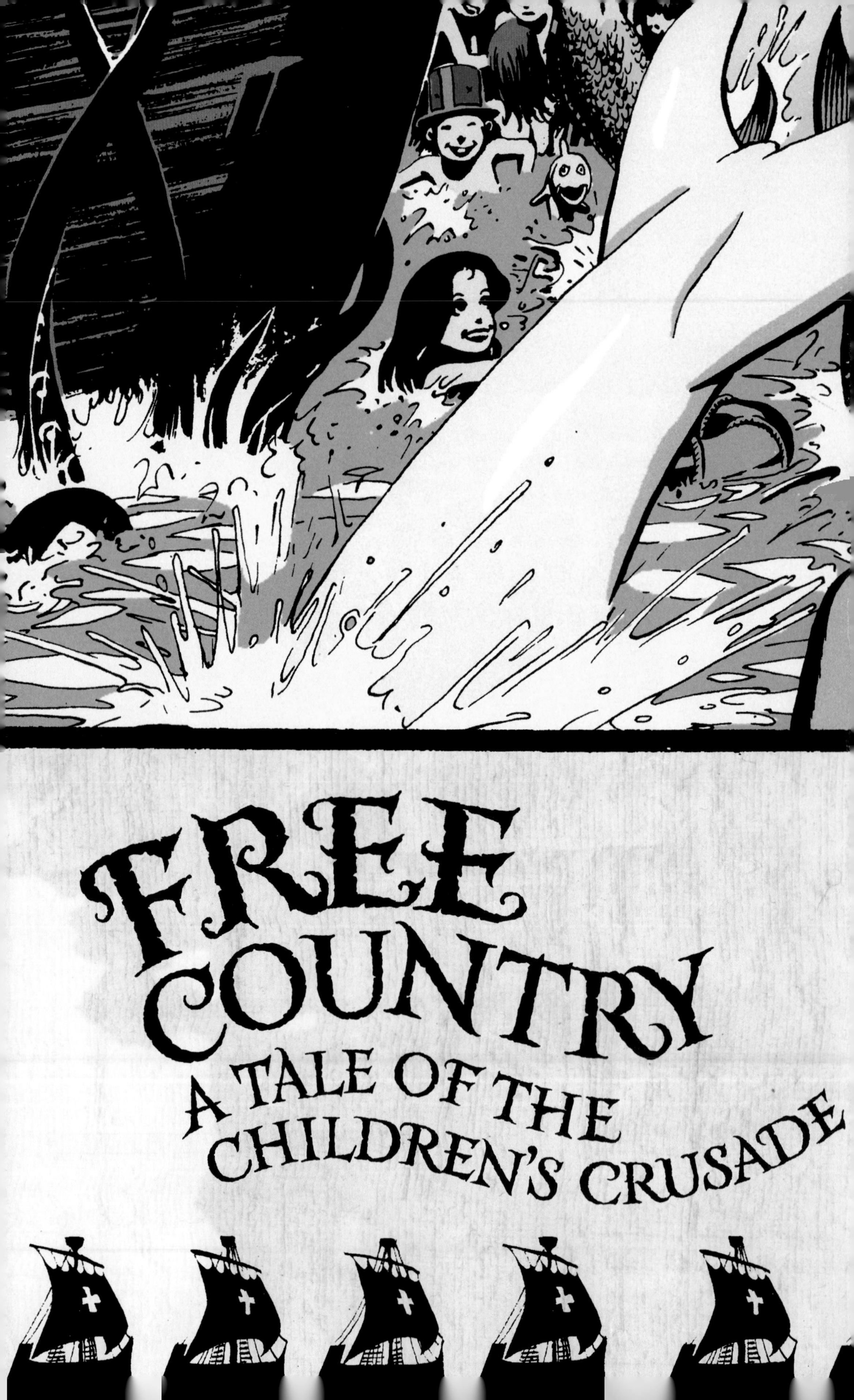

FREE COUNTRY

A TALE OF THE CHILDREN'S CRUSADE

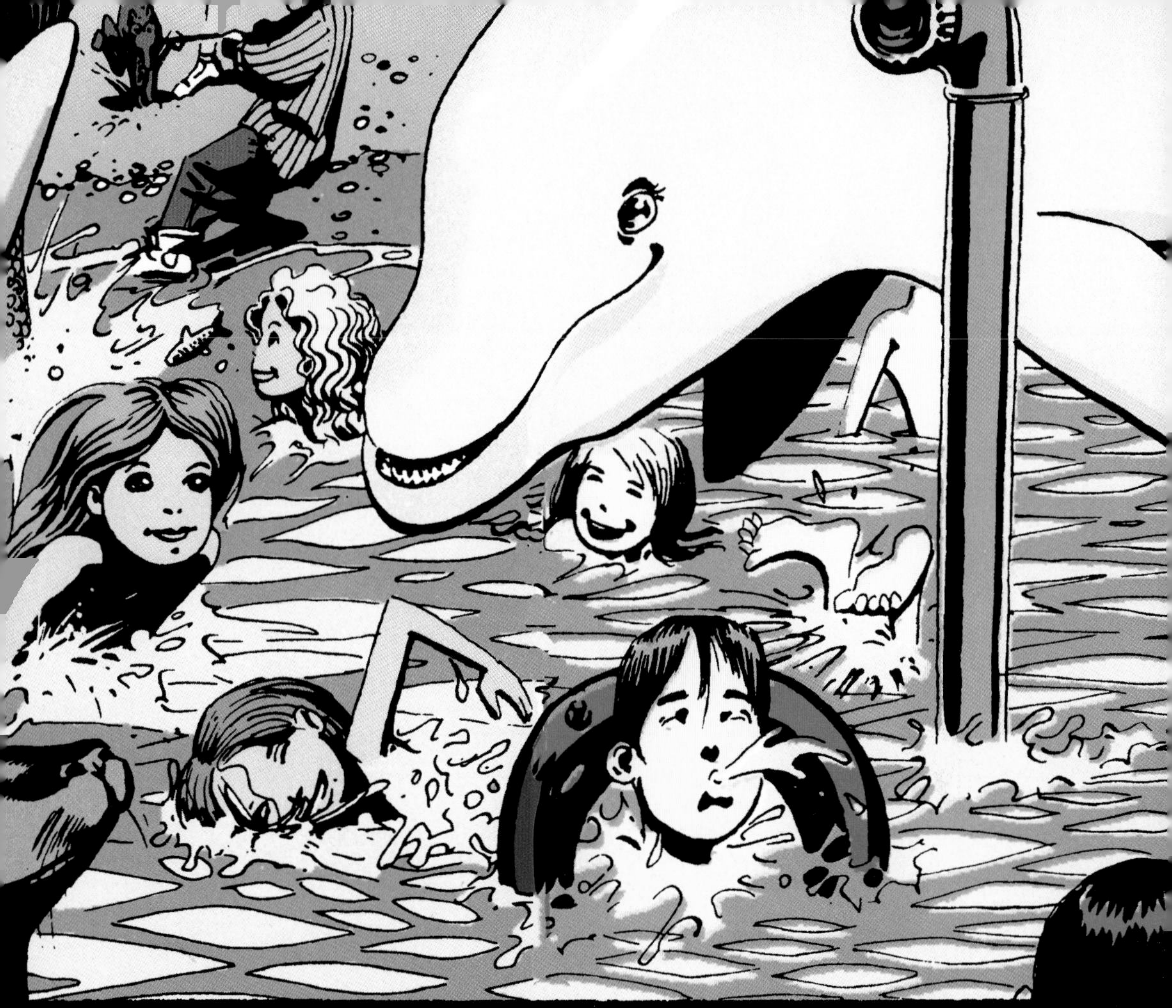

ACT ONE

Writer: Neil Gaiman
Penciller: Chris Bachalo
Inker: Mike Barreiro
Colorist: Daniel Vozzo
Letterer: John Costanza

ACT TWO

Writers: Toby Litt & Rachel Pollack
Artists: Peter Gross & Al Davison
Colorist: Jeanne McGee
Letterer: Todd Klein

ACT THREE

Writers: Neil Gaiman, Alisa Kwitney
Jamie Delano & Toby Litt
Artists: Peter Snejbjerg & Peter Gross
Colorists: Daniel Vozzo & Jeanne McGee
Letterers: John Costanza & Todd Klein

Special thanks to Travis Moore & Megan Levens
Cover art: Mark Buckingham
Cover color: D'Israeli

Stuart Moore Editor-Original Series
Julie Rottenberg Assistant Editor-Original Series
Lou Stathis & Tom Peyer Consulting Editors-Original Series
Rowena Yow Editor
Louis Prandi Publication Design
Shelly Bond VP & Executive Editor - Vertigo

Diane Nelson President
Dan DiDio and Jim Lee Co-Publishers
Geoff Johns Chief Creative Officer
Amit Desai Senior VP – Marketing & Global Franchise Management
Nairi Gardiner Senior VP – Finance
Sam Ades VP – Digital Marketing
Bobbie Chase VP – Talent Development
Mark Chiarello Senior VP – Art, Design & Collected Editions
John Cunningham VP – Content Strategy
Anne DePies VP – Strategy Planning & Reporting
Don Falletti VP – Manufacturing Operations
Lawrence Ganem VP – Editorial Administration & Talent Relations
Alison Gill Senior VP – Manufacturing & Operations
Hank Kanalz Senior VP – Editorial Strategy & Administration
Jay Kogan VP – Legal Affairs
Derek Maddalena Senior VP – Sales & Business Development
Dan Miron VP – Sales Planning & Trade Development
Nick Napolitano VP – Manufacturing Administration
Carol Roeder VP – Marketing
Eddie Scannell VP – Mass Account & Digital Sales
Courtney Simmons Senior VP – Publicity & Communications
Jim (Ski) Sokolowski VP – Comic Book Specialty & Newsstand Sales

Logo design by Nancy Ogami

FREE COUNTRY: A TALE OF THE CHILDREN'S CRUSADE

DC Comics, 4000 Warner Blvd., Burbank, CA 91522
A Warner Bros. Entertainment Company.
Printed in Canada. First Printing.
ISBN: 978-1-4012-4241-1

Library of Congress Cataloging-in-Publication Data

Gaiman, Neil, author.
Free Country : a tale of the Children's Crusade/ Written by Toby Litt, Alisa
Kwitney, Jamie Delano; illustrated by Peter Snejberg.
pages cm

ISBN 978-1-4012-4241-1 (hardback)
I. Gaiman, Neil II. Litt, Toby III. Title.
PN6728.C565 F74 2015
741.5'973—dc23

2015026884

INTRODUCTION
BY NEIL GAIMAN

Vertigo was a ragbag collection of titles back
then, in the beginning, united only by being
overseen by Vertigo editor-in-chief Karen Berger.
They were "for mature readers," but nobody
knew quite what that meant. We were doing our
own thing, whatever that happened to be.

We didn't do superheroes, though. Except for
Animal Man and the Doom Patrol, who were sort of
superheroes. And we didn't do crossovers. Except for
this one. And we didn't exactly do this one either.

It started in a hotel, and all the Vertigo writers and
editors were there on a mysterious rural retreat.
It seemed unlikely to me, like herding cats. We
didn't flock together naturally, but perhaps this
would be our opportunity. Somebody not me had
pointed out that if there was one thing that all the
Vertigo titles in question had in common, it was
that they each had a child in them. (Comics for kids
or for young teens didn't have children in them,
but comics for mature readers did. Go figure.)

There was plotting, I remember much plotting.

The Sandman would be represented by Charles
Rowland and Edwin Paine, last seen during the
"Season of Mists" storyline, in their first outing
as detectives. Animal Man's daughter, Maxine,
would represent Animal Man. Doom Patrol was
represented by Dorothy, Swamp Thing by Tefé,
Black Orchid by Suzy, and Tim Hunter, who had
only appeared in the original "Books of Magic"
series at that point, by himself, in a one-off called
ARCANA. It was the last time I wrote Tim Hunter,
and I took an enormous amount of joy in it.

We'd never done this before.

I took all of my love for children's fiction, for
Robert Browning, for the Iona and Peter Opie
books of children's rhymes and games, and put
it into the opening, and waited to see what came
back while I started to do the other side of the
bookend, the one that wrapped up the plot.

Jamie Delano and Alisa Kwitney came
in and took sections of the closer, and I
added dialogue to Alisa's bits, too.

I remember the main problem being that bits
of plot that had been handed out to the other
books weren't actually in those books when they
were done. In retrospect, it's not even surprising:

Nobody told any of the Vertigo writers what to do, the editors actually overseeing things had never done a crossover, and actually, herding cats is easier than persuading writers to take part in a crossover once the rural retreat is over.

Alisa and Jamie and I found ourselves squeezing enormous amounts of plot into the end of the book. It had started well (or I thought it had, anyway) and then it fragmented, and then it closed.

Time passed. It never made sense to collect THE CHILDREN'S CRUSADE into one book. The chapters in the middle were all so very much part of their own stories. But there was a beginning there, and an end.

Shelly Bond, editor extraordinaire, had been pondering the problem for years: It was she who suggested bringing in Toby Litt and Peter Gross to create a whole new middle, to help build something that could be book-shaped, and to help open up the end, where the strain of having to squeeze rather more plot and dialogue in than we had originally expected had begun to show.

That they have done it seamlessly is a relief and a delight. That you can now read THE CHILDREN'S CRUSADE from beginning to end, and get a story out of it, makes me surprisingly happy.

Rereading THE CHILDREN'S CRUSADE now, it reads like a missing link. While it shows that Vertigo, all those years ago, was not a place for a crossover, it also contains some of my favourite comics moments. (I asked Alisa Kwitney, who cowrote much of the second half of THE CHILDREN'S CRUSADE, if there was anything she wanted me to point out and she said yes, I should tell people that in the double-page spread with the mermaids and the magic, she had instructed artist Peter Snejbjerg to draw a very young Neil Gaiman reading a book, oblivious to the wonders around him.)

And I tell you that here, with pleasure, because if I had ever known that I was in Free Country reading, I had forgotten.

Welcome to a book that is out a little late. Welcome to Flaxdown. Welcome to Free Country.

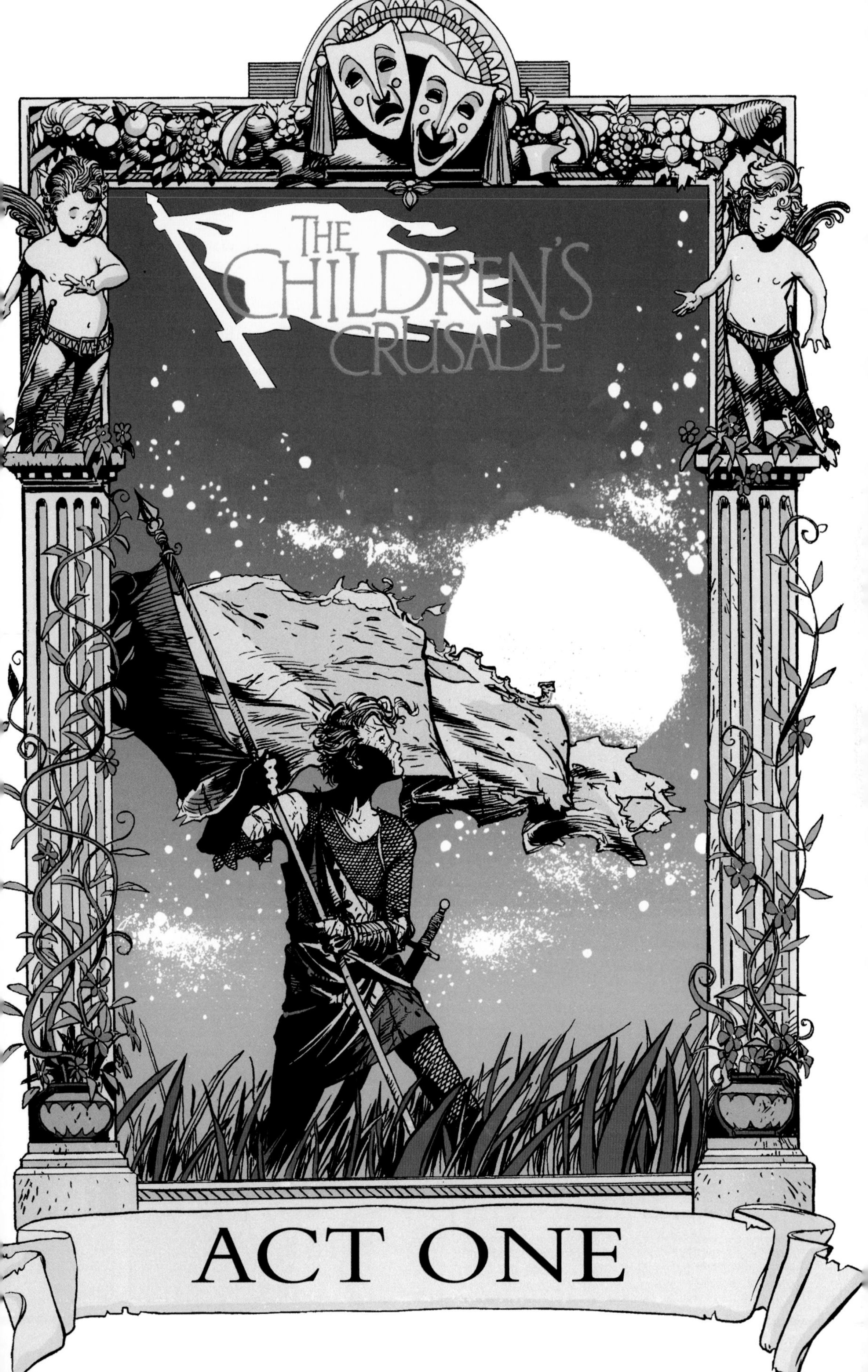
THE CHILDREN'S CRUSADE
ACT ONE

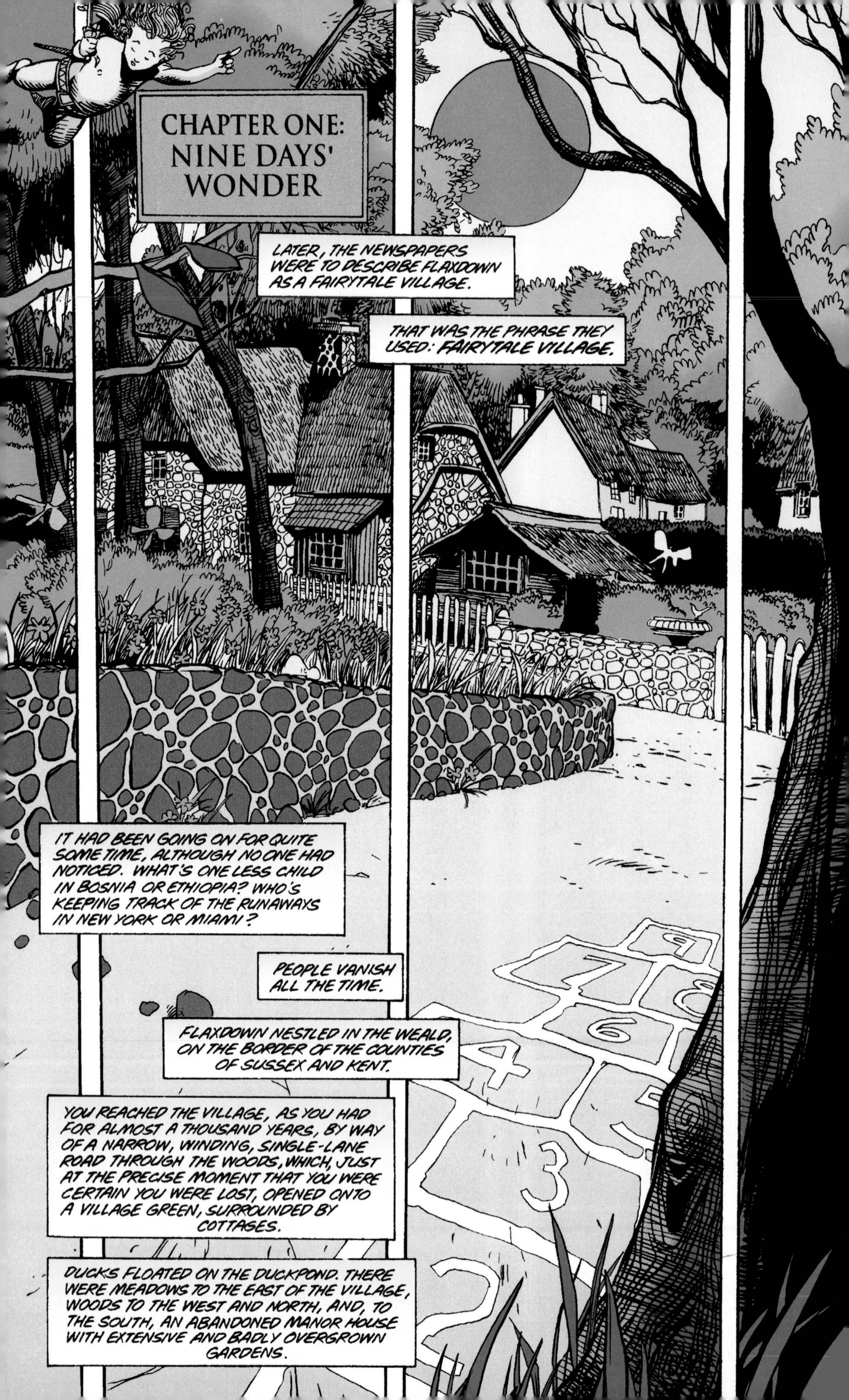
CHAPTER ONE: NINE DAYS' WONDER
LATER, THE NEWSPAPERS WERE TO DESCRIBE FLAXDOWN AS A FAIRYTALE VILLAGE.
THAT WAS THE PHRASE THEY USED: FAIRYTALE VILLAGE.
IT HAD BEEN GOING ON FOR QUITE SOME TIME, ALTHOUGH NO ONE HAD NOTICED. WHAT'S ONE LESS CHILD IN BOSNIA OR ETHIOPIA? WHO'S KEEPING TRACK OF THE RUNAWAYS IN NEW YORK OR MIAMI?
PEOPLE VANISH ALL THE TIME.
FLAXDOWN NESTLED IN THE WEALD, ON THE BORDER OF THE COUNTIES OF SUSSEX AND KENT.
YOU REACHED THE VILLAGE, AS YOU HAD FOR ALMOST A THOUSAND YEARS, BY WAY OF A NARROW, WINDING, SINGLE-LANE ROAD THROUGH THE WOODS, WHICH, JUST AT THE PRECISE MOMENT THAT YOU WERE CERTAIN YOU WERE LOST, OPENED ONTO A VILLAGE GREEN, SURROUNDED BY COTTAGES.
DUCKS FLOATED ON THE DUCKPOND. THERE WERE MEADOWS TO THE EAST OF THE VILLAGE, WOODS TO THE WEST AND NORTH, AND, TO THE SOUTH, AN ABANDONED MANOR HOUSE WITH EXTENSIVE AND BADLY OVERGROWN GARDENS.

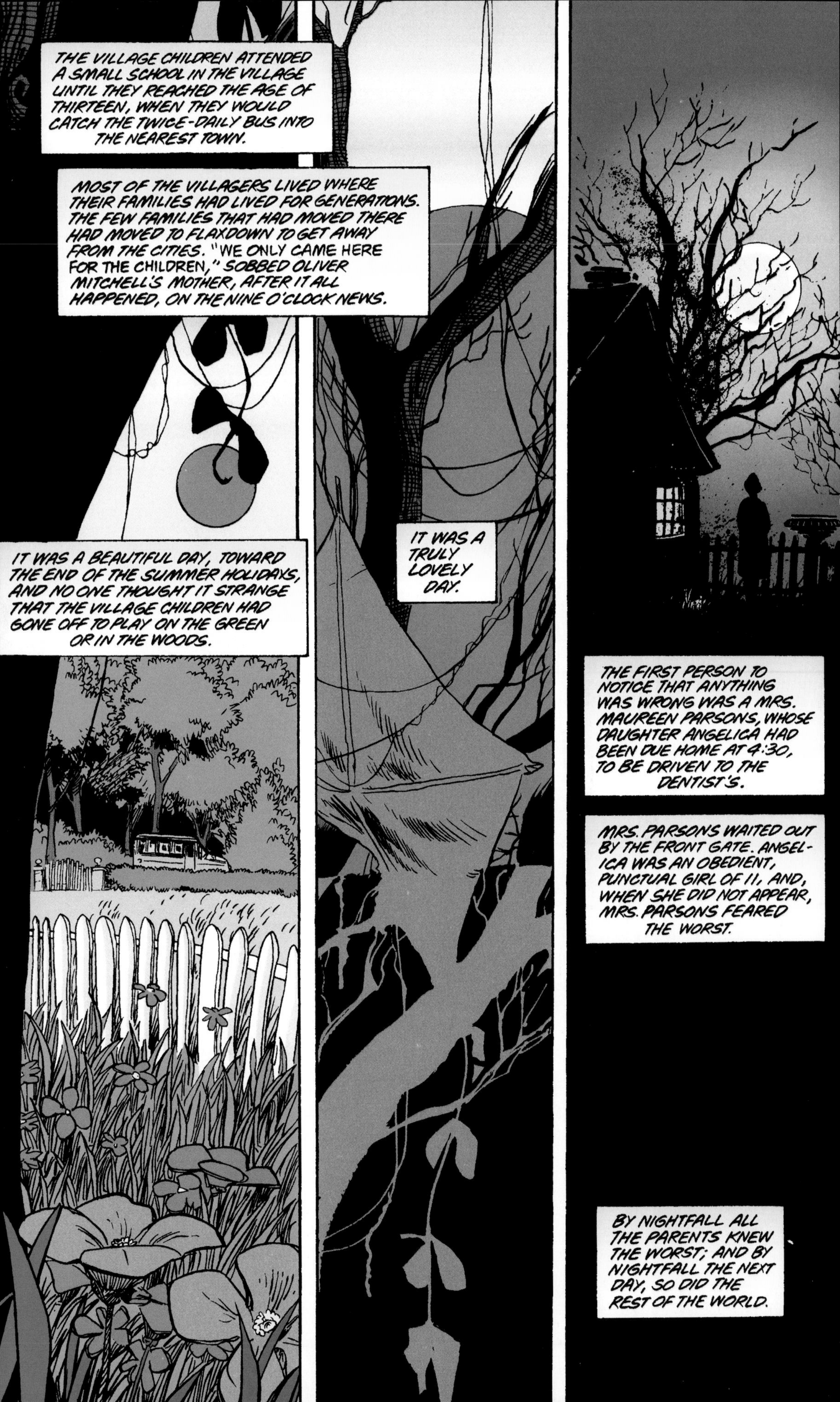
THE VILLAGE CHILDREN ATTENDED A SMALL SCHOOL IN THE VILLAGE UNTIL THEY REACHED THE AGE OF THIRTEEN, WHEN THEY WOULD CATCH THE TWICE-DAILY BUS INTO THE NEAREST TOWN.
MOST OF THE VILLAGERS LIVED WHERE THEIR FAMILIES HAD LIVED FOR GENERATIONS. THE FEW FAMILIES THAT HAD MOVED THERE HAD MOVED TO FLAXDOWN TO GET AWAY FROM THE CITIES. "WE ONLY CAME HERE FOR THE CHILDREN," SOBBED OLIVER MITCHELL'S MOTHER, AFTER IT ALL HAPPENED, ON THE NINE O'CLOCK NEWS.
IT WAS A BEAUTIFUL DAY, TOWARD THE END OF THE SUMMER HOLIDAYS, AND NO ONE THOUGHT IT STRANGE THAT THE VILLAGE CHILDREN HAD GONE OFF TO PLAY ON THE GREEN OR IN THE WOODS.
IT WAS A TRULY LOVELY DAY.
THE FIRST PERSON TO NOTICE THAT ANYTHING WAS WRONG WAS A MRS. MAUREEN PARSONS, WHOSE DAUGHTER ANGELICA HAD BEEN DUE HOME AT 4:30, TO BE DRIVEN TO THE DENTIST'S.
MRS. PARSONS WAITED OUT BY THE FRONT GATE. ANGELICA WAS AN OBEDIENT, PUNCTUAL GIRL OF 11, AND, WHEN SHE DID NOT APPEAR, MRS. PARSONS FEARED THE WORST.
BY NIGHTFALL ALL THE PARENTS KNEW THE WORST; AND BY NIGHTFALL THE NEXT DAY, SO DID THE REST OF THE WORLD.

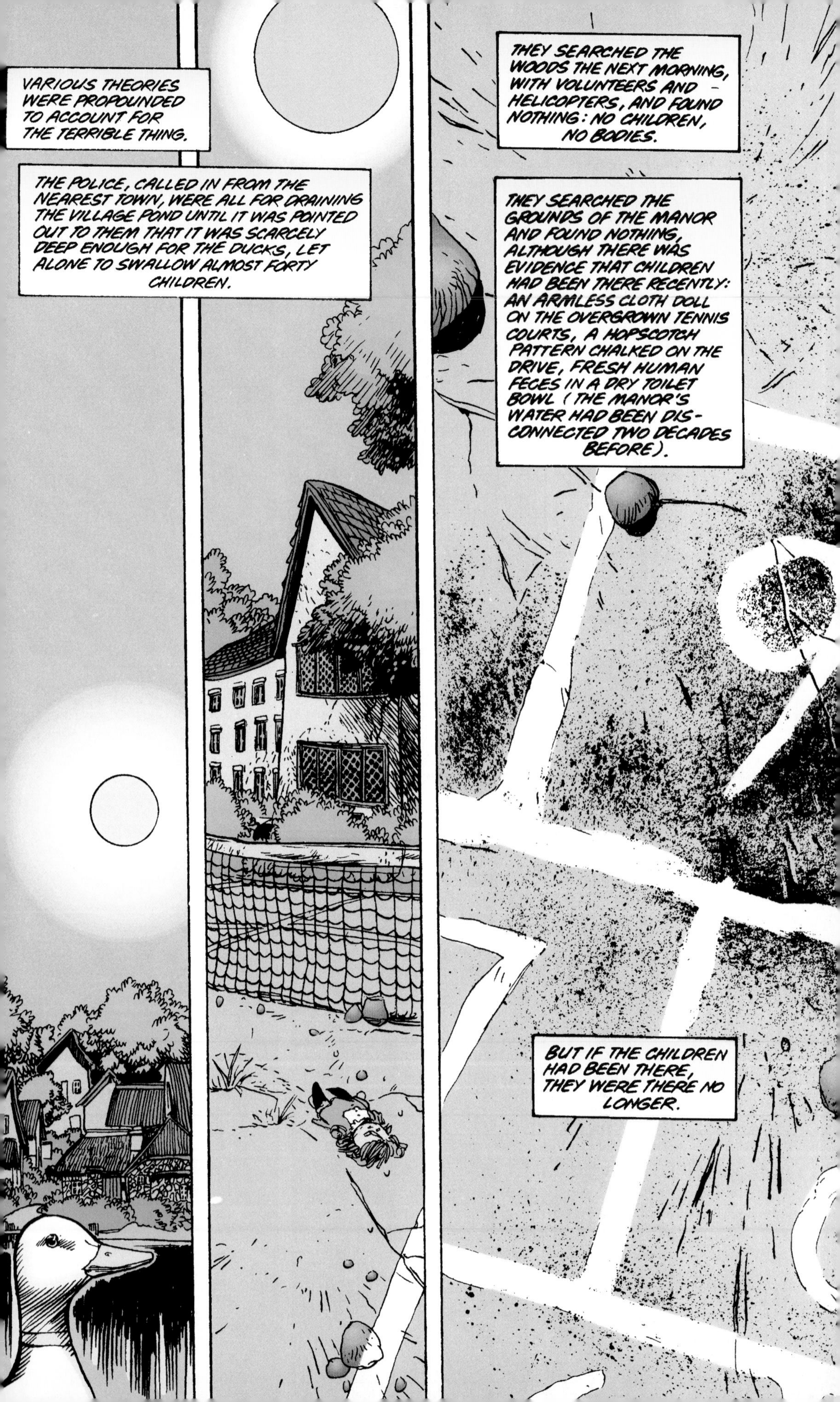
VARIOUS THEORIES WERE PROPOUNDED TO ACCOUNT FOR THE TERRIBLE THING.
THE POLICE, CALLED IN FROM THE NEAREST TOWN, WERE ALL FOR DRAINING THE VILLAGE POND UNTIL IT WAS POINTED OUT TO THEM THAT IT WAS SCARCELY DEEP ENOUGH FOR THE DUCKS, LET ALONE TO SWALLOW ALMOST FORTY CHILDREN.
THEY SEARCHED THE WOODS THE NEXT MORNING, WITH VOLUNTEERS AND HELICOPTERS, AND FOUND NOTHING: NO CHILDREN, NO BODIES.
THEY SEARCHED THE GROUNDS OF THE MANOR AND FOUND NOTHING, ALTHOUGH THERE WAS EVIDENCE THAT CHILDREN HAD BEEN THERE RECENTLY: AN ARMLESS CLOTH DOLL ON THE OVERGROWN TENNIS COURTS, A HOPSCOTCH PATTERN CHALKED ON THE DRIVE, FRESH HUMAN FECES IN A DRY TOILET BOWL (THE MANOR'S WATER HAD BEEN DIS-CONNECTED TWO DECADES BEFORE).
BUT IF THE CHILDREN HAD BEEN THERE, THEY WERE THERE NO LONGER.

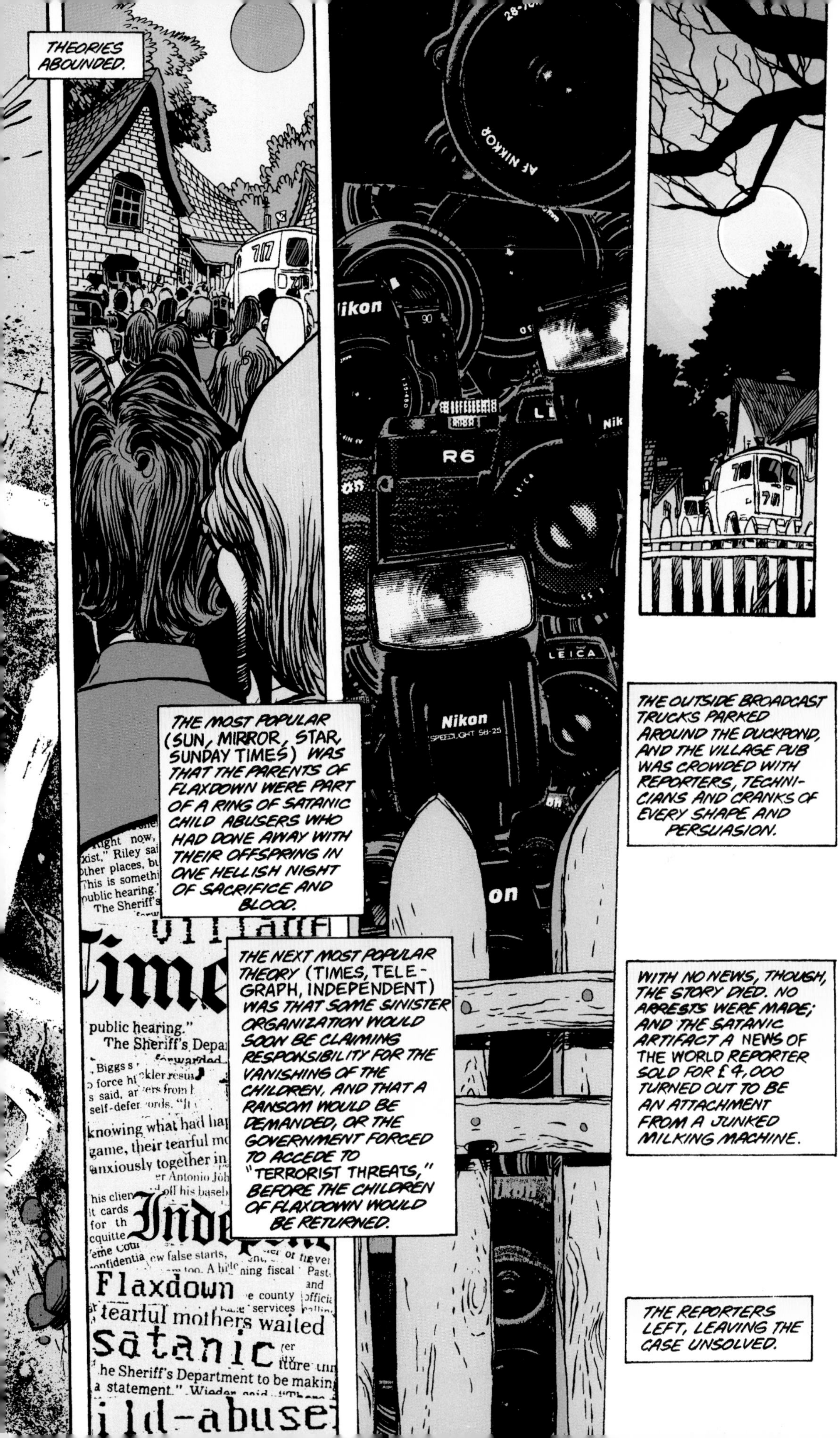
THEORIES ABOUNDED.
THE MOST POPULAR (SUN, MIRROR, STAR, SUNDAY TIMES) WAS THAT THE PARENTS OF FLAXDOWN WERE PART OF A RING OF SATANIC CHILD ABUSERS WHO HAD DONE AWAY WITH THEIR OFFSPRING IN ONE HELLISH NIGHT OF SACRIFICE AND BLOOD.
THE NEXT MOST POPULAR THEORY (TIMES, TELEGRAPH, INDEPENDENT) WAS THAT SOME SINISTER ORGANIZATION WOULD SOON BE CLAIMING RESPONSIBILITY FOR THE VANISHING OF THE CHILDREN, AND THAT A RANSOM WOULD BE DEMANDED, OR THE GOVERNMENT FORCED TO ACCEDE TO "TERRORIST THREATS," BEFORE THE CHILDREN OF FLAXDOWN WOULD BE RETURNED.
THE OUTSIDE BROADCAST TRUCKS PARKED AROUND THE DUCKPOND, AND THE VILLAGE PUB WAS CROWDED WITH REPORTERS, TECHNICIANS AND CRANKS OF EVERY SHAPE AND PERSUASION.
WITH NO NEWS, THOUGH, THE STORY DIED. NO ARRESTS WERE MADE; AND THE SATANIC ARTIFACT A NEWS OF THE WORLD REPORTER SOLD FOR £4,000 TURNED OUT TO BE AN ATTACHMENT FROM A JUNKED MILKING MACHINE.
THE REPORTERS LEFT, LEAVING THE CASE UNSOLVED.

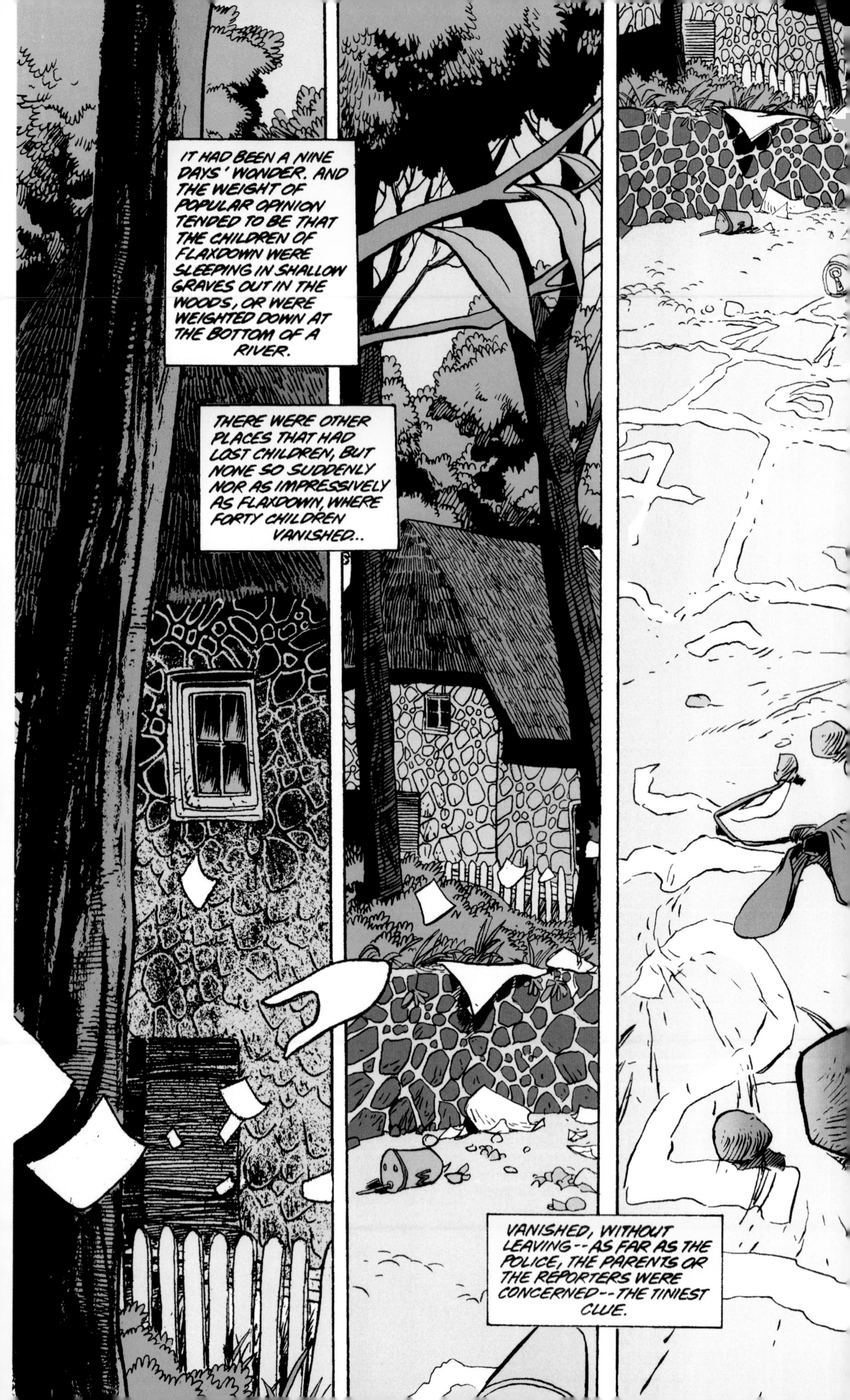
IT HAD BEEN A NINE DAYS' WONDER. AND THE WEIGHT OF POPULAR OPINION TENDED TO BE THAT THE CHILDREN OF FLAXDOWN WERE SLEEPING IN SHALLOW GRAVES OUT IN THE WOODS, OR WERE WEIGHTED DOWN AT THE BOTTOM OF A RIVER.
THERE WERE OTHER PLACES THAT HAD LOST CHILDREN, BUT NONE SO SUDDENLY NOR AS IMPRESSIVELY AS FLAXDOWN, WHERE FORTY CHILDREN VANISHED...
VANISHED, WITHOUT LEAVING--AS FAR AS THE POLICE, THE PARENTS OR THE REPORTERS WERE CONCERNED--THE TINIEST CLUE.

CHAPTER TWO: TRUE DETECTIVE STORIES

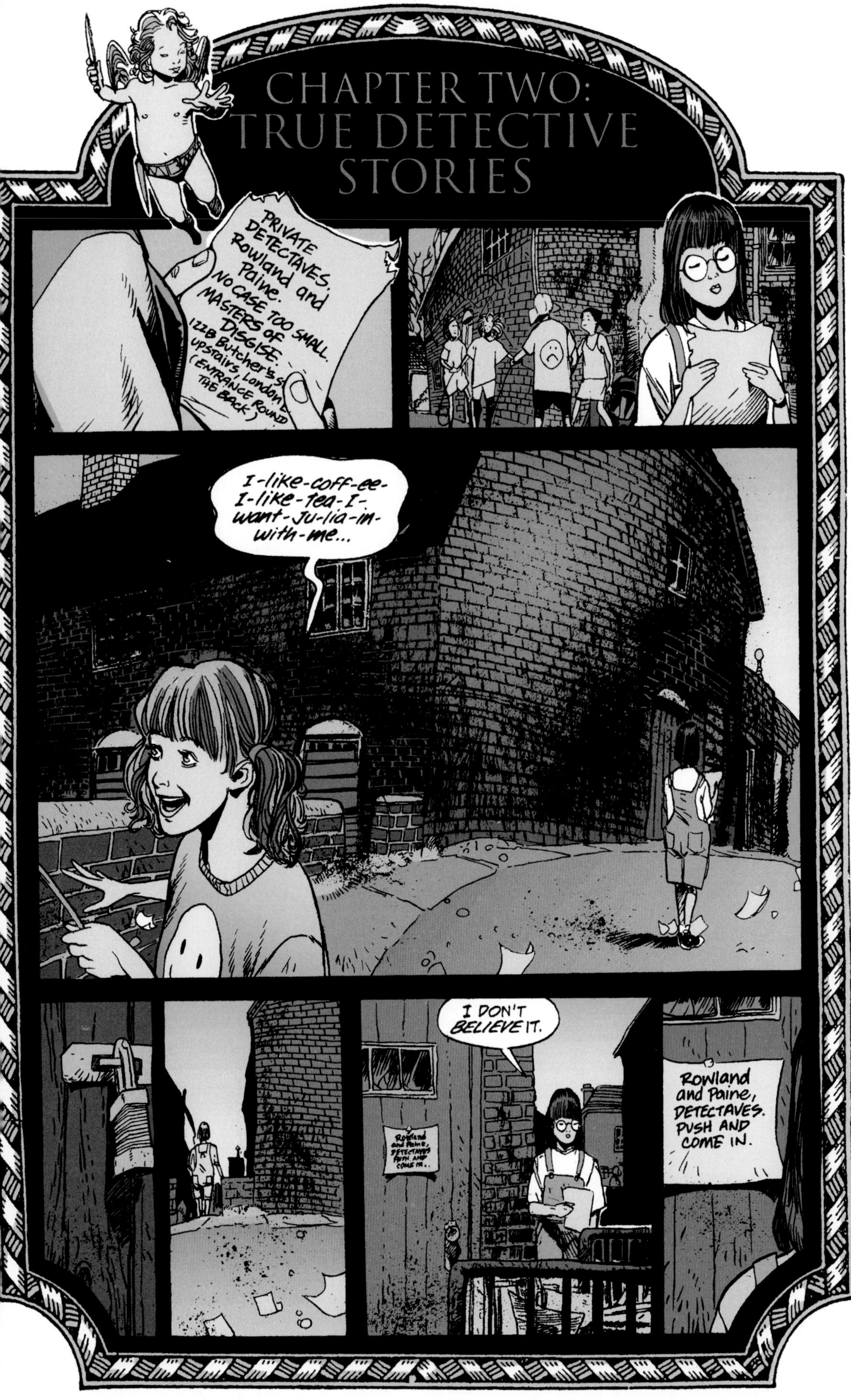
PRIVATE DETECTAVES.
Rowland and Paine.
NO CASE TOO SMALL.
MASTERS OF DISGISE.
122B Butcher's St
upstairs, London
(ENTRANCE ROUND THE BACK)
I-like-coff-ee-I-like-tea-I-want-Ju-lia-in-with-me...
I DON'T BELIEVE IT.
Rowland and Paine, DETECTAVES. PUSH AND COME IN.

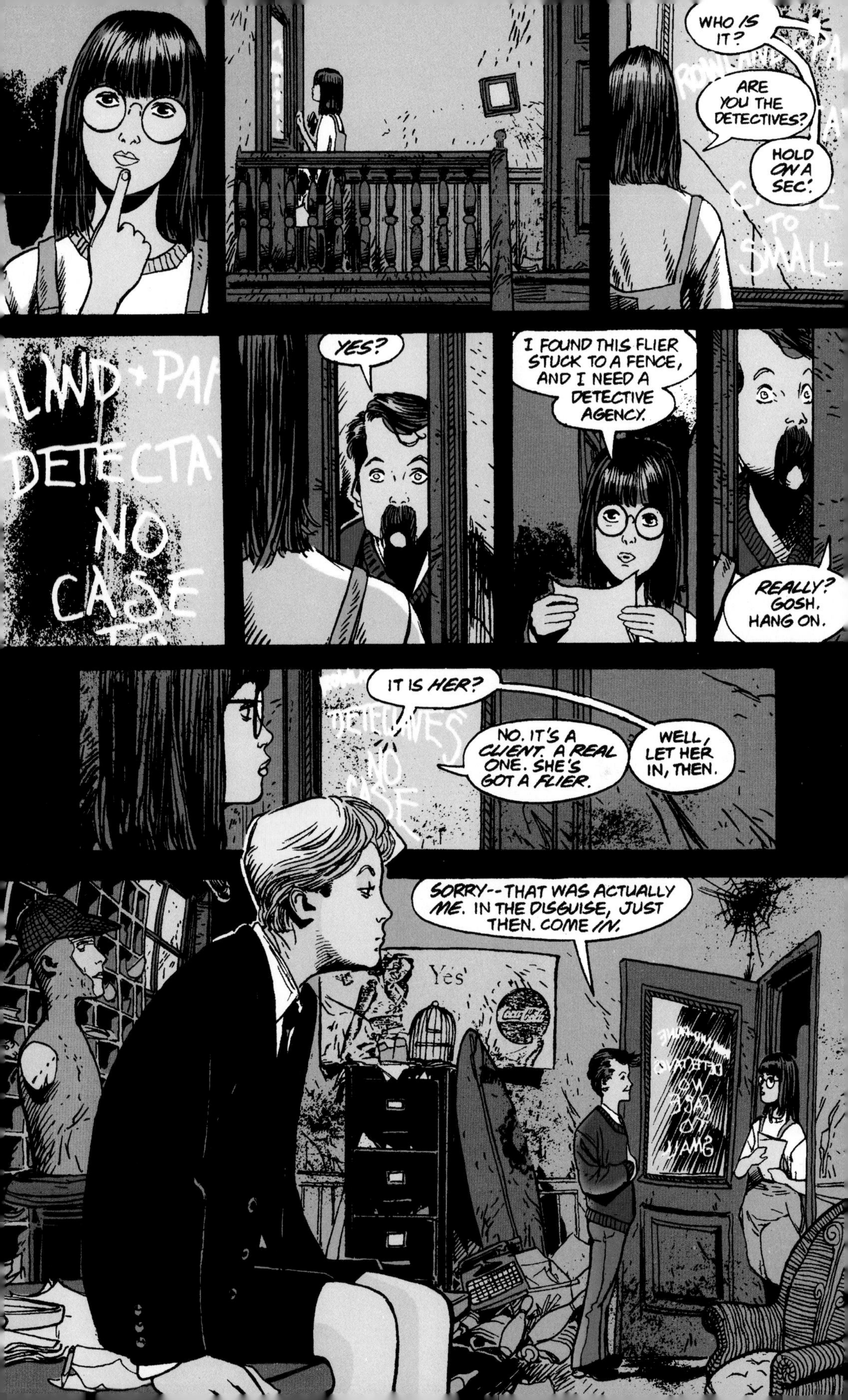
WHO IS IT?
ARE YOU THE DETECTIVES?
HOLD ON A SEC!
YES?
I FOUND THIS FLIER STUCK TO A FENCE, AND I NEED A DETECTIVE AGENCY.
REALLY? GOSH. HANG ON.
IT IS HER?
NO. IT'S A CLIENT. A REAL ONE. SHE'S GOT A FLIER.
WELL, LET HER IN, THEN.
SORRY--THAT WAS ACTUALLY ME. IN THE DISGUISE, JUST THEN. COME IN.
Yes

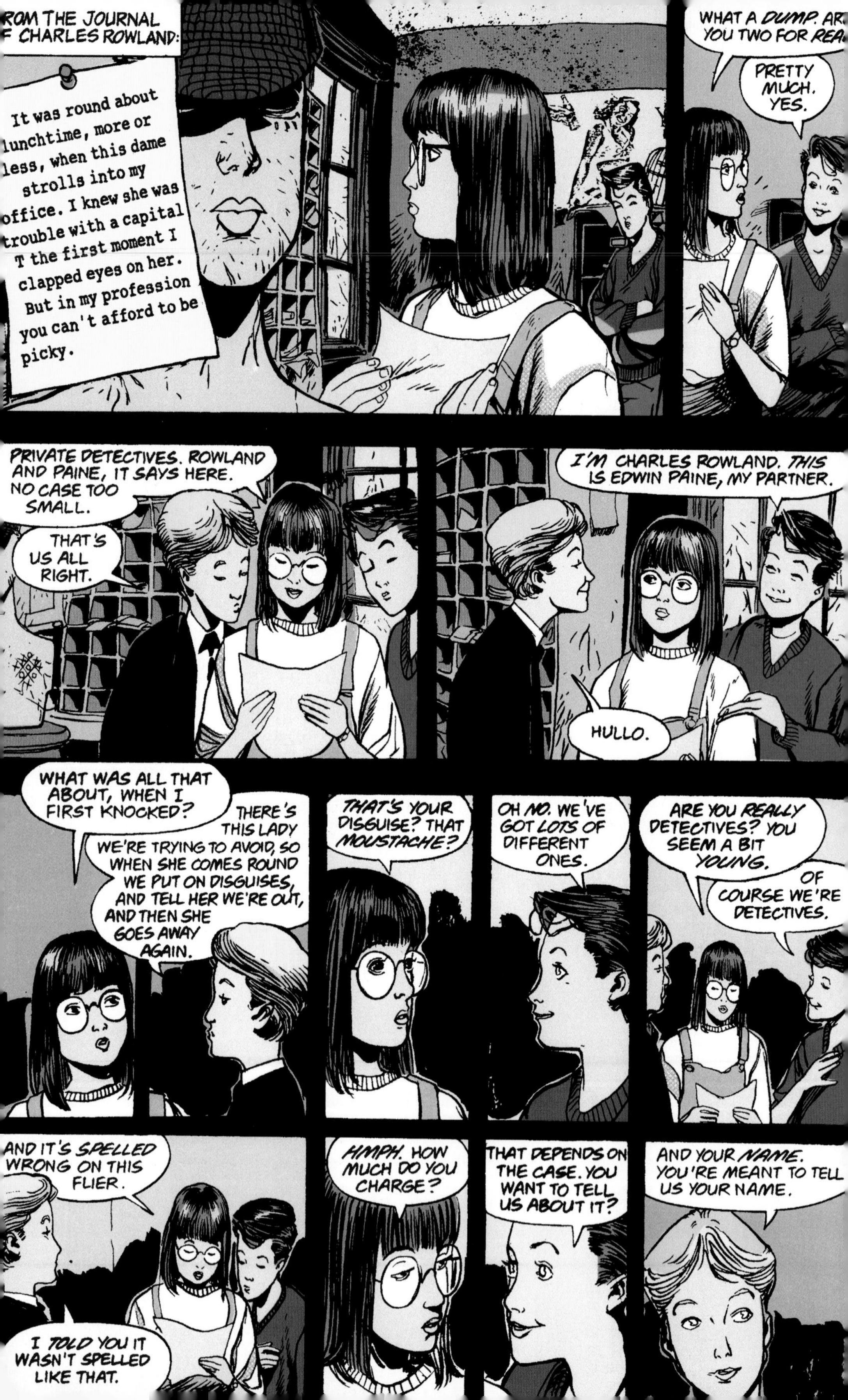
ROM THE JOURNAL
F CHARLES ROWLAND:
It was round about lunchtime, more or less, when this dame strolls into my office. I knew she was trouble with a capital T the first moment I clapped eyes on her. But in my profession you can't afford to be picky.
WHAT A DUMP. AR
YOU TWO FOR REA
PRETTY MUCH. YES.
PRIVATE DETECTIVES. ROWLAND AND PAINE, IT SAYS HERE. NO CASE TOO SMALL.
THAT'S US ALL RIGHT.
I'M CHARLES ROWLAND. THIS IS EDWIN PAINE, MY PARTNER.
HULLO.
WHAT WAS ALL THAT ABOUT, WHEN I FIRST KNOCKED?
THERE'S THIS LADY WE'RE TRYING TO AVOID, SO WHEN SHE COMES ROUND WE PUT ON DISGUISES, AND TELL HER WE'RE OUT, AND THEN SHE GOES AWAY AGAIN.
THAT'S YOUR DISGUISE? THAT MOUSTACHE?
OH NO. WE'VE GOT LOTS OF DIFFERENT ONES.
ARE YOU REALLY DETECTIVES? YOU SEEM A BIT YOUNG.
OF COURSE WE'RE DETECTIVES.
AND IT'S SPELLED WRONG ON THIS FLIER.
I TOLD YOU IT WASN'T SPELLED LIKE THAT.
HMPH. HOW MUCH DO YOU CHARGE?
THAT DEPENDS ON THE CASE. YOU WANT TO TELL US ABOUT IT?
AND YOUR NAME. YOU'RE MEANT TO TELL US YOUR NAME.

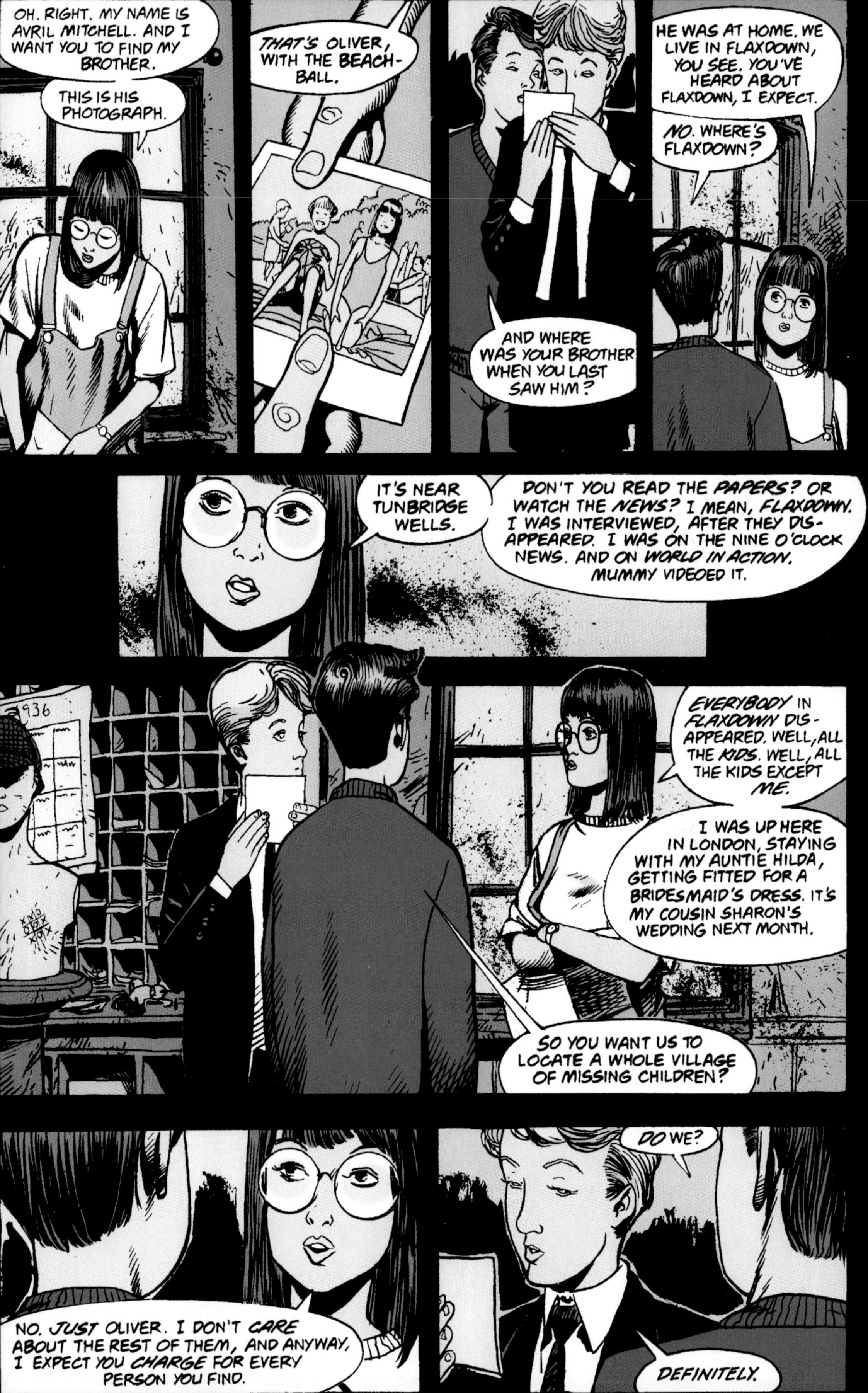

OH. RIGHT. MY NAME IS AVRIL MITCHELL. AND I WANT YOU TO FIND MY BROTHER.
THIS IS HIS PHOTOGRAPH.
THAT'S OLIVER, WITH THE **BEACH**-BALL.
AND WHERE WAS YOUR BROTHER WHEN YOU LAST SAW HIM?
HE WAS AT HOME. WE LIVE IN FLAXDOWN, *YOU SEE. YOU'VE* HEARD ABOUT FLAXDOWN, I EXPECT.
NO. WHERE'S FLAXDOWN?
IT'S NEAR TUNBRIDGE WELLS.
DON'T *YOU* READ THE *PAPERS?* OR WATCH THE *NEWS?* I MEAN, *FLAXDOWN.* I WAS INTERVIEWED, AFTER THEY DIS-APPEARED. I WAS ON THE NINE O'CLOCK NEWS. AND ON *WORLD IN ACTION*. *MUMMY* VIDEOED IT.
1936
EVERYBODY IN *FLAXDOWN* DIS-APPEARED. WELL, ALL THE *KIDS*. WELL, ALL THE KIDS EXCEPT *ME*.
I WAS UP HERE IN LONDON, STAYING WITH MY AUNTIE HILDA, GETTING FITTED FOR A BRIDESMAID'S DRESS. IT'S MY COUSIN SHARON'S WEDDING NEXT MONTH.
SO YOU WANT US TO LOCATE A WHOLE VILLAGE OF MISSING CHILDREN?
NO. *JUST* OLIVER. I DON'T *CARE* ABOUT THE REST OF THEM, AND ANYWAY, I EXPECT *YOU CHARGE* FOR EVERY PERSON YOU FIND.
DO WE?
DEFINITELY.

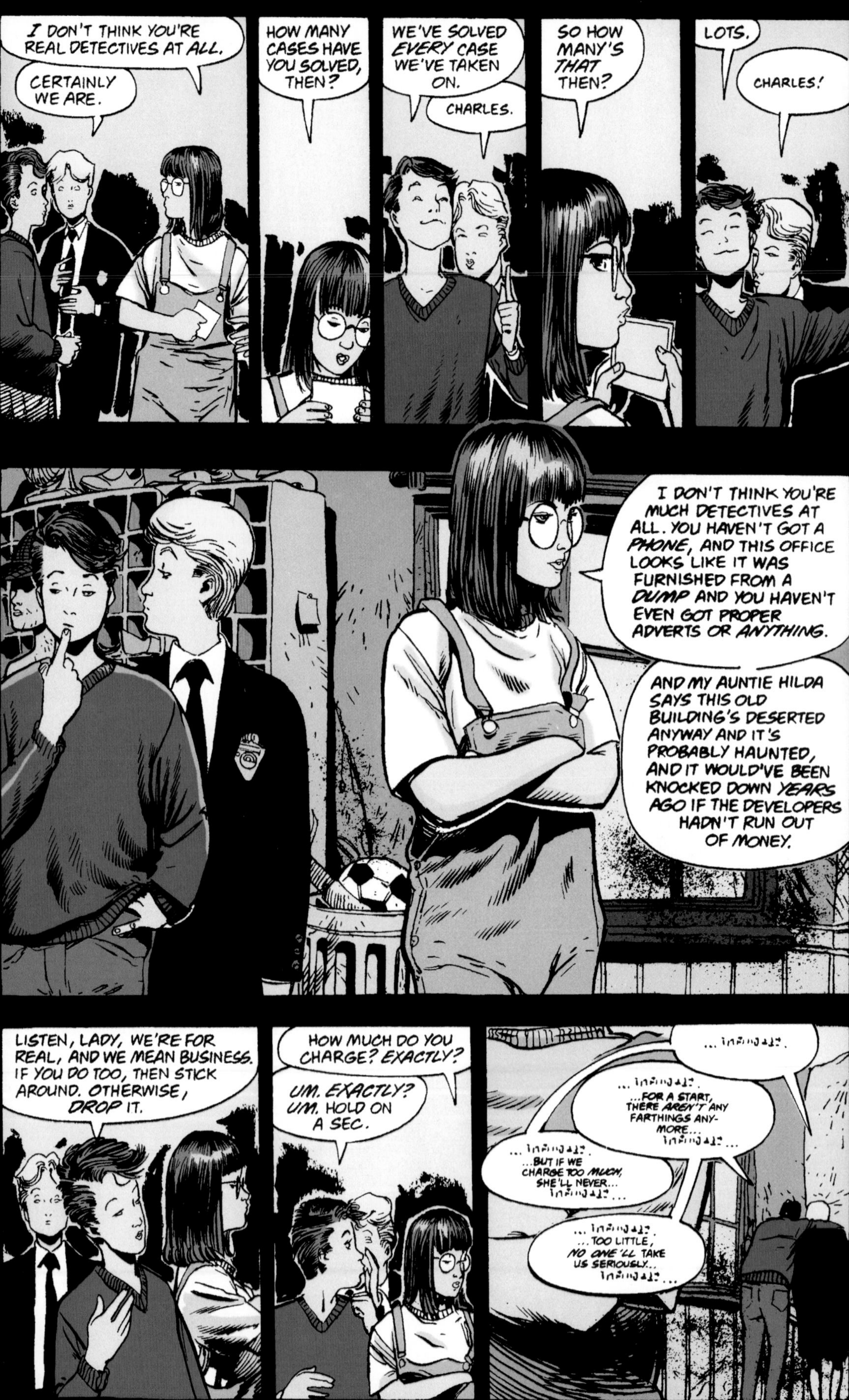
I DON'T THINK YOU'RE REAL DETECTIVES AT ALL.
CERTAINLY WE ARE.
HOW MANY CASES HAVE YOU SOLVED, THEN?
WE'VE SOLVED EVERY CASE WE'VE TAKEN ON.
CHARLES.
SO HOW MANY'S THAT THEN?
LOTS.
CHARLES!
I DON'T THINK YOU'RE MUCH DETECTIVES AT ALL. YOU HAVEN'T GOT A PHONE, AND THIS OFFICE LOOKS LIKE IT WAS FURNISHED FROM A DUMP AND YOU HAVEN'T EVEN GOT PROPER ADVERTS OR ANYTHING.
AND MY AUNTIE HILDA SAYS THIS OLD BUILDING'S DESERTED ANYWAY AND IT'S PROBABLY HAUNTED, AND IT WOULD'VE BEEN KNOCKED DOWN YEARS AGO IF THE DEVELOPERS HADN'T RUN OUT OF MONEY.
LISTEN, LADY, WE'RE FOR REAL, AND WE MEAN BUSINESS. IF YOU DO TOO, THEN STICK AROUND. OTHERWISE, DROP IT.
HOW MUCH DO YOU CHARGE? EXACTLY?
UM. EXACTLY? UM. HOLD ON A SEC.
...FOR A START, THERE AREN'T ANY FARTHINGS ANY-MORE...
...BUT IF WE CHARGE TOO MUCH, SHE'LL NEVER...
...TOO LITTLE, NO ONE'LL TAKE US SERIOUSLY...

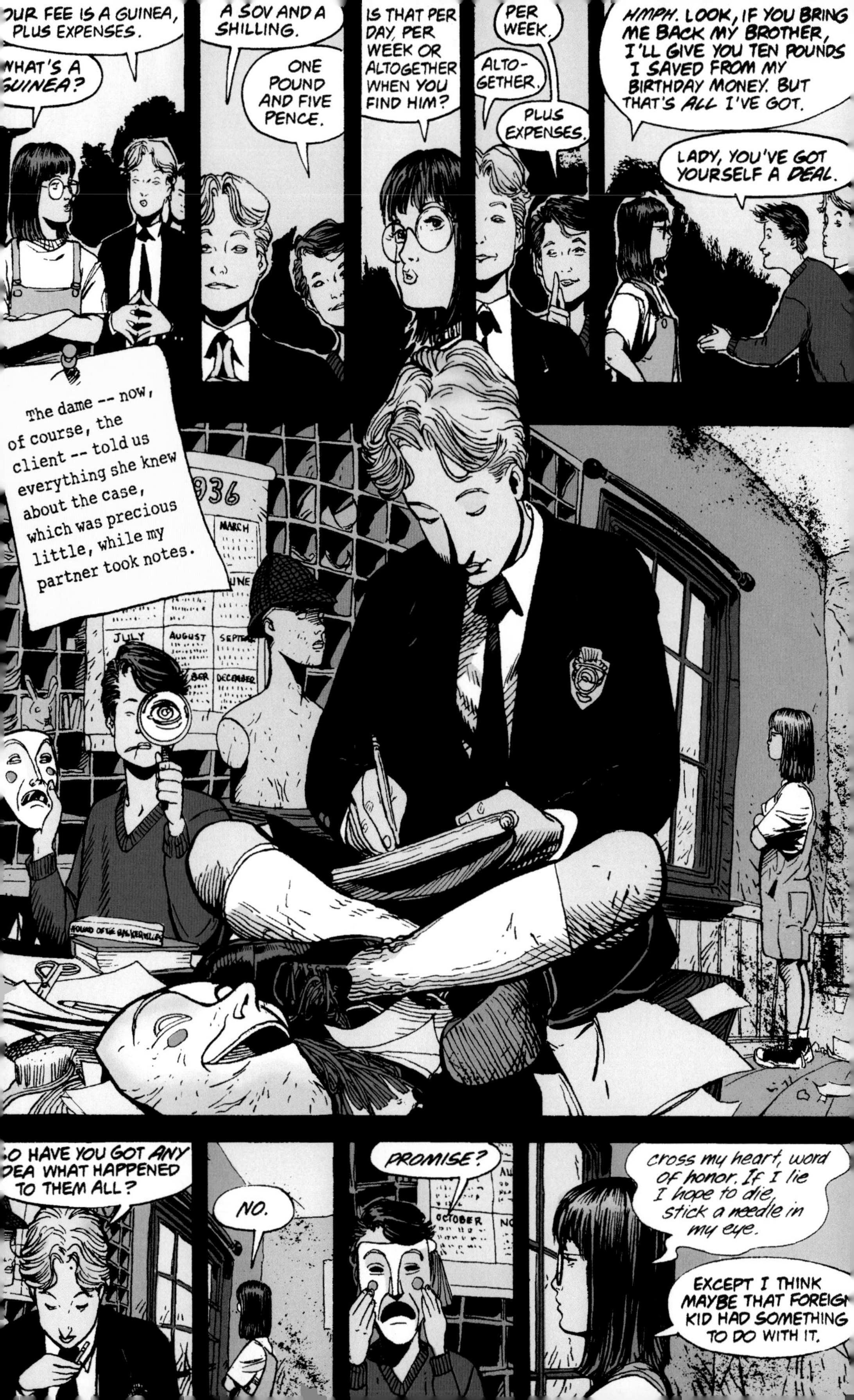
OUR FEE IS A GUINEA, PLUS EXPENSES.
WHAT'S A GUINEA?
A SOV AND A SHILLING.
ONE POUND AND FIVE PENCE.
IS THAT PER DAY, PER WEEK OR ALTOGETHER WHEN YOU FIND HIM?
PER WEEK.
ALTO-GETHER.
PLUS EXPENSES.
HMPH. LOOK, IF YOU BRING ME BACK MY BROTHER, I'LL GIVE YOU TEN POUNDS I SAVED FROM MY BIRTHDAY MONEY. BUT THAT'S ALL I'VE GOT.
LADY, YOU'VE GOT YOURSELF A DEAL.
The dame -- now, of course, the client -- told us everything she knew about the case, which was precious little, while my partner took notes.
1936
MARCH
JULY
AUGUST
DECEMBER
SO HAVE YOU GOT ANY IDEA WHAT HAPPENED TO THEM ALL?
NO.
PROMISE?
OCTOBER
cross my heart, word of honor. If I lie I hope to die, stick a needle in my eye.
EXCEPT I THINK MAYBE THAT FOREIGN KID HAD SOMETHING TO DO WITH IT.

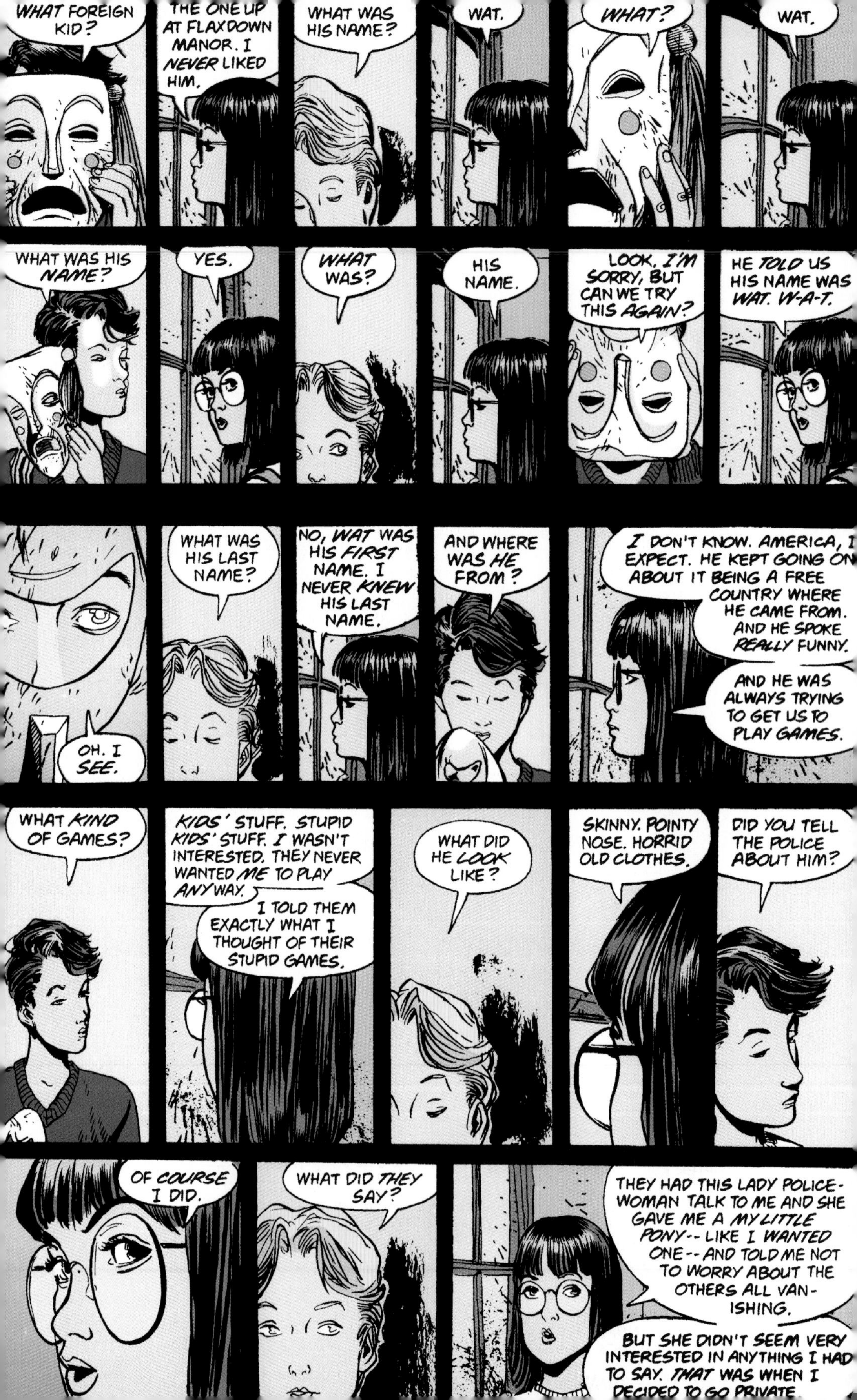
WHAT FOREIGN KID?
THE ONE UP AT FLAXDOWN MANOR. I NEVER LIKED HIM.
WHAT WAS HIS NAME?
WAT.
WHAT?
WAT.
WHAT WAS HIS NAME?
YES.
WHAT WAS?
HIS NAME.
LOOK, I'M SORRY, BUT CAN WE TRY THIS AGAIN?
HE TOLD US HIS NAME WAS WAT. W-A-T.
OH. I SEE.
WHAT WAS HIS LAST NAME?
NO, WAT WAS HIS FIRST NAME. I NEVER KNEW HIS LAST NAME.
AND WHERE WAS HE FROM?
I DON'T KNOW. AMERICA, I EXPECT. HE KEPT GOING ON ABOUT IT BEING A FREE COUNTRY WHERE HE CAME FROM. AND HE SPOKE REALLY FUNNY.
AND HE WAS ALWAYS TRYING TO GET US TO PLAY GAMES.
WHAT KIND OF GAMES?
KIDS' STUFF. STUPID KIDS' STUFF. I WASN'T INTERESTED. THEY NEVER WANTED ME TO PLAY ANYWAY.
I TOLD THEM EXACTLY WHAT I THOUGHT OF THEIR STUPID GAMES.
WHAT DID HE LOOK LIKE?
SKINNY. POINTY NOSE. HORRID OLD CLOTHES.
DID YOU TELL THE POLICE ABOUT HIM?
OF COURSE I DID.
WHAT DID THEY SAY?
THEY HAD THIS LADY POLICE-WOMAN TALK TO ME AND SHE GAVE ME A MY LITTLE PONY-- LIKE I WANTED ONE-- AND TOLD ME NOT TO WORRY ABOUT THE OTHERS ALL VAN-ISHING.
BUT SHE DIDN'T SEEM VERY INTERESTED IN ANYTHING I HAD TO SAY. THAT WAS WHEN I DECIDED TO GO PRIVATE.

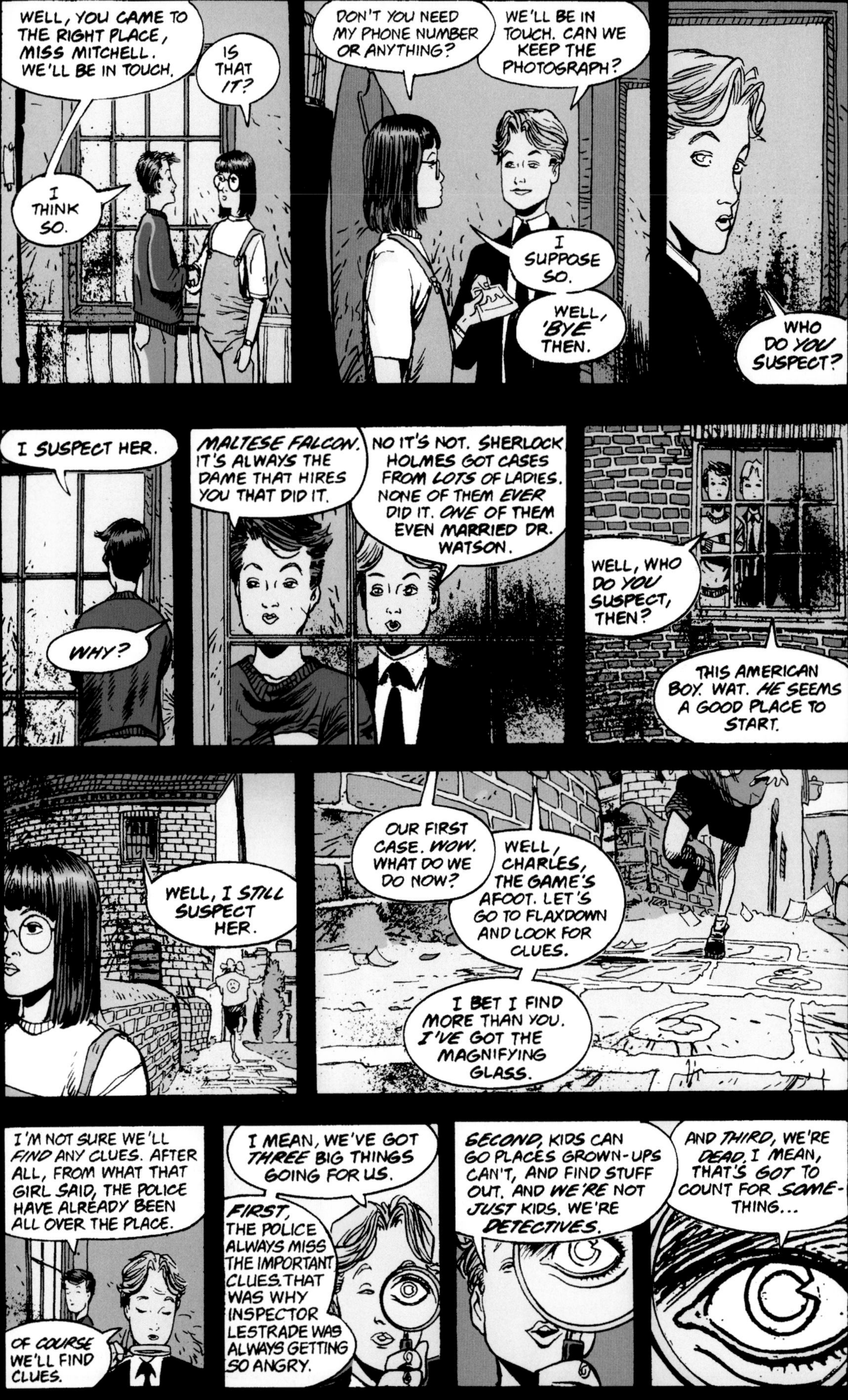
WELL, YOU CAME TO THE RIGHT PLACE, MISS MITCHELL. WE'LL BE IN TOUCH.
IS THAT IT?
I THINK SO.
DON'T YOU NEED MY PHONE NUMBER OR ANYTHING?
WE'LL BE IN TOUCH. CAN WE KEEP THE PHOTOGRAPH?
I SUPPOSE SO.
WELL, 'BYE THEN.
WHO DO YOU SUSPECT?
I SUSPECT HER.
WHY?
MALTESE FALCON. IT'S ALWAYS THE DAME THAT HIRES YOU THAT DID IT.
NO IT'S NOT. SHERLOCK HOLMES GOT CASES FROM LOTS OF LADIES. NONE OF THEM EVER DID IT. ONE OF THEM EVEN MARRIED DR. WATSON.
WELL, WHO DO YOU SUSPECT, THEN?
THIS AMERICAN BOY. WAT. HE SEEMS A GOOD PLACE TO START.
WELL, I STILL SUSPECT HER.
OUR FIRST CASE. WOW. WHAT DO WE DO NOW?
WELL, CHARLES, THE GAME'S AFOOT. LET'S GO TO FLAXDOWN AND LOOK FOR CLUES.
I BET I FIND MORE THAN YOU. I'VE GOT THE MAGNIFYING GLASS.
I'M NOT SURE WE'LL FIND ANY CLUES. AFTER ALL, FROM WHAT THAT GIRL SAID, THE POLICE HAVE ALREADY BEEN ALL OVER THE PLACE.
OF COURSE WE'LL FIND CLUES.
I MEAN, WE'VE GOT THREE BIG THINGS GOING FOR US.
FIRST, THE POLICE ALWAYS MISS THE IMPORTANT CLUES. THAT WAS WHY INSPECTOR LESTRADE WAS ALWAYS GETTING SO ANGRY.
SECOND, KIDS CAN GO PLACES GROWN-UPS CAN'T, AND FIND STUFF OUT. AND WE'RE NOT JUST KIDS. WE'RE DETECTIVES.
AND THIRD, WE'RE DEAD. I MEAN, THAT'S GOT TO COUNT FOR SOME-THING...

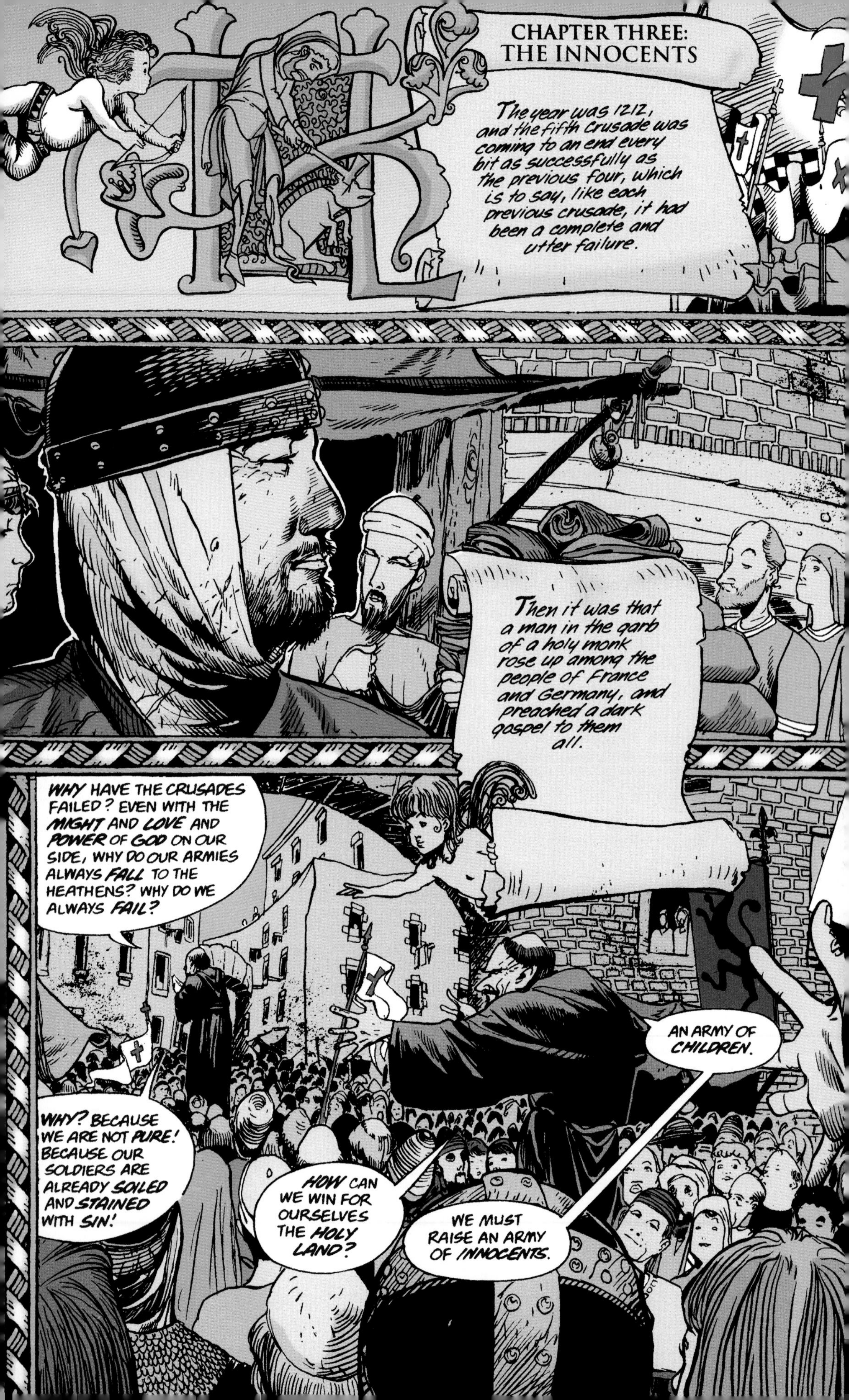
CHAPTER THREE:
THE INNOCENTS
The year was 1212, and the fifth crusade was coming to an end every bit as successfully as the previous four, which is to say, like each previous crusade, it had been a complete and utter failure.
Then it was that a man in the garb of a holy monk rose up among the people of France and Germany, and preached a dark gospel to them all.
WHY HAVE THE CRUSADES FAILED? EVEN WITH THE MIGHT AND LOVE AND POWER OF GOD ON OUR SIDE, WHY DO OUR ARMIES ALWAYS FALL TO THE HEATHENS? WHY DO WE ALWAYS FAIL?
WHY? BECAUSE WE ARE NOT PURE! BECAUSE OUR SOLDIERS ARE ALREADY SOILED AND STAINED WITH SIN!
HOW CAN WE WIN FOR OURSELVES THE HOLY LAND?
WE MUST RAISE AN ARMY OF INNOCENTS.
AN ARMY OF CHILDREN.

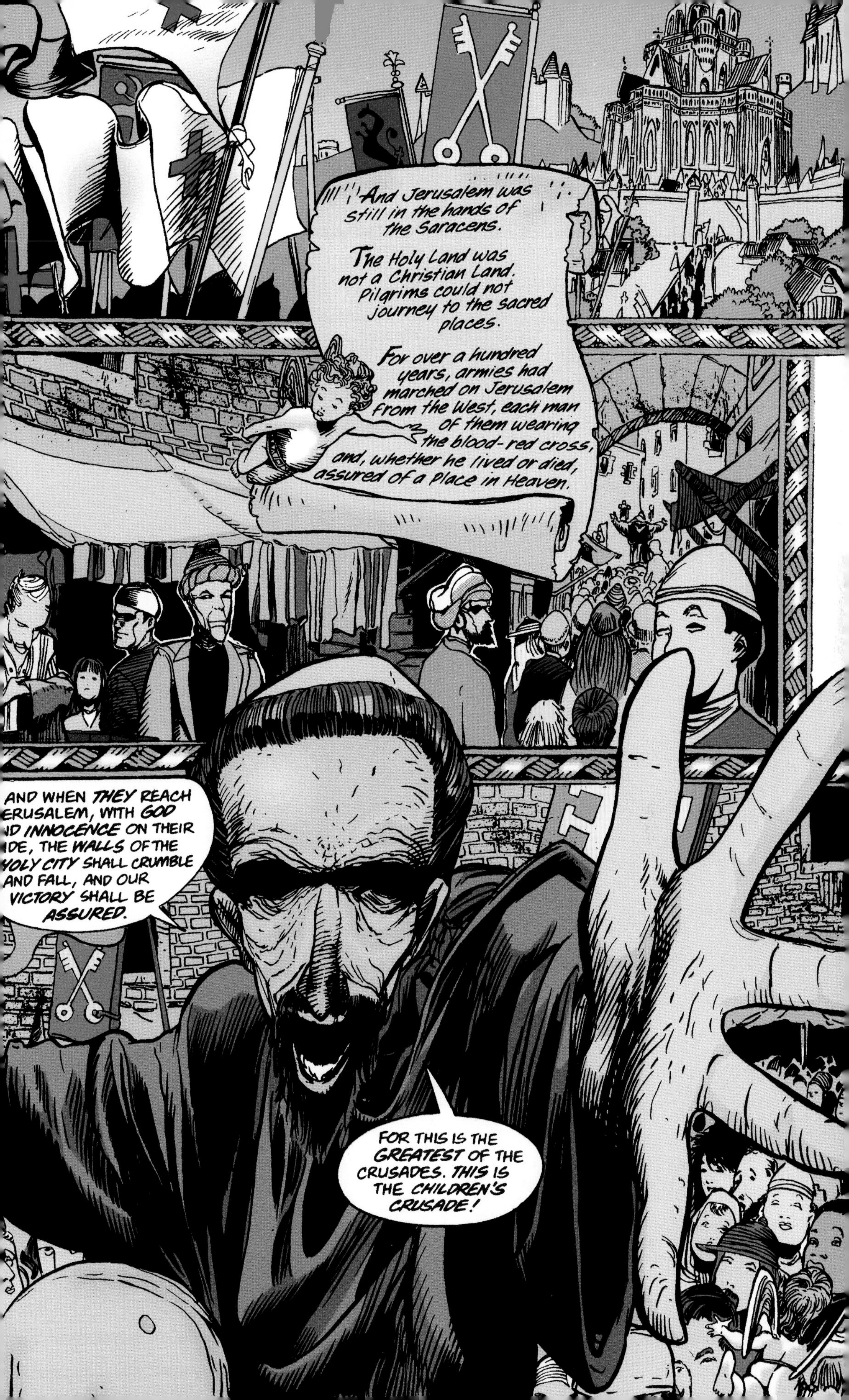
And Jerusalem was still in the hands of the Saracens.
The Holy Land was not a Christian Land. Pilgrims could not journey to the sacred places.
For over a hundred years, armies had marched on Jerusalem from the West, each man of them wearing the blood-red cross, and, whether he lived or died, assured of a place in Heaven.
AND WHEN THEY REACH ERUSALEM, WITH GOD ID INNOCENCE ON THEIR IDE, THE WALLS OF THE YOLY CITY SHALL CRUMBLE AND FALL, AND OUR VICTORY SHALL BE ASSURED.
FOR THIS IS THE GREATEST OF THE CRUSADES. THIS IS THE CHILDREN'S CRUSADE!

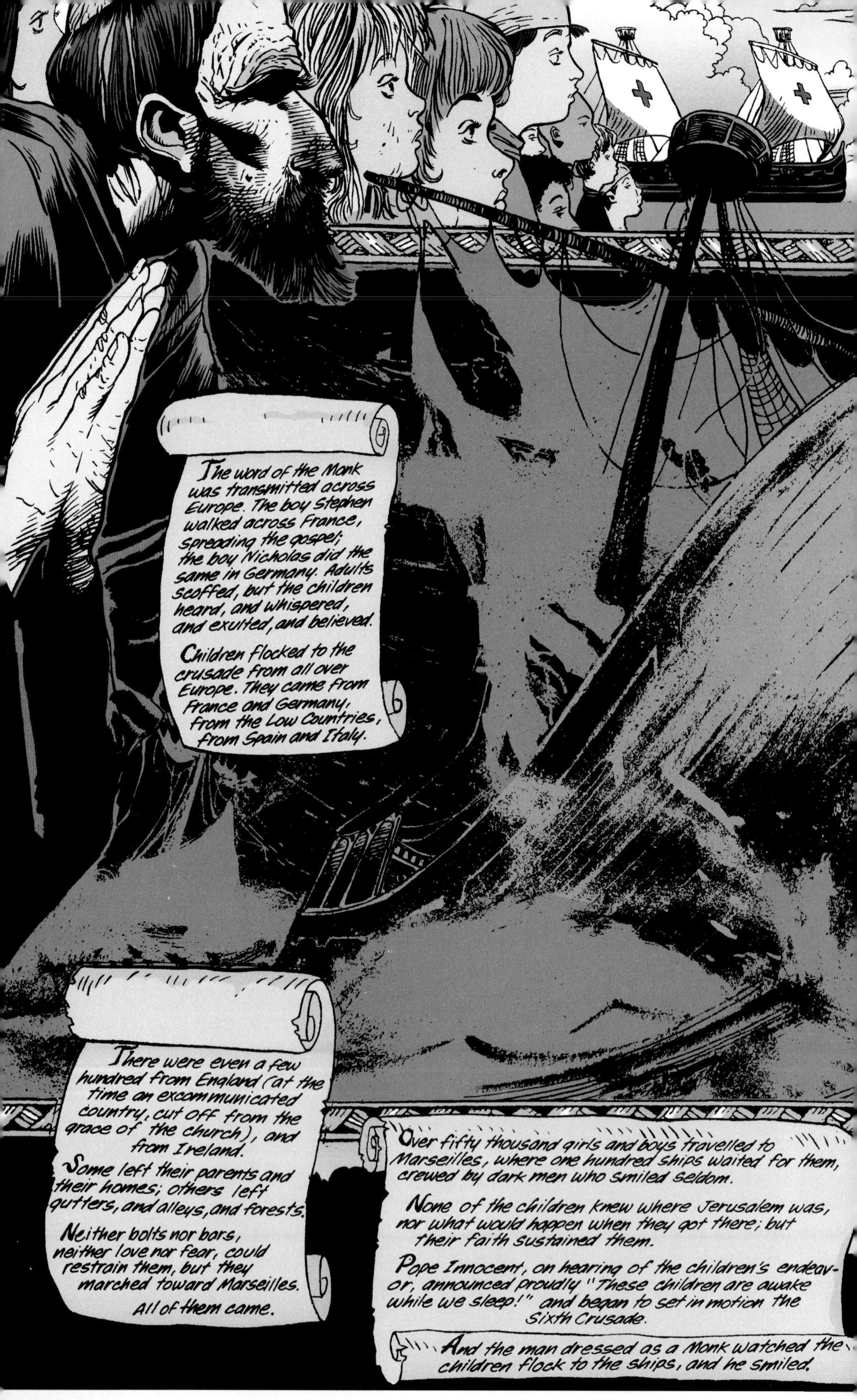
The word of the Monk was transmitted across Europe. The boy Stephen walked across France, spreading the gospel; the boy Nicholas did the same in Germany. Adults scoffed, but the children heard, and whispered, and exulted, and believed.
Children flocked to the crusade from all over Europe. They came from France and Germany, from the Low Countries, from Spain and Italy.
There were even a few hundred from England (at the time an excommunicated country, cut off from the grace of the church), and from Ireland.
Some left their parents and their homes; others left gutters, and alleys, and forests.
Neither bolts nor bars, neither love nor fear, could restrain them, but they marched toward Marseilles.
All of them came.
Over fifty thousand girls and boys travelled to Marseilles, where one hundred ships waited for them, crewed by dark men who smiled seldom.
None of the children knew where Jerusalem was, nor what would happen when they got there; but their faith sustained them.
Pope Innocent, on hearing of the children's endeavor, announced proudly "These children are awake while we sleep!" and began to set in motion the Sixth Crusade.
And the man dressed as a Monk watched the children flock to the ships, and he smiled.

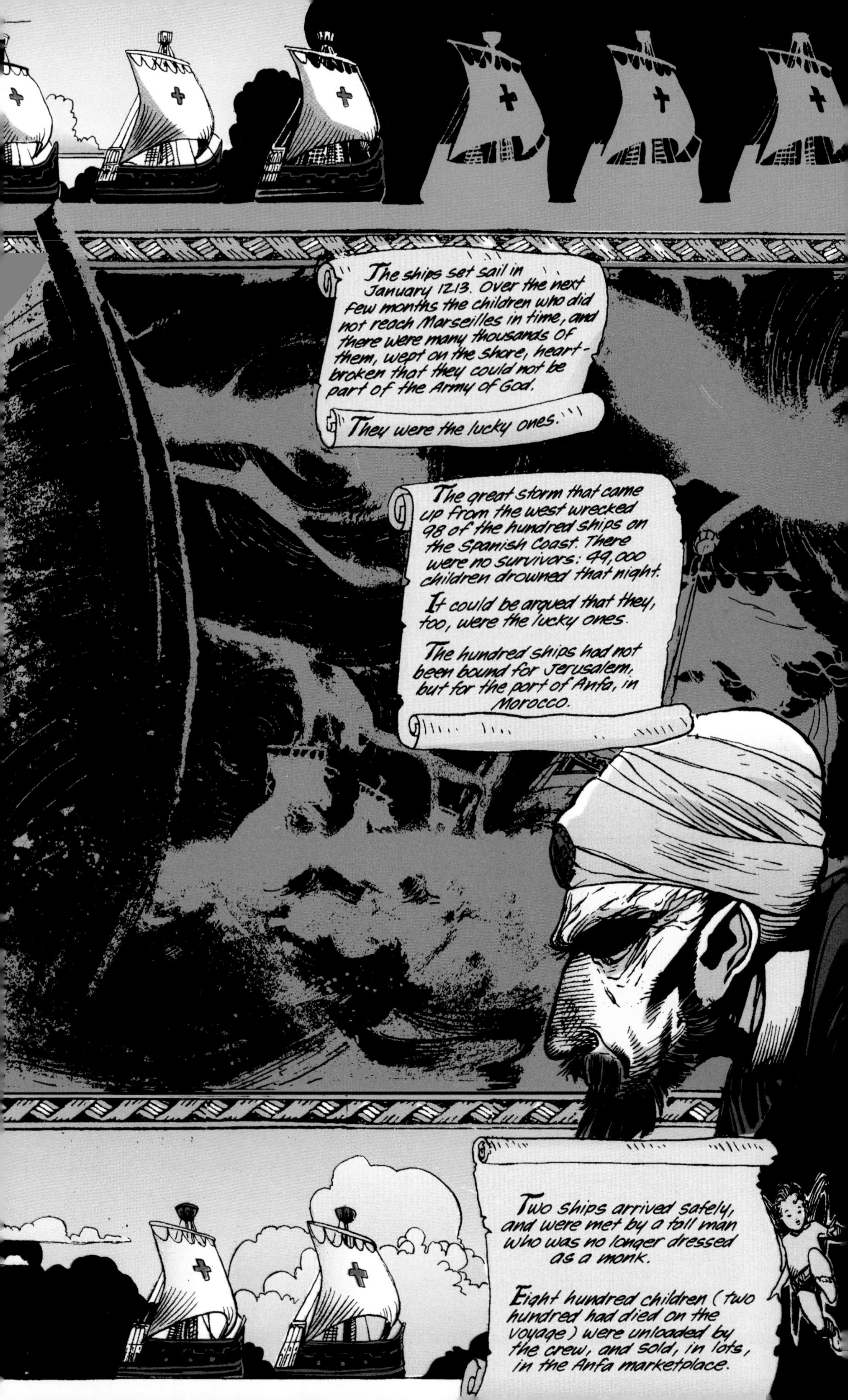
The ships set sail in January 1213. Over the next few months the children who did not reach Marseilles in time, and there were many thousands of them, wept on the shore, heart-broken that they could not be part of the Army of God.
They were the lucky ones.
The great storm that came up from the west wrecked 98 of the hundred ships on the Spanish Coast. There were no survivors: 49,000 children drowned that night.
It could be argued that they, too, were the lucky ones.
The hundred ships had not been bound for Jerusalem, but for the port of Anfa, in Morocco.
Two ships arrived safely, and were met by a tall man who was no longer dressed as a monk.
Eight hundred children (two hundred had died on the voyage) were unloaded by the crew, and sold, in lots, in the Anfa marketplace.

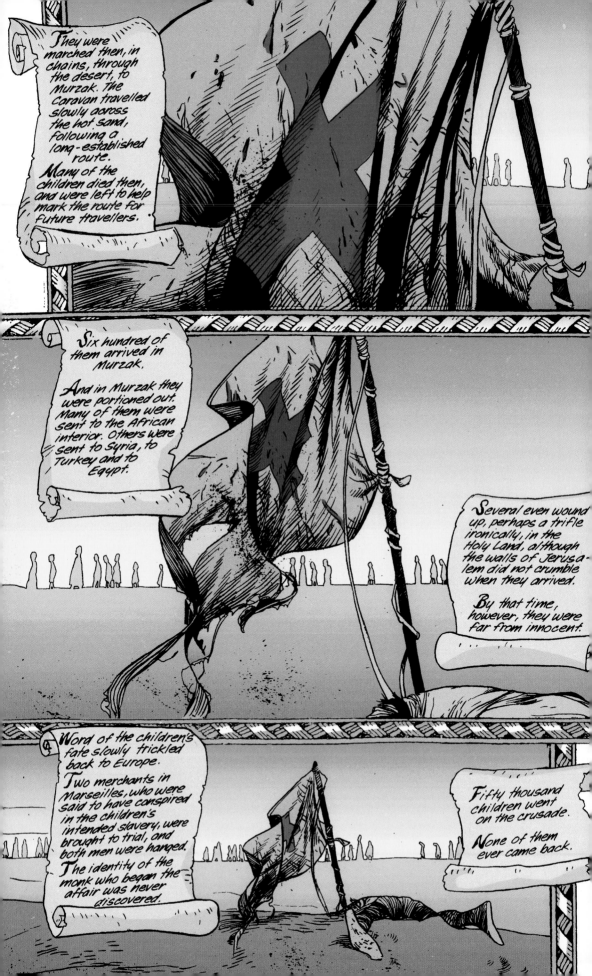

They were marched then, in chains, through the desert, to Murzak. The Caravan travelled slowly across the hot sand, following a long-established route.

Many of the children died then, and were left to help mark the route for future travellers.

Six hundred of them arrived in Murzak.

And in Murzak they were portioned out. Many of them were sent to the African interior. Others were sent to Syria, to Turkey and to Egypt.

Several even wound up, perhaps a trifle ironically, in the Holy Land, although the walls of Jerusalem did not crumble when they arrived.

By that time, however, they were far from innocent.

Word of the children's fate slowly trickled back to Europe.

Two merchants in Marseilles, who were said to have conspired in the children's intended slavery, were brought to trial, and both men were hanged.

The identity of the monk who began the affair was never discovered.

Fifty thousand children went on the crusade.

None of them ever came back.

CHAPTER FOUR:
THE FAT BEGINS TO FRY

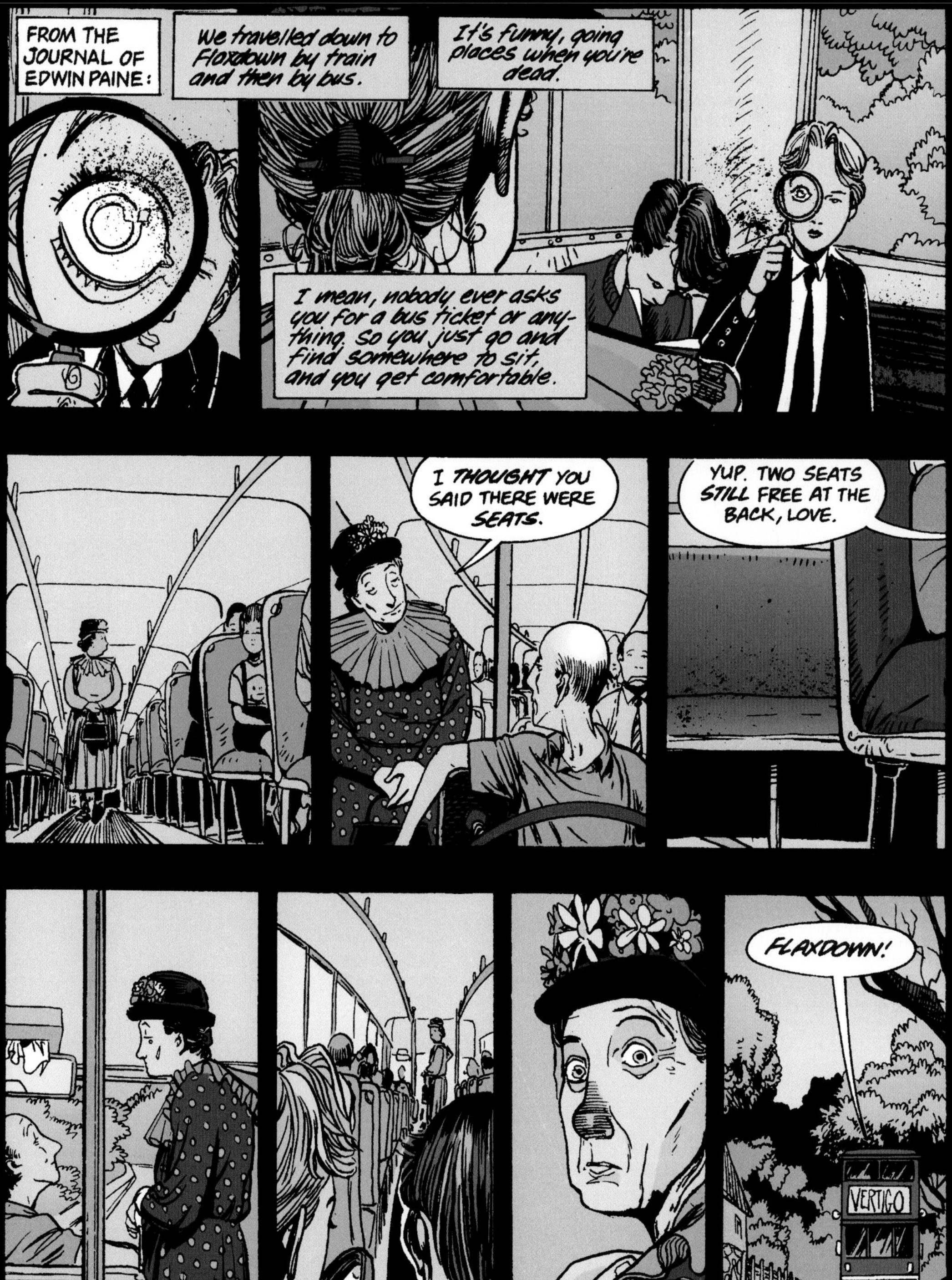
FROM THE JOURNAL OF EDWIN PAINE:
We travelled down to Floxdown by train and then by bus.
It's funny, going places when you're dead.
I mean, nobody ever asks you for a bus ticket or anything. So you just go and find somewhere to sit, and you get comfortable.
I THOUGHT YOU SAID THERE WERE SEATS.
YUP. TWO SEATS STILL FREE AT THE BACK, LOVE.
FLAXDOWN!
VERTIGO

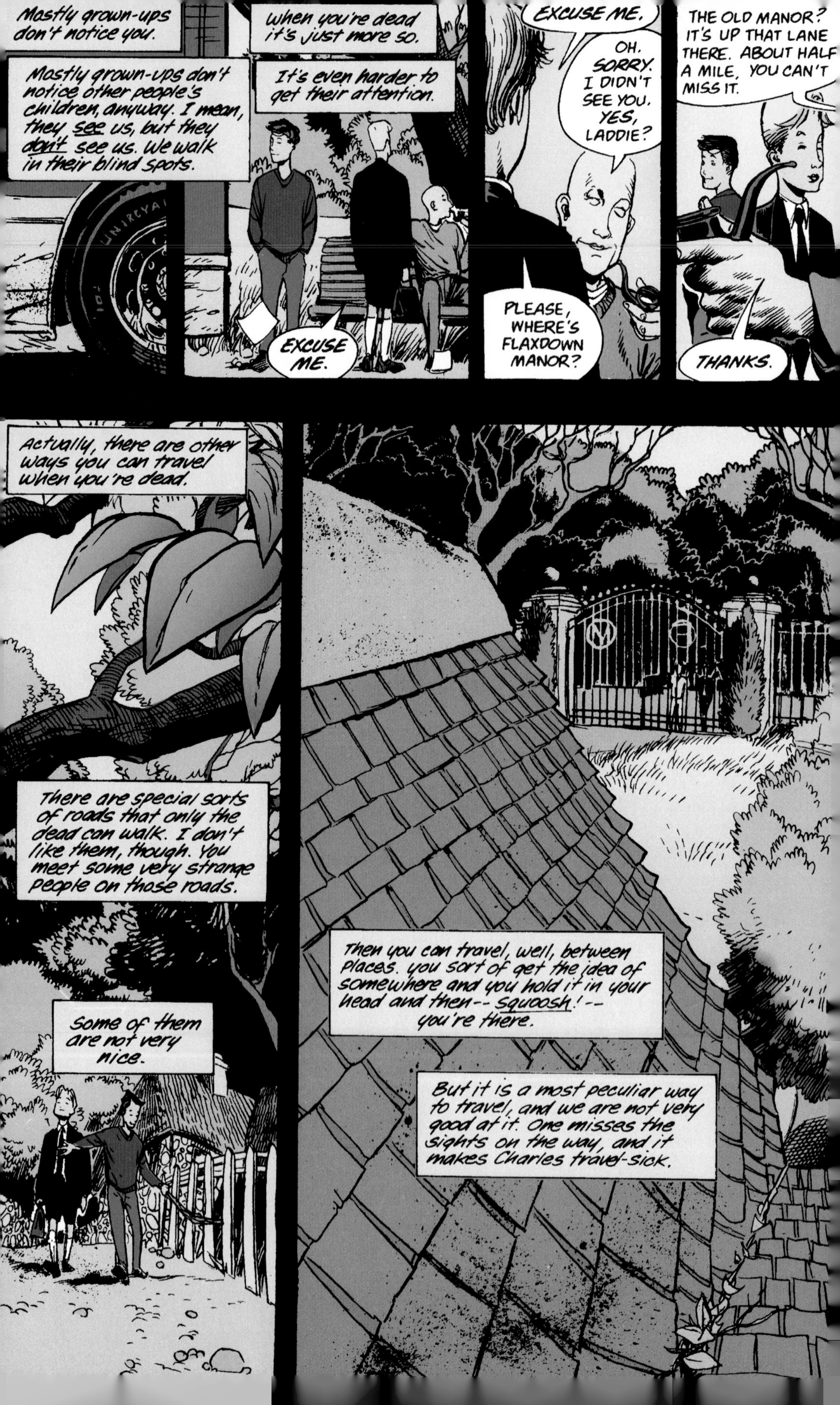
Mostly grown-ups don't notice you.
Mostly grown-ups don't notice other people's children, anyway. I mean, they see us, but they don't see us. We walk in their blind spots.
When you're dead it's just more so.
It's even harder to get their attention.
EXCUSE ME.
EXCUSE ME.
OH. SORRY. I DIDN'T SEE YOU. YES, LADDIE?
PLEASE, WHERE'S FLAXDOWN MANOR?
THE OLD MANOR? IT'S UP THAT LANE THERE. ABOUT HALF A MILE. YOU CAN'T MISS IT.
THANKS.
Actually, there are other ways you can travel when you're dead.
There are special sorts of roads that only the dead can walk. I don't like them, though. You meet some very strange people on those roads.
Some of them are not very nice.
Then you can travel, well, between places. you sort of get the idea of somewhere and you hold it in your head and then-- squoosh!-- you're there.
But it is a most peculiar way to travel, and we are not very good at it. One misses the sights on the way, and it makes Charles travel-sick.

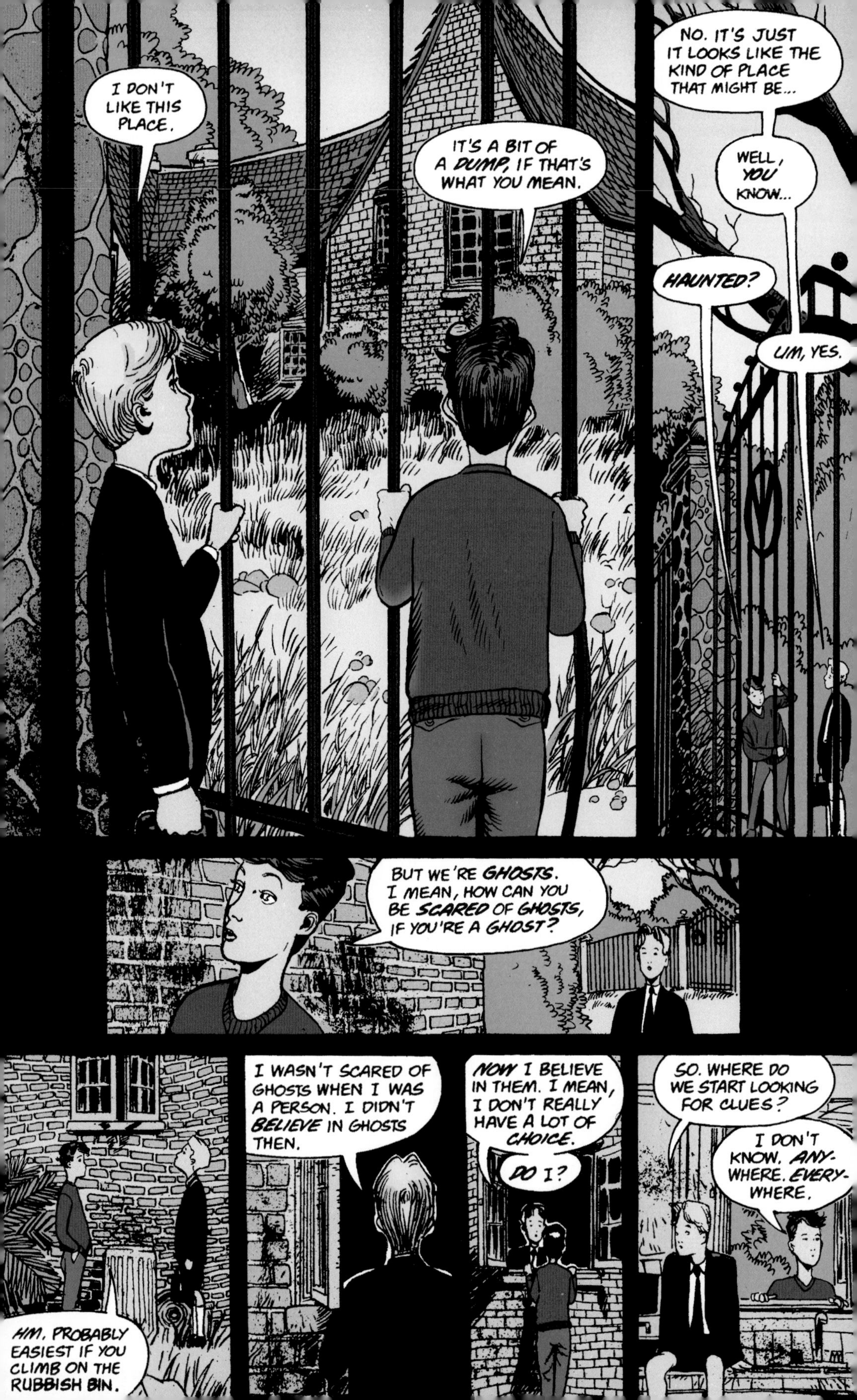
I DON'T LIKE THIS PLACE.
IT'S A BIT OF A DUMP, IF THAT'S WHAT YOU MEAN.
NO. IT'S JUST IT LOOKS LIKE THE KIND OF PLACE THAT MIGHT BE...
WELL, YOU KNOW...
HAUNTED?
UM, YES.
BUT WE'RE GHOSTS. I MEAN, HOW CAN YOU BE SCARED OF GHOSTS, IF YOU'RE A GHOST?
HM. PROBABLY EASIEST IF YOU CLIMB ON THE RUBBISH BIN.
I WASN'T SCARED OF GHOSTS WHEN I WAS A PERSON. I DIDN'T BELIEVE IN GHOSTS THEN.
NOW I BELIEVE IN THEM. I MEAN, I DON'T REALLY HAVE A LOT OF CHOICE.
DO I?
SO. WHERE DO WE START LOOKING FOR CLUES?
I DON'T KNOW. ANY-WHERE. EVERY-WHERE.

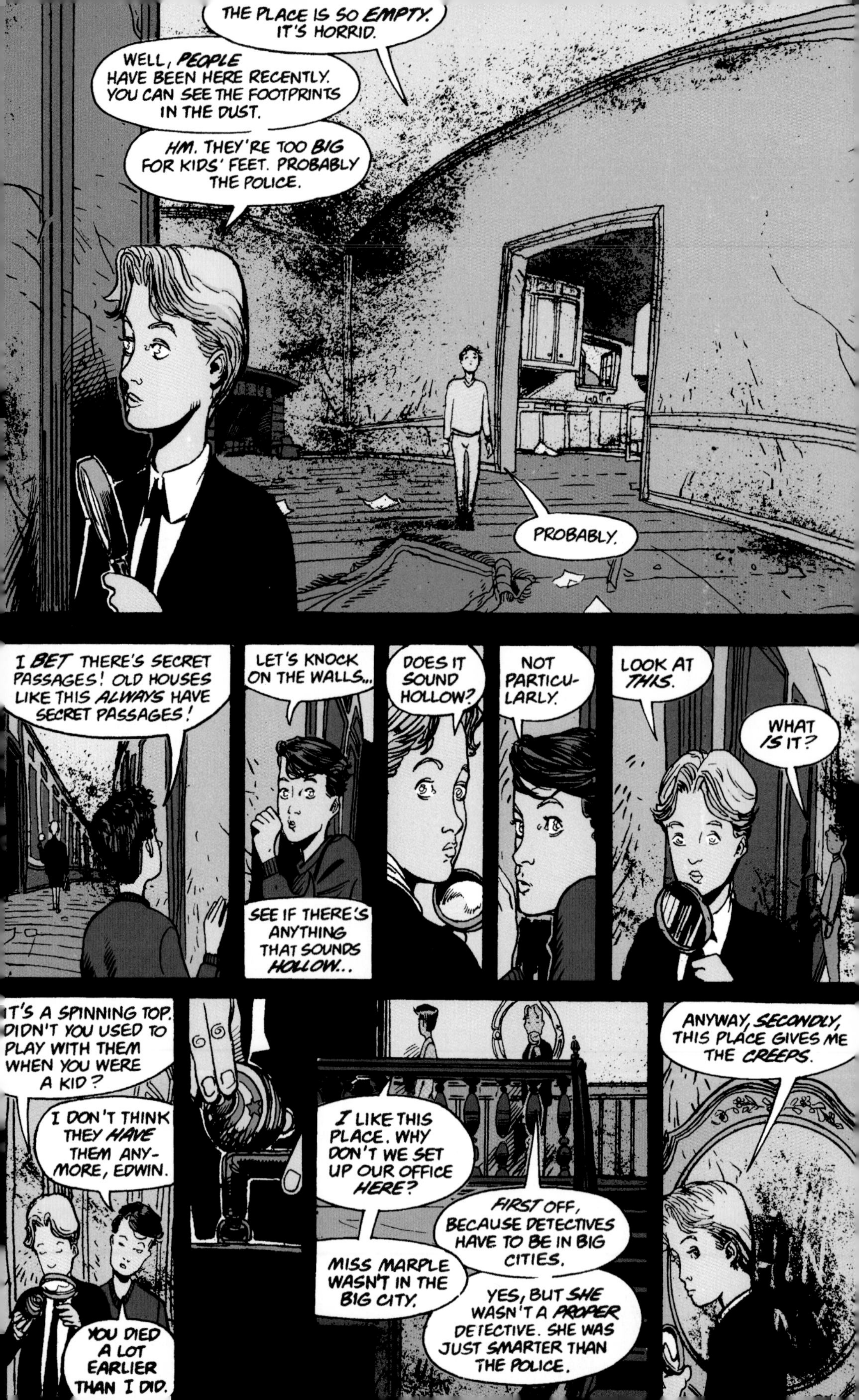
THE PLACE IS SO EMPTY. IT'S HORRID.
WELL, PEOPLE HAVE BEEN HERE RECENTLY. YOU CAN SEE THE FOOTPRINTS IN THE DUST.
HM. THEY'RE TOO BIG FOR KIDS' FEET. PROBABLY THE POLICE.
PROBABLY.
I BET THERE'S SECRET PASSAGES! OLD HOUSES LIKE THIS ALWAYS HAVE SECRET PASSAGES!
LET'S KNOCK ON THE WALLS...
SEE IF THERE'S ANYTHING THAT SOUNDS HOLLOW...
DOES IT SOUND HOLLOW?
NOT PARTICU-LARLY.
LOOK AT THIS.
WHAT IS IT?
IT'S A SPINNING TOP. DIDN'T YOU USED TO PLAY WITH THEM WHEN YOU WERE A KID?
I DON'T THINK THEY HAVE THEM ANY-MORE, EDWIN.
YOU DIED A LOT EARLIER THAN I DID.
I LIKE THIS PLACE. WHY DON'T WE SET UP OUR OFFICE HERE?
FIRST OFF, BECAUSE DETECTIVES HAVE TO BE IN BIG CITIES.
MISS MARPLE WASN'T IN THE BIG CITY.
YES, BUT SHE WASN'T A PROPER DETECTIVE. SHE WAS JUST SMARTER THAN THE POLICE.
ANYWAY, SECONDLY, THIS PLACE GIVES ME THE CREEPS.

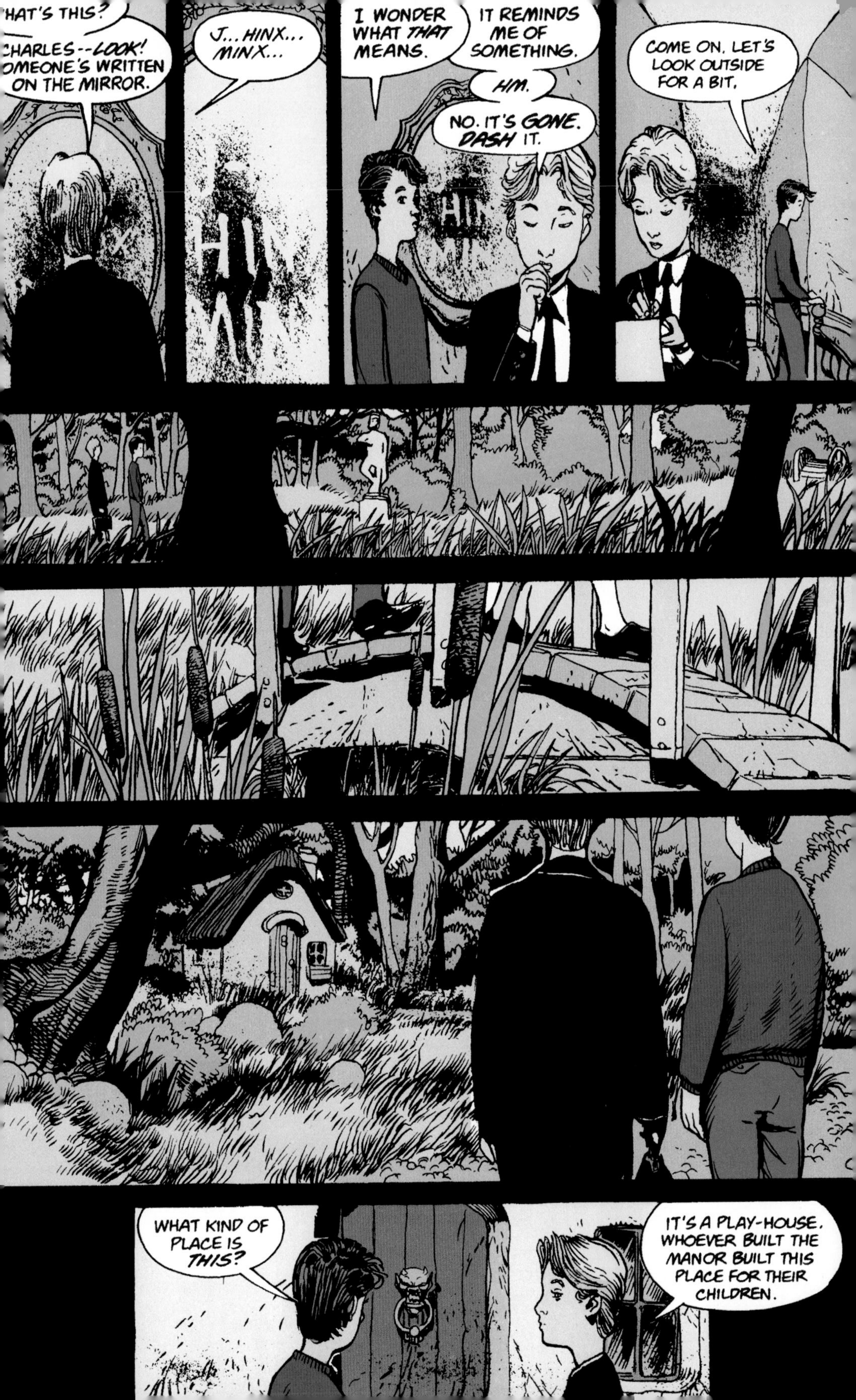

HAT'S THIS?
CHARLES--LOOK! OMEONE'S WRITTEN ON THE MIRROR.
J...HINX... MINX...
I WONDER WHAT THAT MEANS.
IT REMINDS ME OF SOMETHING.
HM.
NO. IT'S GONE. DASH IT.
COME ON. LET'S LOOK OUTSIDE FOR A BIT.
WHAT KIND OF PLACE IS THIS?
IT'S A PLAY-HOUSE. WHOEVER BUILT THE MANOR BUILT THIS PLACE FOR THEIR CHILDREN.

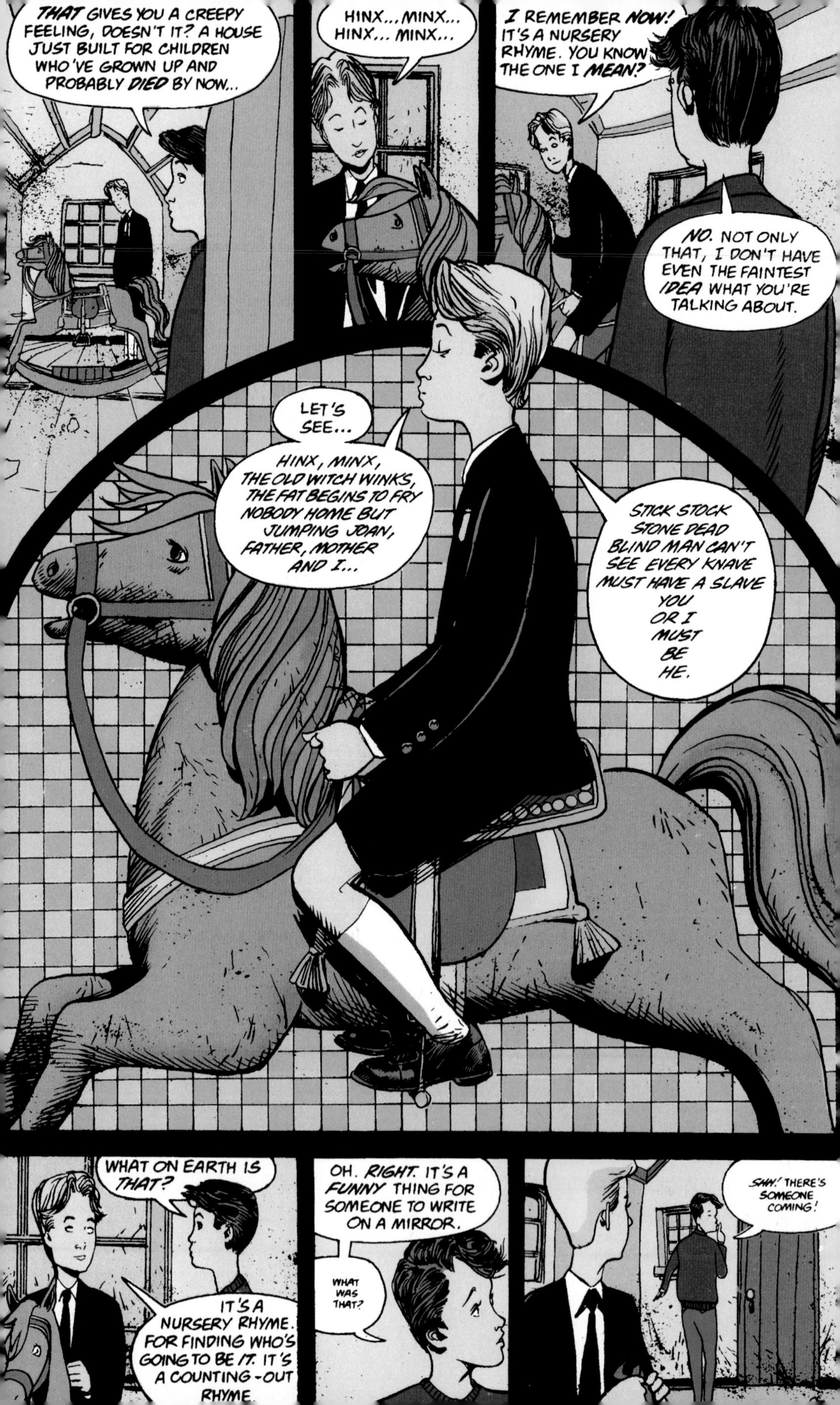
THAT GIVES YOU A CREEPY FEELING, DOESN'T IT? A HOUSE JUST BUILT FOR CHILDREN WHO'VE GROWN UP AND PROBABLY DIED BY NOW...
HINX... MINX... HINX... MINX...
I REMEMBER NOW! IT'S A NURSERY RHYME. YOU KNOW THE ONE I MEAN?
NO. NOT ONLY THAT, I DON'T HAVE EVEN THE FAINTEST IDEA WHAT YOU'RE TALKING ABOUT.
LET'S SEE...
HINX, MINX, THE OLD WITCH WINKS, THE FAT BEGINS TO FRY NOBODY HOME BUT JUMPING JOAN, FATHER, MOTHER AND I...
STICK STOCK STONE DEAD BLIND MAN CAN'T SEE EVERY KNAVE MUST HAVE A SLAVE YOU OR I MUST BE HE.
WHAT ON EARTH IS THAT?
IT'S A NURSERY RHYME. FOR FINDING WHO'S GOING TO BE IT. IT'S A COUNTING-OUT RHYME.
OH. RIGHT. IT'S A FUNNY THING FOR SOMEONE TO WRITE ON A MIRROR.
WHAT WAS THAT?
SHH! THERE'S SOMEONE COMING!

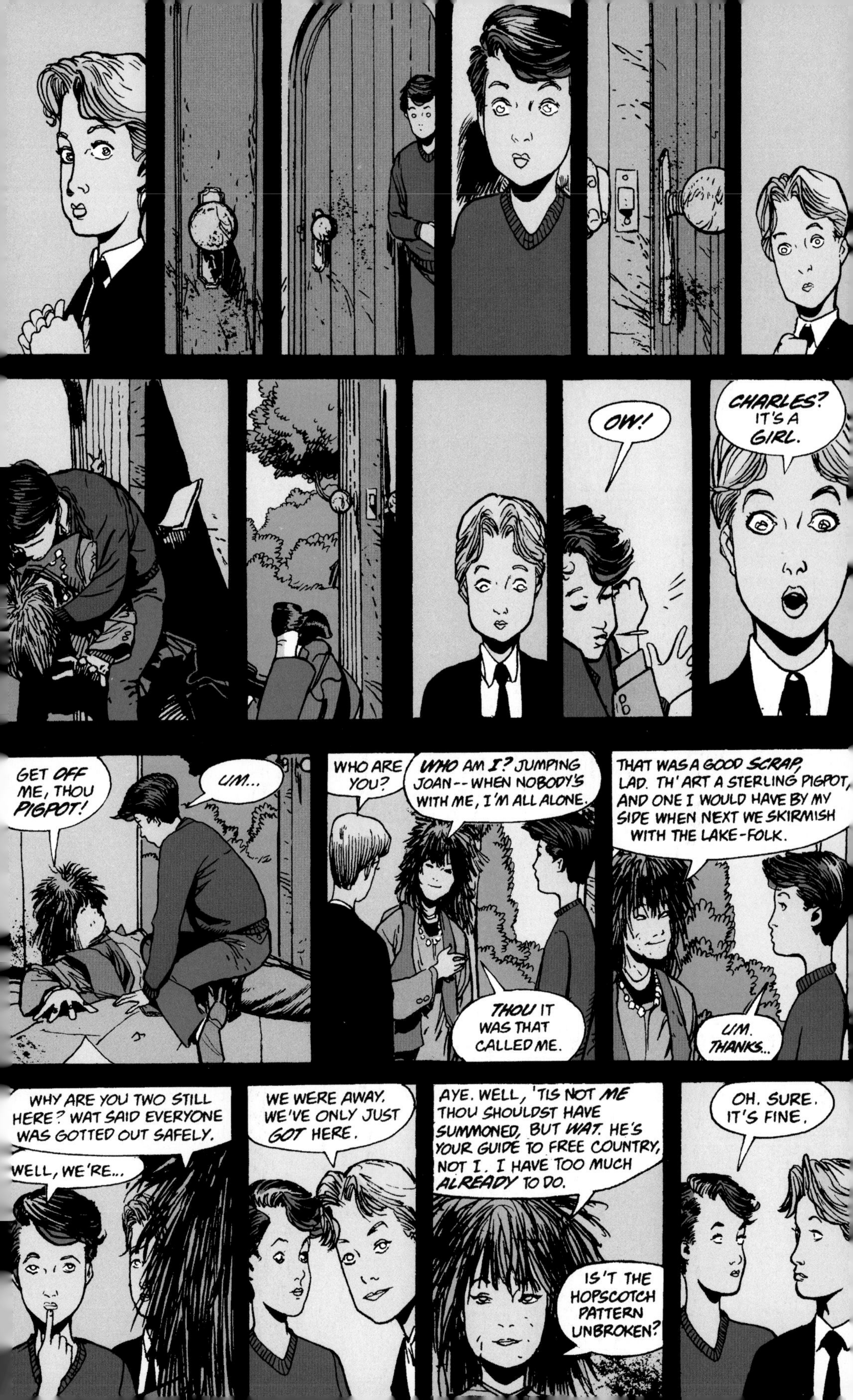
OW!
CHARLES? IT'S A GIRL.
GET OFF ME, THOU PIGPOT!
UM...
WHO ARE YOU?
WHO AM I? JUMPING JOAN--WHEN NOBODY'S WITH ME, I'M ALL ALONE.
THOU IT WAS THAT CALLED ME.
THAT WAS A GOOD SCRAP, LAD. TH' ART A STERLING PIGPOT, AND ONE I WOULD HAVE BY MY SIDE WHEN NEXT WE SKIRMISH WITH THE LAKE-FOLK.
UM. THANKS...
WHY ARE YOU TWO STILL HERE? WAT SAID EVERYONE WAS GOTTED OUT SAFELY.
WELL, WE'RE...
WE WERE AWAY. WE'VE ONLY JUST GOT HERE.
AYE. WELL, 'TIS NOT ME THOU SHOULDST HAVE SUMMONED, BUT WAT. HE'S YOUR GUIDE TO FREE COUNTRY, NOT I. I HAVE TOO MUCH ALREADY TO DO.
IS'T THE HOPSCOTCH PATTERN UNBROKEN?
OH. SURE. IT'S FINE.

VERY WELL, THEN. I'LL BE AWAY. PUT OUT THY FISTS.

LIKE *THIS*.

A *GIFT*, A *GHOST*, A *FRIEND*, A *FOE*, A *LETTER* TO *COME*, A *JOURNEY* TO--

HUH?

NOBODY HOME BUT JUMPING JOAN... THAT WAS PRETTY PECULIAR, IF YOU ASK ME.

WAS SHE AN ALIVE PERSON? I COULDN'T TELL.

SHE WAS WARM, *AND* BREATHING. I COULD FEEL HER.

YES, BUT *SHE* COULD FEEL YOU, TOO. REGULAR LIVING PEOPLE SHOULDN'T BE ABLE TO DO *THAT*.

YOU'LL HAVE A PROPER *SHINER* ON THAT EYE, COME TOMORROW.

WELL, MAYBE SHE'S *NOT* A REGULAR LIVING PERSON, THEN.

WHERE DO YOU THINK SHE WAS FROM?

I HAVEN'T A...

HULLO.

SHE *DROPPED* SOMETHING.

PROBABLY WHEN YOU WERE FIGHTING.

SUZY-- JUNKIN
BUCKLEY
MAXINE BAKER--
JACK RABBIT
TEFÉ HOLLAND--
PETER/PUCK
DOROTHY SPI
LIAN
TIMOTHY HUNT
KERWYN

WELL, I THINK WE'VE GOT OURSELVES A *PROPER* CLUE.

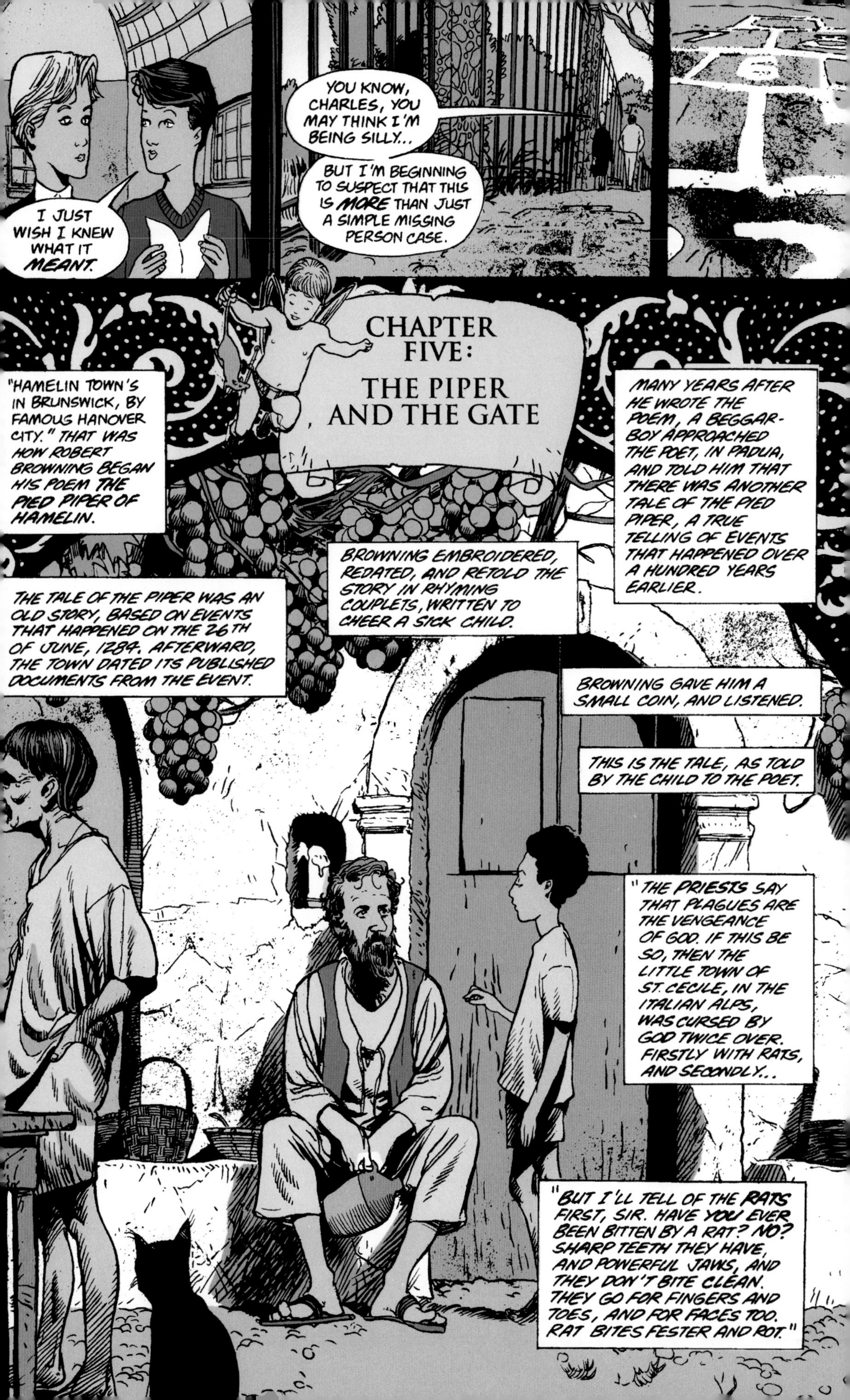
I JUST WISH I KNEW WHAT IT MEANT.
YOU KNOW, CHARLES, YOU MAY THINK I'M BEING SILLY...
BUT I'M BEGINNING TO SUSPECT THAT THIS IS MORE THAN JUST A SIMPLE MISSING PERSON CASE.
CHAPTER FIVE: THE PIPER AND THE GATE
"HAMELIN TOWN'S IN BRUNSWICK, BY FAMOUS HANOVER CITY." THAT WAS HOW ROBERT BROWNING BEGAN HIS POEM THE PIED PIPER OF HAMELIN.
THE TALE OF THE PIPER WAS AN OLD STORY, BASED ON EVENTS THAT HAPPENED ON THE 26TH OF JUNE, 1284. AFTERWARD, THE TOWN DATED ITS PUBLISHED DOCUMENTS FROM THE EVENT.
BROWNING EMBROIDERED, REDATED, AND RETOLD THE STORY IN RHYMING COUPLETS, WRITTEN TO CHEER A SICK CHILD.
MANY YEARS AFTER HE WROTE THE POEM, A BEGGAR-BOY APPROACHED THE POET, IN PADUA, AND TOLD HIM THAT THERE WAS ANOTHER TALE OF THE PIED PIPER, A TRUE TELLING OF EVENTS THAT HAPPENED OVER A HUNDRED YEARS EARLIER.
BROWNING GAVE HIM A SMALL COIN, AND LISTENED.
THIS IS THE TALE, AS TOLD BY THE CHILD TO THE POET.
"THE PRIESTS SAY THAT PLAGUES ARE THE VENGEANCE OF GOD. IF THIS BE SO, THEN THE LITTLE TOWN OF ST. CECILE, IN THE ITALIAN ALPS, WAS CURSED BY GOD TWICE OVER. FIRSTLY WITH RATS, AND SECONDLY...
"BUT I'LL TELL OF THE RATS FIRST, SIR. HAVE YOU EVER BEEN BITTEN BY A RAT? NO? SHARP TEETH THEY HAVE, AND POWERFUL JAWS, AND THEY DON'T BITE CLEAN. THEY GO FOR FINGERS AND TOES, AND FOR FACES TOO. RAT BITES FESTER AND ROT."

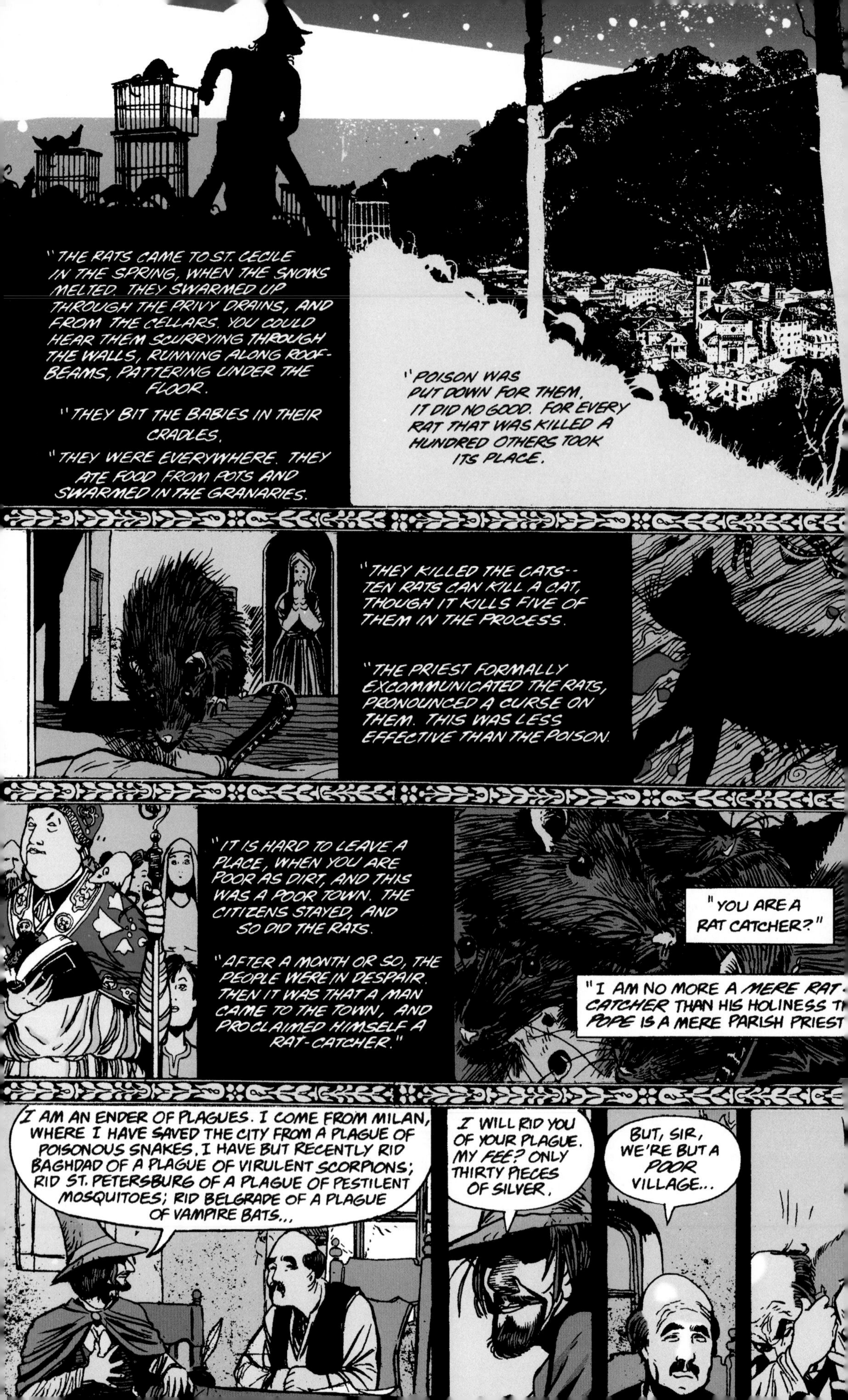

"THE RATS CAME TO ST. CECILE IN THE SPRING, WHEN THE SNOWS MELTED. THEY SWARMED UP THROUGH THE PRIVY DRAINS, AND FROM THE CELLARS. YOU COULD HEAR THEM SCURRYING THROUGH THE WALLS, RUNNING ALONG ROOF-BEAMS, PATTERING UNDER THE FLOOR.
"THEY BIT THE BABIES IN THEIR CRADLES.
"THEY WERE EVERYWHERE. THEY ATE FOOD FROM POTS AND SWARMED IN THE GRANARIES.
"POISON WAS PUT DOWN FOR THEM. IT DID NO GOOD. FOR EVERY RAT THAT WAS KILLED A HUNDRED OTHERS TOOK ITS PLACE.
"THEY KILLED THE CATS-- TEN RATS CAN KILL A CAT, THOUGH IT KILLS FIVE OF THEM IN THE PROCESS.
"THE PRIEST FORMALLY EXCOMMUNICATED THE RATS, PRONOUNCED A CURSE ON THEM. THIS WAS LESS EFFECTIVE THAN THE POISON.
"IT IS HARD TO LEAVE A PLACE, WHEN YOU ARE POOR AS DIRT, AND THIS WAS A POOR TOWN. THE CITIZENS STAYED, AND SO DID THE RATS.
"AFTER A MONTH OR SO, THE PEOPLE WERE IN DESPAIR. THEN IT WAS THAT A MAN CAME TO THE TOWN, AND PROCLAIMED HIMSELF A RAT-CATCHER."
"YOU ARE A RAT CATCHER?"
"I AM NO MORE A MERE RAT-CATCHER THAN HIS HOLINESS TH POPE IS A MERE PARISH PRIEST
I AM AN ENDER OF PLAGUES. I COME FROM MILAN, WHERE I HAVE SAVED THE CITY FROM A PLAGUE OF POISONOUS SNAKES. I HAVE BUT RECENTLY RID BAGHDAD OF A PLAGUE OF VIRULENT SCORPIONS; RID ST. PETERSBURG OF A PLAGUE OF PESTILENT MOSQUITOES; RID BELGRADE OF A PLAGUE OF VAMPIRE BATS...
I WILL RID YOU OF YOUR PLAGUE. MY FEE? ONLY THIRTY PIECES OF SILVER.
BUT, SIR, WE'RE BUT A POOR VILLAGE...

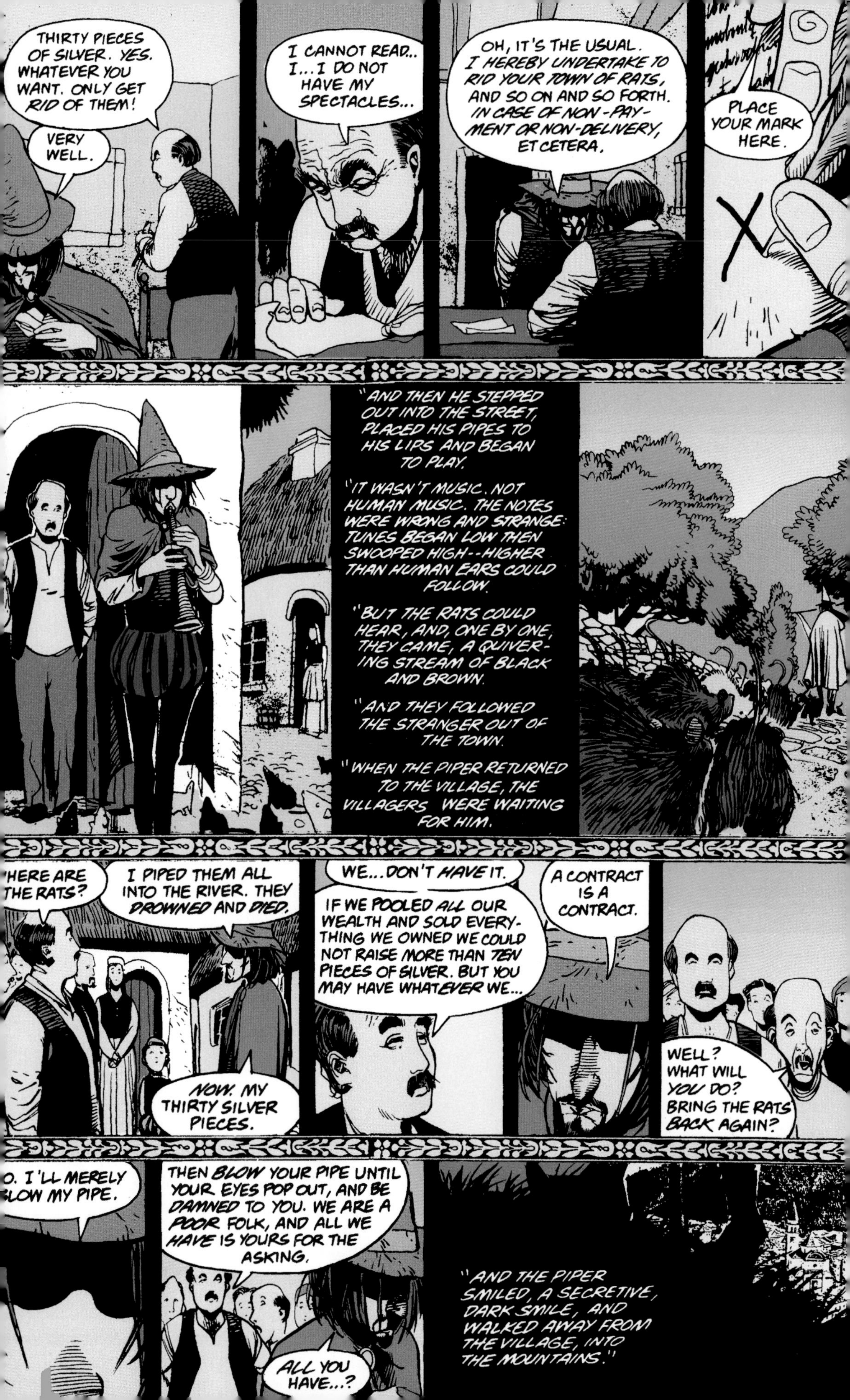
THIRTY PIECES OF SILVER. YES. WHATEVER YOU WANT. ONLY GET *RID* OF THEM!
VERY WELL.
I CANNOT READ.. I... I DO NOT HAVE MY SPECTACLES...
OH, IT'S THE USUAL. I HEREBY UNDERTAKE TO RID YOUR TOWN OF RATS, AND SO ON AND SO FORTH. *IN CASE OF NON-PAYMENT OR NON-DELIVERY,* ETCETERA.
PLACE YOUR MARK HERE.
"AND THEN HE STEPPED OUT INTO THE STREET, PLACED HIS PIPES TO HIS LIPS AND BEGAN TO PLAY.
"IT WASN'T MUSIC. NOT HUMAN MUSIC. THE NOTES WERE WRONG AND STRANGE: TUNES BEGAN LOW THEN SWOOPED HIGH--HIGHER THAN HUMAN EARS COULD FOLLOW.
"BUT THE RATS COULD HEAR, AND, ONE BY ONE, THEY CAME, A QUIVERING STREAM OF BLACK AND BROWN.
"AND THEY FOLLOWED THE STRANGER OUT OF THE TOWN.
"WHEN THE PIPER RETURNED TO THE VILLAGE, THE VILLAGERS WERE WAITING FOR HIM.
HERE ARE THE RATS?
I PIPED THEM ALL INTO THE RIVER. THEY *DROWNED* AND *DIED.*
NOW. MY THIRTY SILVER PIECES.
WE... DON'T *HAVE* IT.
IF WE POOLED *ALL* OUR WEALTH AND SOLD EVERYTHING WE OWNED WE COULD NOT RAISE *MORE* THAN *TEN* PIECES OF SILVER. BUT YOU MAY HAVE WHAT*EVER* WE...
A CONTRACT IS A CONTRACT.
WELL? WHAT WILL *YOU DO?* BRING THE RATS *BACK* AGAIN?
O. I'LL MERELY LOW MY PIPE.
THEN *BLOW* YOUR PIPE UNTIL YOUR EYES POP OUT, AND BE *DAMNED* TO YOU. WE ARE A *POOR* FOLK, AND ALL WE *HAVE* IS YOURS FOR THE ASKING.
ALL YOU HAVE...?
"AND THE PIPER SMILED, A SECRETIVE, DARK SMILE, AND WALKED AWAY FROM THE VILLAGE, INTO THE MOUNTAINS."

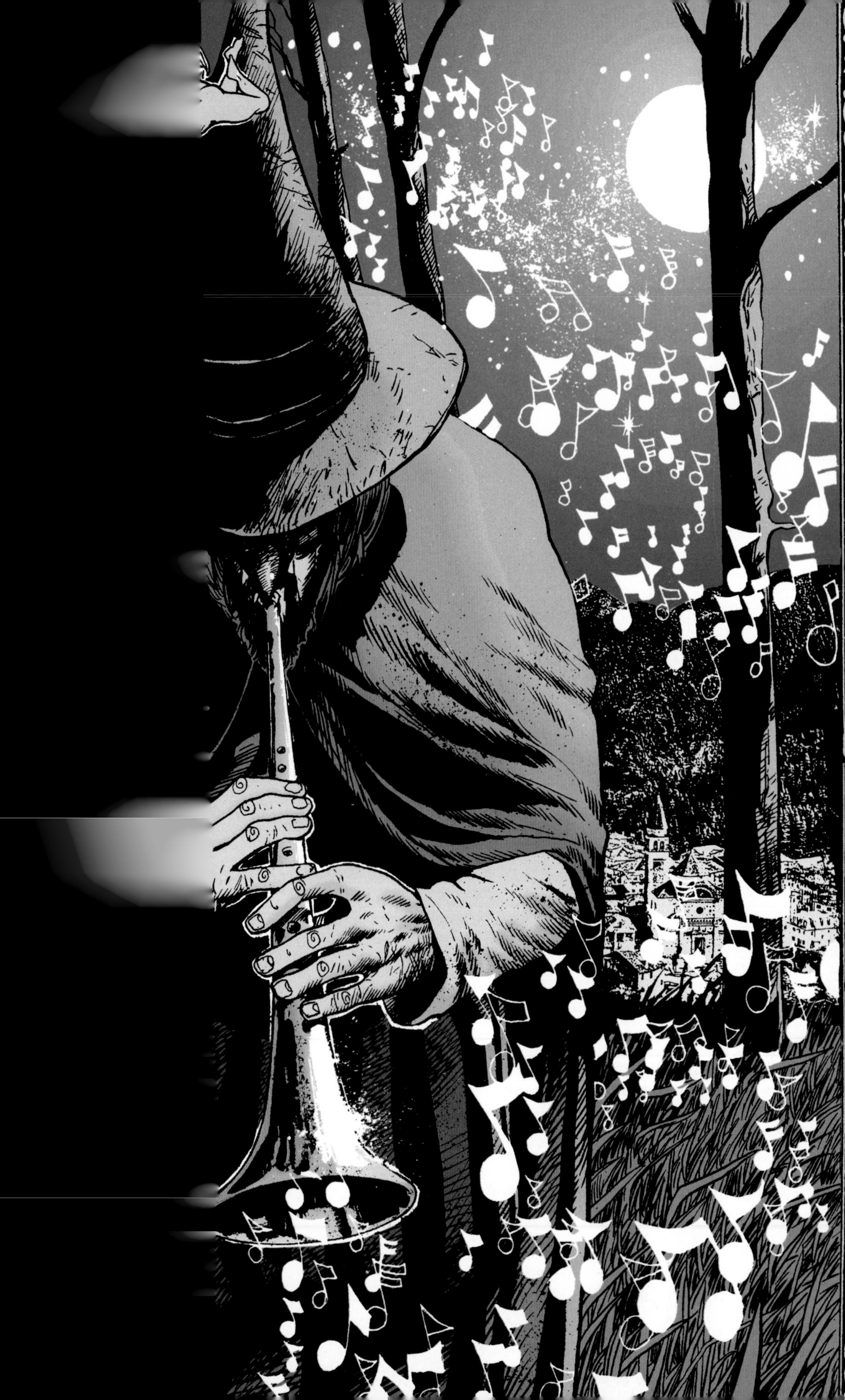

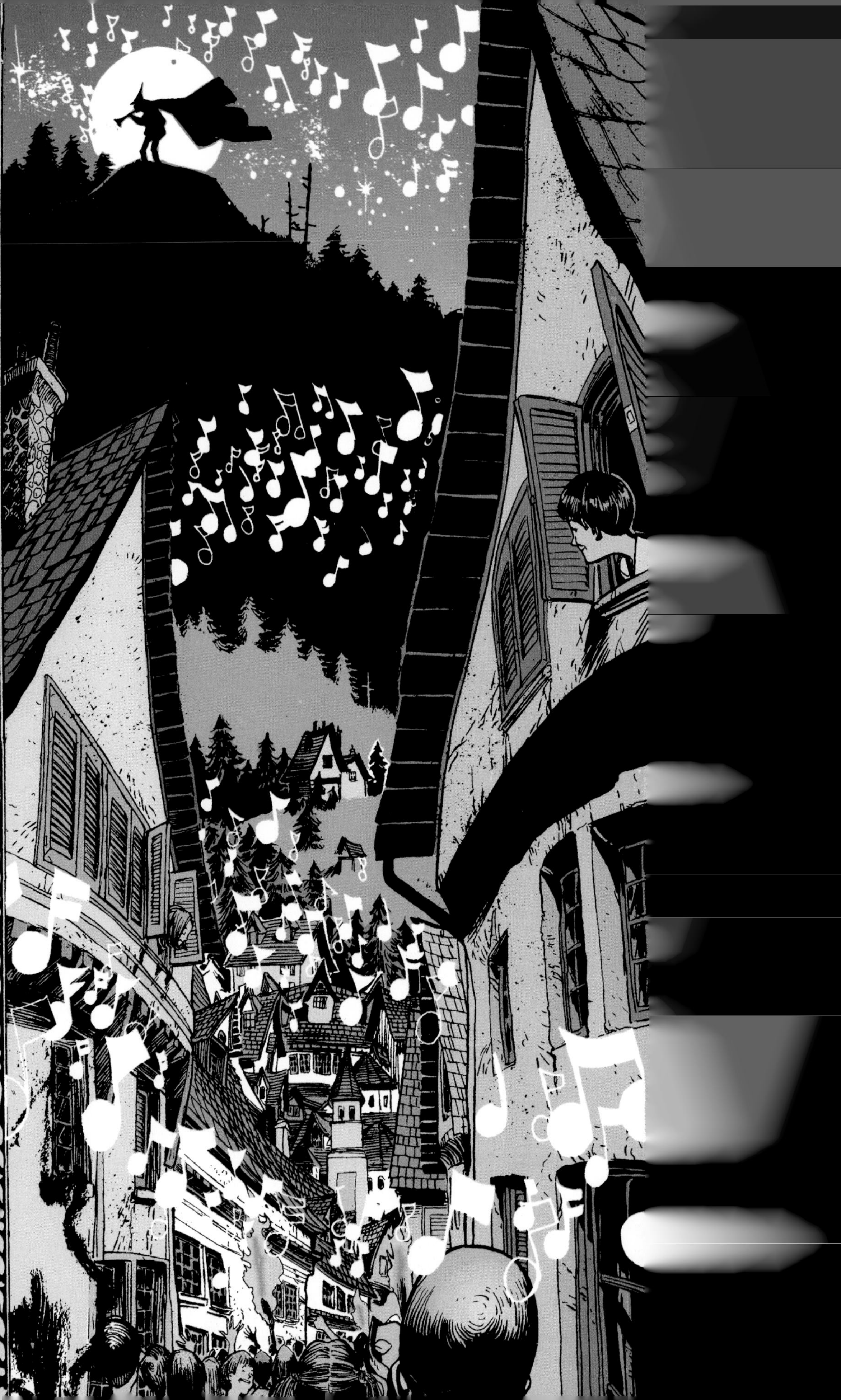

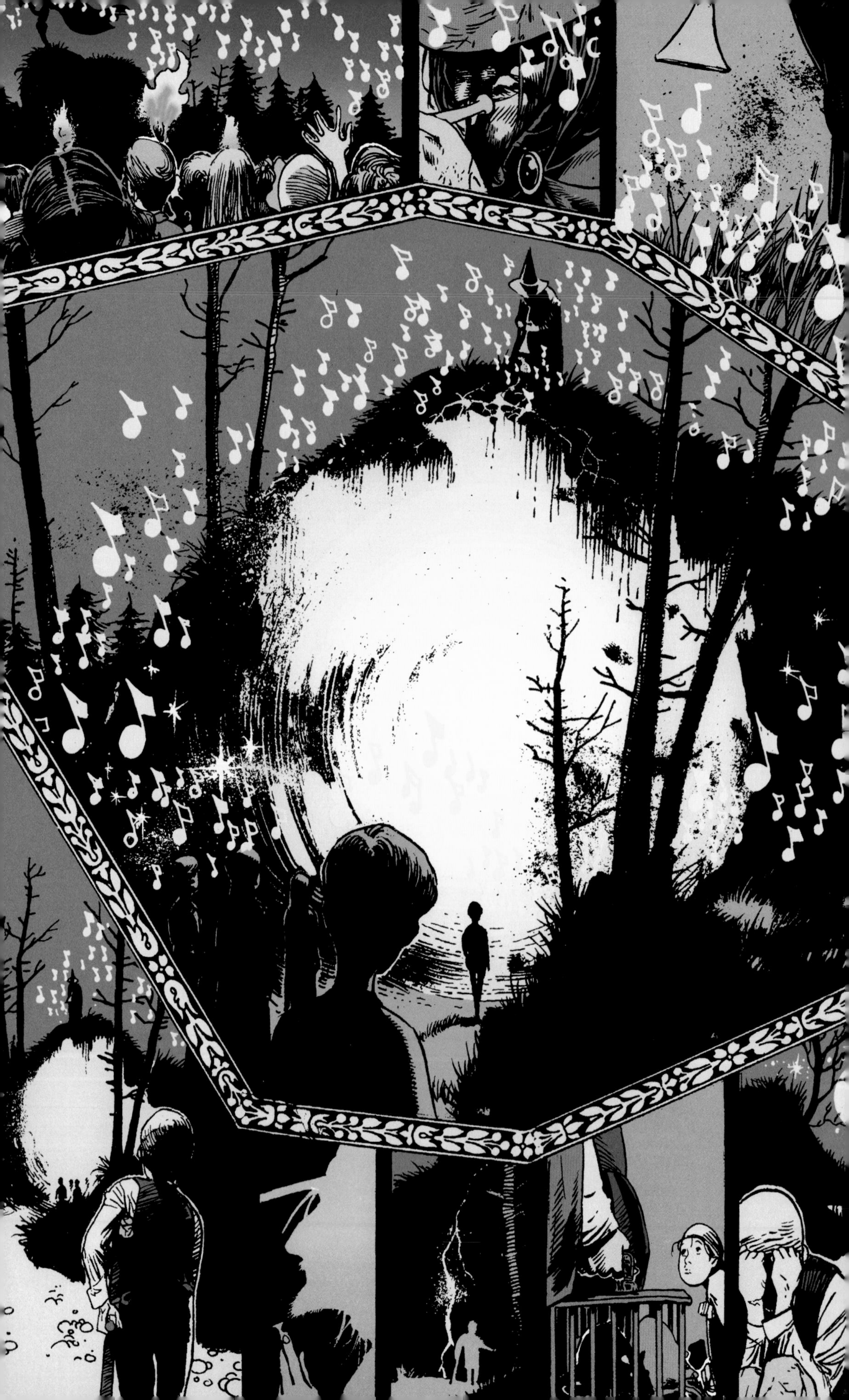

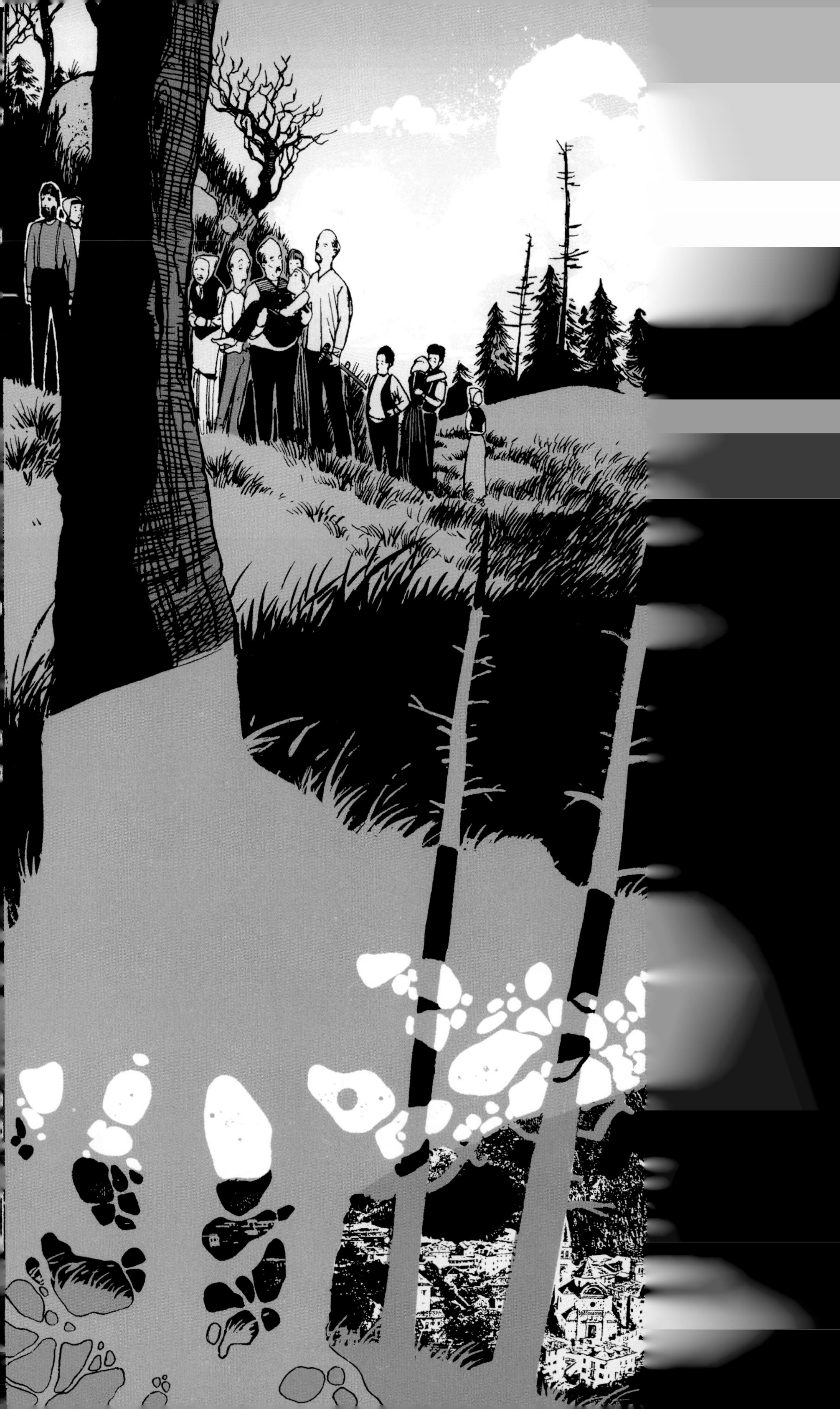

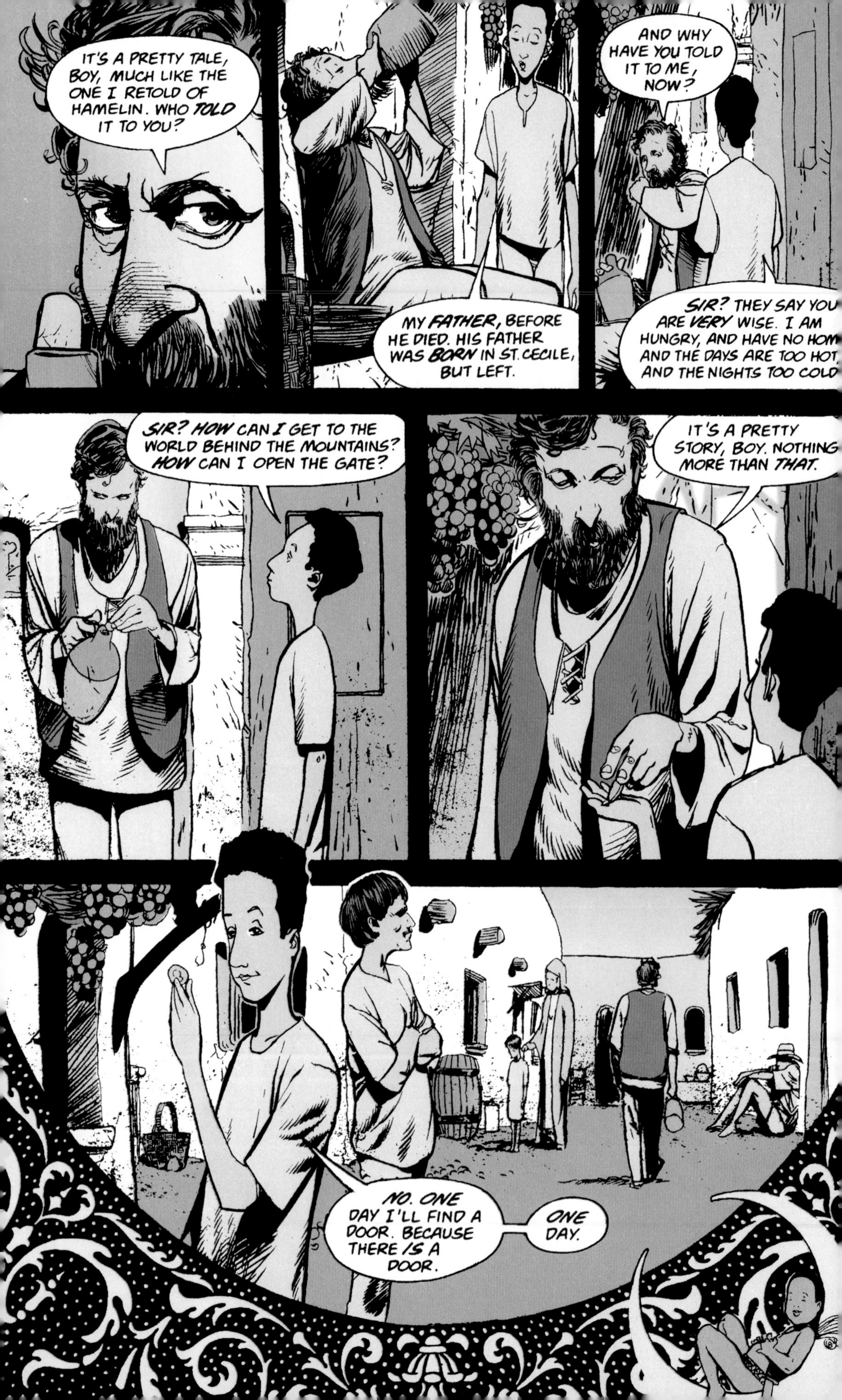
IT'S A PRETTY TALE, BOY, MUCH LIKE THE ONE I RETOLD OF HAMELIN. WHO TOLD IT TO YOU?
MY FATHER, BEFORE HE DIED. HIS FATHER WAS BORN IN ST. CECILE, BUT LEFT.
AND WHY HAVE YOU TOLD IT TO ME, NOW?
SIR? THEY SAY YOU ARE VERY WISE. I AM HUNGRY, AND HAVE NO HOM AND THE DAYS ARE TOO HOT AND THE NIGHTS TOO COLD
SIR? HOW CAN I GET TO THE WORLD BEHIND THE MOUNTAINS? HOW CAN I OPEN THE GATE?
IT'S A PRETTY STORY, BOY. NOTHING MORE THAN THAT.
NO. ONE DAY I'LL FIND A DOOR. BECAUSE THERE IS A DOOR.
ONE DAY.

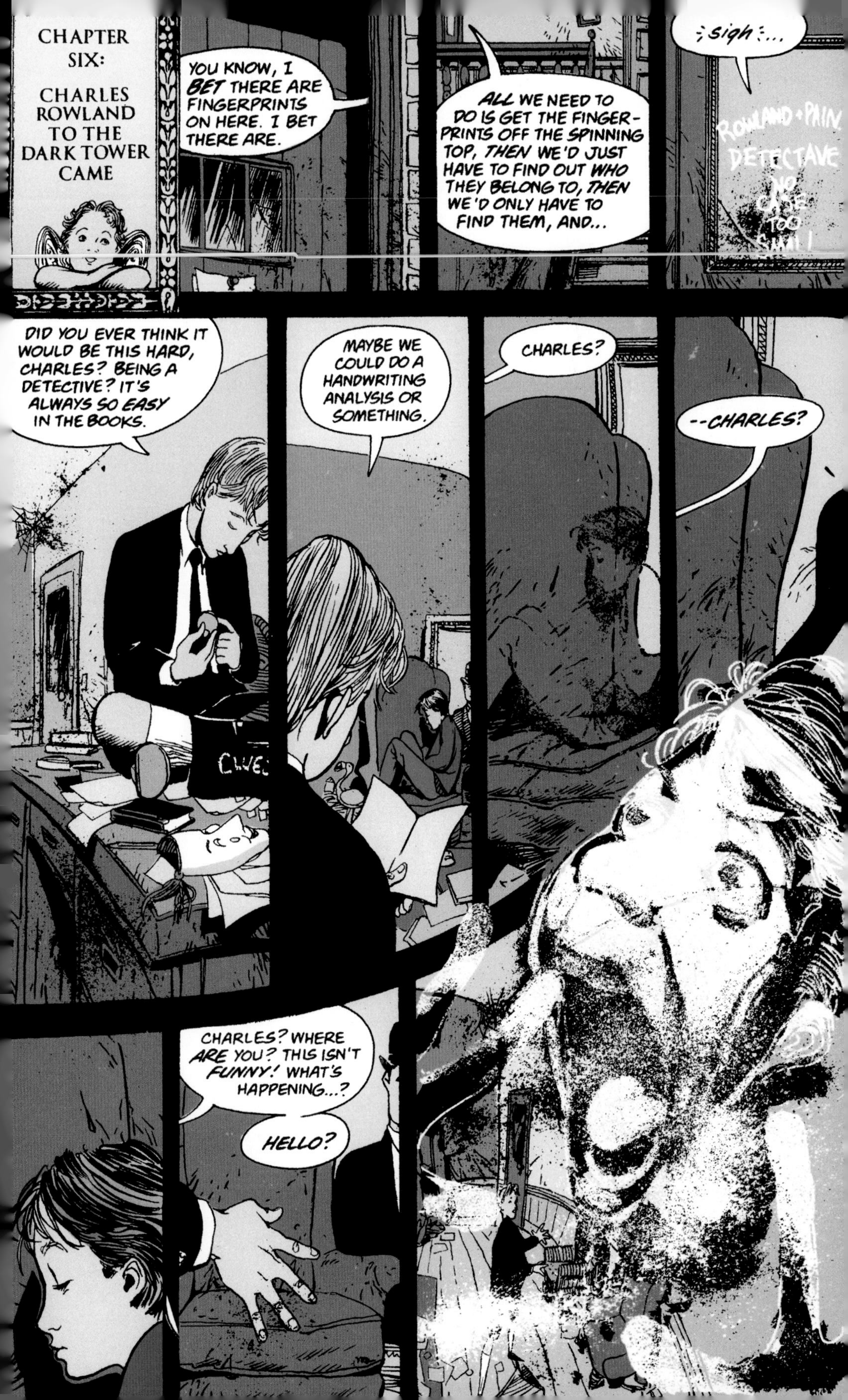
CHAPTER SIX: CHARLES ROWLAND TO THE DARK TOWER CAME
YOU KNOW, I *BET* THERE ARE FINGERPRINTS ON HERE. I BET THERE ARE.
ALL WE NEED TO DO IS GET THE FINGER-PRINTS OFF THE SPINNING TOP, *THEN* WE'D JUST HAVE TO FIND OUT *WHO* THEY BELONG TO, *THEN* WE'D ONLY HAVE TO FIND THEM, AND...
ROWLAND + PAIN.
DETECTAVE
:sigh:...
DID YOU EVER THINK IT WOULD BE THIS HARD, CHARLES? BEING A DETECTIVE? IT'S ALWAYS SO *EASY* IN THE BOOKS.
MAYBE WE COULD DO A HANDWRITING ANALYSIS OR SOMETHING.
CHARLES?
--CHARLES?
CHARLES? WHERE *ARE* YOU? THIS ISN'T *FUNNY!* WHAT'S HAPPENING...?
HELLO?

CHARLES? WHAT HAPPENED TO YOU?

I...I'M NOT SURE.

EDWIN? I THINK I WAS... I THINK I MUST HAVE BEEN... ASLEEP.

I DON'T UNDER-STAND.

EDWIN. I WAS DREAMING.

I DIDN'T THINK DEAD PEOPLE DREAMED.

OR SLEPT.

I DON'T.

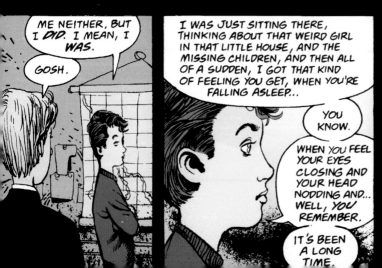

ME NEITHER, BUT I DID. I MEAN, I WAS.

GOSH.

I WAS JUST SITTING THERE, THINKING ABOUT THAT WEIRD GIRL IN THAT LITTLE HOUSE, AND THE MISSING CHILDREN, AND THEN ALL OF A SUDDEN, I GOT THAT KIND OF FEELING YOU GET, WHEN YOU'RE FALLING ASLEEP...

YOU KNOW.

WHEN YOU FEEL YOUR EYES CLOSING AND YOUR HEAD NODDING AND... WELL, YOU REMEMBER.

IT'S BEEN A LONG TIME.

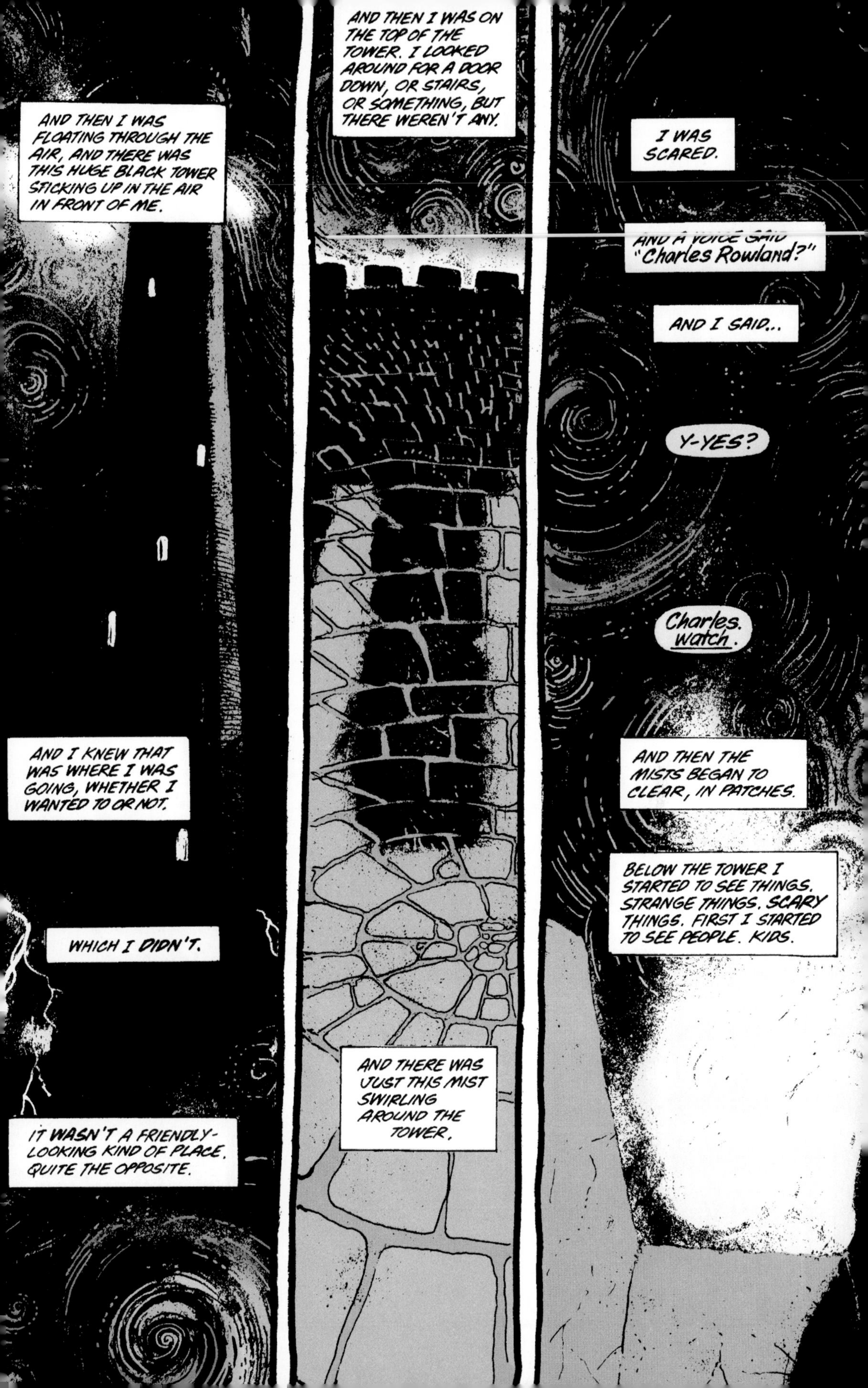
AND THEN I WAS FLOATING THROUGH THE AIR, AND THERE WAS THIS HUGE BLACK TOWER STICKING UP IN THE AIR IN FRONT OF ME.
AND I KNEW THAT WAS WHERE I WAS GOING, WHETHER I WANTED TO OR NOT.
WHICH I DIDN'T.
IT WASN'T A FRIENDLY-LOOKING KIND OF PLACE. QUITE THE OPPOSITE.
AND THEN I WAS ON THE TOP OF THE TOWER. I LOOKED AROUND FOR A DOOR DOWN, OR STAIRS, OR SOMETHING, BUT THERE WEREN'T ANY.
AND THERE WAS JUST THIS MIST SWIRLING AROUND THE TOWER.
I WAS SCARED.
AND A VOICE SAID "Charles Rowland?"
AND I SAID...
Y-YES?
Charles. watch.
AND THEN THE MISTS BEGAN TO CLEAR, IN PATCHES.
BELOW THE TOWER I STARTED TO SEE THINGS. STRANGE THINGS. SCARY THINGS. FIRST I STARTED TO SEE PEOPLE. KIDS.

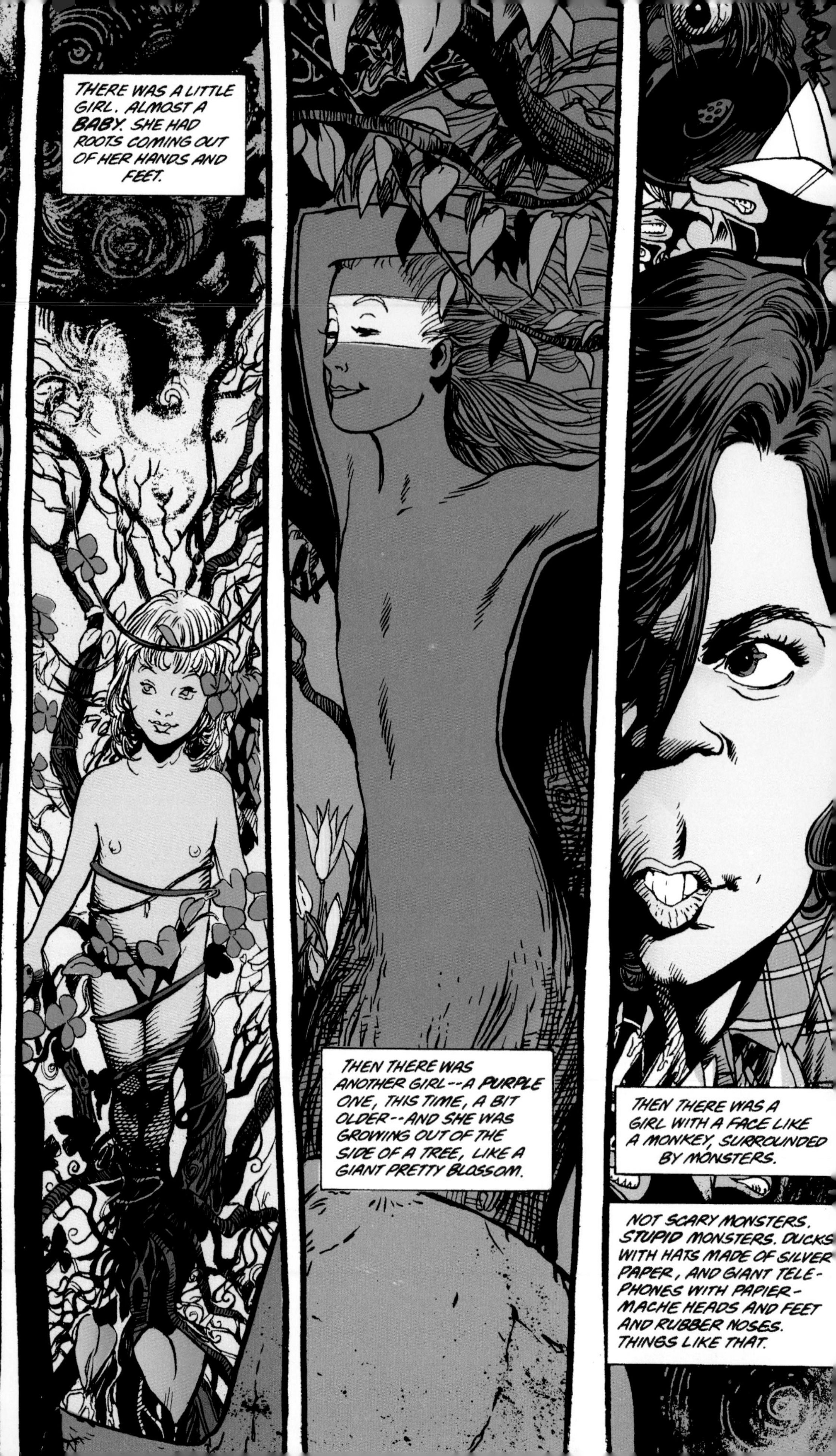
THERE WAS A LITTLE GIRL. ALMOST A BABY. SHE HAD ROOTS COMING OUT OF HER HANDS AND FEET.
THEN THERE WAS ANOTHER GIRL--A PURPLE ONE, THIS TIME, A BIT OLDER--AND SHE WAS GROWING OUT OF THE SIDE OF A TREE, LIKE A GIANT PRETTY BLOSSOM.
THEN THERE WAS A GIRL WITH A FACE LIKE A MONKEY, SURROUNDED BY MONSTERS.
NOT SCARY MONSTERS. STUPID MONSTERS. DUCKS WITH HATS MADE OF SILVER PAPER, AND GIANT TELE-PHONES WITH PAPIER-MACHE HEADS AND FEET AND RUBBER NOSES. THINGS LIKE THAT.

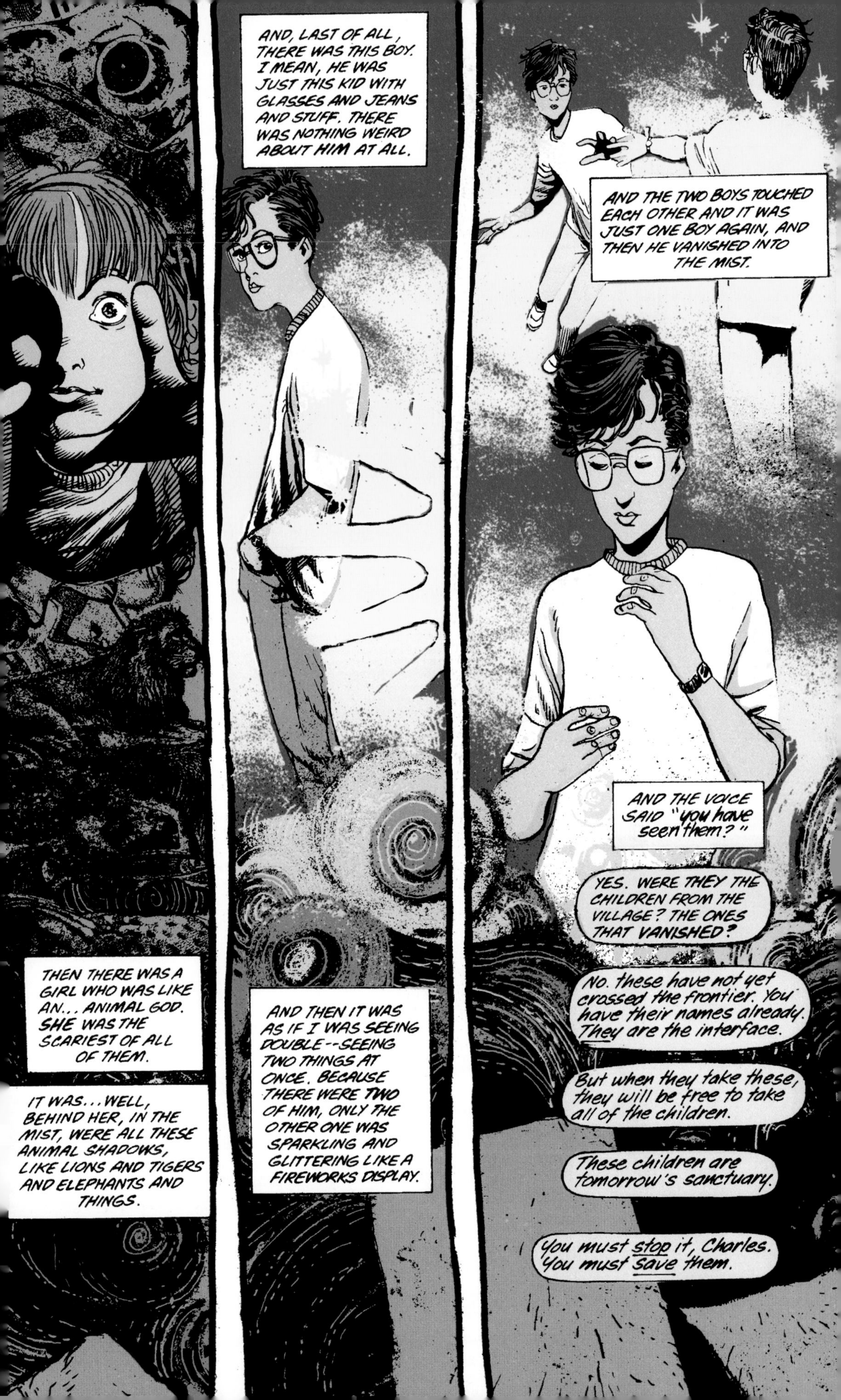
THEN THERE WAS A GIRL WHO WAS LIKE AN... ANIMAL GOD. SHE WAS THE SCARIEST OF ALL OF THEM.
IT WAS...WELL, BEHIND HER, IN THE MIST, WERE ALL THESE ANIMAL SHADOWS, LIKE LIONS AND TIGERS AND ELEPHANTS AND THINGS.
AND, LAST OF ALL, THERE WAS THIS BOY. I MEAN, HE WAS JUST THIS KID WITH GLASSES AND JEANS AND STUFF. THERE WAS NOTHING WEIRD ABOUT HIM AT ALL.
AND THEN IT WAS AS IF I WAS SEEING DOUBLE--SEEING TWO THINGS AT ONCE. BECAUSE THERE WERE TWO OF HIM, ONLY THE OTHER ONE WAS SPARKLING AND GLITTERING LIKE A FIREWORKS DISPLAY.
AND THE TWO BOYS TOUCHED EACH OTHER AND IT WAS JUST ONE BOY AGAIN, AND THEN HE VANISHED INTO THE MIST.
AND THE VOICE SAID "you have seen them?"
YES. WERE THEY THE CHILDREN FROM THE VILLAGE? THE ONES THAT VANISHED?
No. these have not yet crossed the frontier. You have their names already. They are the interface.
But when they take these, they will be free to take all of the children.
These children are tomorrow's sanctuary.
You must stop it, Charles. You must save them.

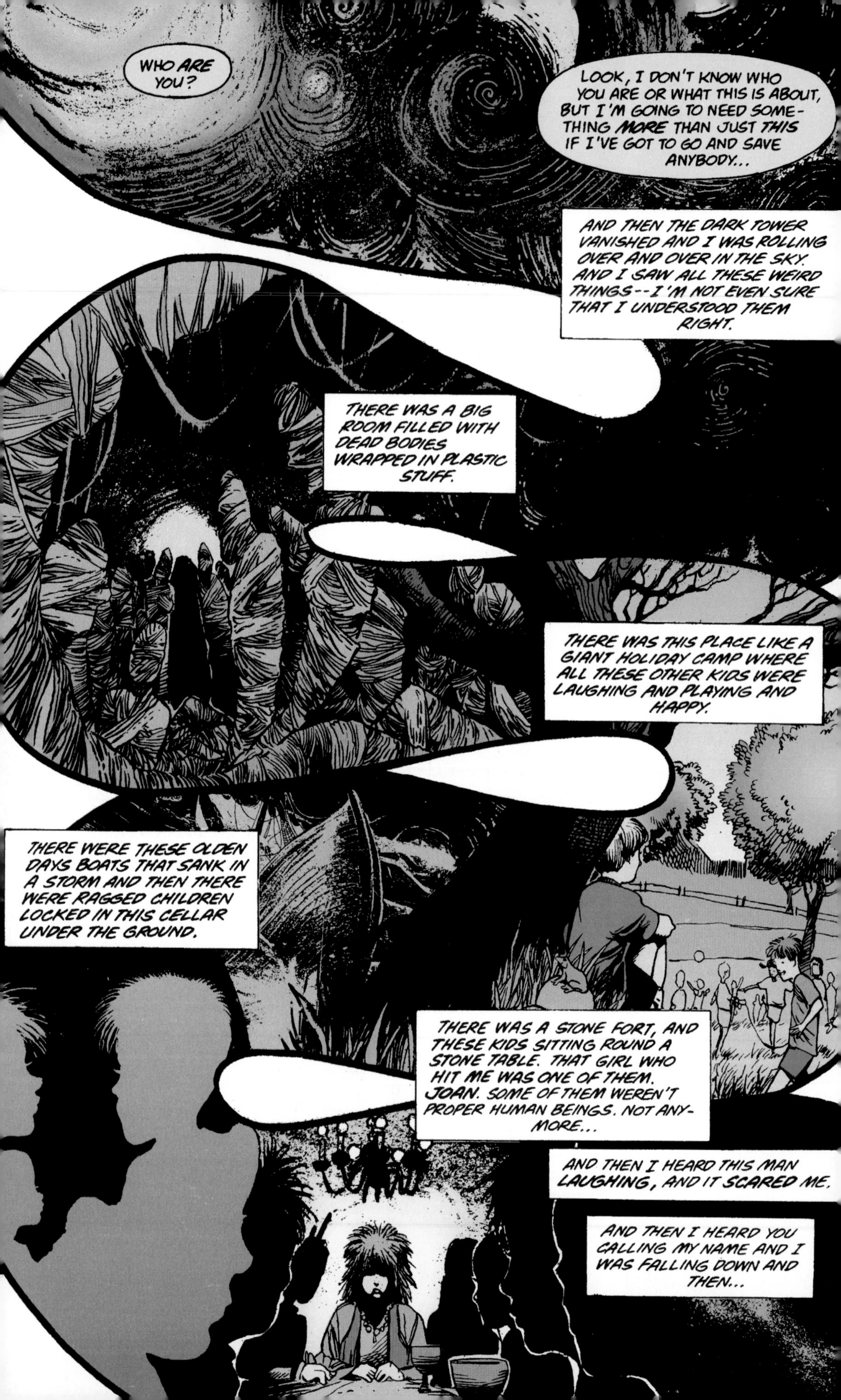

WHO ARE YOU?
LOOK, I DON'T KNOW WHO YOU ARE OR WHAT THIS IS ABOUT, BUT I'M GOING TO NEED SOME-THING MORE THAN JUST THIS IF I'VE GOT TO GO AND SAVE ANYBODY...
AND THEN THE DARK TOWER VANISHED AND I WAS ROLLING OVER AND OVER IN THE SKY. AND I SAW ALL THESE WEIRD THINGS--I'M NOT EVEN SURE THAT I UNDERSTOOD THEM RIGHT.
THERE WAS A BIG ROOM FILLED WITH DEAD BODIES WRAPPED IN PLASTIC STUFF.
THERE WAS THIS PLACE LIKE A GIANT HOLIDAY CAMP WHERE ALL THESE OTHER KIDS WERE LAUGHING AND PLAYING AND HAPPY.
THERE WERE THESE OLDEN DAYS BOATS THAT SANK IN A STORM AND THEN THERE WERE RAGGED CHILDREN LOCKED IN THIS CELLAR UNDER THE GROUND.
THERE WAS A STONE FORT, AND THESE KIDS SITTING ROUND A STONE TABLE. THAT GIRL WHO HIT ME WAS ONE OF THEM. JOAN. SOME OF THEM WEREN'T PROPER HUMAN BEINGS. NOT ANY-MORE...
AND THEN I HEARD THIS MAN LAUGHING, AND IT SCARED ME.
AND THEN I HEARD YOU CALLING MY NAME AND I WAS FALLING DOWN AND THEN...

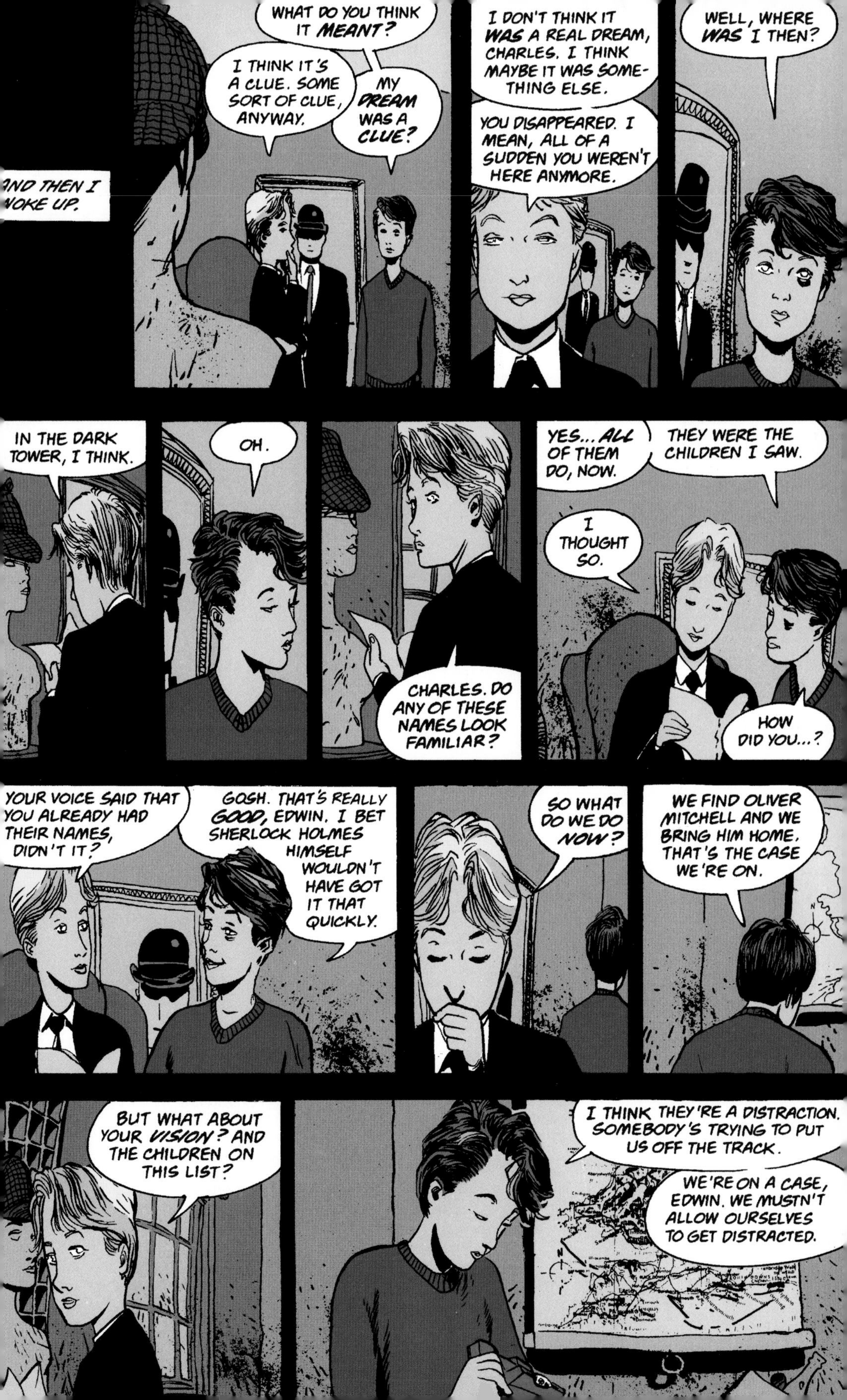

AND THEN I WOKE UP.
WHAT DO YOU THINK IT MEANT?
I THINK IT'S A CLUE. SOME SORT OF CLUE, ANYWAY.
MY DREAM WAS A CLUE?
I DON'T THINK IT WAS A REAL DREAM, CHARLES. I THINK MAYBE IT WAS SOMETHING ELSE.
YOU DISAPPEARED. I MEAN, ALL OF A SUDDEN YOU WEREN'T HERE ANYMORE.
WELL, WHERE WAS I THEN?
IN THE DARK TOWER, I THINK.
OH.
CHARLES. DO ANY OF THESE NAMES LOOK FAMILIAR?
YES... ALL OF THEM DO, NOW.
THEY WERE THE CHILDREN I SAW.
I THOUGHT SO.
HOW DID YOU...?
YOUR VOICE SAID THAT YOU ALREADY HAD THEIR NAMES, DIDN'T IT?
GOSH. THAT'S REALLY GOOD, EDWIN. I BET SHERLOCK HOLMES HIMSELF WOULDN'T HAVE GOT IT THAT QUICKLY.
SO WHAT DO WE DO NOW?
WE FIND OLIVER MITCHELL AND WE BRING HIM HOME. THAT'S THE CASE WE'RE ON.
BUT WHAT ABOUT YOUR VISION? AND THE CHILDREN ON THIS LIST?
I THINK THEY'RE A DISTRACTION. SOMEBODY'S TRYING TO PUT US OFF THE TRACK.
WE'RE ON A CASE, EDWIN. WE MUSTN'T ALLOW OURSELVES TO GET DISTRACTED.

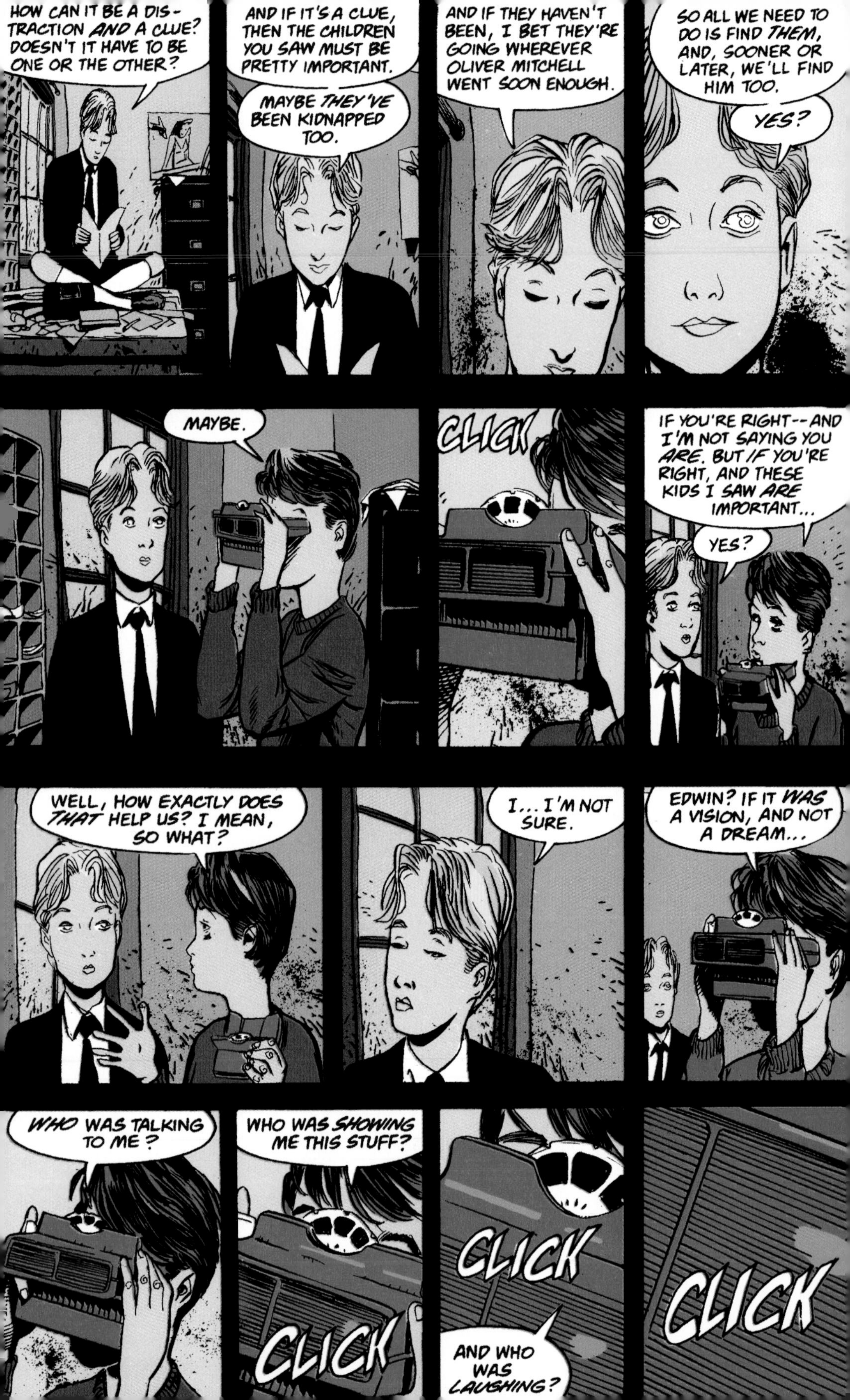
HOW CAN IT BE A DIS-TRACTION AND A CLUE? DOESN'T IT HAVE TO BE ONE OR THE OTHER?
AND IF IT'S A CLUE, THEN THE CHILDREN YOU SAW MUST BE PRETTY IMPORTANT.
MAYBE THEY'VE BEEN KIDNAPPED TOO.
AND IF THEY HAVEN'T BEEN, I BET THEY'RE GOING WHEREVER OLIVER MITCHELL WENT SOON ENOUGH.
SO ALL WE NEED TO DO IS FIND THEM, AND, SOONER OR LATER, WE'LL FIND HIM TOO.
YES?
MAYBE.
CLICK
IF YOU'RE RIGHT-- AND I'M NOT SAYING YOU ARE. BUT IF YOU'RE RIGHT, AND THESE KIDS I SAW ARE IMPORTANT...
YES?
WELL, HOW EXACTLY DOES THAT HELP US? I MEAN, SO WHAT?
I... I'M NOT SURE.
EDWIN? IF IT WAS A VISION, AND NOT A DREAM...
WHO WAS TALKING TO ME?
WHO WAS SHOWING ME THIS STUFF?
CLICK
CLICK
AND WHO WAS LAUGHING?
CLICK

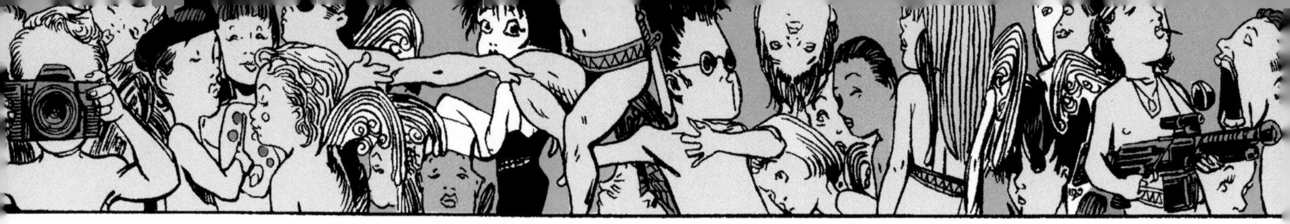

CHAPTER 7: THE HOLE

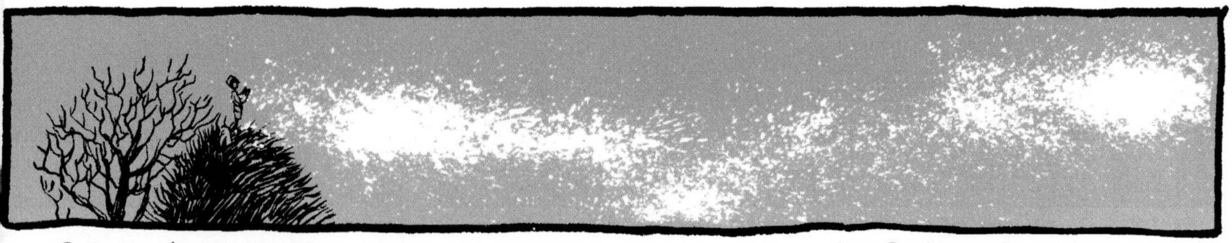

RIGHT. I'M AIKEN DRUM, I AM, AND THIS IS MY TELLING. ATTEND AND BE STILL, ALL WHO WOULD LISTEN, ALL WHO WOULD LEARN.

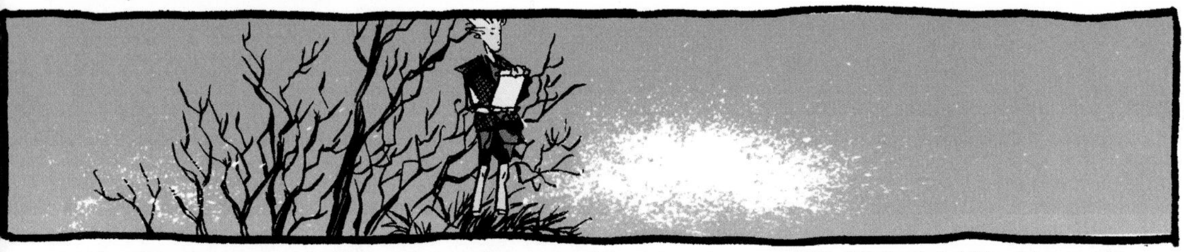

IT WAS THE THIRTEENTH YEAR OF THE TWELFTH CENTURY IN THE YEAR OF OUR LORD. AND IT WAS FOR OUR LORD WE HAD TRAVELLED THE DARK ROADS WE HAD TRAVELLED, AND FALLEN INTO THE PIT THAT HELD US.

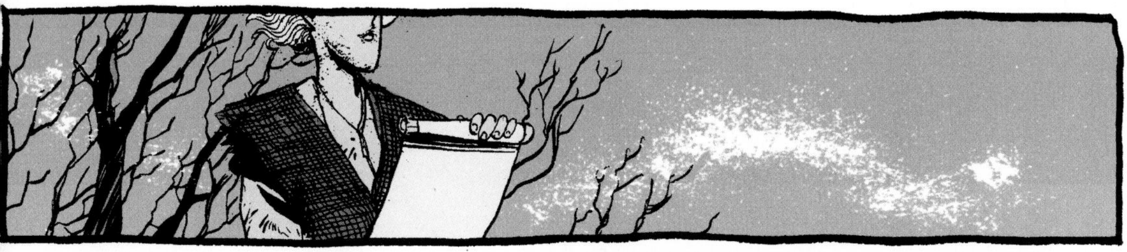

NOT THAT ANY OF US TURNED OUR FACE FROM OUR LORD. WE STILL BELIEVED IN MIRACLES. AND WITH GOOD REASON.

IT WAS A MIRACLE ANY ONE OF US WAS ALIVE. AFTER THE SEA AND THE STORMS HAD HAD THEIR WAY WITH US, AND AFTER THEY SOLD US ON THE BLOCK, LIKE SHEEP, THEN MARCHED US ACROSS THE BURNING SANDS.

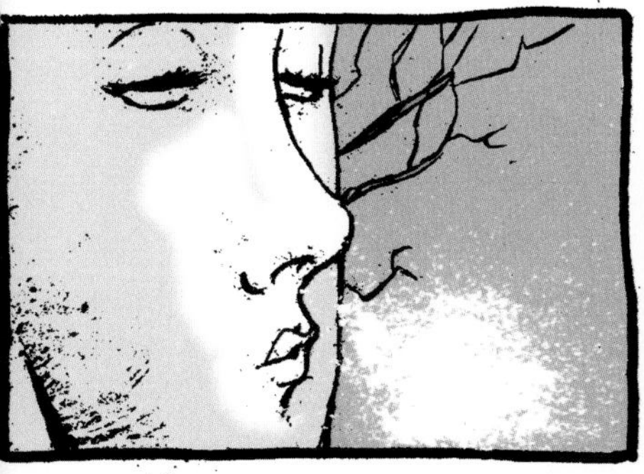

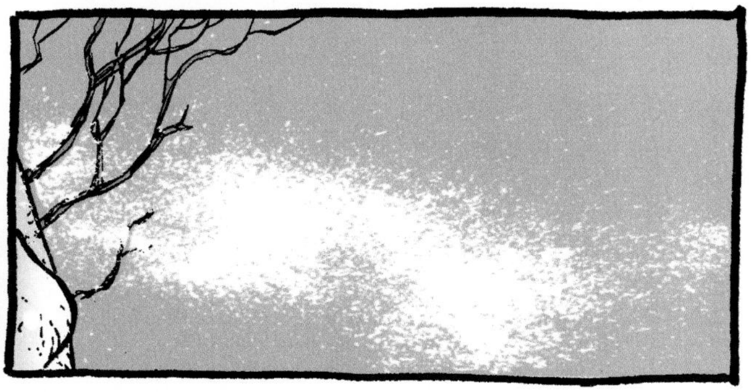

MY SISTER MWYFANY AND I HAD TRAVELLED FOR SO LONG, OVER LAND AND OVER SEA, AND THEN IT TURNED TO STINKING SHITE AND WE WERE LOST IN A FOREIGN WORLD, WITH ONLY EACH OTHER TO TALK TO.

MWYFANY FELL IN THE DESERT, AND THEY WOULDN'T LET ME STOP TO SAY A PRAYER FOR HER, OR WAIT BESIDE HER, OR ANYTHING. WE JUST LEFT HER THERE, TO DIE ALONE.

SHE WAS CALLING TO ME, AS THEY MARCHED US AWAY ACROSS THE SEARING SAND, BUT HER VOICE WAS PARCHED AND WEAK, AND HER WORDS WERE CARRIED AWAY BY THE WIND. I WOULD HAVE KILLED OUR CAPTORS THEN, IF I COULD, I THINK.

WE LEFT THE DESERT.

WE TRAVELLED BY BARGE, AND THEN ACROSS A FOREST.

THERE WERE FOURTEEN OF US, IN THE HOLE. FOURTEEN, AT FIRST. WE DID NOT KNOW THE NAME OF THE LAND IN WHICH WE FOUND OUR-SELVES AT THE LAST. WE DID NOT SPEAK THE LANGUAGE OF OUR CAPTORS.

STILL, WE COULD SPEAK TO EACH OTHER, AFTER OUR FASHION. A FEW WORDS OF GERMAN, A FEW WORDS OF FRENCH, OR ENGLISH, ITALIAN, SPANISH. SOME OF THE BOYS SPOKE A LITTLE LATIN.

THE DESERT SAND BURNED OUR FEET BY DAY AND FROZE OUR BALLOCKS BY NIGHT. WE DRANK FOUL WATER, AND WERE GRATEFUL FOR IT, SUCKED IT UP LIKE MOTHER'S MILK.

FOR WE CAME TO THE CITY LATE ONE STARLESS NIGHT, AND WE WERE LED THROUGH DARK STREETS INTO A HUGE BUILDING, AND PUSHED INTO A HOLE THAT LED TO A CELLAR, AND WERE LEFT THERE, IN THE DARKNESS, IN THE PIT, TO ROT.

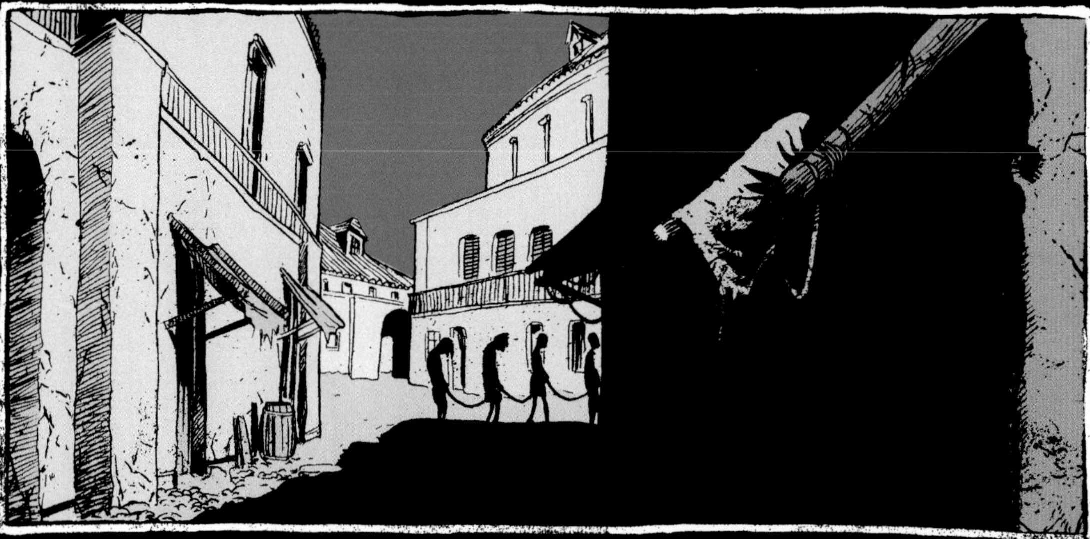

FROM TIME TO TIME THE DOOR IN THE CEILING WOULD OPEN, AND FOOD WOULD BE TOSSED DOWN ON US: SPOILED FRUIT, OR ROTTEN MEAT, LIVE WITH VERMIN, AND WE WOULD FIGHT OVER IT IN THE DARKNESS LIKE CROWS QUARRELLING OVER A STILLBORN LAMB.

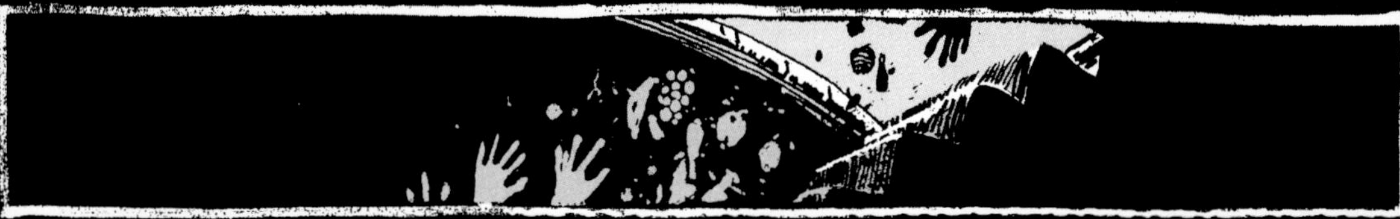

WATER THEY WOULD LOWER IN A BUCKET, ONCE A DAY-- OR SO WE SUPPOSED, FOR THERE WAS NO DAY NOR NIGHT IN THAT HOLE. WE SET ASIDE A CORNER OF THE ROOM TO PISS AND SHIT IN, AND THE STENCH WAS SO BAD WE COULD SCARCELY BREATHE.

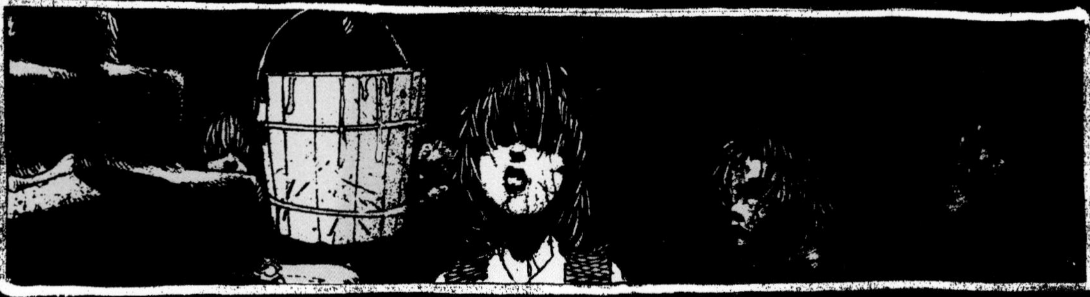

WE TALKED IN WHISPERS IN THE DARKNESS. WHAT WOULD OUR CAPTORS DO TO US? WHAT DID THEY PLAN? WE DID NOT KNOW.

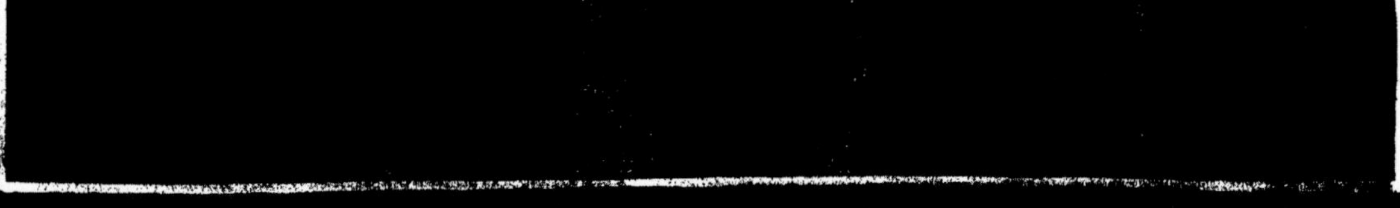

OUR SPIRITS WERE BROKEN; BUT WE DID NOT DESPAIR. WE WERE ONLY CHILDREN, BUT WE WERE STILL ALIVE. WE HAD COME THROUGH HELL AFTER HELL AND WE WERE STILL ALIVE.

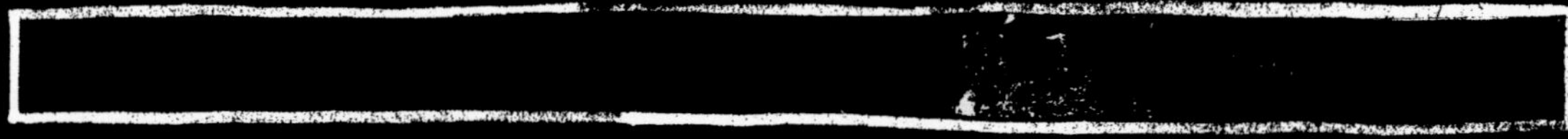

THEY CAME DOWN INTO OUR PRISON WITH LAMPS AND SWORDS, AND TOOK YOLINDE WITH THEM.

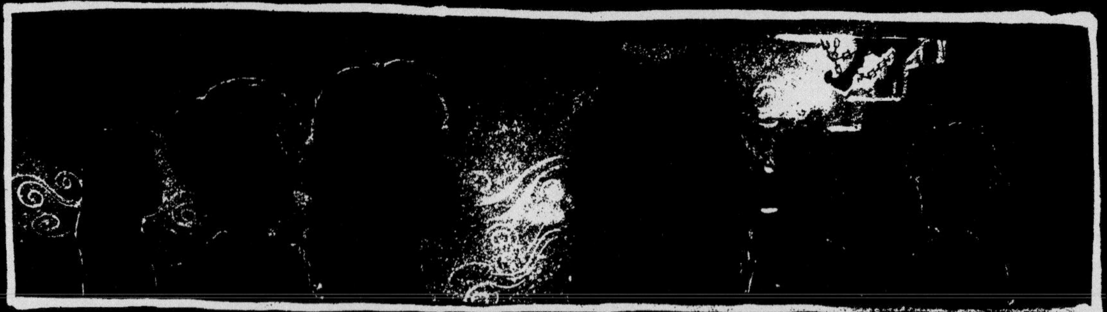

WE HEARD HER SCREAMS ABOVE US; FELT HER WARM BLOOD TRICKLE THROUGH THE GRATING IN THE CEILING. THAT, THEN, WAS THE FATE THAT AWAITED US.

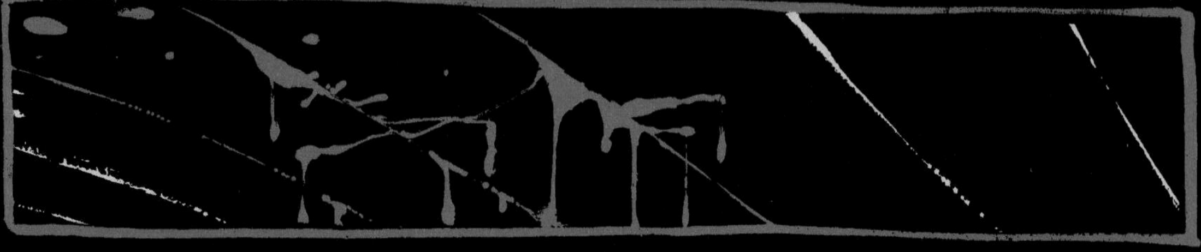

THE MEAT THEY GAVE US NEXT WAS STILL WARM AND RAW, AND-- STARVED THOUGH WE WERE-- NONE OF US DARED EAT OF IT.

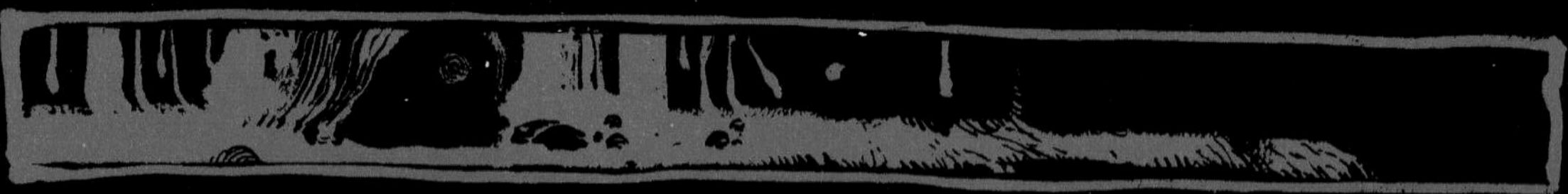

SHE CAME TO US AS A DREAM. NOT TO ONE OF US, TO ALL OF US. WE WOKE, ONE BY ONE, INTO DARKNESS, AND WE KNEW. WE HAD DREAMED OF YOLINDE. "THERE IS A WAY OUT," SHE TOLD US, EACH IN OUR OWN TONGUE. "THERE IS A PLACE TO GO." AND WHEN WE WOKE, WE KNEW: THE GATE, AND HOW TO OPEN IT.

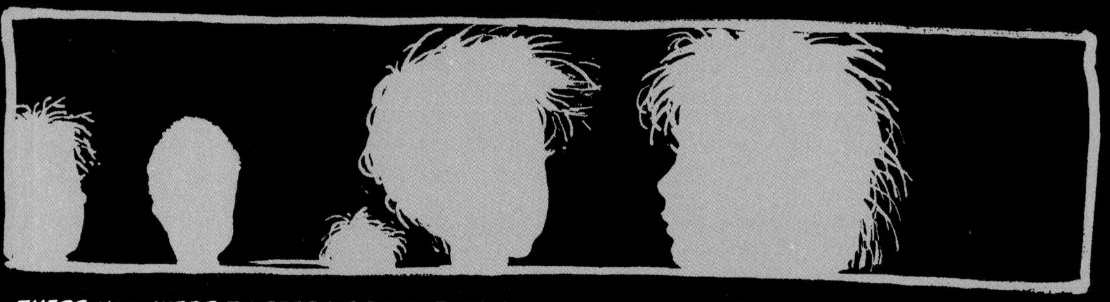

THERE NOW WERE THIRTEEN OF US. THIN AS TWIGS, NONE OLDER THAN TWELVE YEARS NOR YOUNGER THAN SEVEN, ALL PALE AND ILL AND WRETCHED. OUR EYES HAD ADJUSTED TO THE DIM LIGHT: WE WERE NOT BLIND, ALTHOUGH WE LIVED IN DARKNESS, AND WE STARED AT EACH OTHER IN DESPERATION.

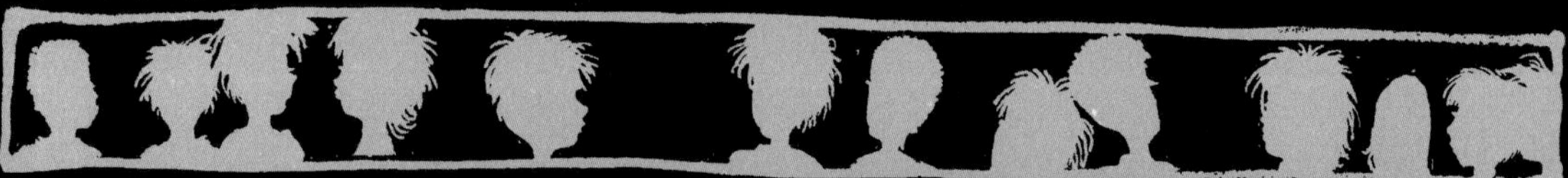

THERE WAS NO OTHER WAY. WE STOOD IN A CIRCLE. WE PLAYED ROCK, SCISSORS, SKIN, UNTIL ONE OF US WAS LEFT. IT WAS KERWYN. KERWYN, THEN, DID THE DIP, THE COUNTING RHYME.

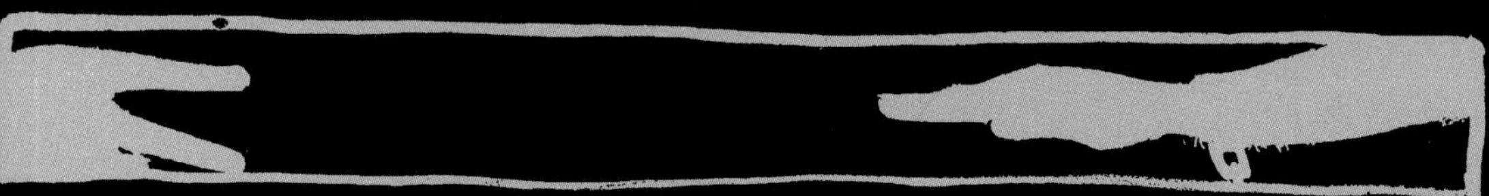

ONE BY ONE, WE STEPPED OUT OF THE CIRCLE. EVENTUALLY, IT WAS JUST ME AND JACOMO, THE GOLD-SMITH'S SON, FROM NAPLES. "DIE, PUSSY, DIE," CHANTED KERWYN, HIS FINGER POINTING TO ONE OF US, THEN TO THE OTHER. "SHUT YOUR LITTLE EYE. WHEN YOU WAKE, BAKE A CAKE, DIE PUSSY, DIE."

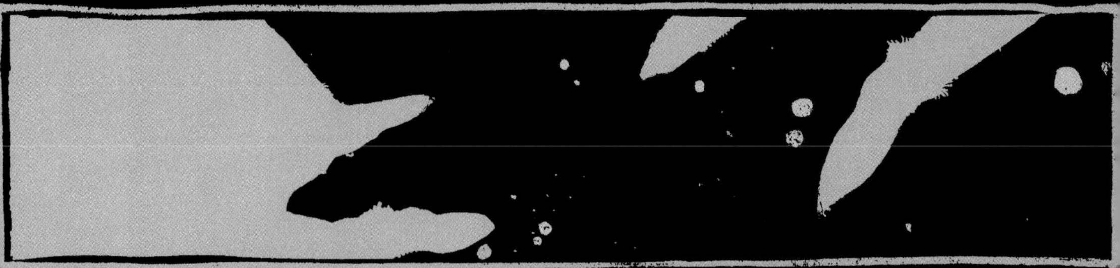

HE WAS POINTING TO ME, AND I STEPPED BACK.

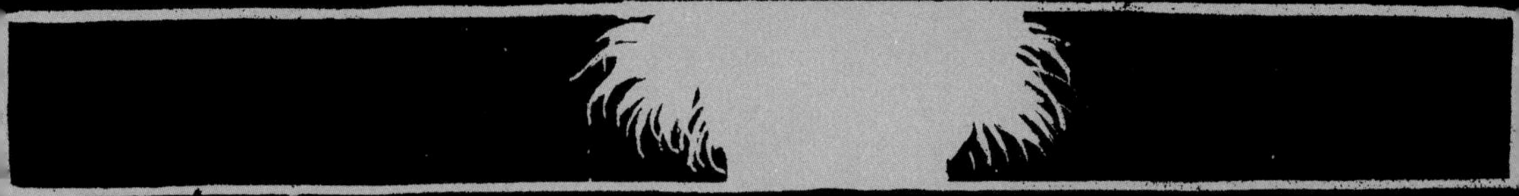

JACOMO WAS SOBBING. ONE BY ONE, WE APOLOGIZED TO HIM. THEN WE STRANGLED HIM WITH OUR CHAINS, AND BROKE HIS HEAD AGAINST THE STONES OF THE FLOOR.
JACOMO MADE NO NOISE AS WE KILLED HIM, SO AS NOT TO ALERT THE ADULTS IN THE ROOMS ABOVE US. I PRAY I COULD HAVE BEEN THAT BRAVE, THAT NOBLE, IN HIS PLACE.
WE DREW THE PATTERN ON THE FLOOR WITH JACOMO'S BLACK BLOOD, WEEPING ALL THE WHILE.

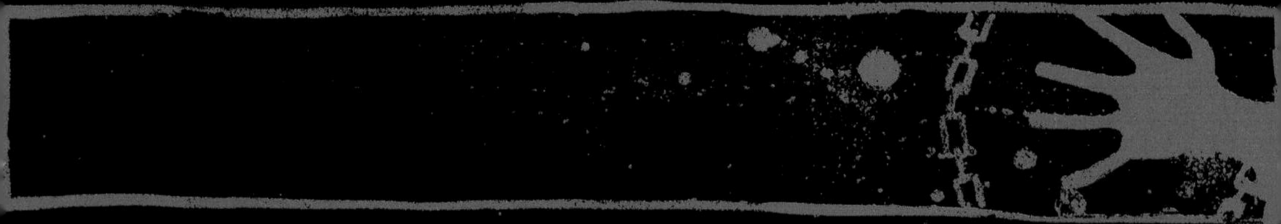

KERWYN WAS THE FIRST TO DANCE ON IT. ONE FOOT, THEN THE OTHER, THEN BOTH FEET TOGETHER, HIS CHAINS RATTLING AS HE WENT.

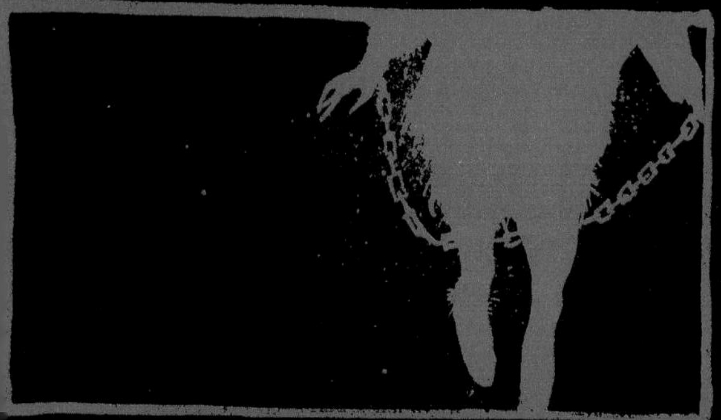

HE REACHED THE END AND HE WAS GONE, AND THE PATTERN BURNED WITH CRIMSON LIGHT, IN THE DARKNESS.

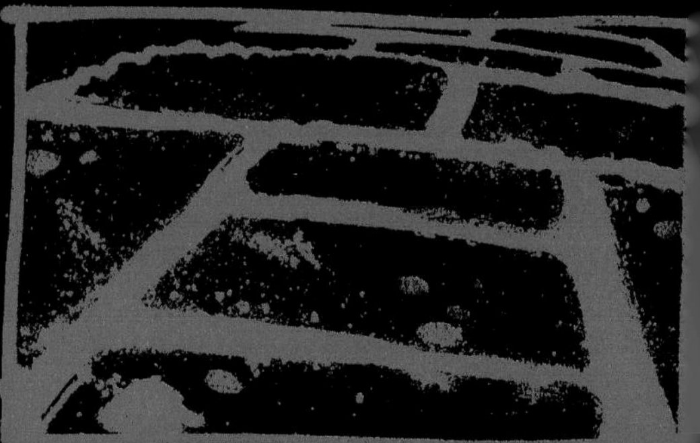

ONE BY ONE WE DANCED AND STUMBLED OUR WAY OUT OF THE PIT.
I WAS THE LAST OF US TO CROSS THE DIVIDE, AS I HAD BEEN THE LAST TO BE CHOSEN.

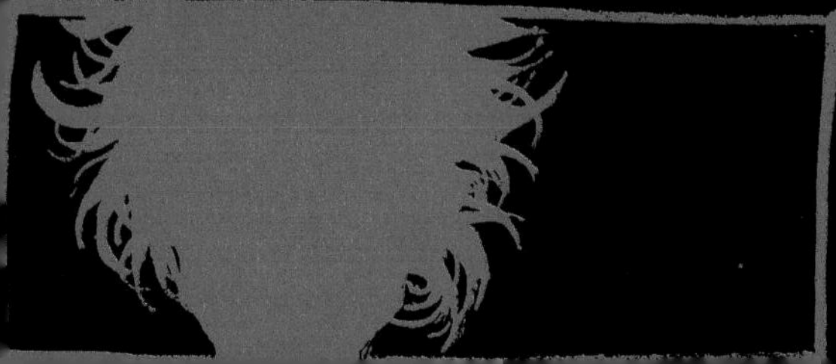

I SPARED ONE FINAL GLANCE FOR JACOMO, WHO HAD DIED THAT WE MIGHT LIVE, AND THEN HOPPED ONTO THE FINAL SQUARE.

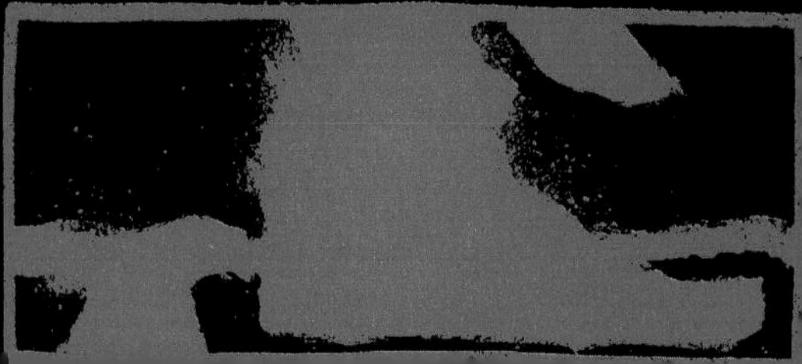

THERE WERE TWELVE OF US, BLINKING AND SHIELDING OUR EYES FROM THE LIGHT OF THE MORNING SUN.

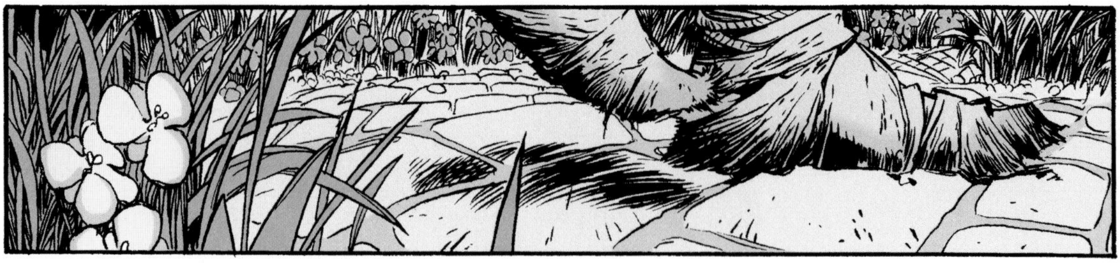

THERE WERE FRUITS ON THE TREES, AND THE SWEET BIRDS SANG A SONG OF WELCOME.
AND WE FELT THE WORLD SHAPING ITSELF TO CARE FOR US. WE WERE IN FREE COUNTRY, AND NOTHING COULD HURT US AGAIN.

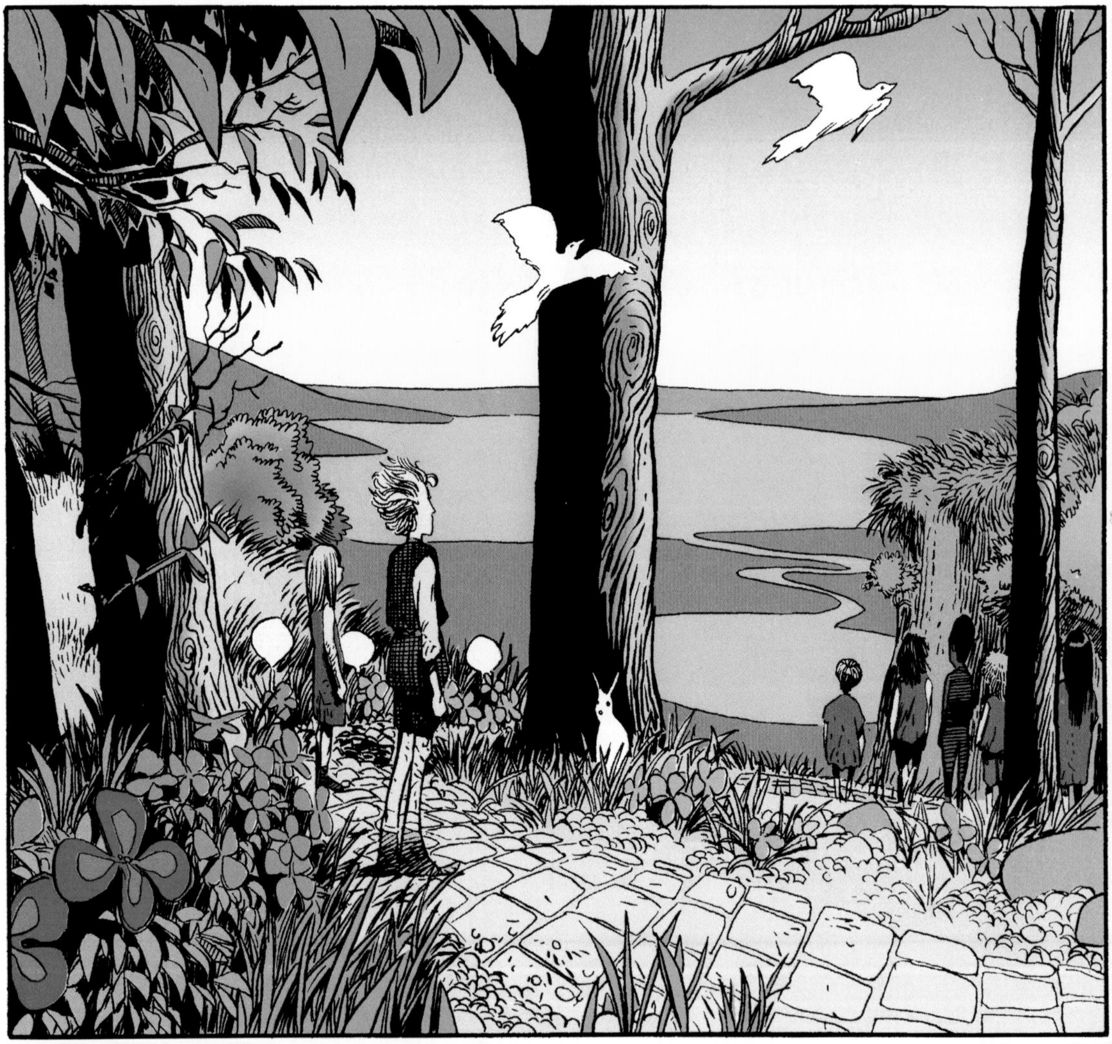

WE WERE IN FREE COUNTRY, WHERE THERE IS NO AGE OR PAIN OR HUNGER OR DEATH.

THERE.

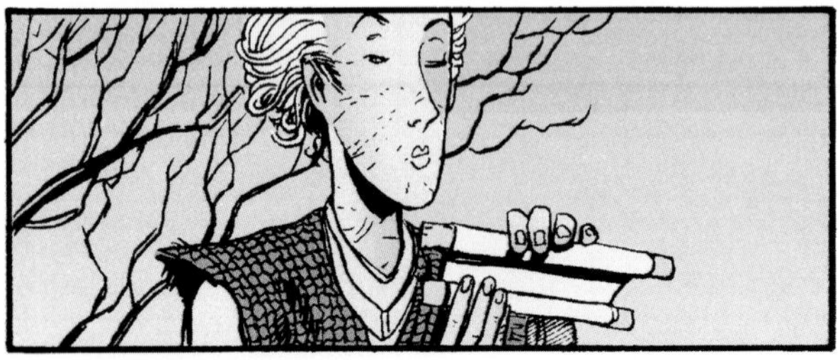

I AM AIKEN DRUM. THAT IS MY TELLING.

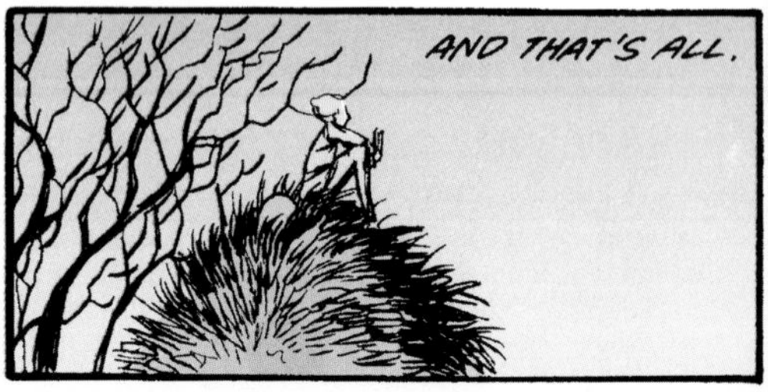
AND THAT'S ALL.

CHAPTER EIGHT: WHAT COMES OUT OF THE CHIMNEY?

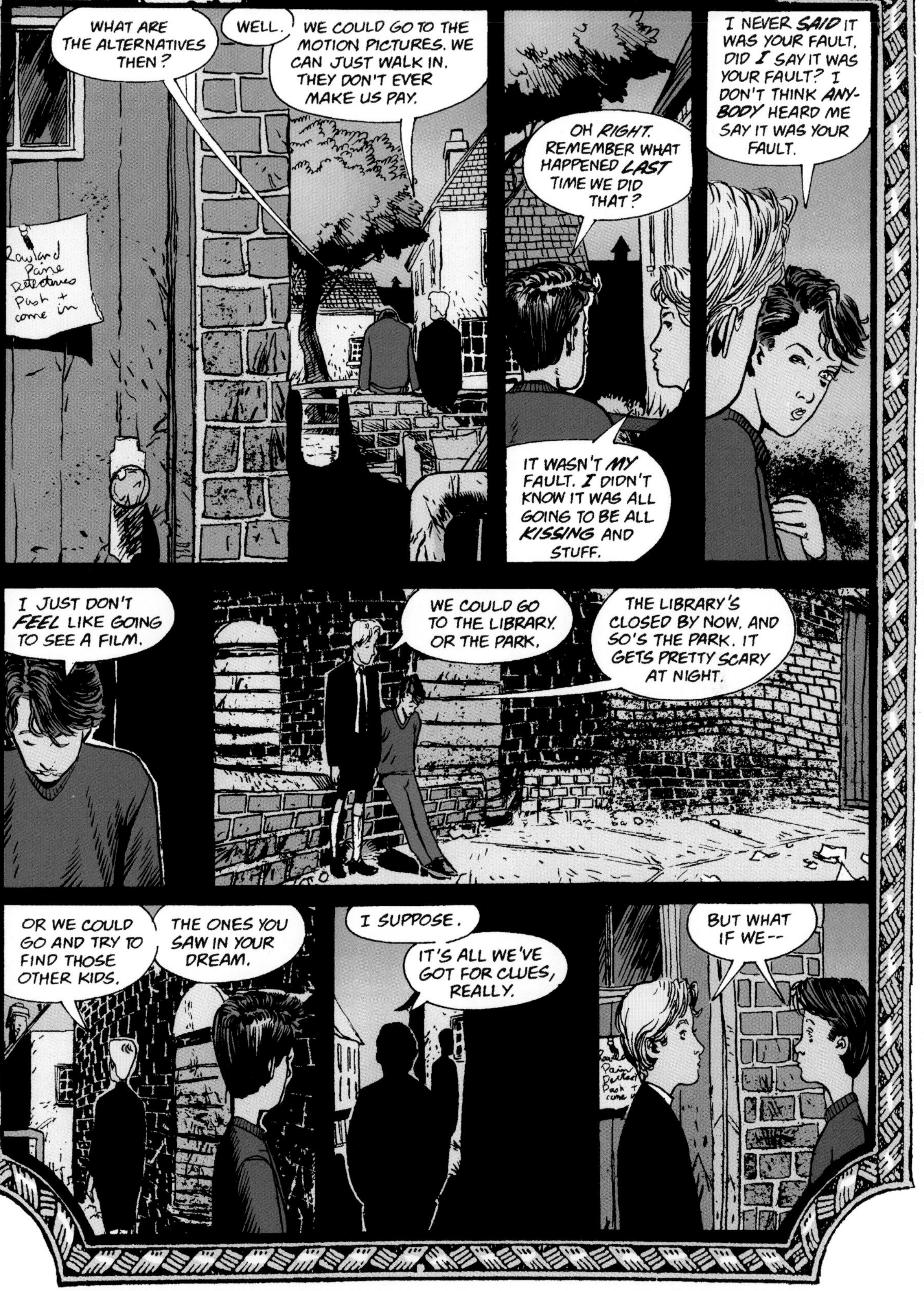
WHAT ARE THE ALTERNATIVES THEN?
WELL.
WE COULD GO TO THE MOTION PICTURES. WE CAN JUST WALK IN. THEY DON'T EVER MAKE US PAY.
Rowland Paine Detectives Push + come in
OH RIGHT. REMEMBER WHAT HAPPENED LAST TIME WE DID THAT?
IT WASN'T MY FAULT. I DIDN'T KNOW IT WAS ALL GOING TO BE ALL KISSING AND STUFF.
I NEVER SAID IT WAS YOUR FAULT. DID I SAY IT WAS YOUR FAULT? I DON'T THINK ANYBODY HEARD ME SAY IT WAS YOUR FAULT.
I JUST DON'T FEEL LIKE GOING TO SEE A FILM.
WE COULD GO TO THE LIBRARY. OR THE PARK.
THE LIBRARY'S CLOSED BY NOW. AND SO'S THE PARK. IT GETS PRETTY SCARY AT NIGHT.
OR WE COULD GO AND TRY TO FIND THOSE OTHER KIDS.
THE ONES YOU SAW IN YOUR DREAM.
I SUPPOSE.
IT'S ALL WE'VE GOT FOR CLUES, REALLY.
BUT WHAT IF WE--

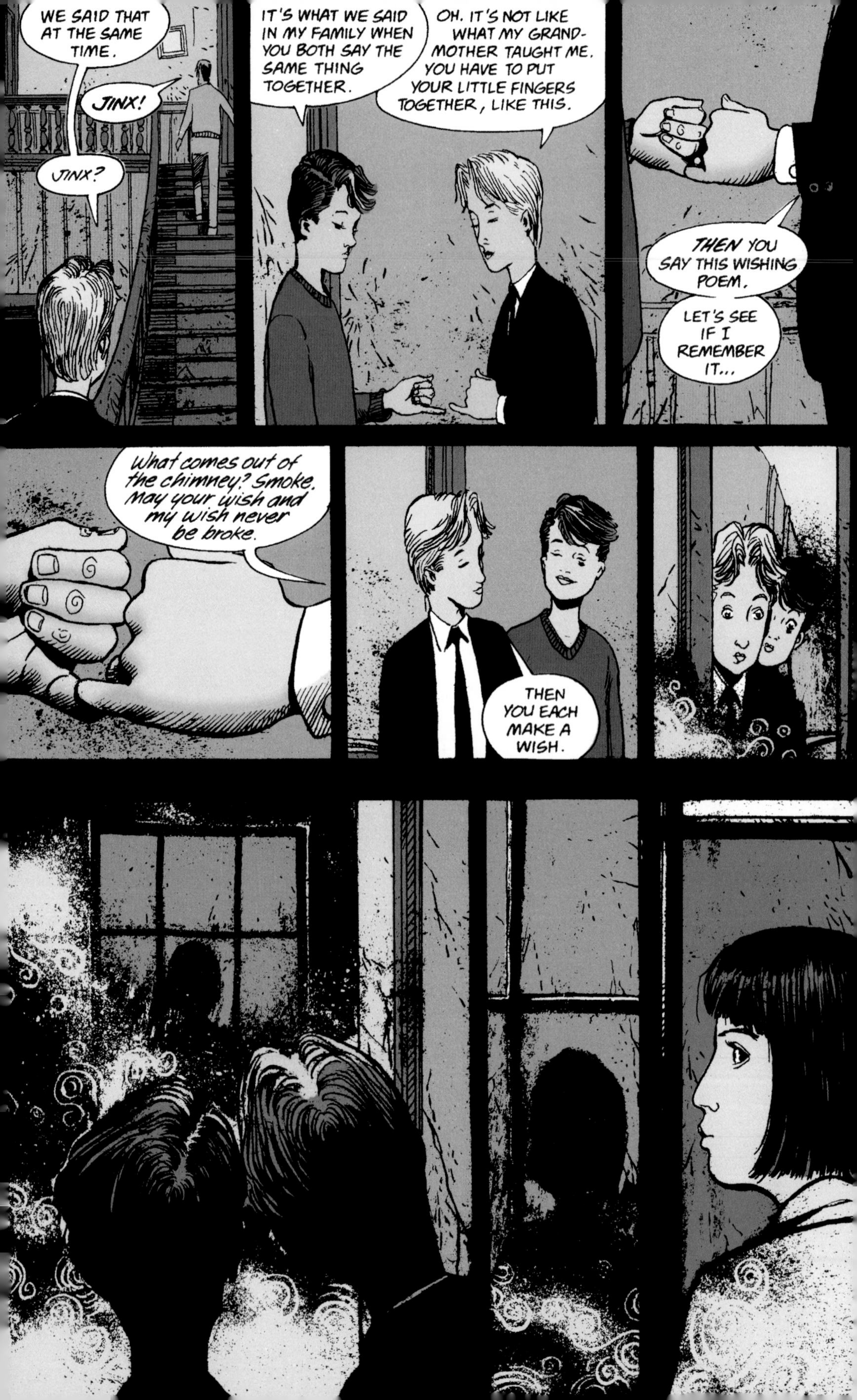
WE SAID THAT AT THE SAME TIME.
JINX!
JINX?
IT'S WHAT WE SAID IN MY FAMILY WHEN YOU BOTH SAY THE SAME THING TOGETHER.
OH. IT'S NOT LIKE WHAT MY GRAND-MOTHER TAUGHT ME. YOU HAVE TO PUT YOUR LITTLE FINGERS TOGETHER, LIKE THIS.
THEN YOU SAY THIS WISHING POEM.
LET'S SEE IF I REMEMBER IT...
What comes out of the chimney? Smoke. May your wish and my wish never be broke.
THEN YOU EACH MAKE A WISH.

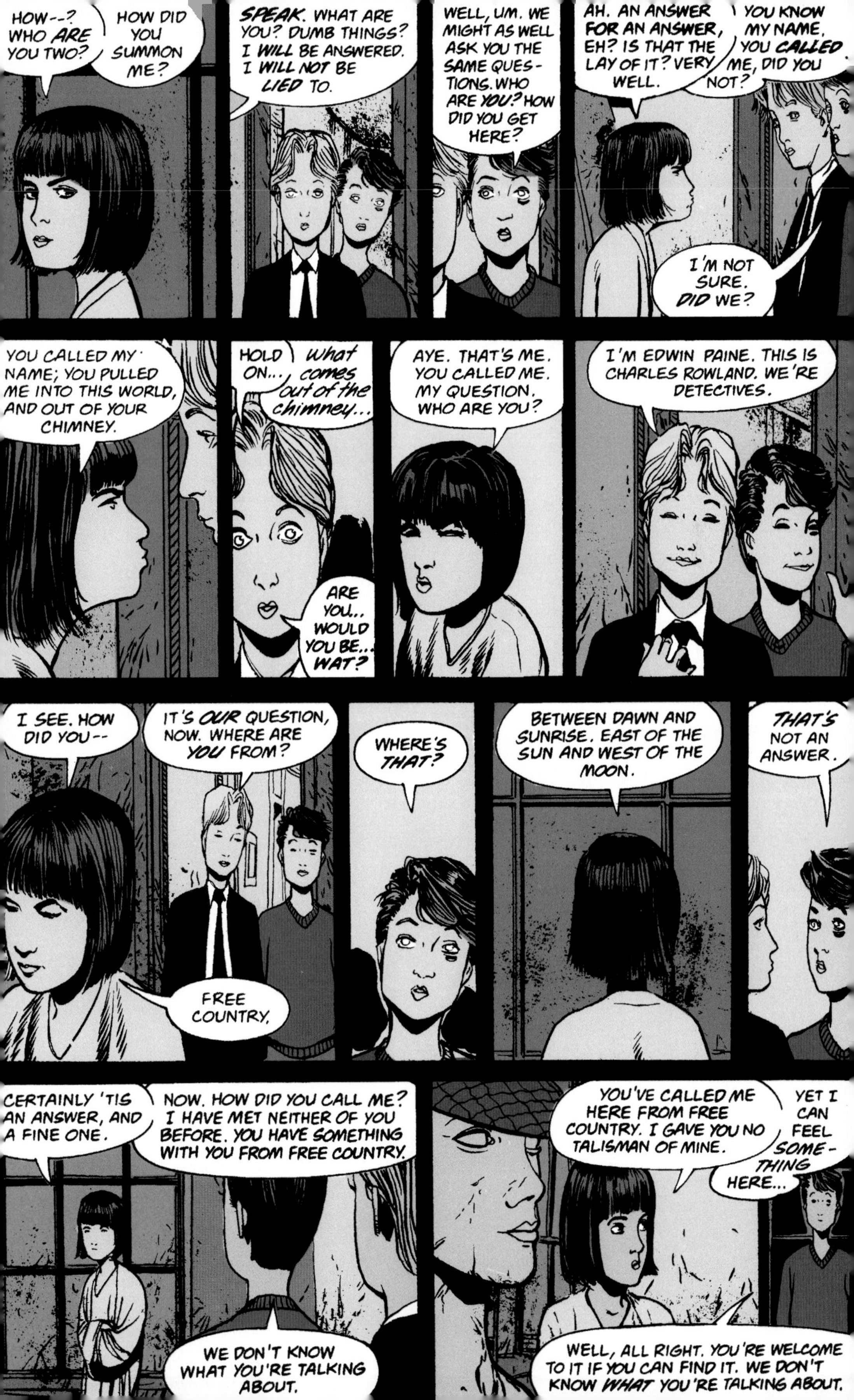
HOW--? WHO ARE YOU TWO?
HOW DID YOU SUMMON ME?
SPEAK. WHAT ARE YOU? DUMB THINGS? I WILL BE ANSWERED. I WILL NOT BE LIED TO.
WELL, UM. WE MIGHT AS WELL ASK YOU THE SAME QUESTIONS. WHO ARE YOU? HOW DID YOU GET HERE?
AH. AN ANSWER FOR AN ANSWER, EH? IS THAT THE LAY OF IT? VERY WELL.
YOU KNOW MY NAME. YOU CALLED ME, DID YOU NOT?
I'M NOT SURE. DID WE?
YOU CALLED MY NAME; YOU PULLED ME INTO THIS WORLD, AND OUT OF YOUR CHIMNEY.
HOLD ON...
what comes out of the chimney...
ARE YOU... WOULD YOU BE... WAT?
AYE. THAT'S ME. YOU CALLED ME. MY QUESTION. WHO ARE YOU?
I'M EDWIN PAINE. THIS IS CHARLES ROWLAND. WE'RE DETECTIVES.
I SEE. HOW DID YOU--
IT'S OUR QUESTION, NOW. WHERE ARE YOU FROM?
FREE COUNTRY.
WHERE'S THAT?
BETWEEN DAWN AND SUNRISE. EAST OF THE SUN AND WEST OF THE MOON.
THAT'S NOT AN ANSWER.
CERTAINLY 'TIS AN ANSWER, AND A FINE ONE.
NOW. HOW DID YOU CALL ME? I HAVE MET NEITHER OF YOU BEFORE. YOU HAVE SOMETHING WITH YOU FROM FREE COUNTRY.
WE DON'T KNOW WHAT YOU'RE TALKING ABOUT.
YOU'VE CALLED ME HERE FROM FREE COUNTRY. I GAVE YOU NO TALISMAN OF MINE.
YET I CAN FEEL SOMETHING HERE...
WELL, ALL RIGHT. YOU'RE WELCOME TO IT IF YOU CAN FIND IT. WE DON'T KNOW WHAT YOU'RE TALKING ABOUT.

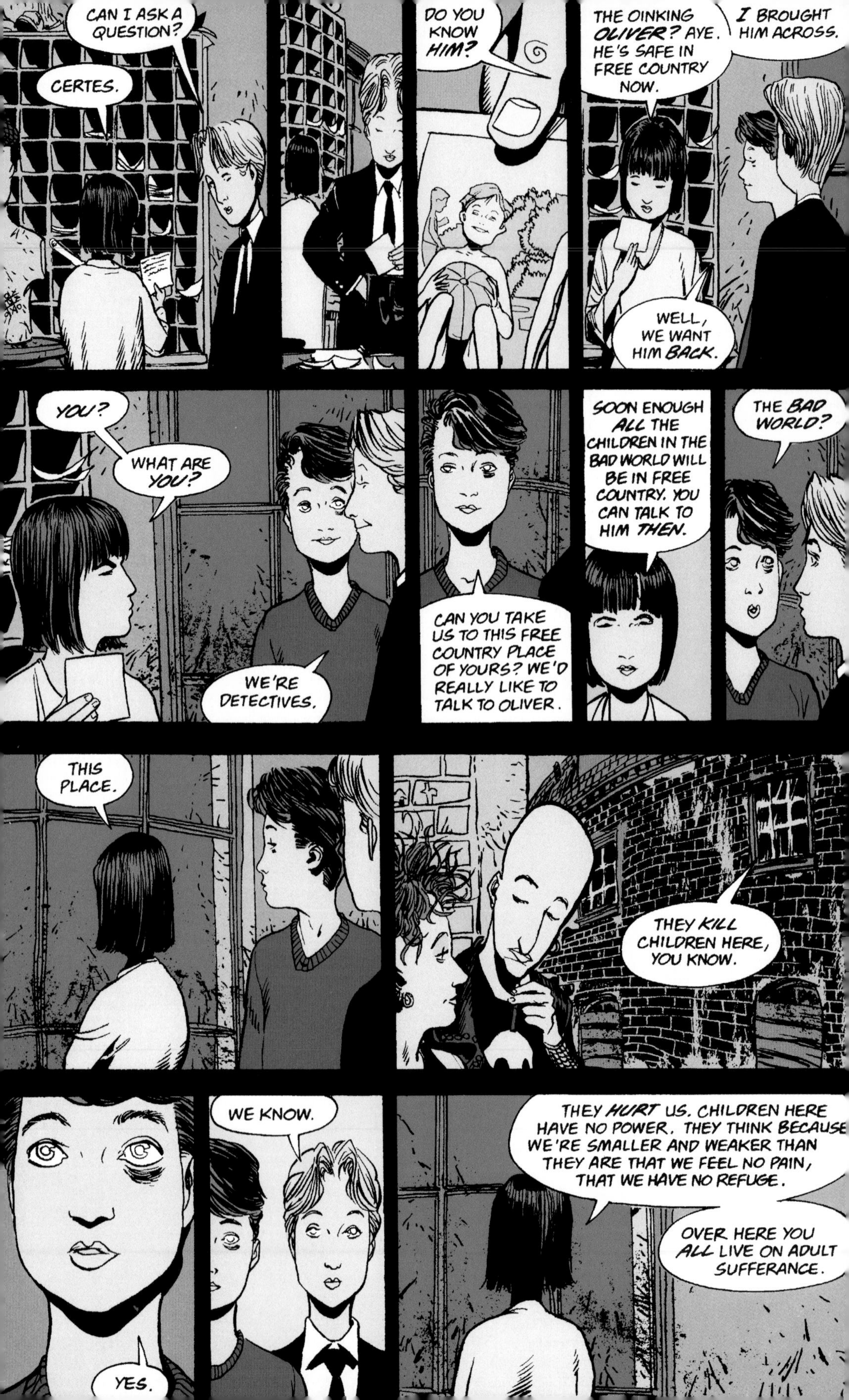

CAN I ASK A QUESTION?
CERTES.
DO YOU KNOW HIM?
THE OINKING OLIVER? AYE. HE'S SAFE IN FREE COUNTRY NOW.
I BROUGHT HIM ACROSS.
WELL, WE WANT HIM BACK.
YOU?
WHAT ARE YOU?
WE'RE DETECTIVES.
CAN YOU TAKE US TO THIS FREE COUNTRY PLACE OF YOURS? WE'D REALLY LIKE TO TALK TO OLIVER.
SOON ENOUGH ALL THE CHILDREN IN THE BAD WORLD WILL BE IN FREE COUNTRY. YOU CAN TALK TO HIM THEN.
THE BAD WORLD?
THIS PLACE.
THEY KILL CHILDREN HERE, YOU KNOW.
YES.
WE KNOW.
THEY HURT US. CHILDREN HERE HAVE NO POWER. THEY THINK BECAUSE WE'RE SMALLER AND WEAKER THAN THEY ARE THAT WE FEEL NO PAIN, THAT WE HAVE NO REFUGE.
OVER HERE YOU ALL LIVE ON ADULT SUFFERANCE.

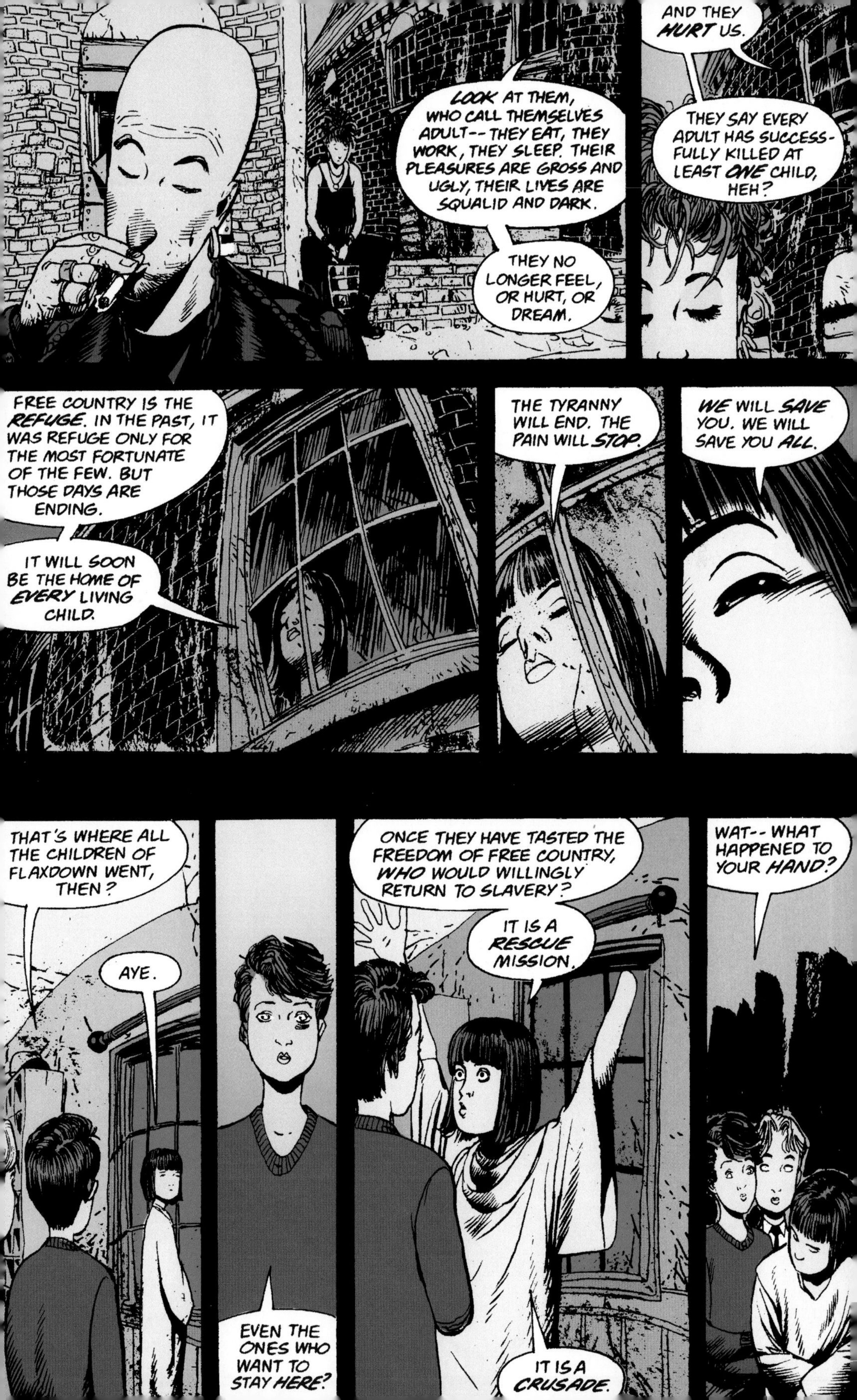
LOOK AT THEM, WHO CALL THEMSELVES ADULT-- THEY EAT, THEY WORK, THEY SLEEP. THEIR PLEASURES ARE GROSS AND UGLY, THEIR LIVES ARE SQUALID AND DARK.
THEY NO LONGER FEEL, OR HURT, OR DREAM.
AND THEY HURT US.
THEY SAY EVERY ADULT HAS SUCCESS-FULLY KILLED AT LEAST ONE CHILD, HEH?
FREE COUNTRY IS THE REFUGE. IN THE PAST, IT WAS REFUGE ONLY FOR THE MOST FORTUNATE OF THE FEW. BUT THOSE DAYS ARE ENDING.
IT WILL SOON BE THE HOME OF EVERY LIVING CHILD.
THE TYRANNY WILL END. THE PAIN WILL STOP.
WE WILL SAVE YOU. WE WILL SAVE YOU ALL.
THAT'S WHERE ALL THE CHILDREN OF FLAXDOWN WENT, THEN?
AYE.
EVEN THE ONES WHO WANT TO STAY HERE?
ONCE THEY HAVE TASTED THE FREEDOM OF FREE COUNTRY, WHO WOULD WILLINGLY RETURN TO SLAVERY?
IT IS A RESCUE MISSION.
IT IS A CRUSADE.
WAT-- WHAT HAPPENED TO YOUR HAND?

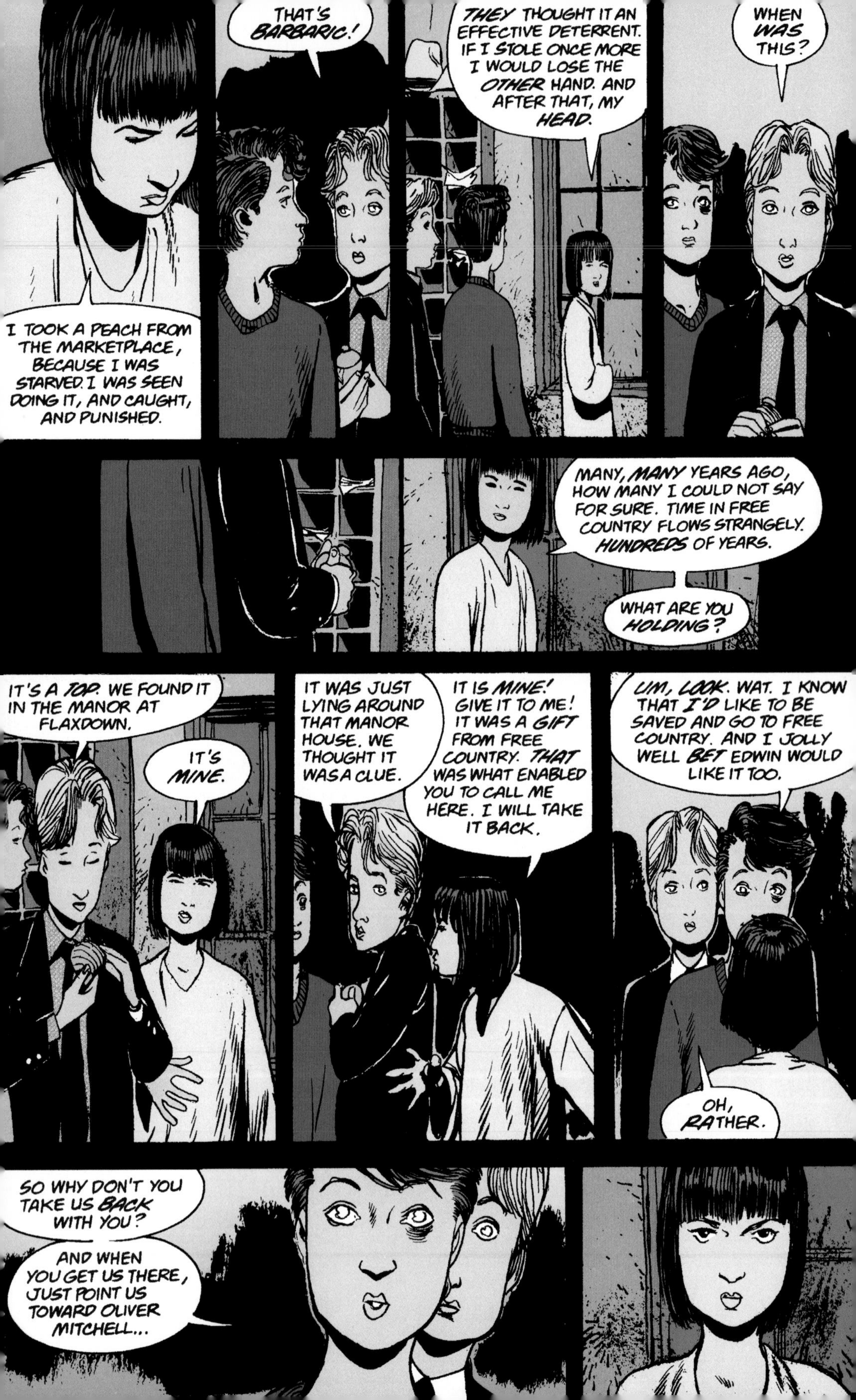
I TOOK A PEACH FROM THE MARKETPLACE, BECAUSE I WAS STARVED. I WAS SEEN DOING IT, AND CAUGHT, AND PUNISHED.
THAT'S BARBARIC!
THEY THOUGHT IT AN EFFECTIVE DETERRENT. IF I STOLE ONCE MORE I WOULD LOSE THE OTHER HAND. AND AFTER THAT, MY HEAD.
WHEN WAS THIS?
MANY, MANY YEARS AGO, HOW MANY I COULD NOT SAY FOR SURE. TIME IN FREE COUNTRY FLOWS STRANGELY. HUNDREDS OF YEARS.
WHAT ARE YOU HOLDING?
IT'S A TOP. WE FOUND IT IN THE MANOR AT FLAXDOWN.
IT'S MINE.
IT WAS JUST LYING AROUND THAT MANOR HOUSE. WE THOUGHT IT WAS A CLUE.
IT IS MINE! GIVE IT TO ME! IT WAS A GIFT FROM FREE COUNTRY. THAT WAS WHAT ENABLED YOU TO CALL ME HERE. I WILL TAKE IT BACK.
UM, LOOK. WAT. I KNOW THAT I'D LIKE TO BE SAVED AND GO TO FREE COUNTRY. AND I JOLLY WELL BET EDWIN WOULD LIKE IT TOO.
OH, RATHER.
SO WHY DON'T YOU TAKE US BACK WITH YOU?
AND WHEN YOU GET US THERE, JUST POINT US TOWARD OLIVER MITCHELL...

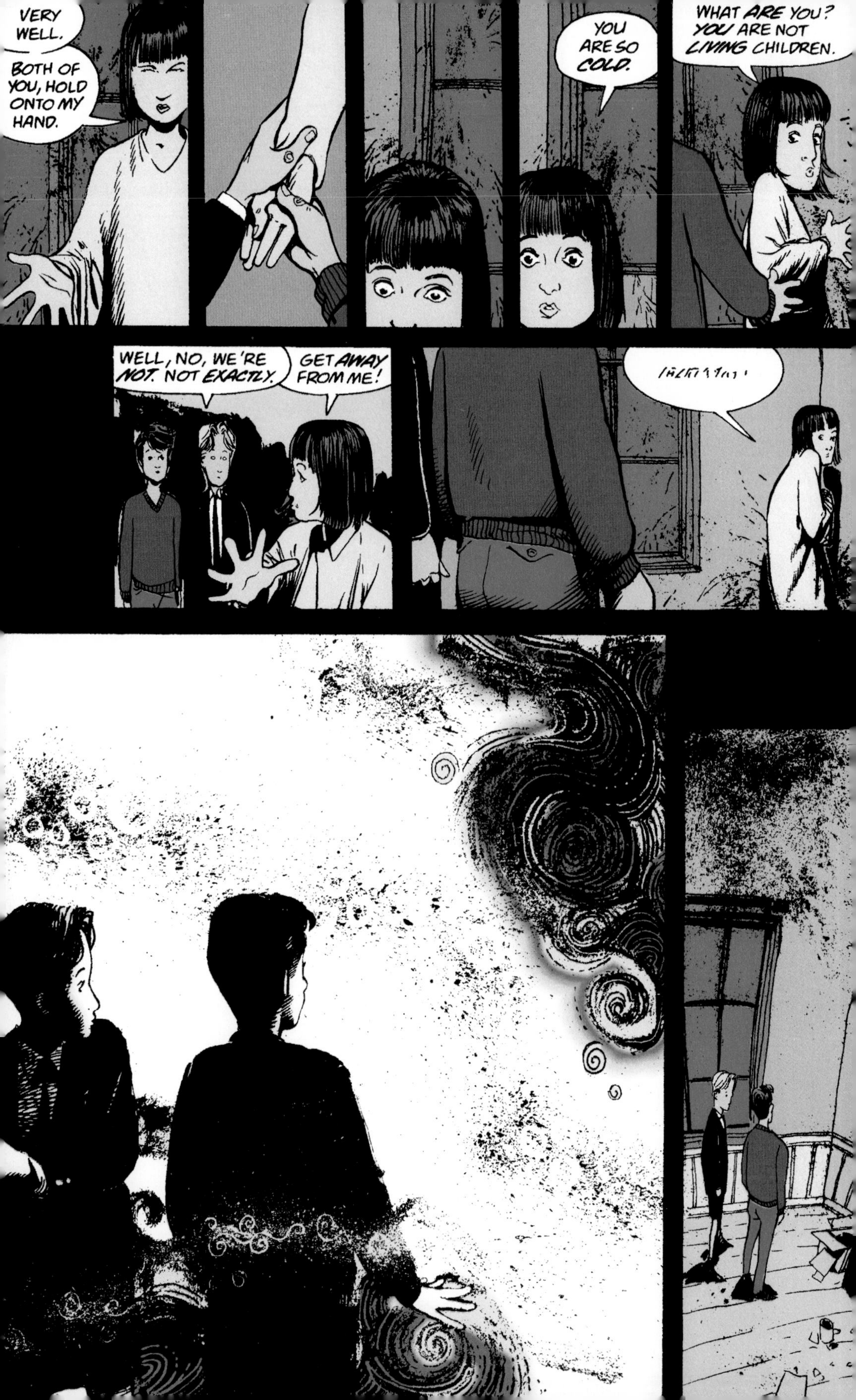
VERY WELL.
BOTH OF YOU, HOLD ONTO MY HAND.
YOU ARE SO COLD.
WHAT ARE YOU? YOU ARE NOT LIVING CHILDREN.
WELL, NO, WE'RE NOT. NOT EXACTLY.
GET AWAY FROM ME!

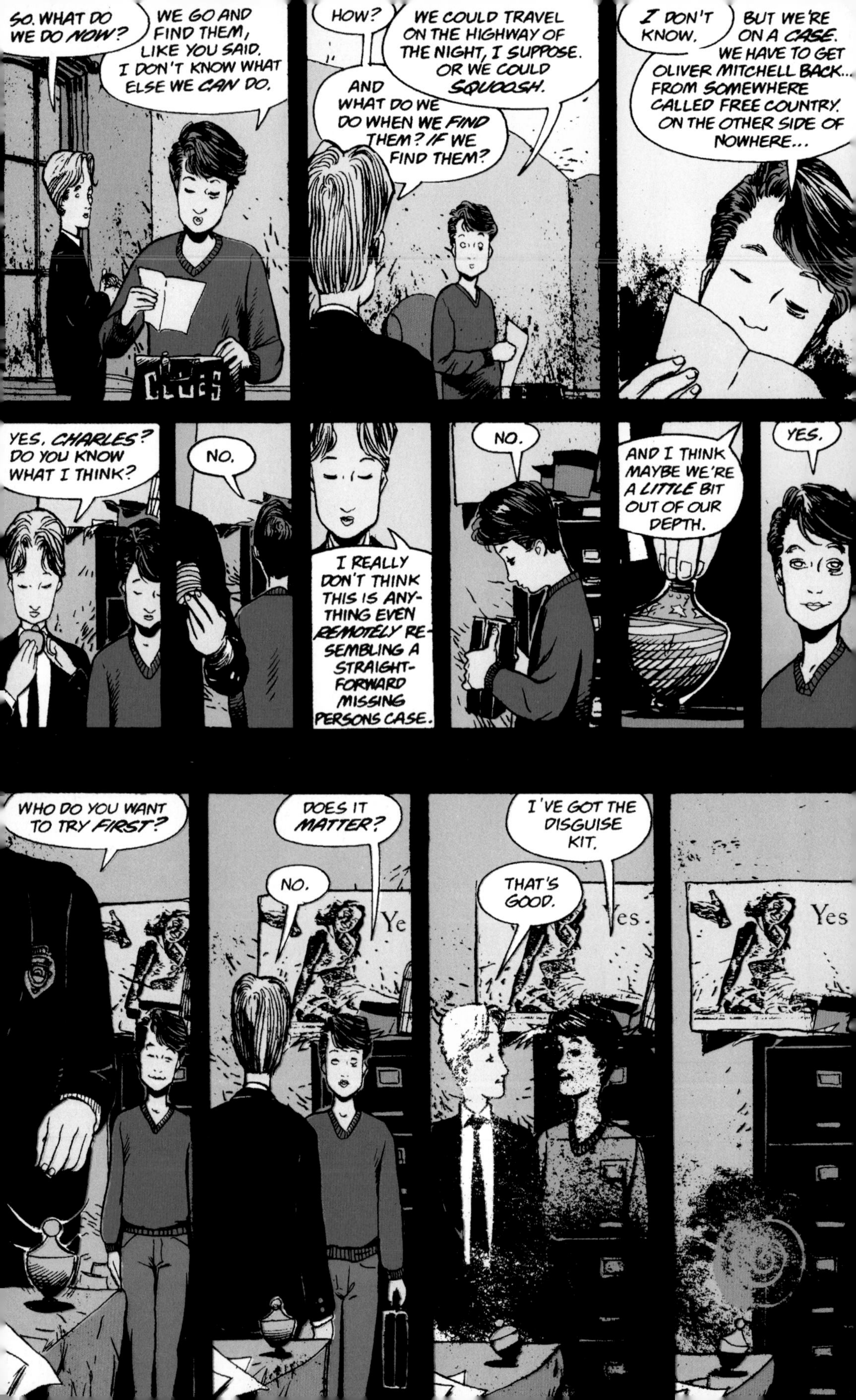
SO. WHAT DO WE DO NOW?
WE GO AND FIND THEM, LIKE YOU SAID. I DON'T KNOW WHAT ELSE WE CAN DO.
CLUES
HOW?
WE COULD TRAVEL ON THE HIGHWAY OF THE NIGHT, I SUPPOSE. OR WE COULD SQUOOSH.
AND WHAT DO WE DO WHEN WE FIND THEM? IF WE FIND THEM?
I DON'T KNOW.
BUT WE'RE ON A CASE. WE HAVE TO GET OLIVER MITCHELL BACK... FROM SOMEWHERE CALLED FREE COUNTRY. ON THE OTHER SIDE OF NOWHERE...
YES, CHARLES? DO YOU KNOW WHAT I THINK?
NO.
I REALLY DON'T THINK THIS IS ANYTHING EVEN REMOTELY RESEMBLING A STRAIGHTFORWARD MISSING PERSONS CASE.
NO.
AND I THINK MAYBE WE'RE A LITTLE BIT OUT OF OUR DEPTH.
YES.
WHO DO YOU WANT TO TRY FIRST?
DOES IT MATTER?
NO.
I'VE GOT THE DISGUISE KIT.
THAT'S GOOD.
Yes
Yes

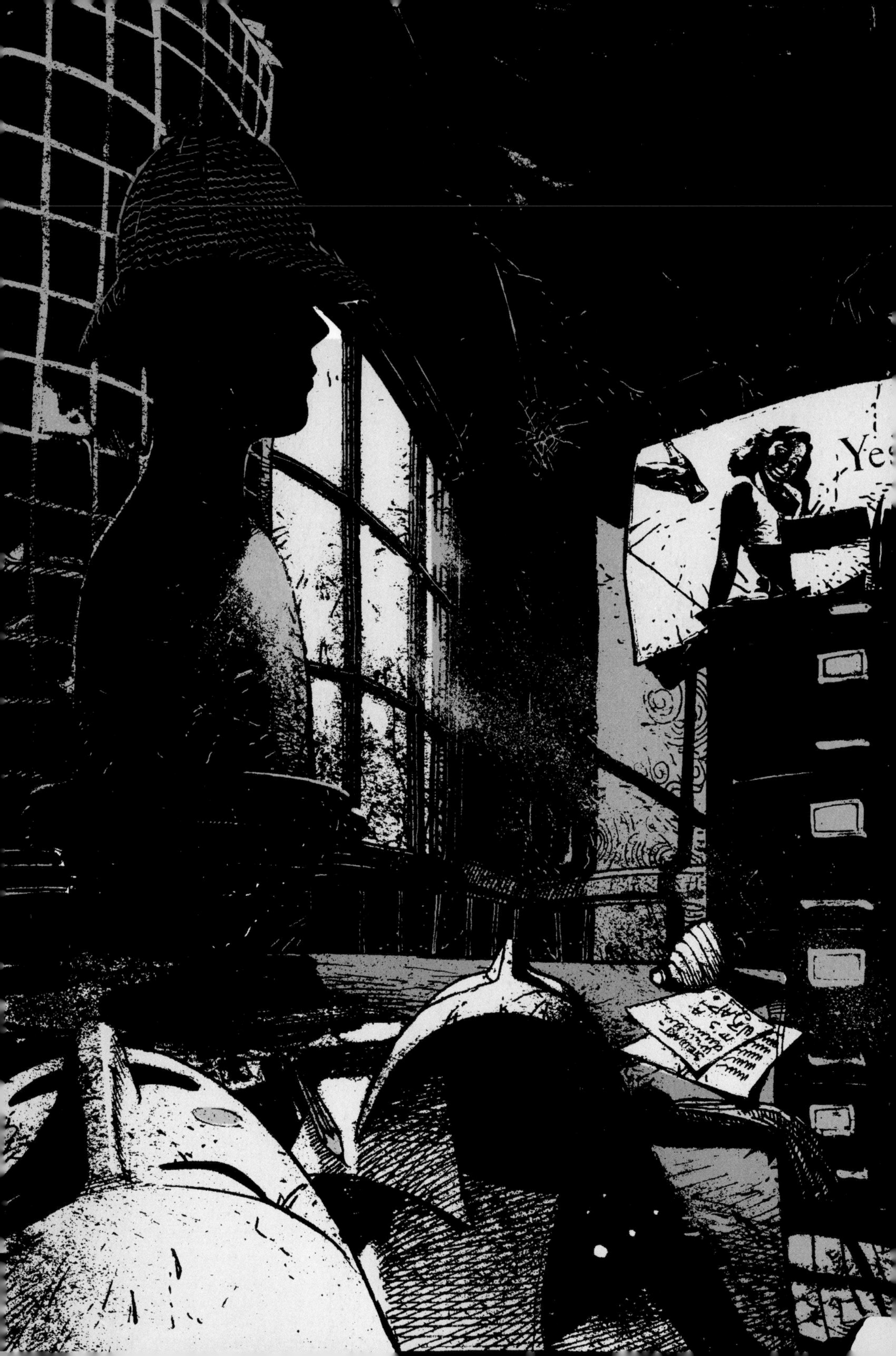

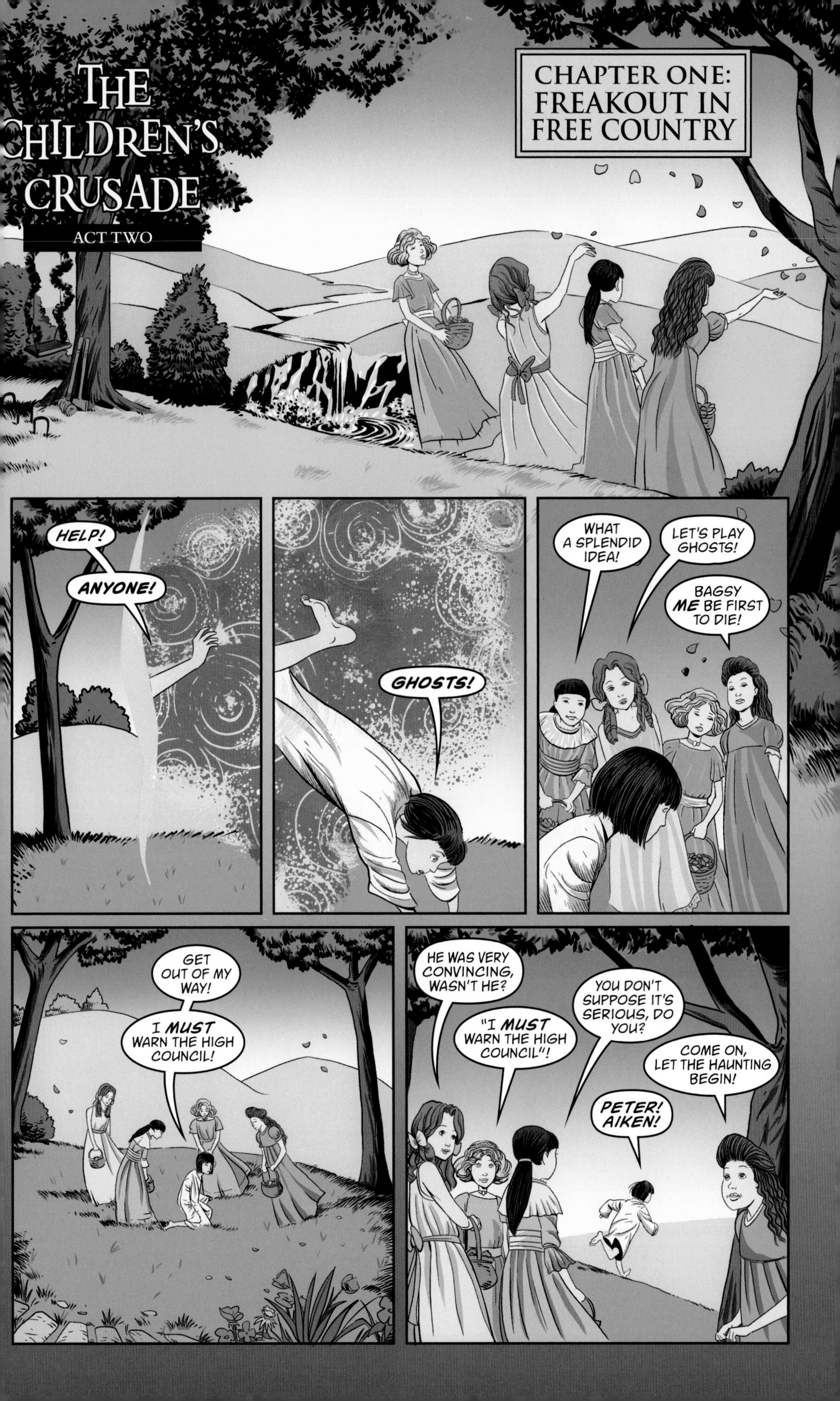

THE CHILDREN'S CRUSADE
ACT TWO
CHAPTER ONE: FREAKOUT IN FREE COUNTRY
HELP!
ANYONE!
GHOSTS!
WHAT A SPLENDID IDEA!
LET'S PLAY GHOSTS!
BAGSY ME BE FIRST TO DIE!
GET OUT OF MY WAY!
I MUST WARN THE HIGH COUNCIL!
HE WAS VERY CONVINCING, WASN'T HE?
"I MUST WARN THE HIGH COUNCIL"!
YOU DON'T SUPPOSE IT'S SERIOUS, DO YOU?
COME ON, LET THE HAUNTING BEGIN!
PETER! AIKEN!

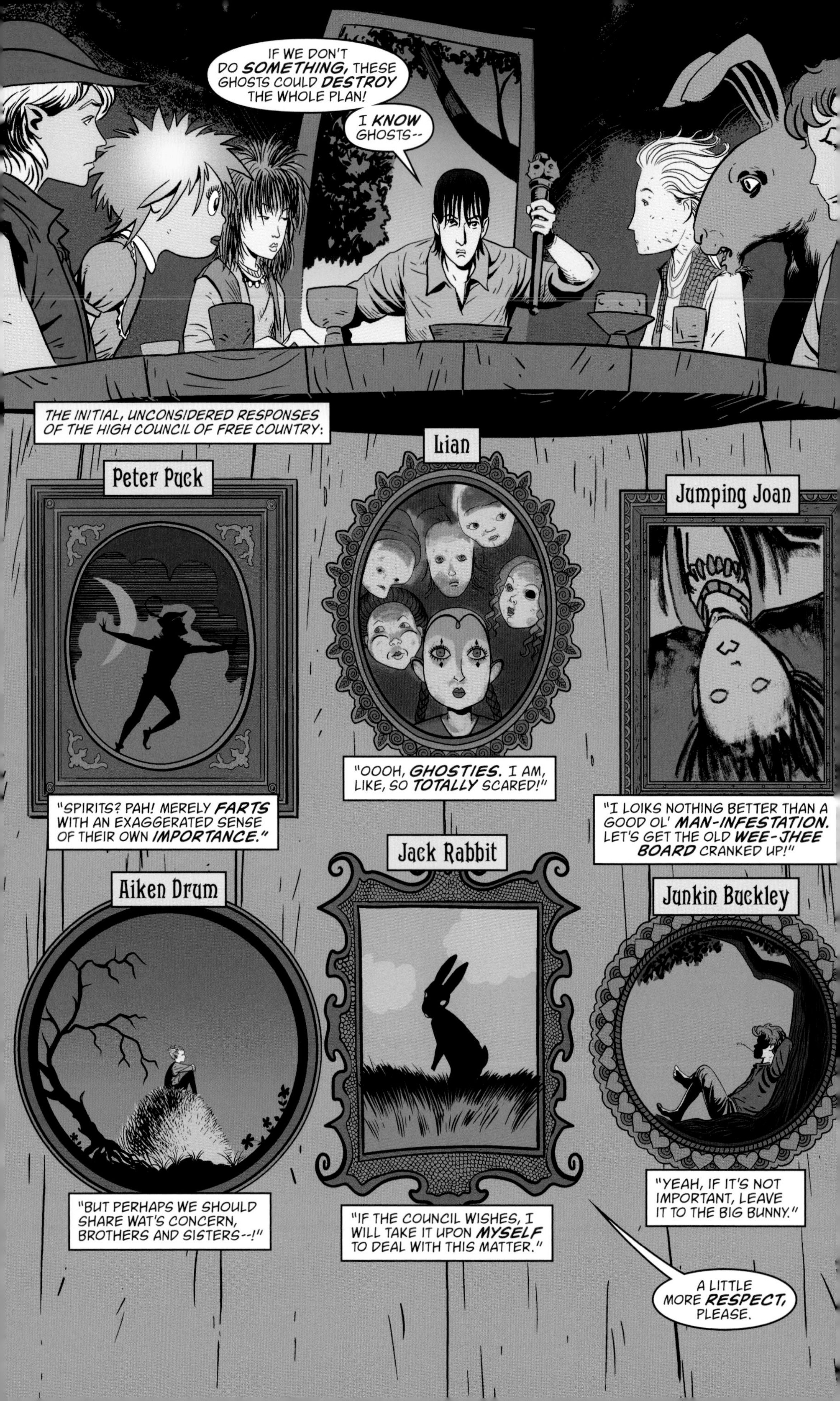
IF WE DON'T DO SOMETHING, THESE GHOSTS COULD DESTROY THE WHOLE PLAN!
I KNOW GHOSTS--
THE INITIAL, UNCONSIDERED RESPONSES OF THE HIGH COUNCIL OF FREE COUNTRY:
Peter Puck
"SPIRITS? PAH! MERELY FARTS WITH AN EXAGGERATED SENSE OF THEIR OWN IMPORTANCE."
Lian
"OOOH, GHOSTIES. I AM, LIKE, SO TOTALLY SCARED!"
Jumping Joan
"I LOIKS NOTHING BETTER THAN A GOOD OL' MAN-INFESTATION. LET'S GET THE OLD WEE-JHEE BOARD CRANKED UP!"
Aiken Drum
"BUT PERHAPS WE SHOULD SHARE WAT'S CONCERN, BROTHERS AND SISTERS--!"
Jack Rabbit
"IF THE COUNCIL WISHES, I WILL TAKE IT UPON MYSELF TO DEAL WITH THIS MATTER."
Junkin Buckley
"YEAH, IF IT'S NOT IMPORTANT, LEAVE IT TO THE BIG BUNNY."
A LITTLE MORE RESPECT, PLEASE.

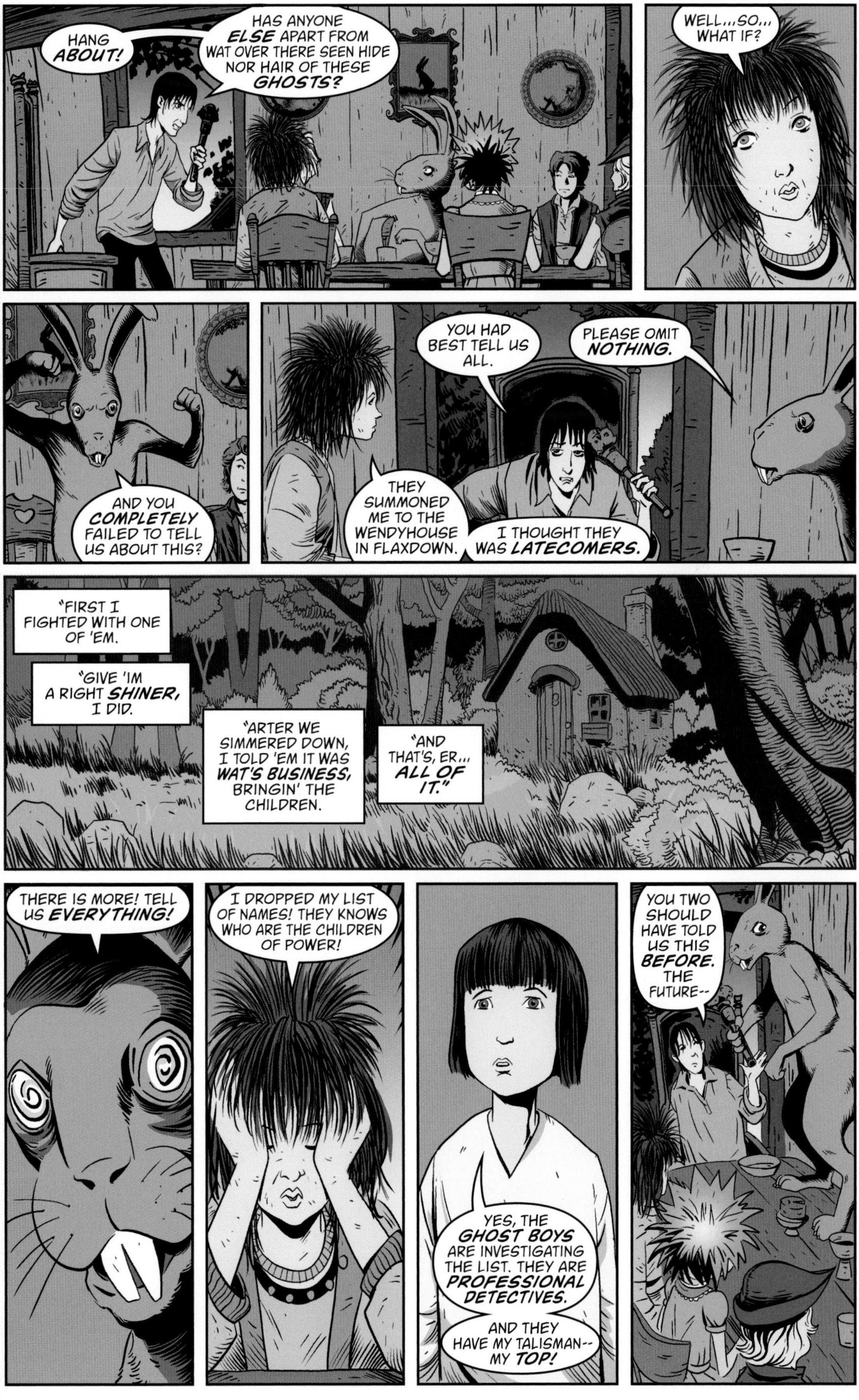

HANG ABOUT!
HAS ANYONE ELSE APART FROM WAT OVER THERE SEEN HIDE NOR HAIR OF THESE GHOSTS?
WELL...SO... WHAT IF?
AND YOU COMPLETELY FAILED TO TELL US ABOUT THIS?
YOU HAD BEST TELL US ALL.
PLEASE OMIT NOTHING.
THEY SUMMONED ME TO THE WENDYHOUSE IN FLAXDOWN.
I THOUGHT THEY WAS LATECOMERS.
"FIRST I FIGHTED WITH ONE OF 'EM.
"GIVE 'IM A RIGHT SHINER, I DID.
"ARTER WE SIMMERED DOWN, I TOLD 'EM IT WAS WAT'S BUSINESS, BRINGIN' THE CHILDREN.
"AND THAT'S, ER... ALL OF IT."
THERE IS MORE! TELL US EVERYTHING!
I DROPPED MY LIST OF NAMES! THEY KNOWS WHO ARE THE CHILDREN OF POWER!
YES, THE GHOST BOYS ARE INVESTIGATING THE LIST. THEY ARE PROFESSIONAL DETECTIVES.
AND THEY HAVE MY TALISMAN-- MY TOP!
YOU TWO SHOULD HAVE TOLD US THIS BEFORE. THE FUTURE--

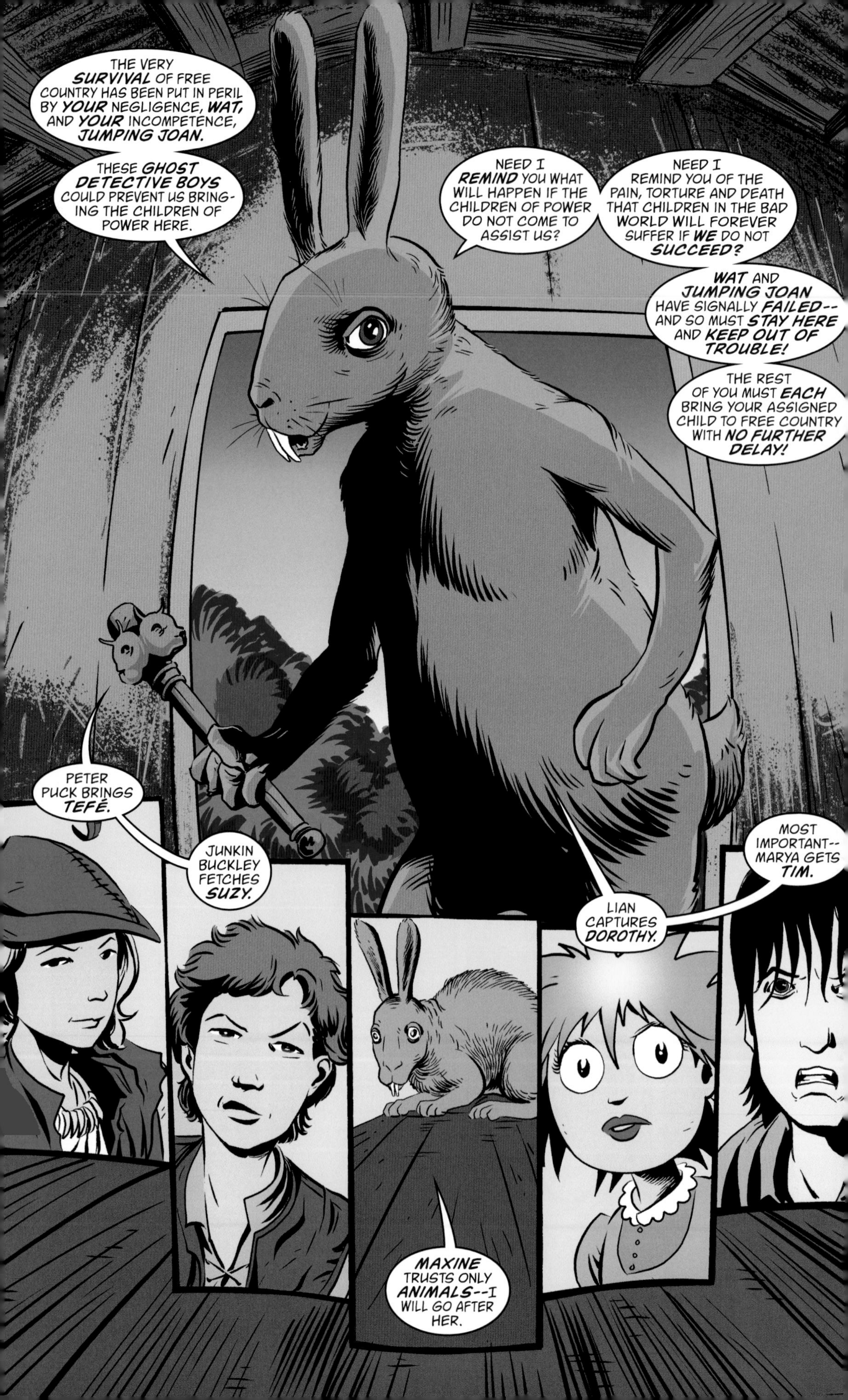
THE VERY SURVIVAL OF FREE COUNTRY HAS BEEN PUT IN PERIL BY YOUR NEGLIGENCE, WAT, AND YOUR INCOMPETENCE, JUMPING JOAN.
THESE GHOST DETECTIVE BOYS COULD PREVENT US BRING-ING THE CHILDREN OF POWER HERE.
NEED I REMIND YOU WHAT WILL HAPPEN IF THE CHILDREN OF POWER DO NOT COME TO ASSIST US?
NEED I REMIND YOU OF THE PAIN, TORTURE AND DEATH THAT CHILDREN IN THE BAD WORLD WILL FOREVER SUFFER IF WE DO NOT SUCCEED?
WAT AND JUMPING JOAN HAVE SIGNALLY FAILED-- AND SO MUST STAY HERE AND KEEP OUT OF TROUBLE!
THE REST OF YOU MUST EACH BRING YOUR ASSIGNED CHILD TO FREE COUNTRY WITH NO FURTHER DELAY!
PETER PUCK BRINGS TEFÉ.
JUNKIN BUCKLEY FETCHES SUZY.
MAXINE TRUSTS ONLY ANIMALS--I WILL GO AFTER HER.
LIAN CAPTURES DOROTHY.
MOST IMPORTANT-- MARYA GETS TIM.

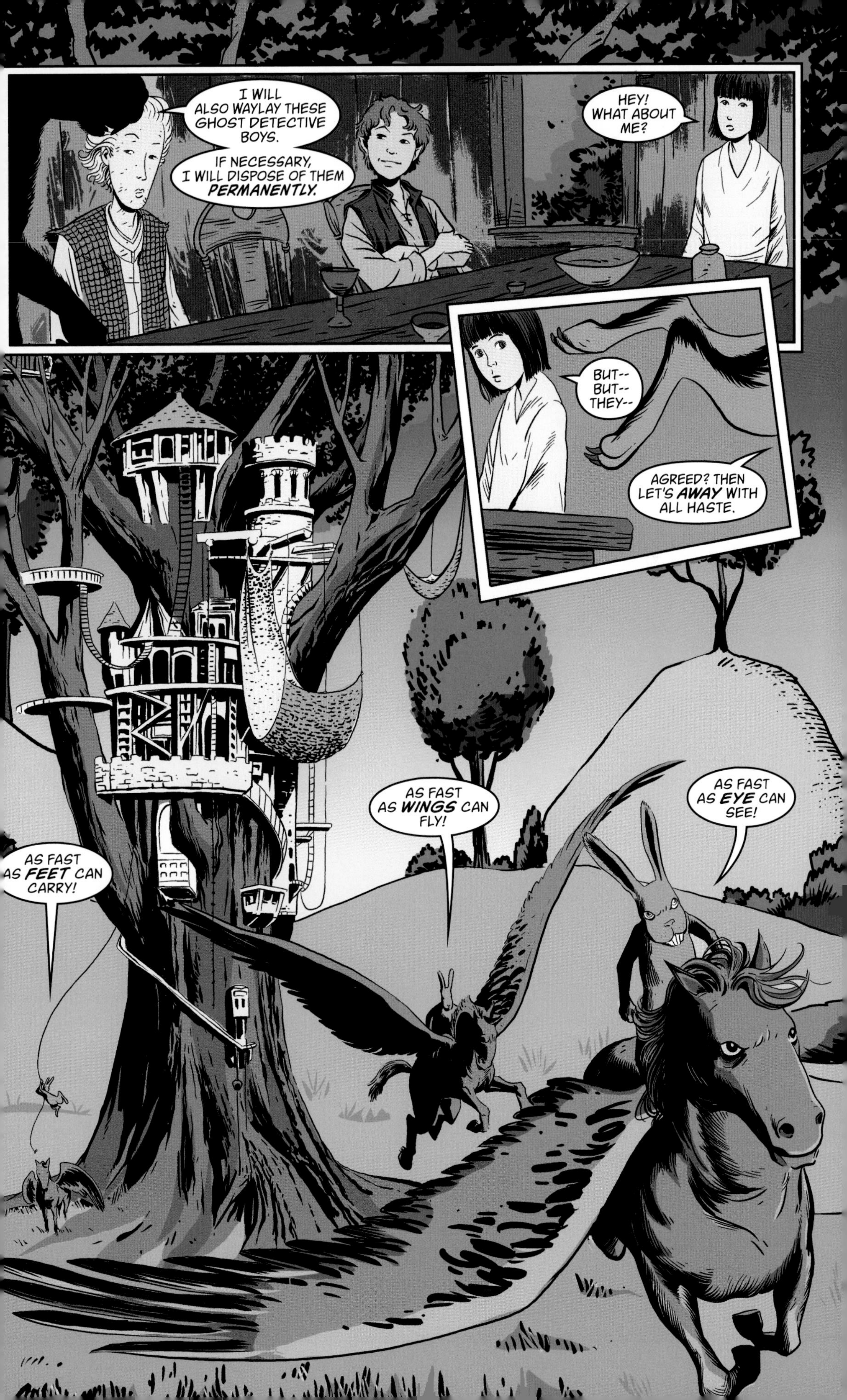
I WILL ALSO WAYLAY THESE GHOST DETECTIVE BOYS.
IF NECESSARY, I WILL DISPOSE OF THEM *PERMANENTLY.*
HEY! WHAT ABOUT ME?
BUT-- BUT-- THEY--
AGREED? THEN LET'S *AWAY* WITH ALL HASTE.
AS FAST AS *FEET* CAN CARRY!
AS FAST AS *WINGS* CAN FLY!
AS FAST AS *EYE* CAN SEE!

CHAPTE

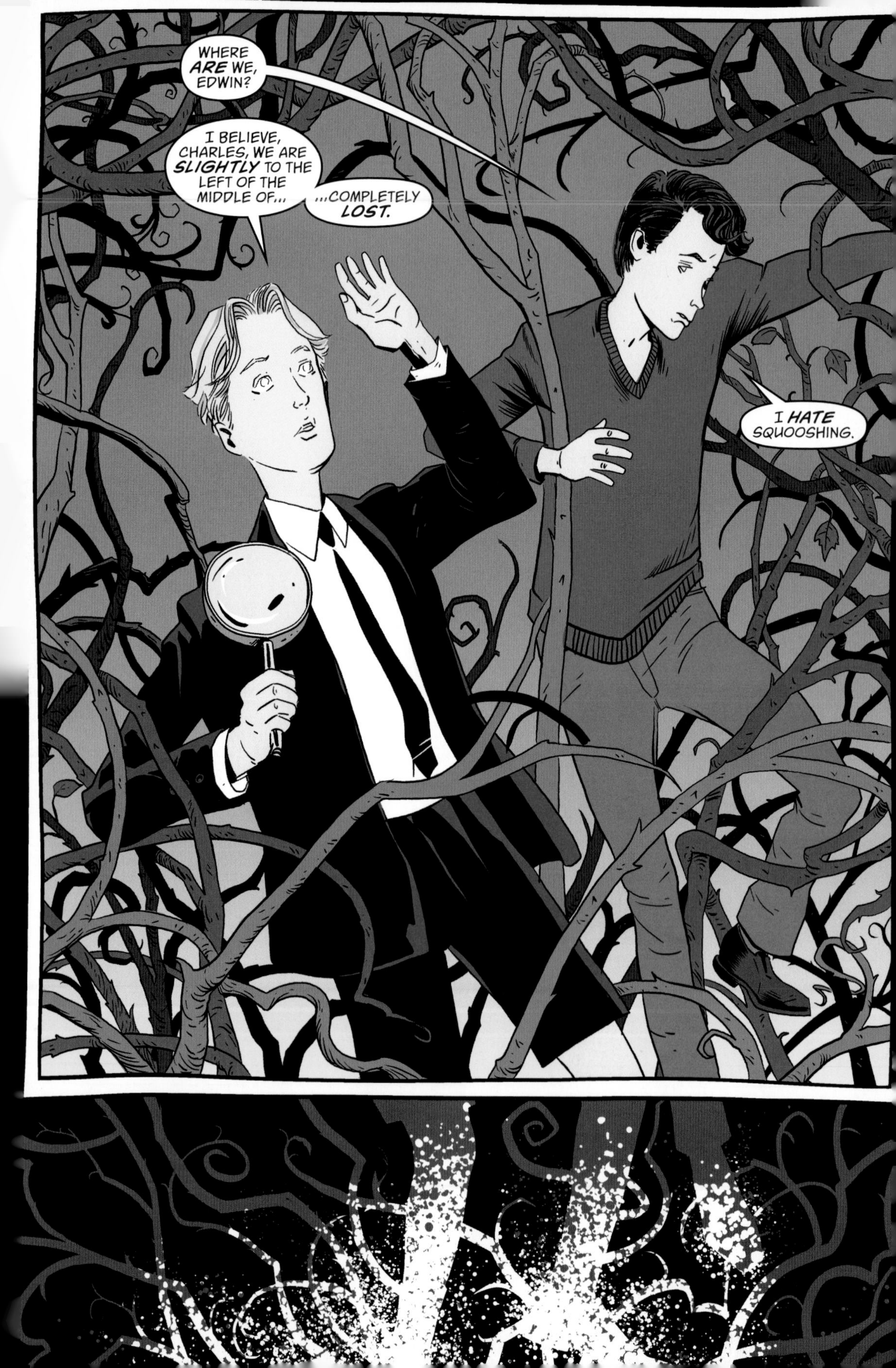
WHERE *ARE* WE, EDWIN?
I BELIEVE, CHARLES, WE ARE *SLIGHTLY* TO THE LEFT OF THE MIDDLE OF...
...COMPLETELY *LOST.*
I *HATE* SQUOOSHING.

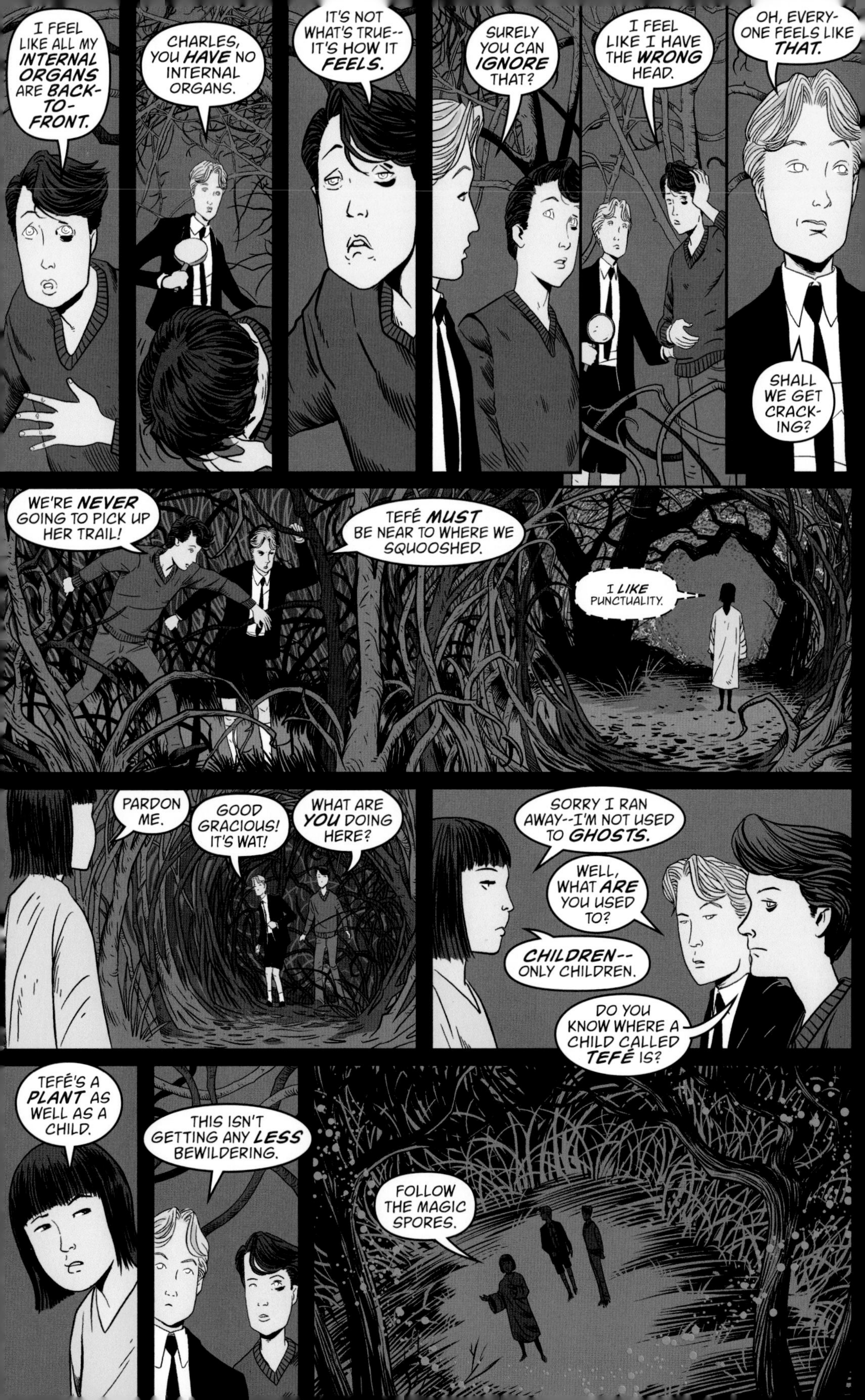
I FEEL LIKE ALL MY INTERNAL ORGANS ARE BACK-TO-FRONT.
CHARLES, YOU HAVE NO INTERNAL ORGANS.
IT'S NOT WHAT'S TRUE-- IT'S HOW IT FEELS.
SURELY YOU CAN IGNORE THAT?
I FEEL LIKE I HAVE THE WRONG HEAD.
OH, EVERY-ONE FEELS LIKE THAT.
SHALL WE GET CRACK-ING?
WE'RE NEVER GOING TO PICK UP HER TRAIL!
TEFÉ MUST BE NEAR TO WHERE WE SQUOOSHED.
I LIKE PUNCTUALITY.
PARDON ME.
GOOD GRACIOUS! IT'S WAT!
WHAT ARE YOU DOING HERE?
SORRY I RAN AWAY--I'M NOT USED TO GHOSTS.
WELL, WHAT ARE YOU USED TO?
CHILDREN-- ONLY CHILDREN.
DO YOU KNOW WHERE A CHILD CALLED TEFÉ IS?
TEFÉ'S A PLANT AS WELL AS A CHILD.
THIS ISN'T GETTING ANY LESS BEWILDERING.
FOLLOW THE MAGIC SPORES.

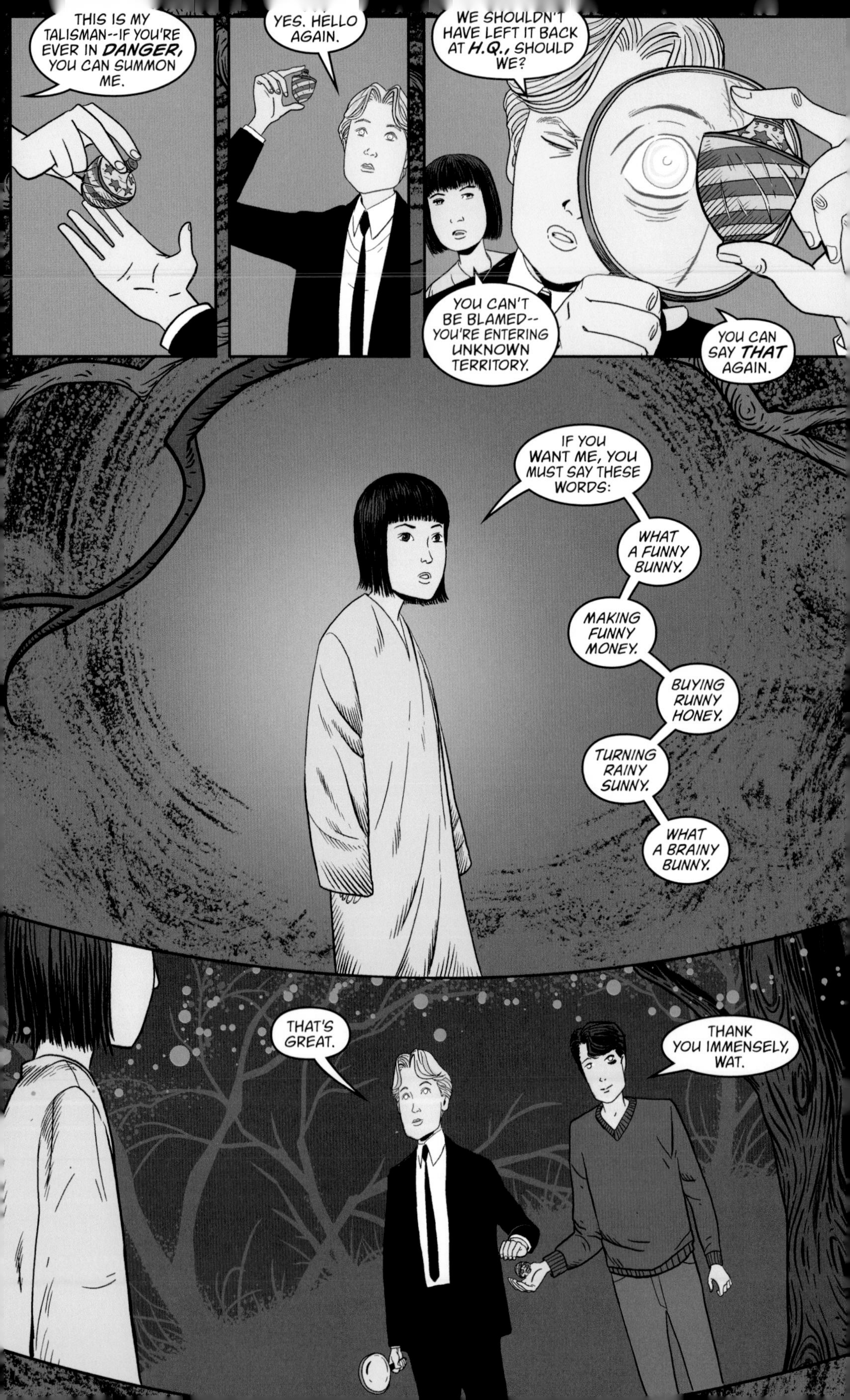

THIS IS MY TALISMAN--IF YOU'RE EVER IN DANGER, YOU CAN SUMMON ME.
YES. HELLO AGAIN.
WE SHOULDN'T HAVE LEFT IT BACK AT H.Q., SHOULD WE?
YOU CAN'T BE BLAMED--YOU'RE ENTERING UNKNOWN TERRITORY.
YOU CAN SAY THAT AGAIN.
IF YOU WANT ME, YOU MUST SAY THESE WORDS:
WHAT A FUNNY BUNNY.
MAKING FUNNY MONEY.
BUYING RUNNY HONEY.
TURNING RAINY SUNNY.
WHAT A BRAINY BUNNY.
THAT'S GREAT.
THANK YOU IMMENSELY, WAT.

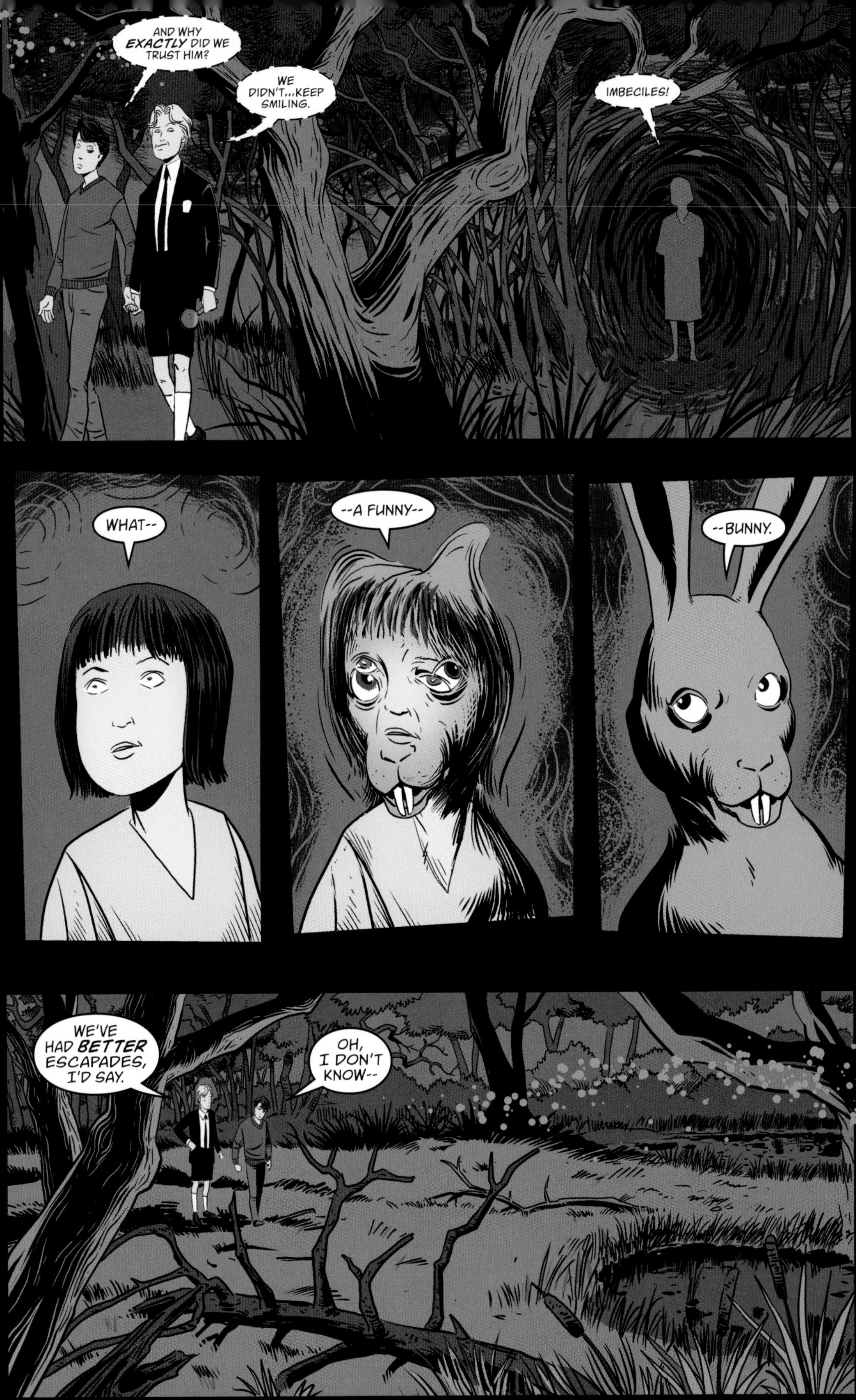
AND WHY EXACTLY DID WE TRUST HIM?
WE DIDN'T...KEEP SMILING.
IMBECILES!
WHAT--
--A FUNNY--
--BUNNY.
WE'VE HAD BETTER ESCAPADES, I'D SAY.
OH, I DON'T KNOW--

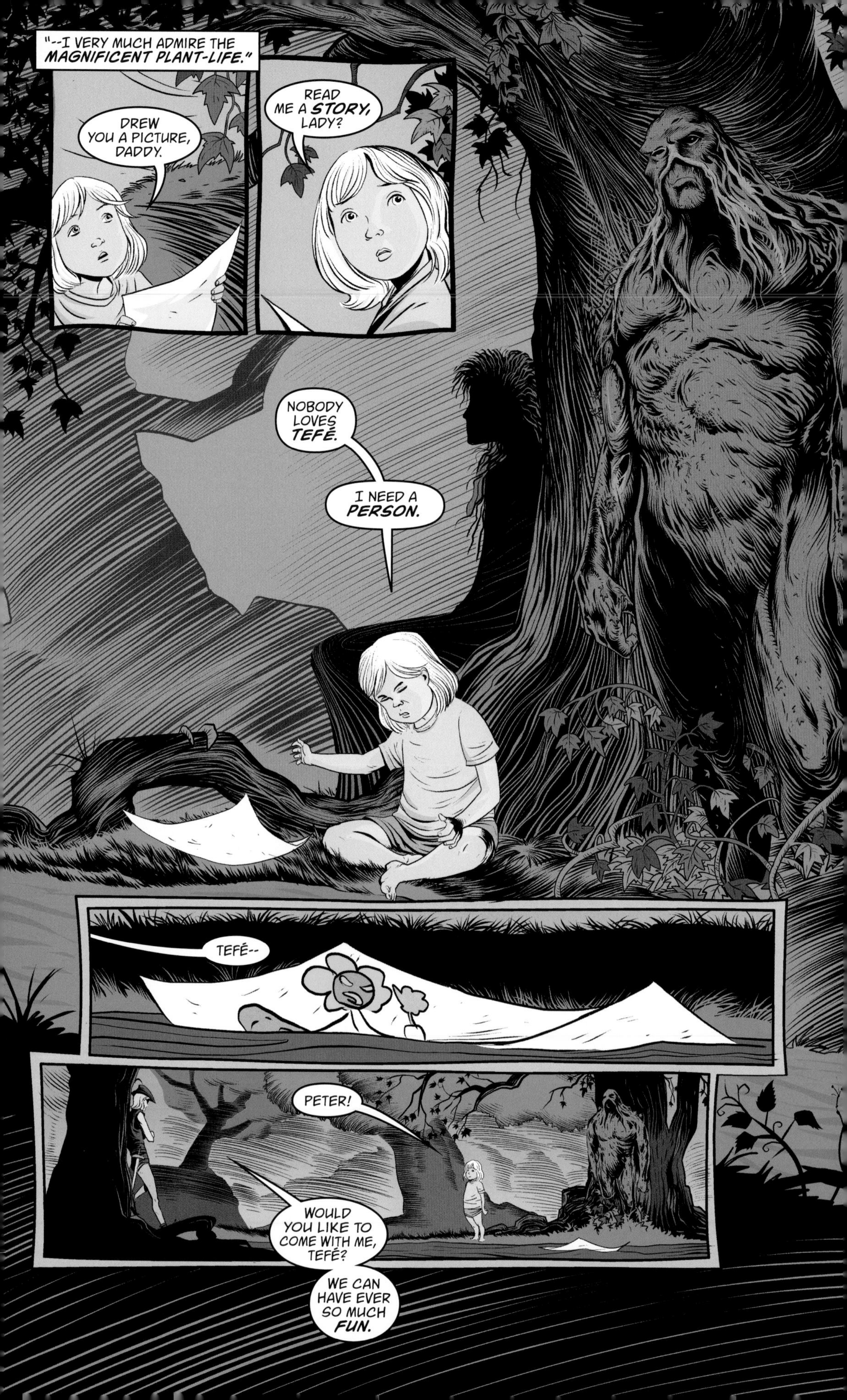
"--I VERY MUCH ADMIRE THE MAGNIFICENT PLANT-LIFE."
DREW YOU A PICTURE, DADDY.
READ ME A STORY, LADY?
NOBODY LOVES TEFÉ.
I NEED A PERSON.
TEFÉ--
PETER!
WOULD YOU LIKE TO COME WITH ME, TEFÉ?
WE CAN HAVE EVER SO MUCH FUN.

CHAPTER THREE: THE BALLAD OF JUNKIN BUCKLEY AND ORCHID SUZY

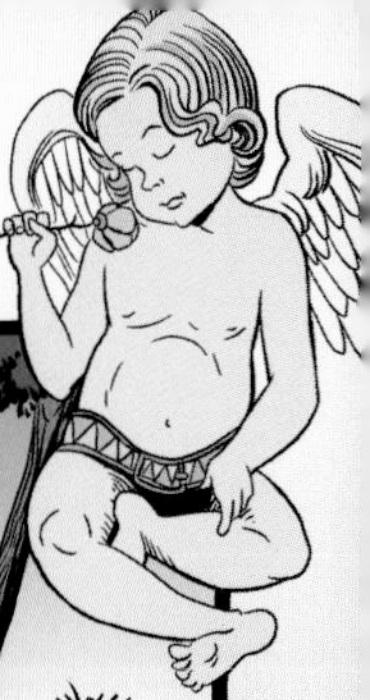

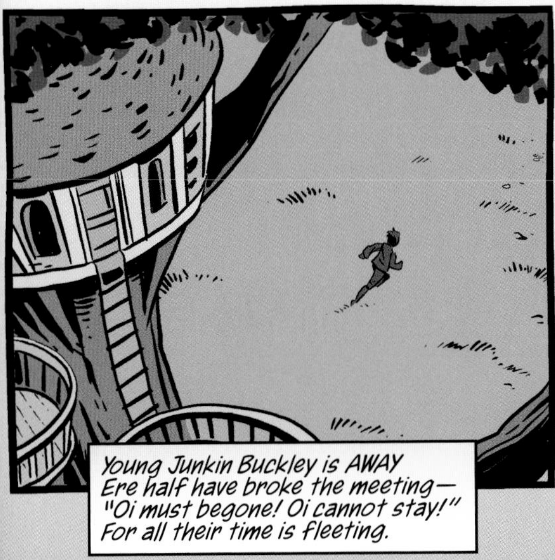
Young Junkin Buckley is AWAY
Ere half have broke the meeting—
"Oi must begone! Oi cannot stay!"
For all their time is fleeting.

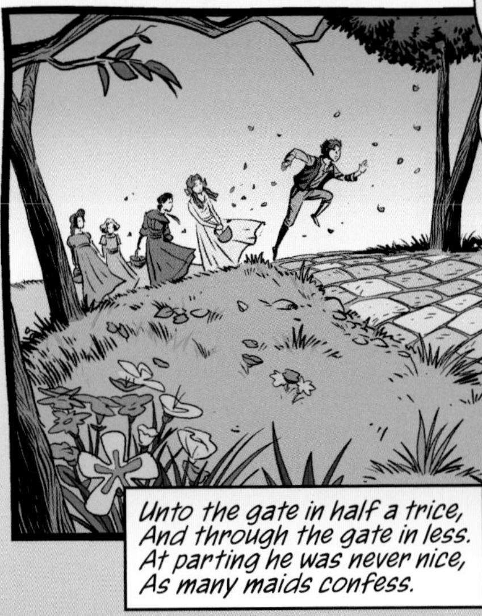
Unto the gate in half a trice,
And through the gate in less.
At parting he was never nice,
As many maids confess.

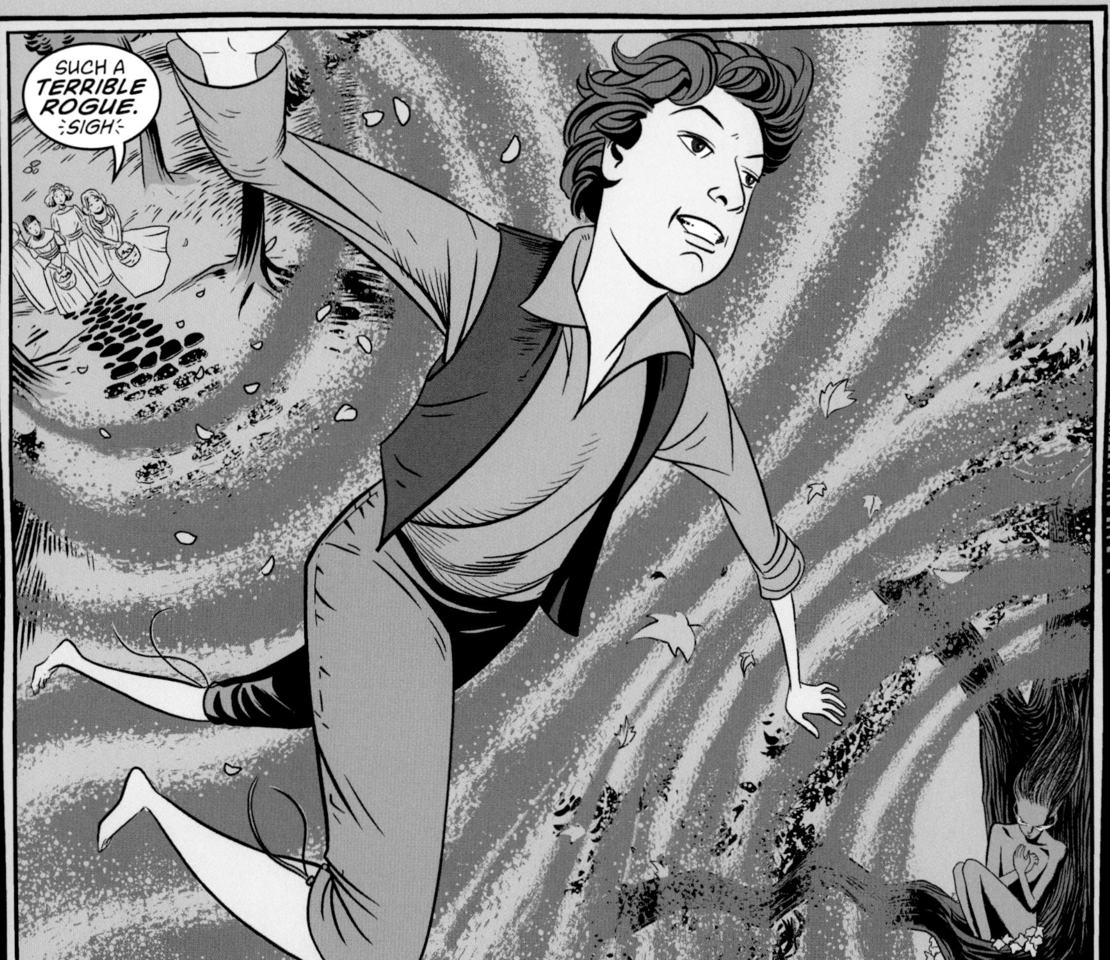
SUCH A TERRIBLE ROGUE. SIGH

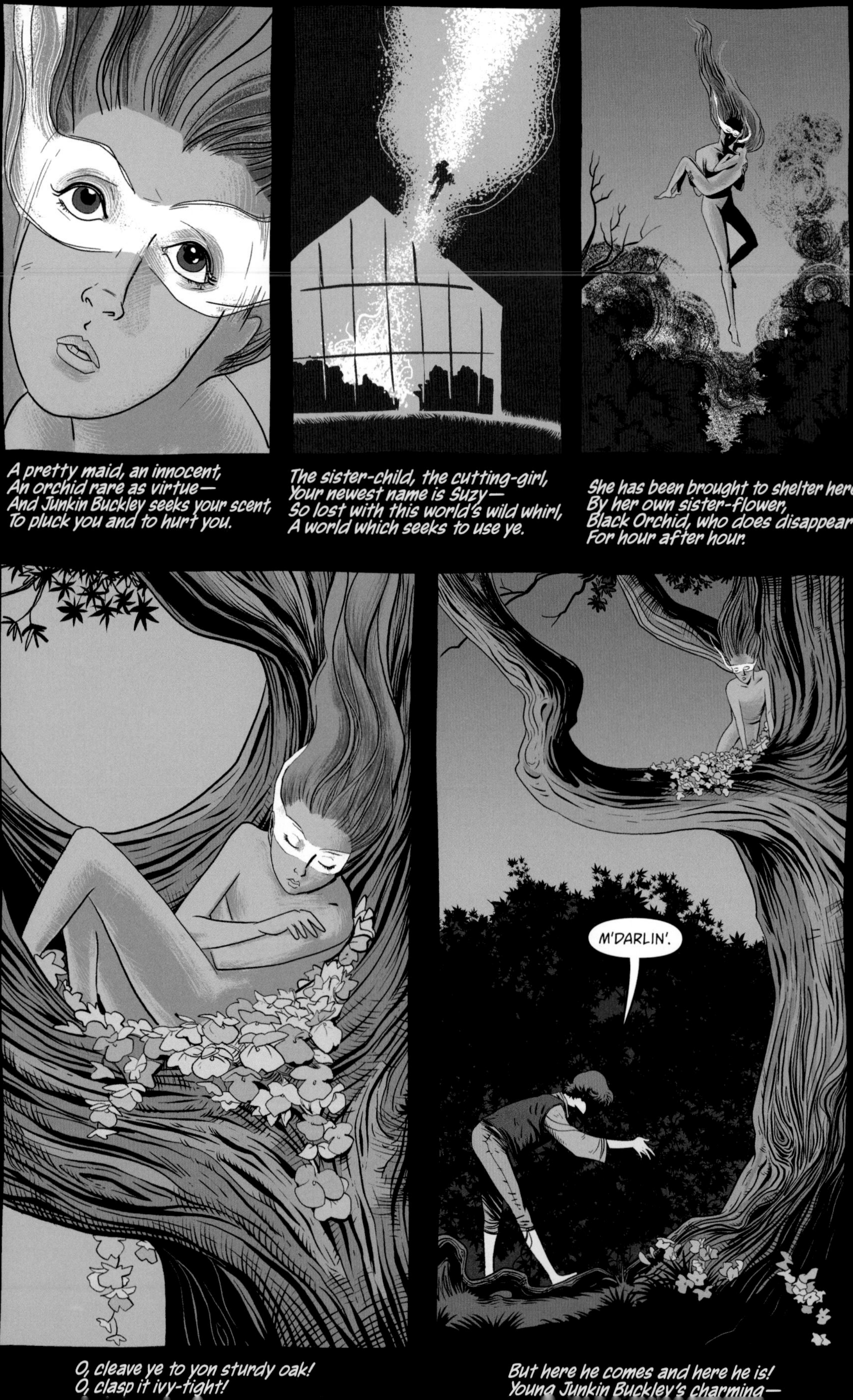
A pretty maid, an innocent,
An orchid rare as virtue—
And Junkin Buckley seeks your scent,
To pluck you and to hurt you.
The sister-child, the cutting-girl,
Your newest name is Suzy—
So lost with this world's wild whirl,
A world which seeks to use ye.
She has been brought to shelter here
By her own sister-flower,
Black Orchid, who does disappear
For hour after hour.
O, cleave ye to yon sturdy oak!
O, clasp it ivy-tight!
M'DARLIN'.
But here he comes and here he is!
Young Junkin Buckley's charming—

And Suzy's never had a friend,
At least, not one so witty,
Who tells her tales that never end,
Who tells her she is pretty.

And Suzy loves the games they play,
The rhymes that Junkin teaches,
His touch is soft as new-dug clay,
His words as sweet as peaches.

But of the world around about
Young Junkin shows her terrors
Of pain and fear and children hur
And children lost in horrors.

Now, Suzy feels a deep despair,
For all of humankind—

"I see such suffering everywhere—
I wish that I were blind.

"I wish that men were more like flowers,
Who feed the earth they eat,
Who rest within more gentle hours,

"I wish that men were more like trees,
Who never force their will,
Who never harm another's face,

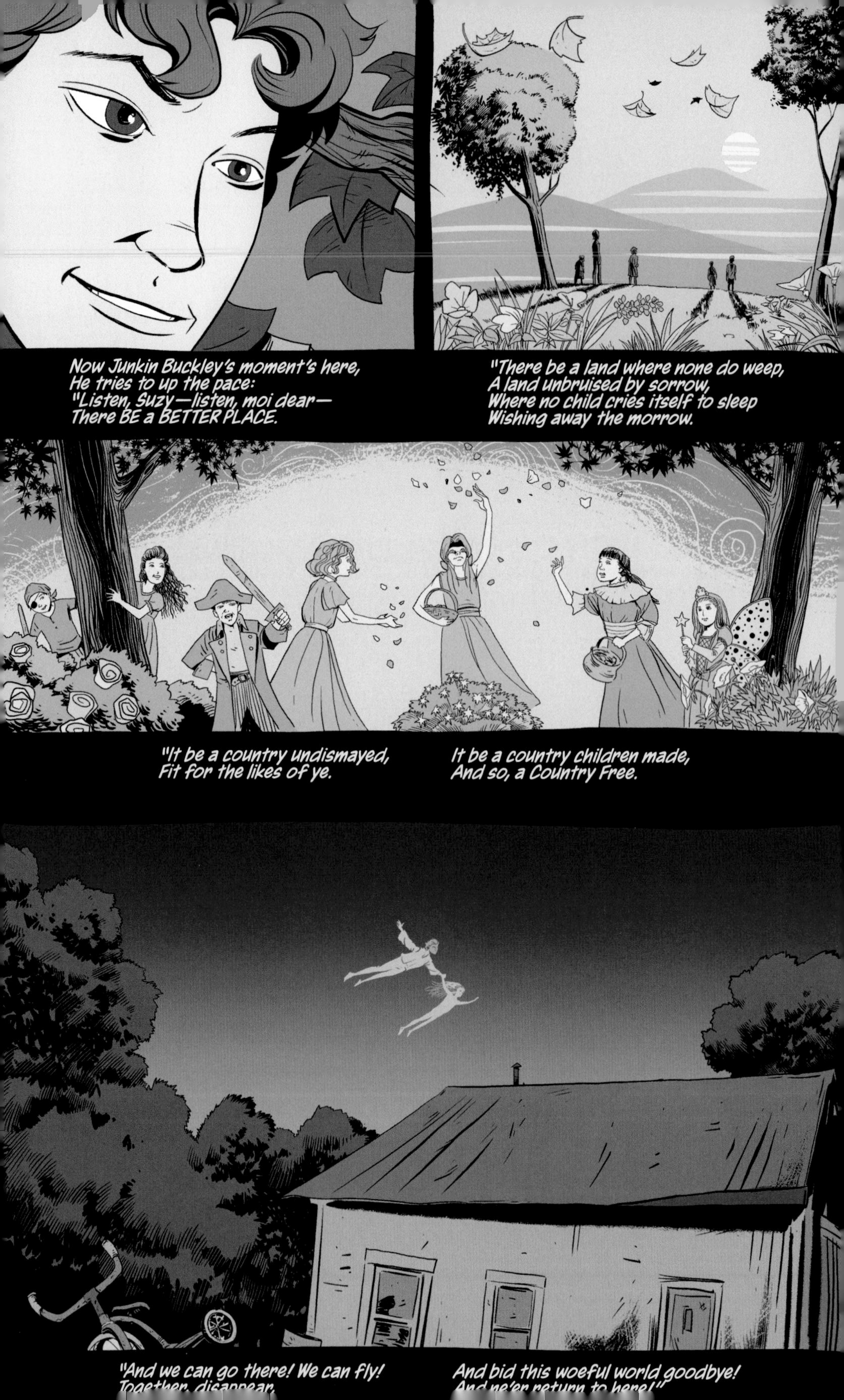
Now Junkin Buckley's moment's here,
He tries to up the pace:
"Listen, Suzy—listen, moi dear—
There BE a BETTER PLACE.
"There be a land where none do weep,
A land unbruised by sorrow,
Where no child cries itself to sleep
Wishing away the morrow.
"It be a country undismayed,
Fit for the likes of ye.
It be a country children made,
And so, a Country Free.
"And we can go there! We can fly!
Together, disappear,
And bid this woeful world goodbye!
And ne'er return to here!"

"But more and better, once ye go
Unto this Country Free,

Ye can bring, from this world of woe
All children after ye."

Poor Suzy is amazed at this,
Though Buckley he deceives.
And when he clasps her in a kiss,
Poor Suzy, she believes!

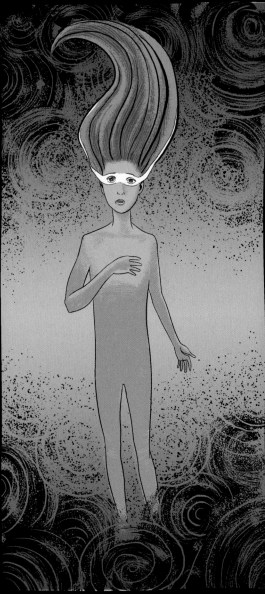

Suzy believes what he avers,
She trusts all promises.
She asks him if his heart is hers,
Just as her heart is his?

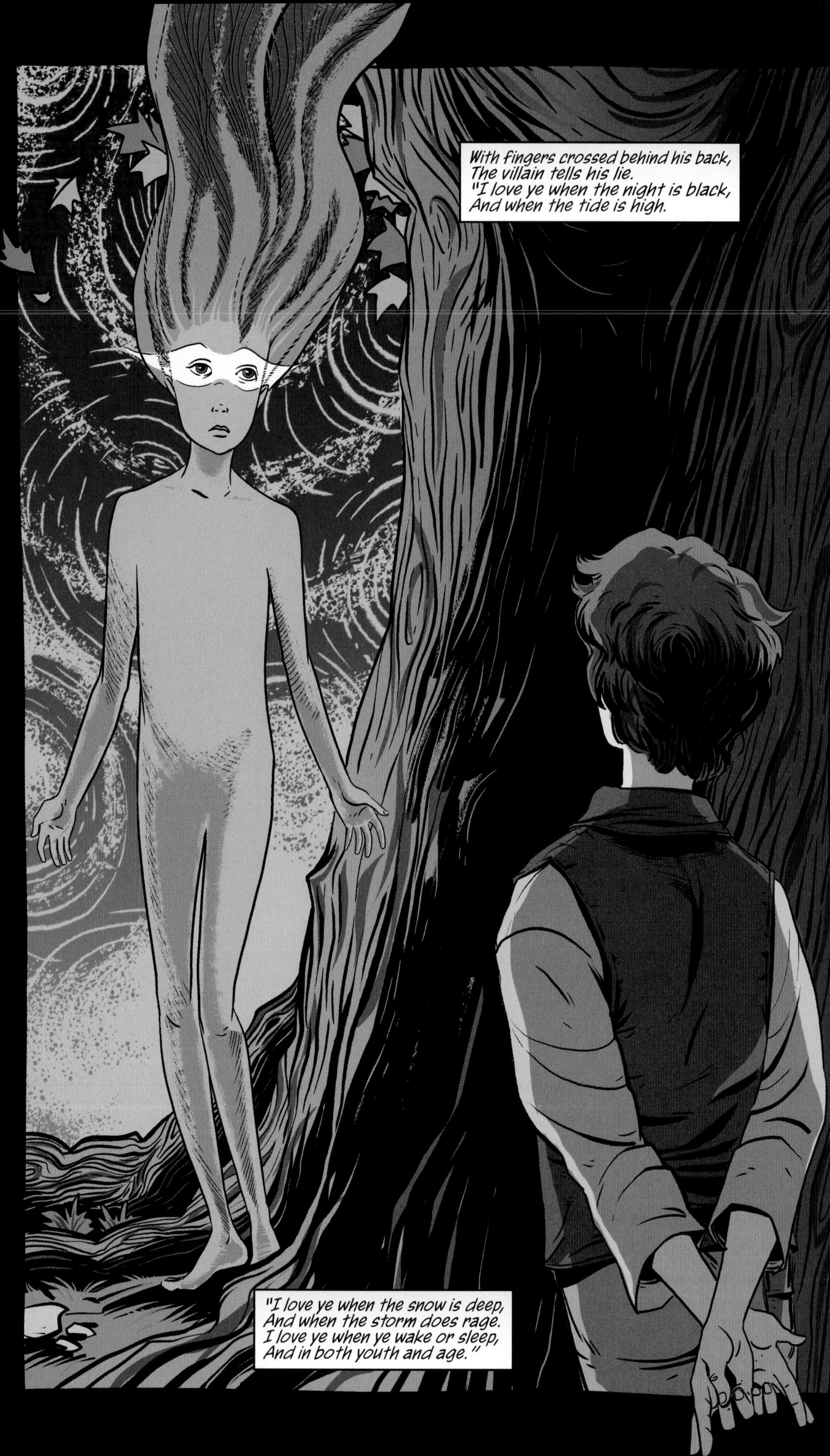
With fingers crossed behind his back,
The villain tells his lie.
"I love ye when the night is black,
And when the tide is high.
"I love ye when the snow is deep,
And when the storm does rage.
I love ye when ye wake or sleep,
And in both youth and age."

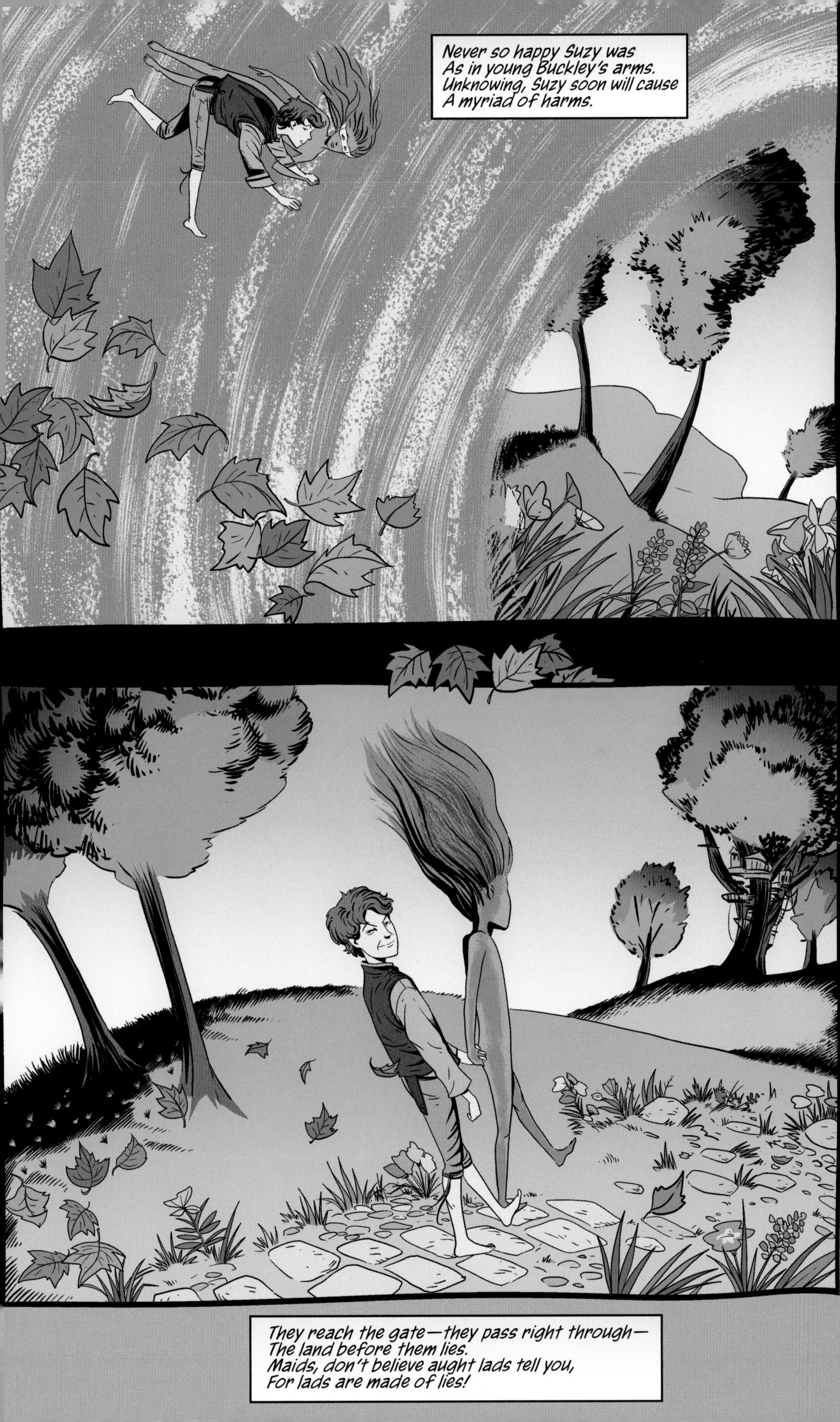
Never so happy Suzy was
As in young Buckley's arms.
Unknowing, Suzy soon will cause
A myriad of harms.
They reach the gate—they pass right through—
The land before them lies.
Maids, don't believe aught lads tell you,
For lads are made of lies!

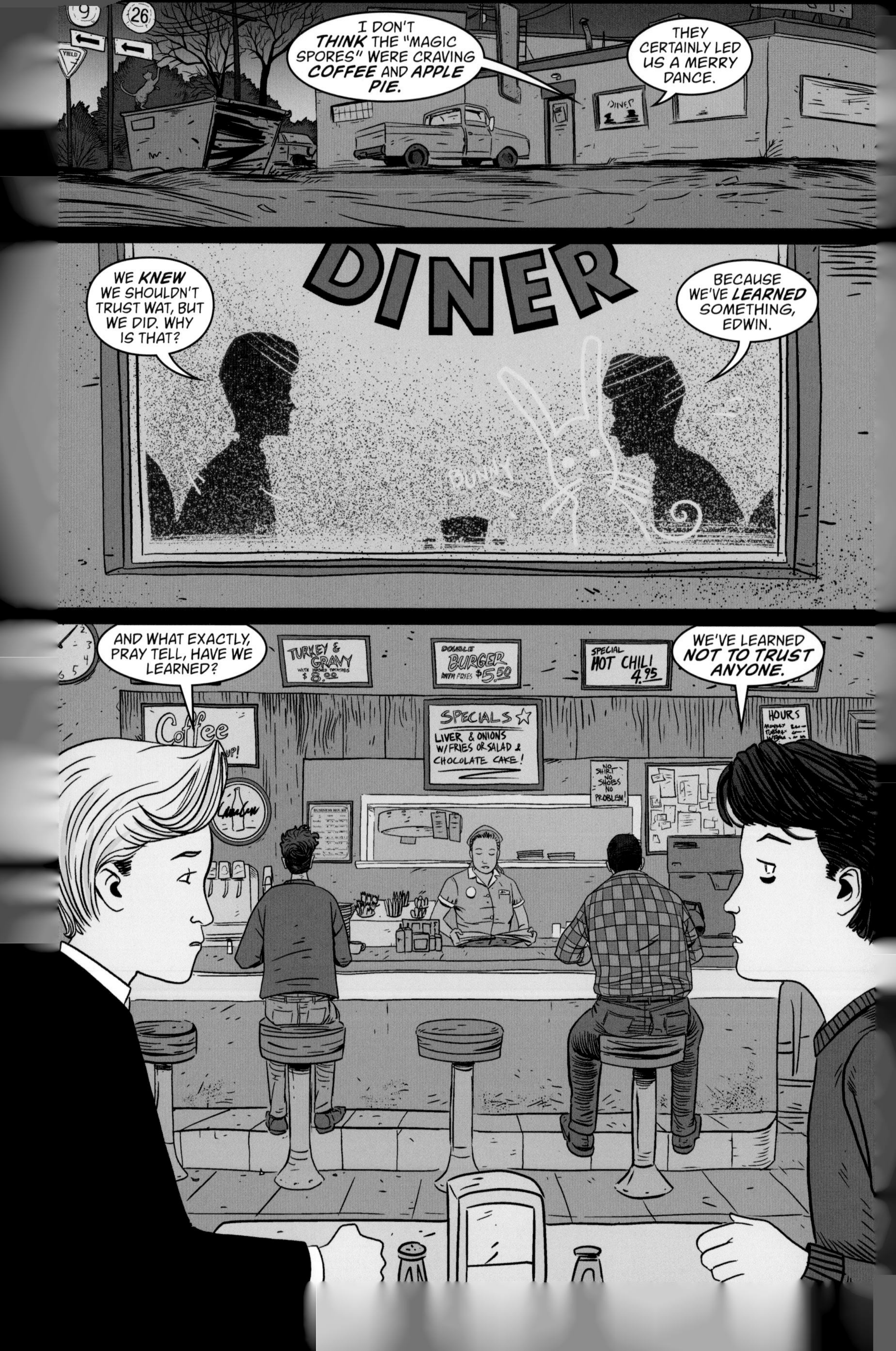

YIELD
I DON'T *THINK* THE "MAGIC SPORES" WERE CRAVING *COFFEE* AND *APPLE PIE.*
THEY CERTAINLY LED US A MERRY DANCE.
DINER
WE *KNEW* WE SHOULDN'T TRUST WAT, BUT WE DID. WHY IS THAT?
BECAUSE WE'VE *LEARNED* SOMETHING, EDWIN.
BUNNY
AND WHAT EXACTLY, PRAY TELL, HAVE WE LEARNED?
WE'VE LEARNED *NOT TO TRUST ANYONE.*
TURKEY & GRAVY WITH MASHED POTATOES $8.00
DOUBLE BURGER WITH FRIES $5.50
SPECIAL HOT CHILI 4.95
SPECIALS LIVER & ONIONS W/FRIES OR SALAD & CHOCOLATE CAKE!
Coffee
NO SHIRT NO SHOES NO PROBLEM!
HOURS

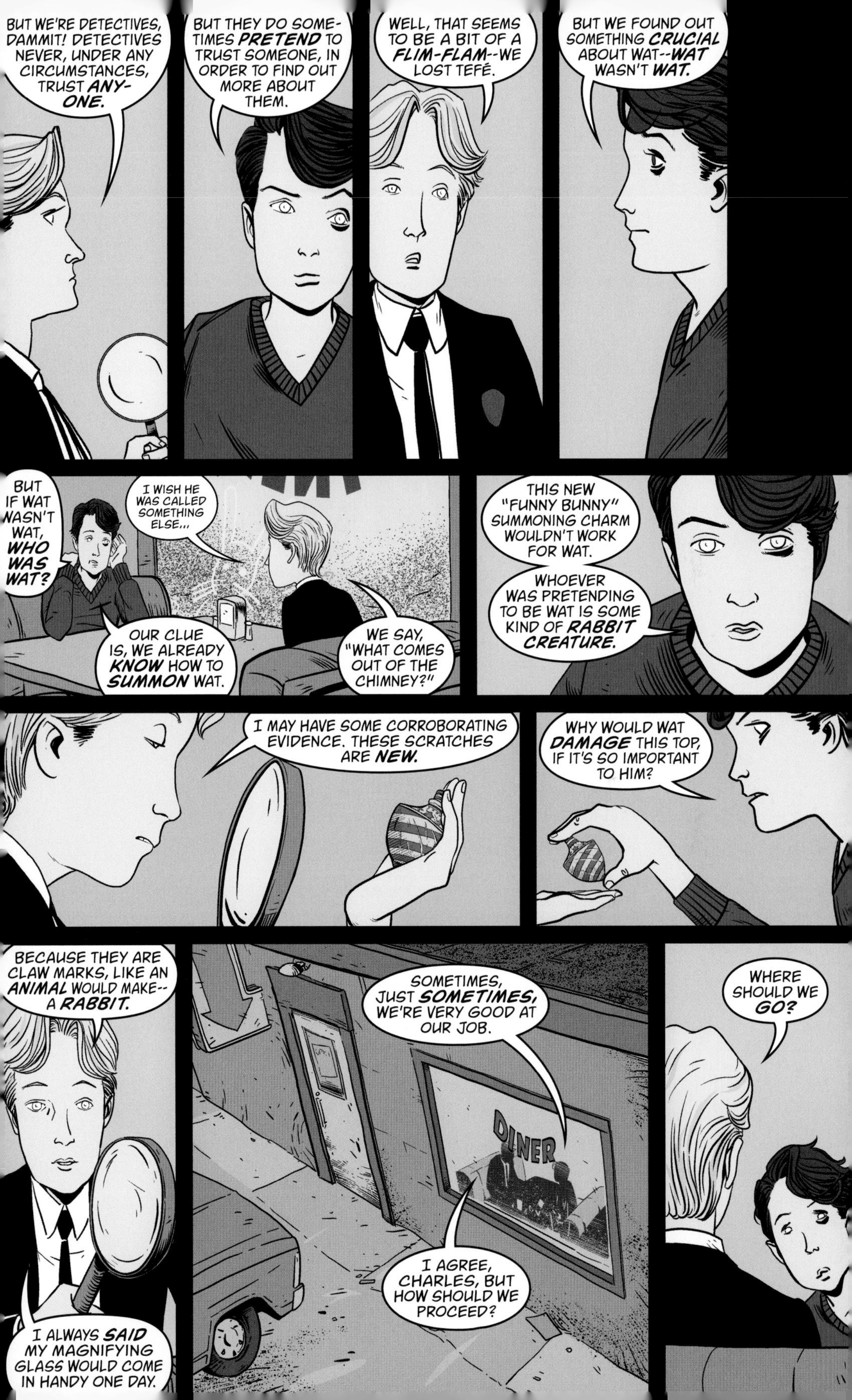
BUT WE'RE DETECTIVES, DAMMIT! DETECTIVES NEVER, UNDER ANY CIRCUMSTANCES, TRUST ANY-ONE.
BUT THEY DO SOME-TIMES PRETEND TO TRUST SOMEONE, IN ORDER TO FIND OUT MORE ABOUT THEM.
WELL, THAT SEEMS TO BE A BIT OF A FLIM-FLAM--WE LOST TEFÉ.
BUT WE FOUND OUT SOMETHING CRUCIAL ABOUT WAT--WAT WASN'T WAT.
BUT IF WAT WASN'T WAT, WHO WAS WAT?
I WISH HE WAS CALLED SOMETHING ELSE...
OUR CLUE IS, WE ALREADY KNOW HOW TO SUMMON WAT.
WE SAY, "WHAT COMES OUT OF THE CHIMNEY?"
THIS NEW "FUNNY BUNNY" SUMMONING CHARM WOULDN'T WORK FOR WAT.
WHOEVER WAS PRETENDING TO BE WAT IS SOME KIND OF RABBIT CREATURE.
I MAY HAVE SOME CORROBORATING EVIDENCE. THESE SCRATCHES ARE NEW.
WHY WOULD WAT DAMAGE THIS TOP, IF IT'S SO IMPORTANT TO HIM?
BECAUSE THEY ARE CLAW MARKS, LIKE AN ANIMAL WOULD MAKE--A RABBIT.
I ALWAYS SAID MY MAGNIFYING GLASS WOULD COME IN HANDY ONE DAY.
SOMETIMES, JUST SOMETIMES, WE'RE VERY GOOD AT OUR JOB.
DINER
I AGREE, CHARLES, BUT HOW SHOULD WE PROCEED?
WHERE SHOULD WE GO?

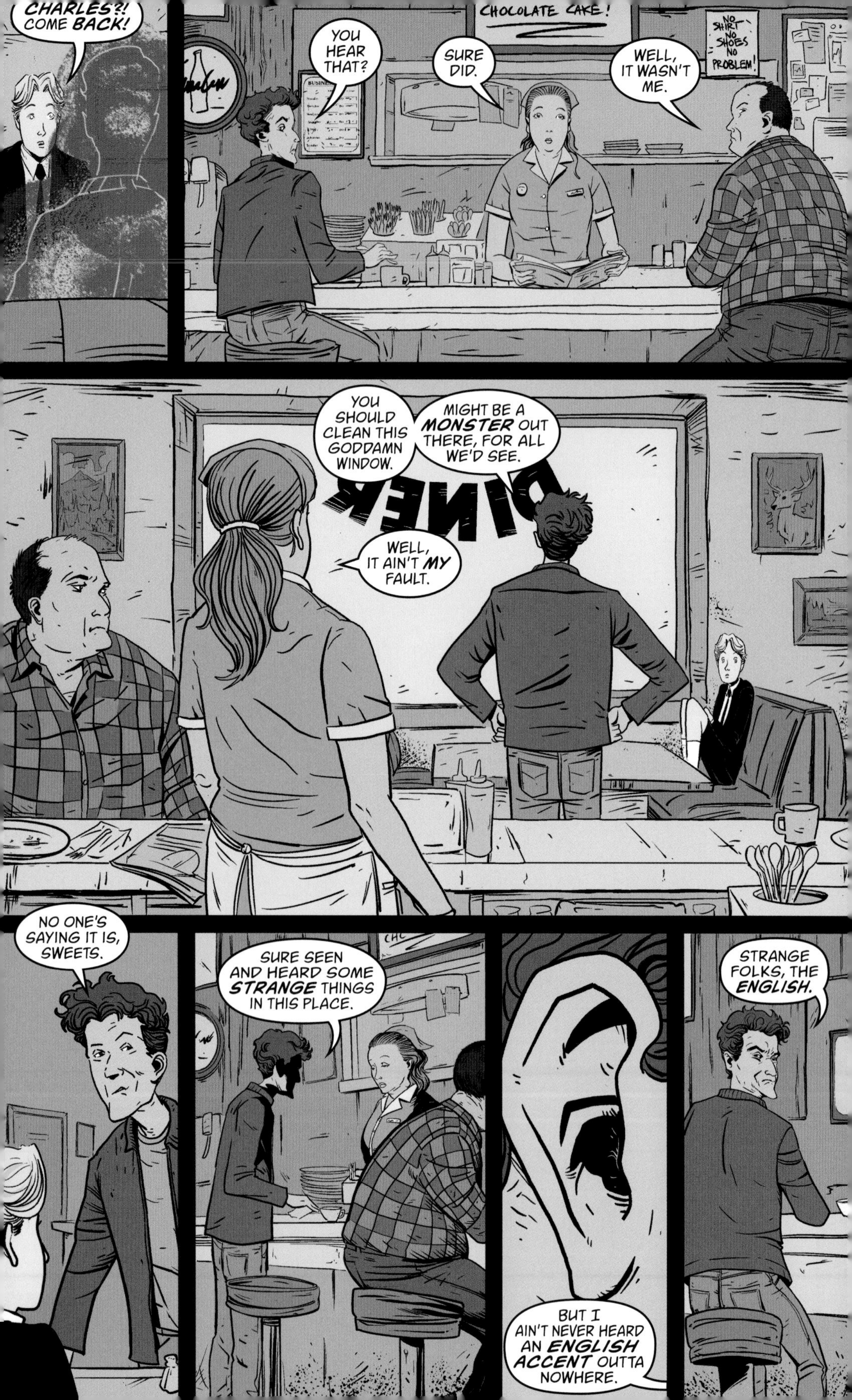
CHARLES?! COME BACK!
CHOCOLATE CAKE!
NO SHIRT NO SHOES NO PROBLEM!
YOU HEAR THAT?
SURE DID.
WELL, IT WASN'T ME.
YOU SHOULD CLEAN THIS GODDAMN WINDOW.
MIGHT BE A MONSTER OUT THERE, FOR ALL WE'D SEE.
DINER
WELL, IT AIN'T MY FAULT.
NO ONE'S SAYING IT IS, SWEETS.
SURE SEEN AND HEARD SOME STRANGE THINGS IN THIS PLACE.
BUT I AIN'T NEVER HEARD AN ENGLISH ACCENT OUTTA NOWHERE.
STRANGE FOLKS, THE ENGLISH.

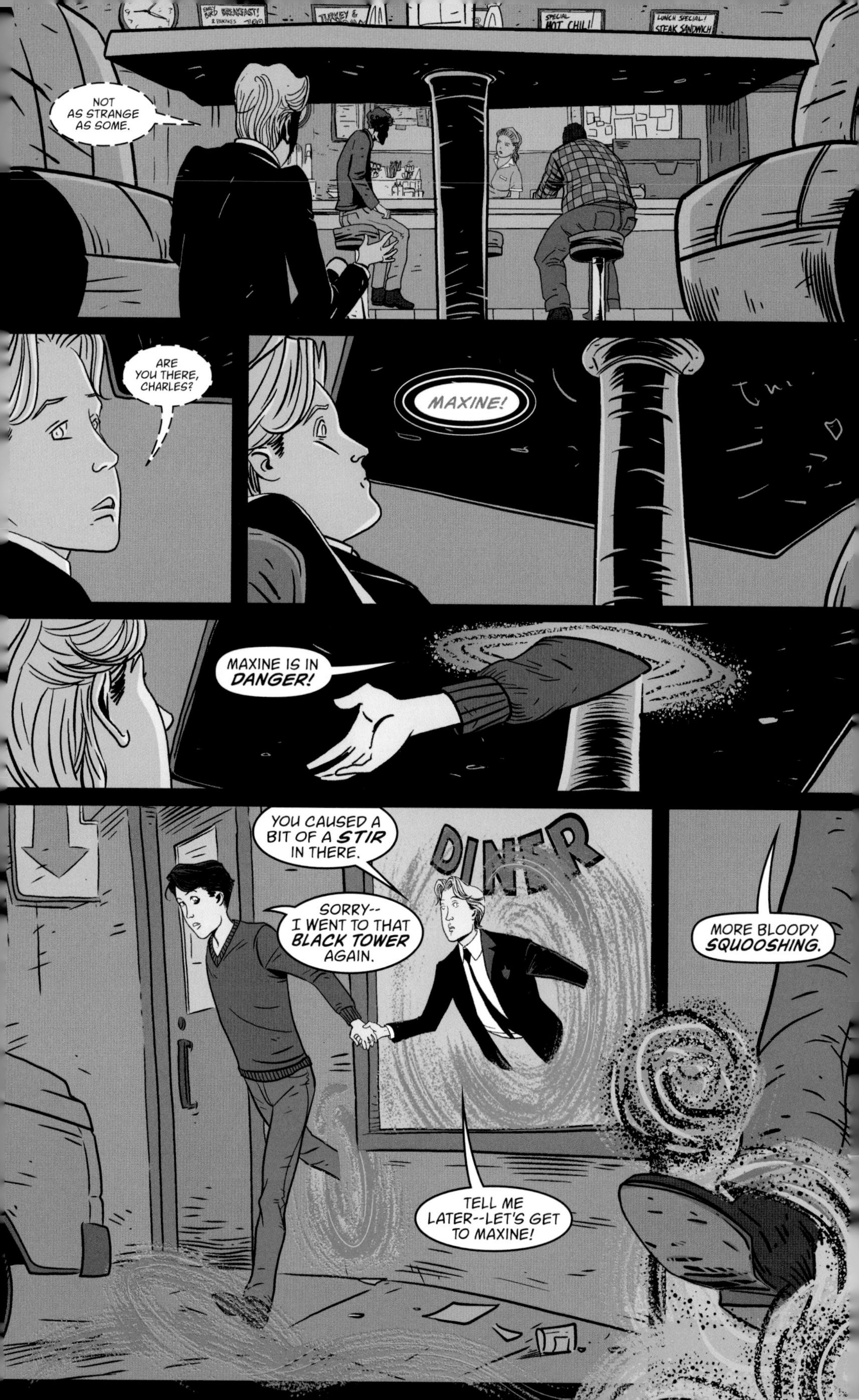
SPECIAL HOT CHILI!
LUNCH SPECIAL! STEAK SANDWICH
NOT AS STRANGE AS SOME.
ARE YOU THERE, CHARLES?
MAXINE!
MAXINE IS IN DANGER!
YOU CAUSED A BIT OF A STIR IN THERE.
DINER
SORRY-- I WENT TO THAT BLACK TOWER AGAIN.
MORE BLOODY SQUOOSHING.
TELL ME LATER--LET'S GET TO MAXINE!

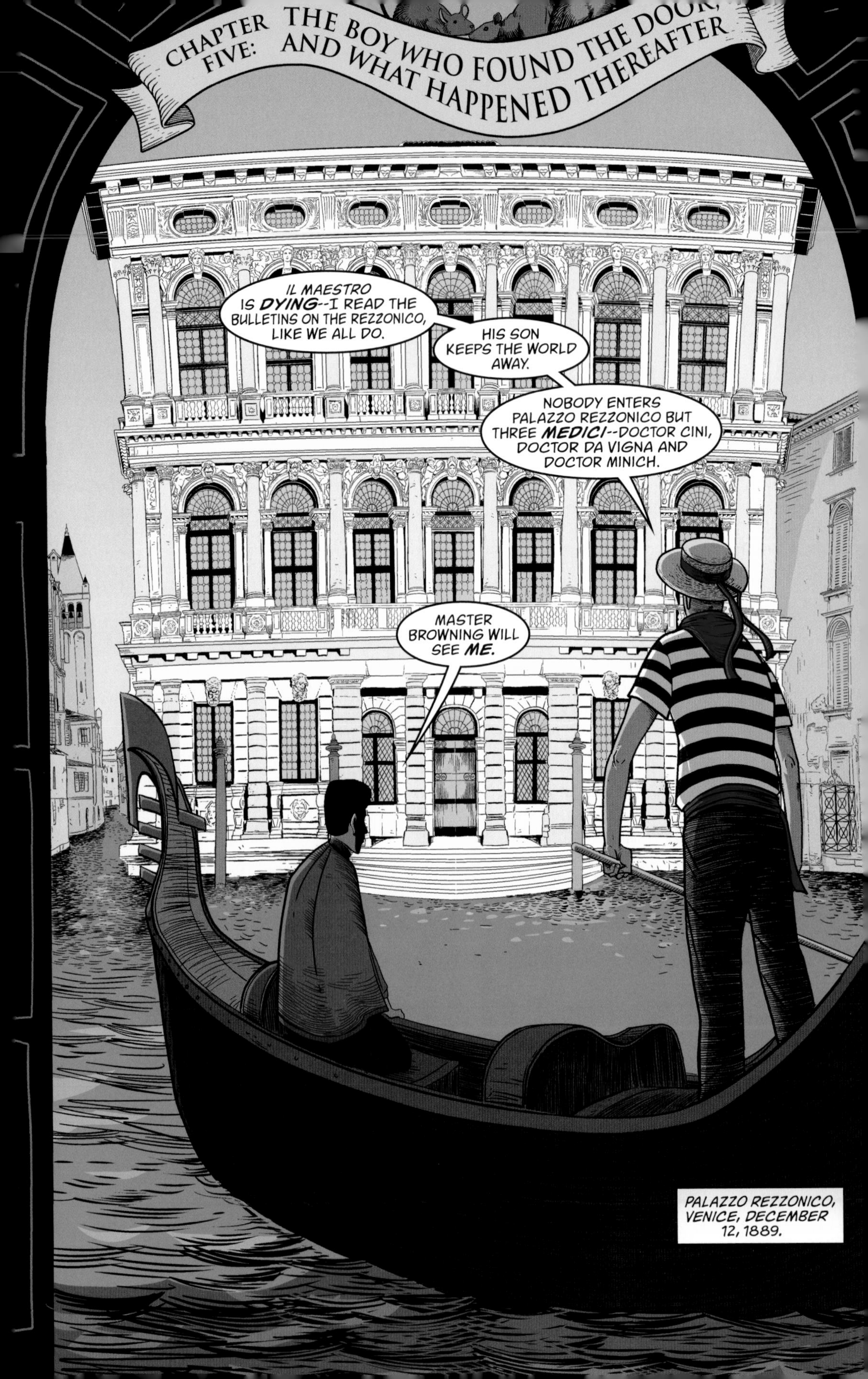
CHAPTER FIVE: THE BOY WHO FOUND THE DOOR, AND WHAT HAPPENED THEREAFTER
IL MAESTRO IS DYING--I READ THE BULLETINS ON THE REZZONICO, LIKE WE ALL DO.
HIS SON KEEPS THE WORLD AWAY.
NOBODY ENTERS PALAZZO REZZONICO BUT THREE MEDICI--DOCTOR CINI, DOCTOR DA VIGNA AND DOCTOR MINICH.
MASTER BROWNING WILL SEE ME.
PALAZZO REZZONICO, VENICE, DECEMBER 12, 1889.

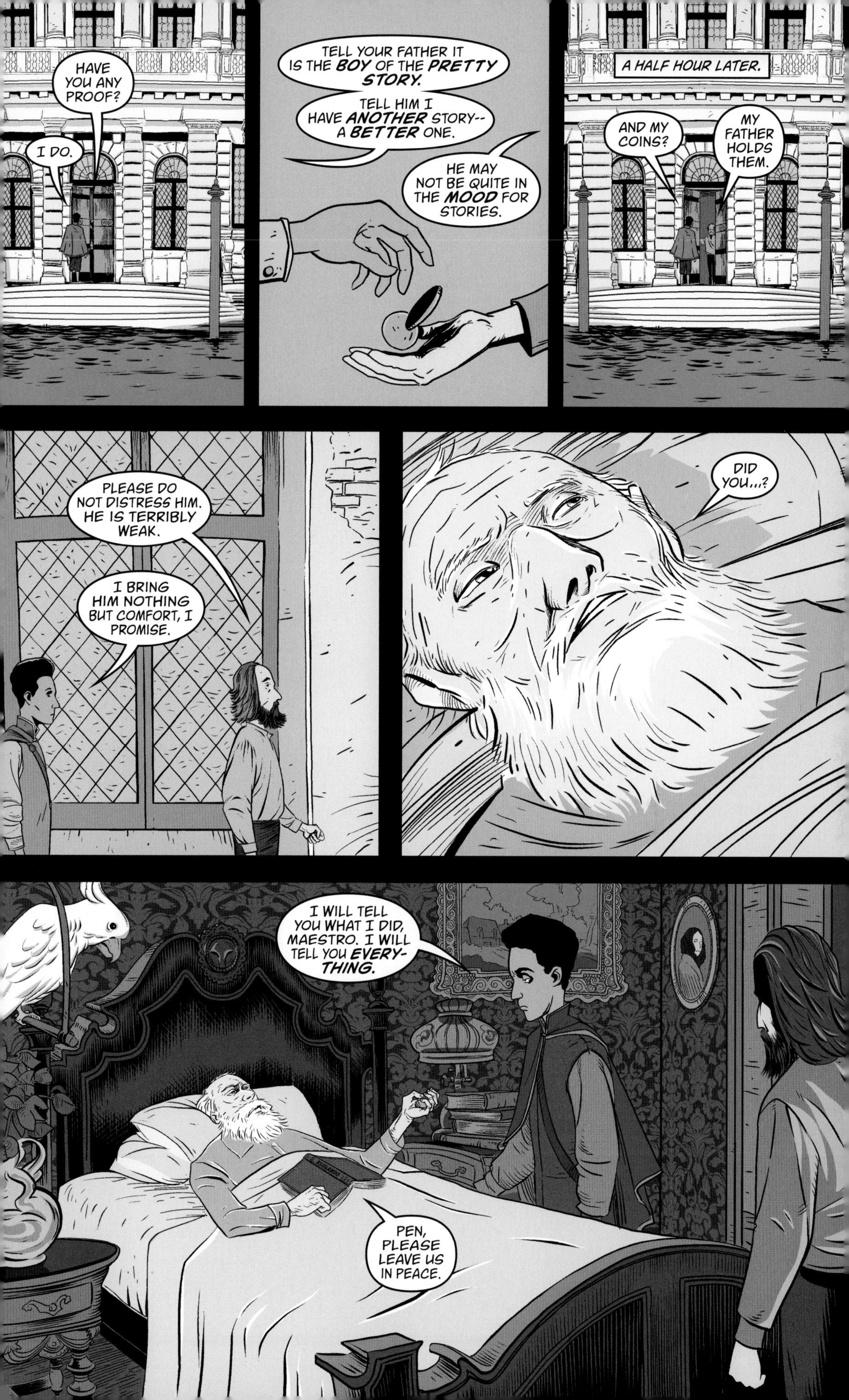
HAVE YOU ANY PROOF?
I DO.
TELL YOUR FATHER IT IS THE BOY OF THE PRETTY STORY.
TELL HIM I HAVE ANOTHER STORY-- A BETTER ONE.
HE MAY NOT BE QUITE IN THE MOOD FOR STORIES.
A HALF HOUR LATER.
AND MY COINS?
MY FATHER HOLDS THEM.
PLEASE DO NOT DISTRESS HIM. HE IS TERRIBLY WEAK.
I BRING HIM NOTHING BUT COMFORT, I PROMISE.
DID YOU...?
I WILL TELL YOU WHAT I DID, MAESTRO. I WILL TELL YOU EVERY-THING.
PEN, PLEASE LEAVE US IN PEACE.

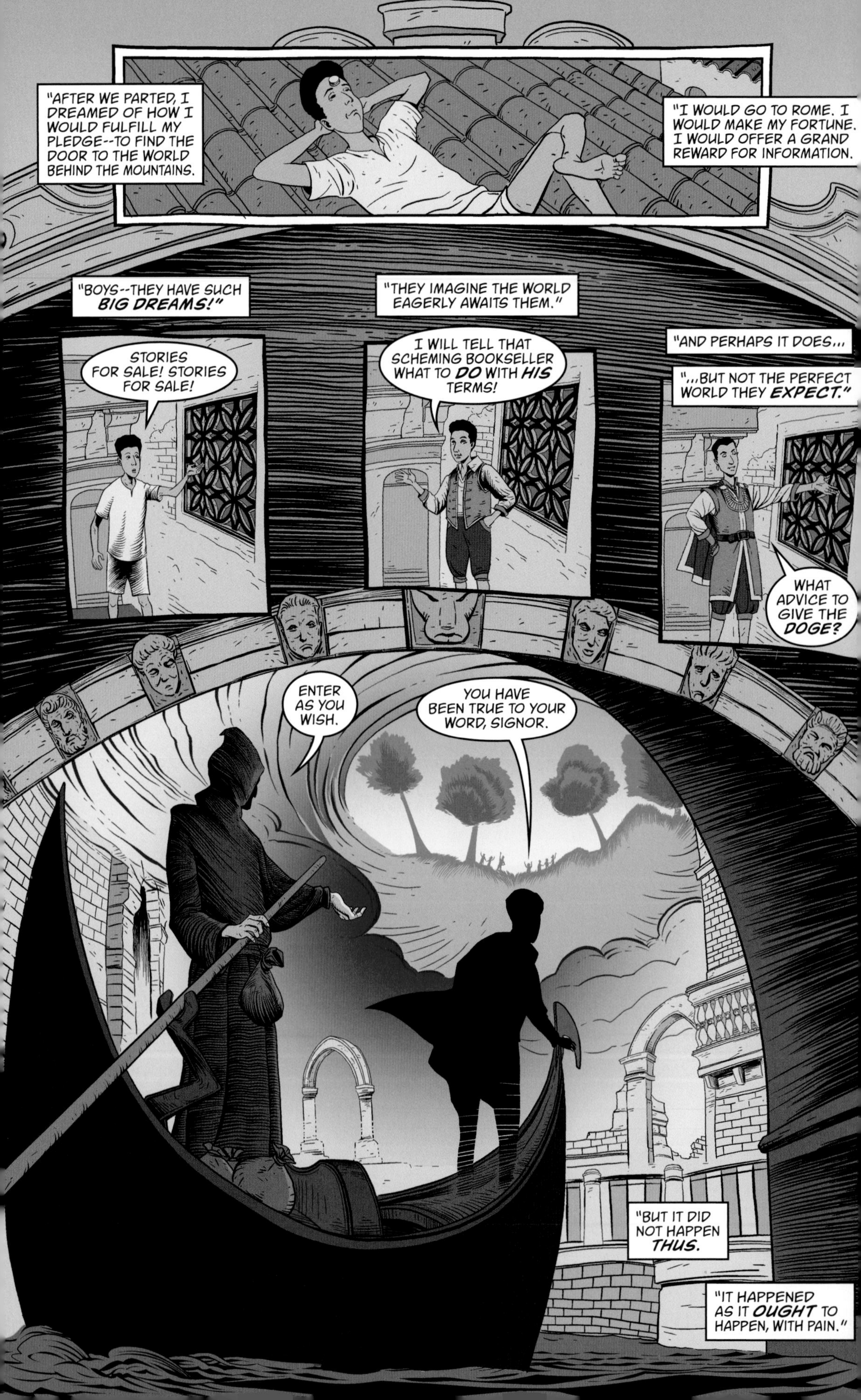
"AFTER WE PARTED, I DREAMED OF HOW I WOULD FULFILL MY PLEDGE--TO FIND THE DOOR TO THE WORLD BEHIND THE MOUNTAINS.
"I WOULD GO TO ROME. I WOULD MAKE MY FORTUNE. I WOULD OFFER A GRAND REWARD FOR INFORMATION.
"BOYS--THEY HAVE SUCH BIG DREAMS!"
"THEY IMAGINE THE WORLD EAGERLY AWAITS THEM."
STORIES FOR SALE! STORIES FOR SALE!
I WILL TELL THAT SCHEMING BOOKSELLER WHAT TO DO WITH HIS TERMS!
"AND PERHAPS IT DOES...
"...BUT NOT THE PERFECT WORLD THEY EXPECT."
WHAT ADVICE TO GIVE THE DOGE?
ENTER AS YOU WISH.
YOU HAVE BEEN TRUE TO YOUR WORD, SIGNOR.
"BUT IT DID NOT HAPPEN THUS.
"IT HAPPENED AS IT OUGHT TO HAPPEN, WITH PAIN."

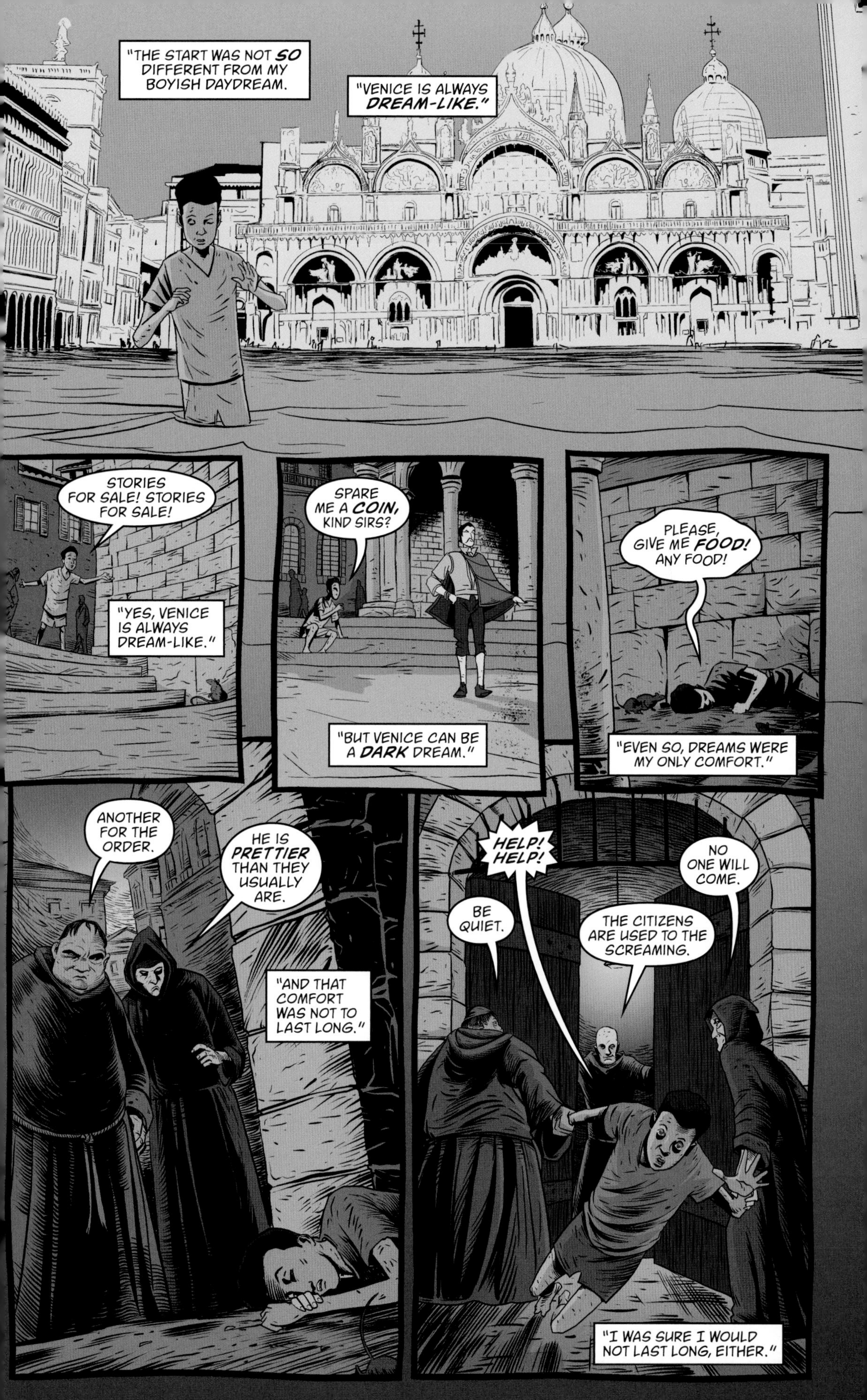
"THE START WAS NOT SO DIFFERENT FROM MY BOYISH DAYDREAM.
"VENICE IS ALWAYS DREAM-LIKE."
STORIES FOR SALE! STORIES FOR SALE!
"YES, VENICE IS ALWAYS DREAM-LIKE."
SPARE ME A COIN, KIND SIRS?
"BUT VENICE CAN BE A DARK DREAM."
PLEASE, GIVE ME FOOD! ANY FOOD!
"EVEN SO, DREAMS WERE MY ONLY COMFORT."
ANOTHER FOR THE ORDER.
HE IS PRETTIER THAN THEY USUALLY ARE.
"AND THAT COMFORT WAS NOT TO LAST LONG."
HELP! HELP!
BE QUIET.
NO ONE WILL COME.
THE CITIZENS ARE USED TO THE SCREAMING.
"I WAS SURE I WOULD NOT LAST LONG, EITHER."

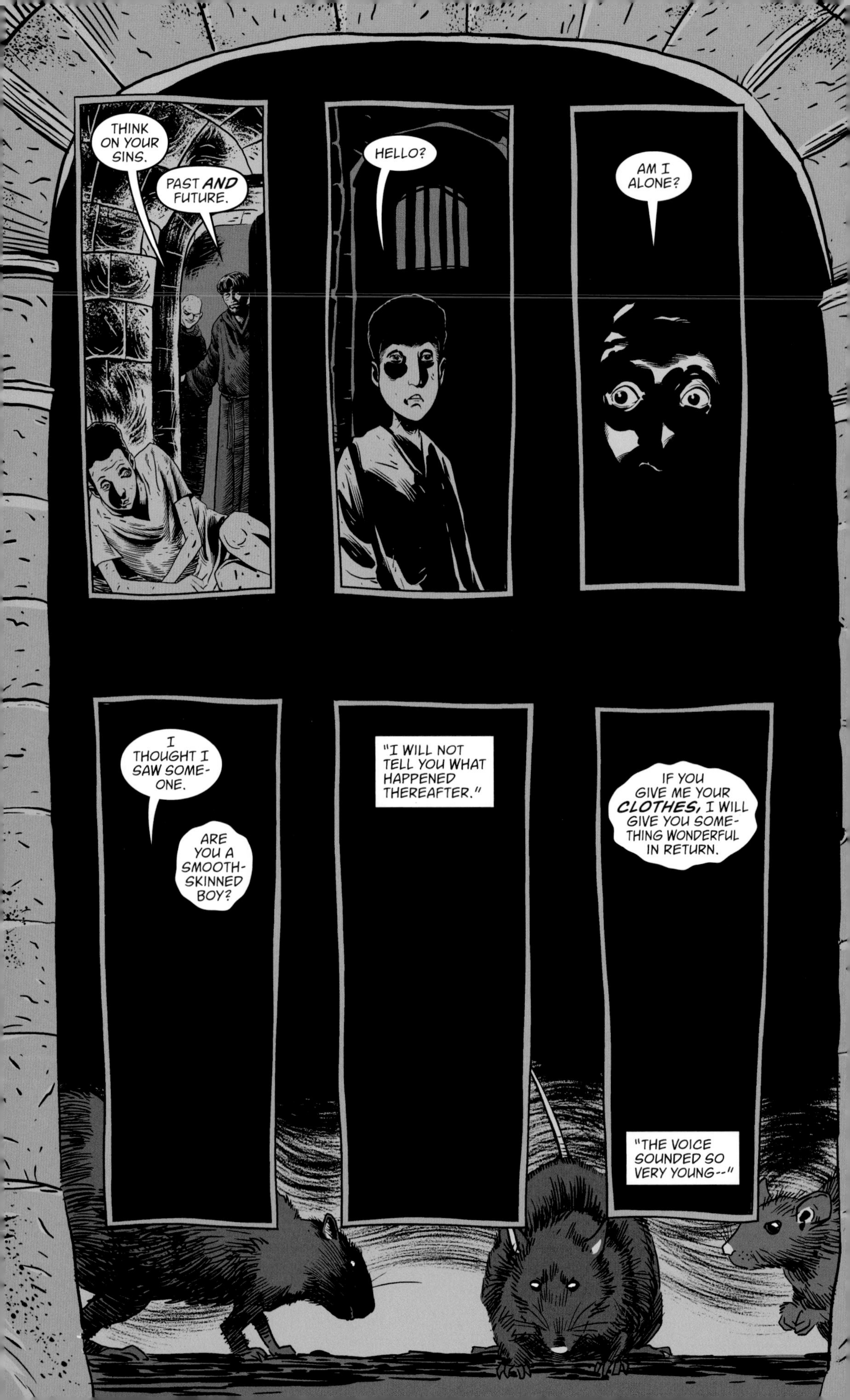
THINK ON YOUR SINS.
PAST **AND** FUTURE.
HELLO?
AM I ALONE?
I THOUGHT I SAW SOME- ONE.
ARE YOU A SMOOTH- SKINNED BOY?
"I WILL NOT TELL YOU WHAT HAPPENED THEREAFTER."
IF YOU GIVE ME YOUR **CLOTHES,** I WILL GIVE YOU SOME- THING WONDERFUL IN RETURN.
"THE VOICE SOUNDED SO VERY YOUNG--"

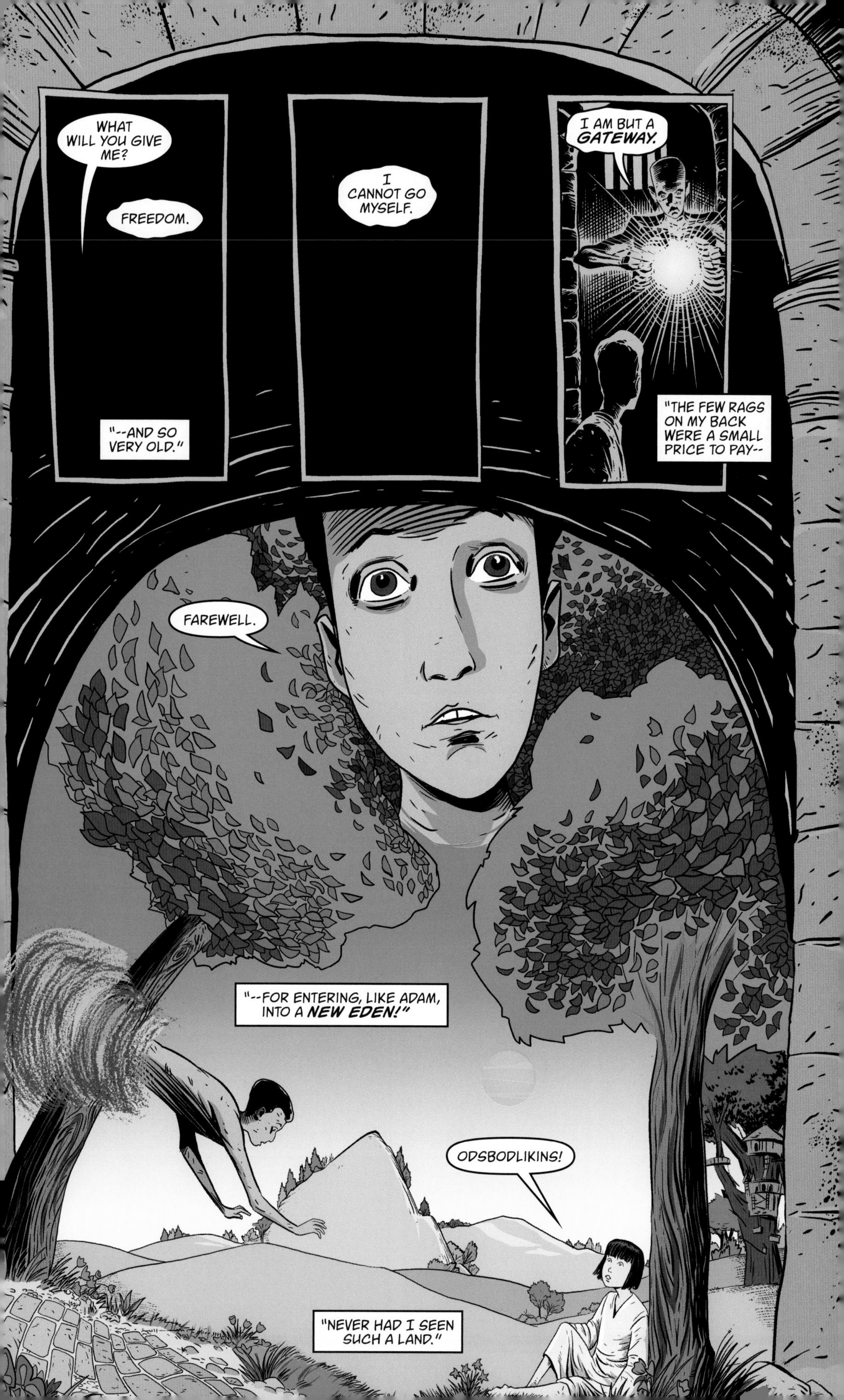
WHAT WILL YOU GIVE ME?
FREEDOM.
"--AND SO VERY OLD."
I CANNOT GO MYSELF.
I AM BUT A GATEWAY.
"THE FEW RAGS ON MY BACK WERE A SMALL PRICE TO PAY--
FAREWELL.
"--FOR ENTERING, LIKE ADAM, INTO A NEW EDEN!"
ODSBODLIKINS!
"NEVER HAD I SEEN SUCH A LAND."

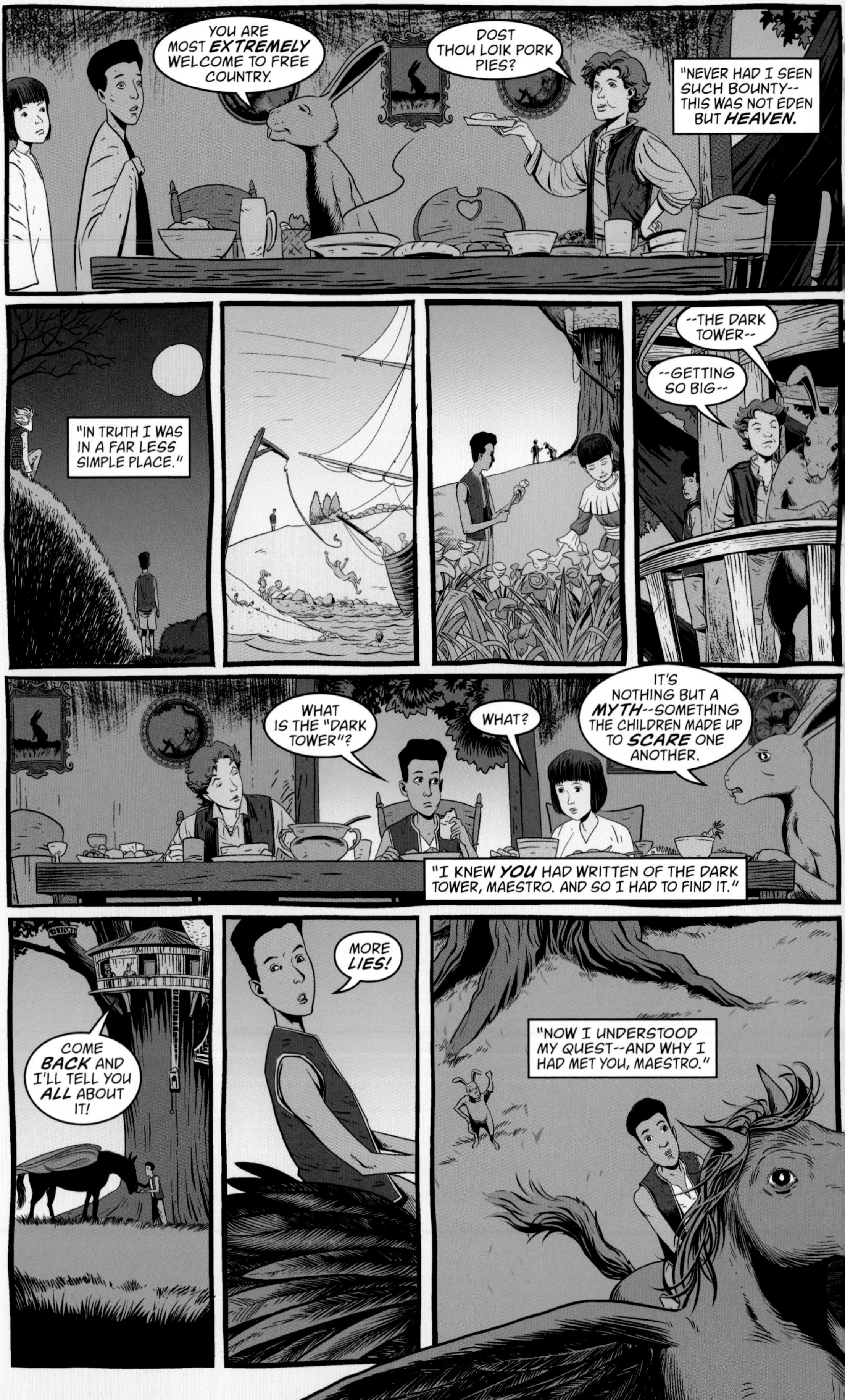
YOU ARE MOST EXTREMELY WELCOME TO FREE COUNTRY.
DOST THOU LOIK PORK PIES?
"NEVER HAD I SEEN SUCH BOUNTY-- THIS WAS NOT EDEN BUT HEAVEN.
"IN TRUTH I WAS IN A FAR LESS SIMPLE PLACE."
--THE DARK TOWER--
--GETTING SO BIG--
WHAT IS THE "DARK TOWER"?
WHAT?
IT'S NOTHING BUT A MYTH--SOMETHING THE CHILDREN MADE UP TO SCARE ONE ANOTHER.
"I KNEW YOU HAD WRITTEN OF THE DARK TOWER, MAESTRO. AND SO I HAD TO FIND IT."
COME BACK AND I'LL TELL YOU ALL ABOUT IT!
MORE LIES!
"NOW I UNDERSTOOD MY QUEST--AND WHY I HAD MET YOU, MAESTRO."

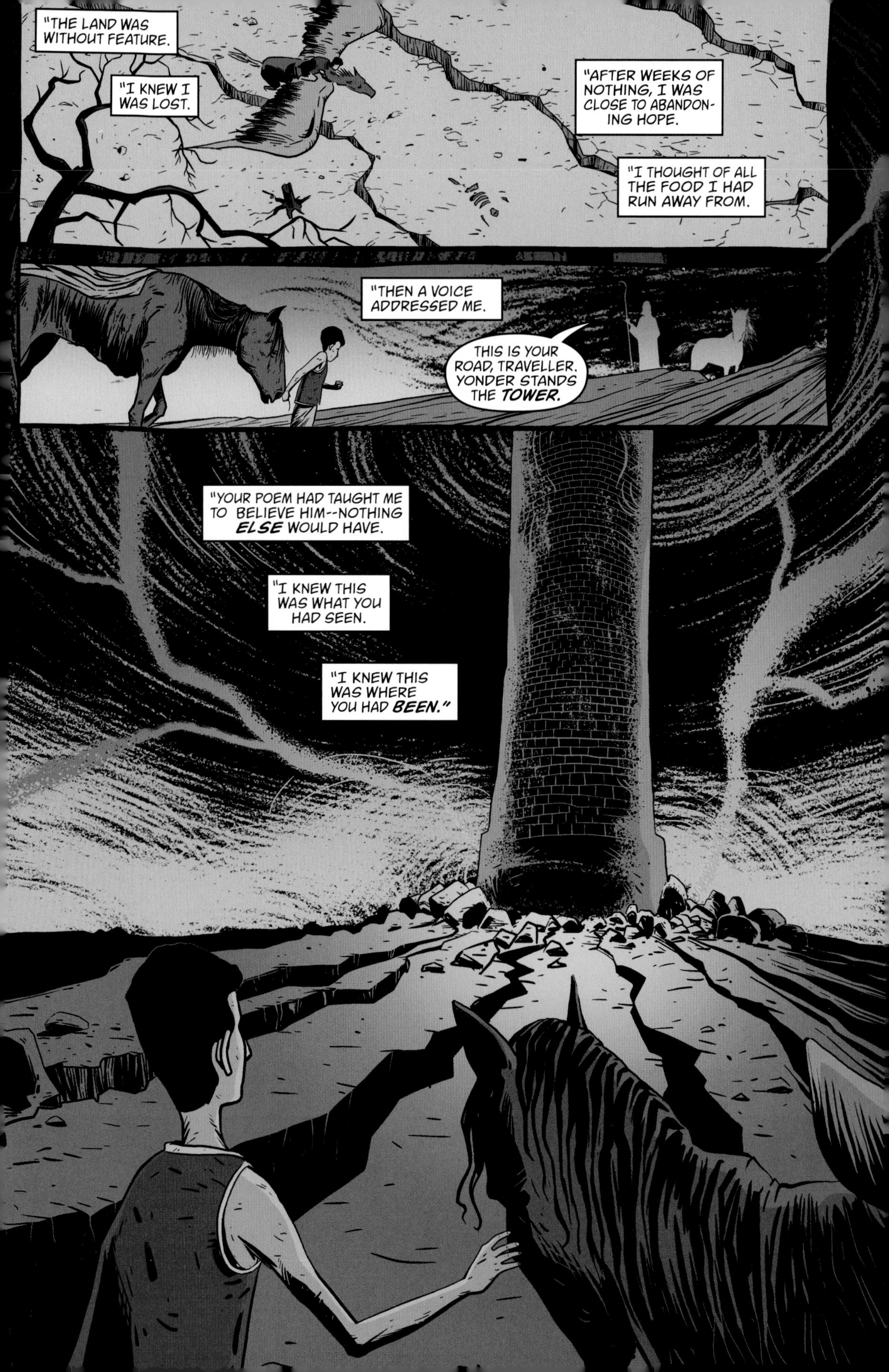
"THE LAND WAS WITHOUT FEATURE.
"I KNEW I WAS LOST.
"AFTER WEEKS OF NOTHING, I WAS CLOSE TO ABANDONING HOPE.
"I THOUGHT OF ALL THE FOOD I HAD RUN AWAY FROM.
"THEN A VOICE ADDRESSED ME.
THIS IS YOUR ROAD, TRAVELLER. YONDER STANDS THE TOWER.
"YOUR POEM HAD TAUGHT ME TO BELIEVE HIM--NOTHING ELSE WOULD HAVE.
"I KNEW THIS WAS WHAT YOU HAD SEEN.
"I KNEW THIS WAS WHERE YOU HAD BEEN."

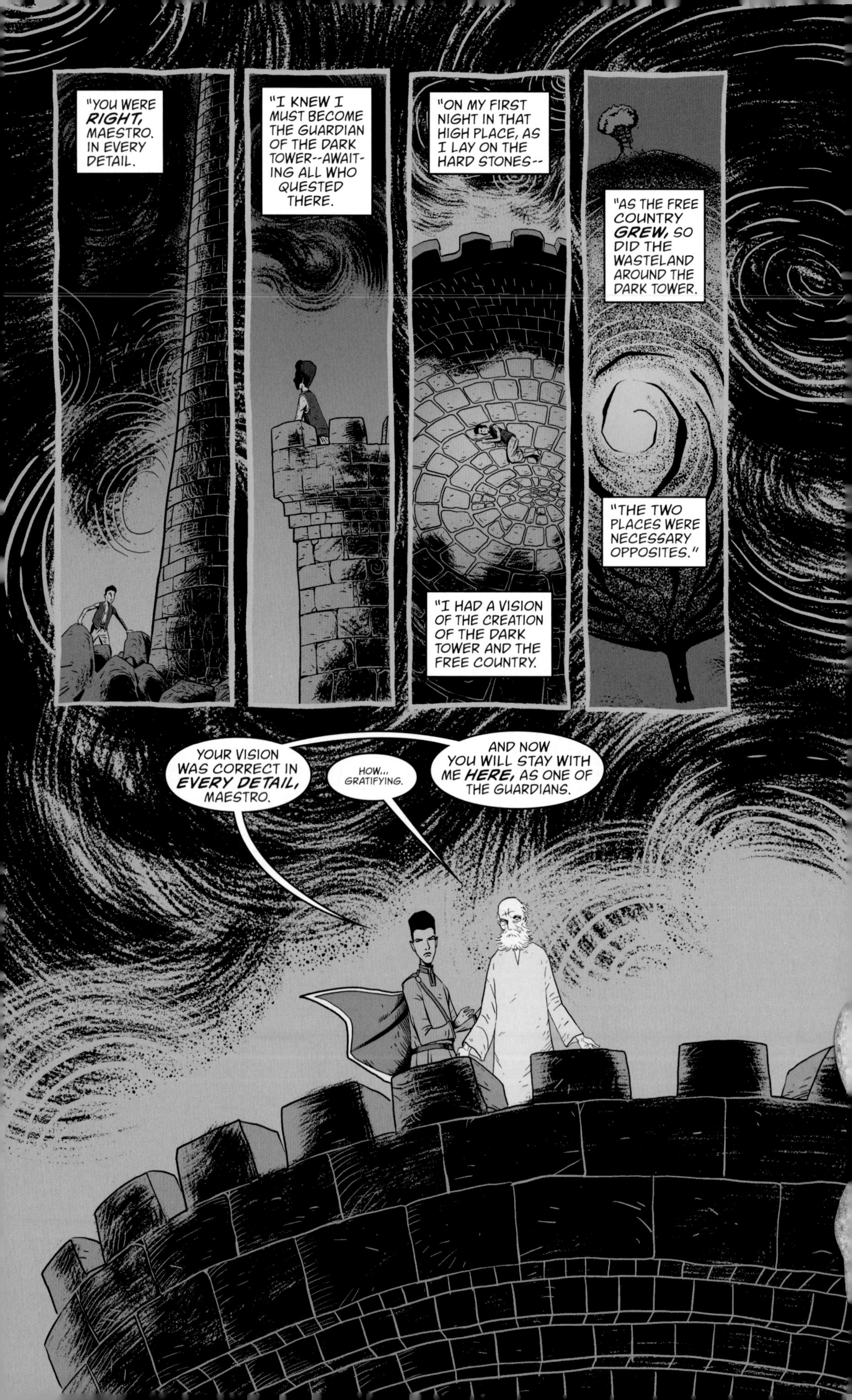
"YOU WERE RIGHT, MAESTRO. IN EVERY DETAIL.
"I KNEW I MUST BECOME THE GUARDIAN OF THE DARK TOWER--AWAITING ALL WHO QUESTED THERE.
"ON MY FIRST NIGHT IN THAT HIGH PLACE, AS I LAY ON THE HARD STONES--
"I HAD A VISION OF THE CREATION OF THE DARK TOWER AND THE FREE COUNTRY.
"AS THE FREE COUNTRY GREW, SO DID THE WASTELAND AROUND THE DARK TOWER.
"THE TWO PLACES WERE NECESSARY OPPOSITES."
YOUR VISION WAS CORRECT IN EVERY DETAIL, MAESTRO.
HOW... GRATIFYING.
AND NOW YOU WILL STAY WITH ME HERE, AS ONE OF THE GUARDIANS.

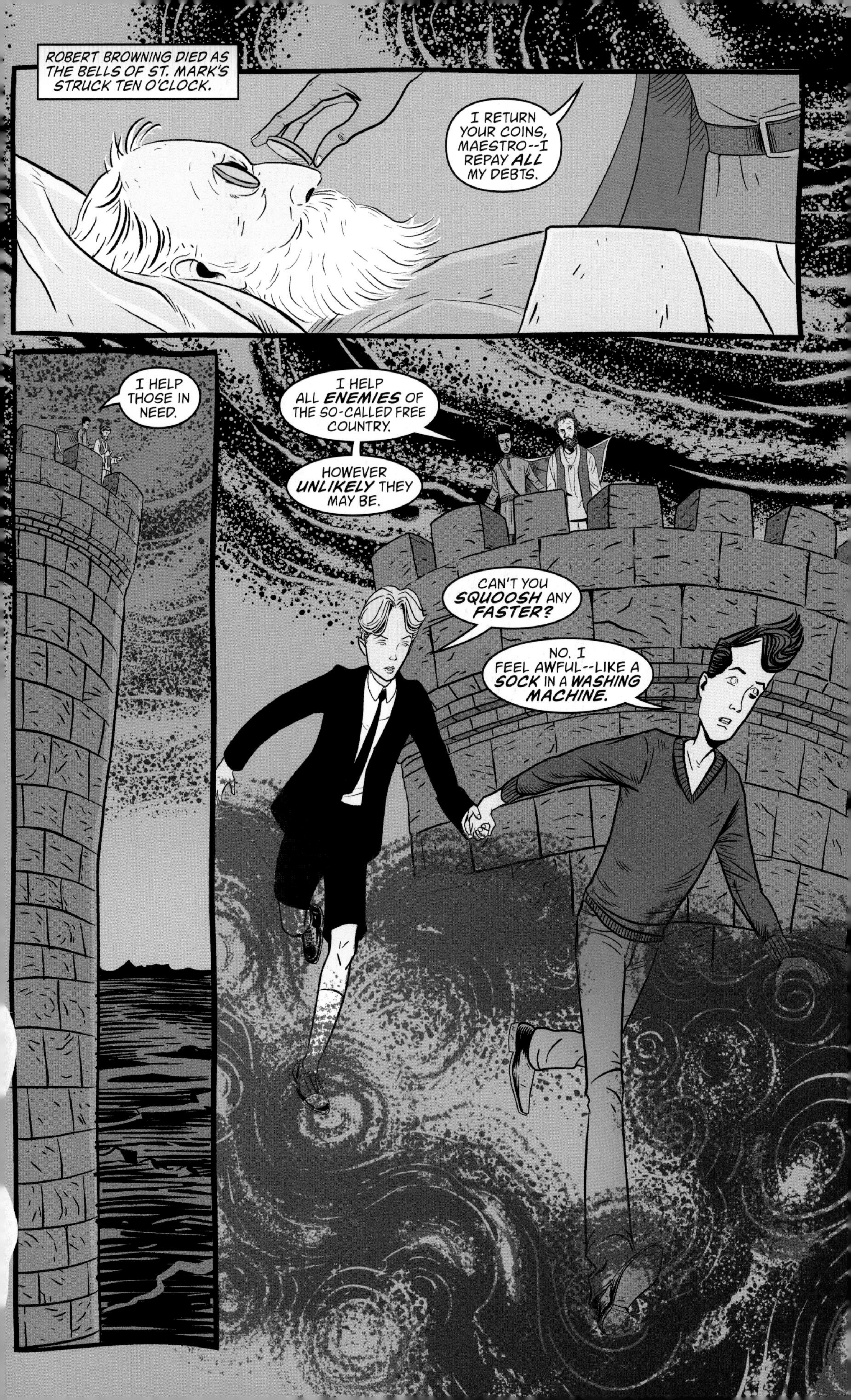
ROBERT BROWNING DIED AS THE BELLS OF ST. MARK'S STRUCK TEN O'CLOCK.
I RETURN YOUR COINS, MAESTRO--I REPAY ALL MY DEBTS.
I HELP THOSE IN NEED.
I HELP ALL ENEMIES OF THE SO-CALLED FREE COUNTRY.
HOWEVER UNLIKELY THEY MAY BE.
CAN'T YOU SQUOOSH ANY FASTER?
NO. I FEEL AWFUL--LIKE A SOCK IN A WASHING MACHINE.

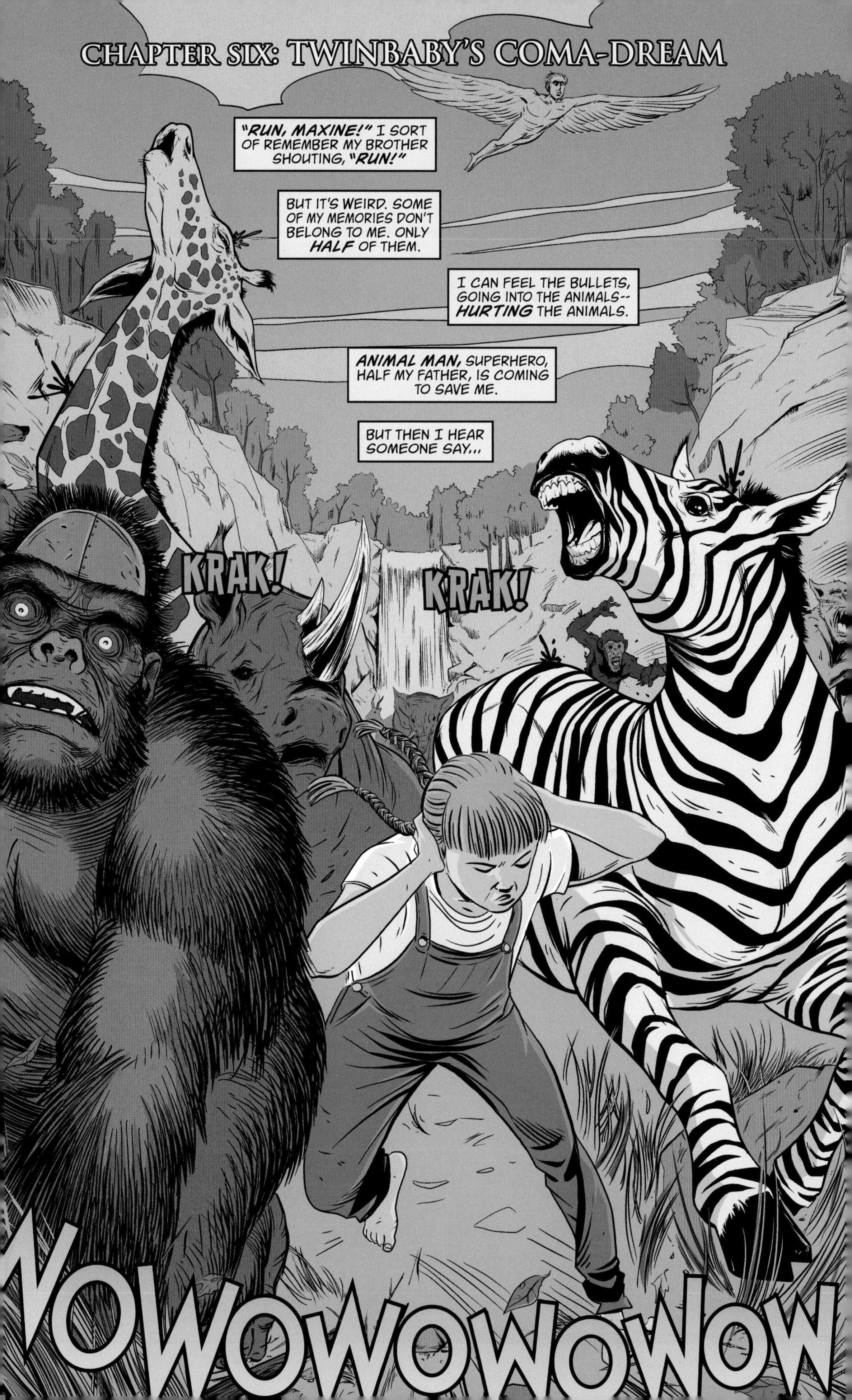
CHAPTER SIX: TWINBABY'S COMA-DREAM
"RUN, MAXINE!" I SORT OF REMEMBER MY BROTHER SHOUTING, "RUN!"
BUT IT'S WEIRD. SOME OF MY MEMORIES DON'T BELONG TO ME. ONLY HALF OF THEM.
I CAN FEEL THE BULLETS, GOING INTO THE ANIMALS-- HURTING THE ANIMALS.
ANIMAL MAN, SUPERHERO, HALF MY FATHER, IS COMING TO SAVE ME.
BUT THEN I HEAR SOMEONE SAY...
KRAK!
KRAK!
WOWOWOWOWOWOW

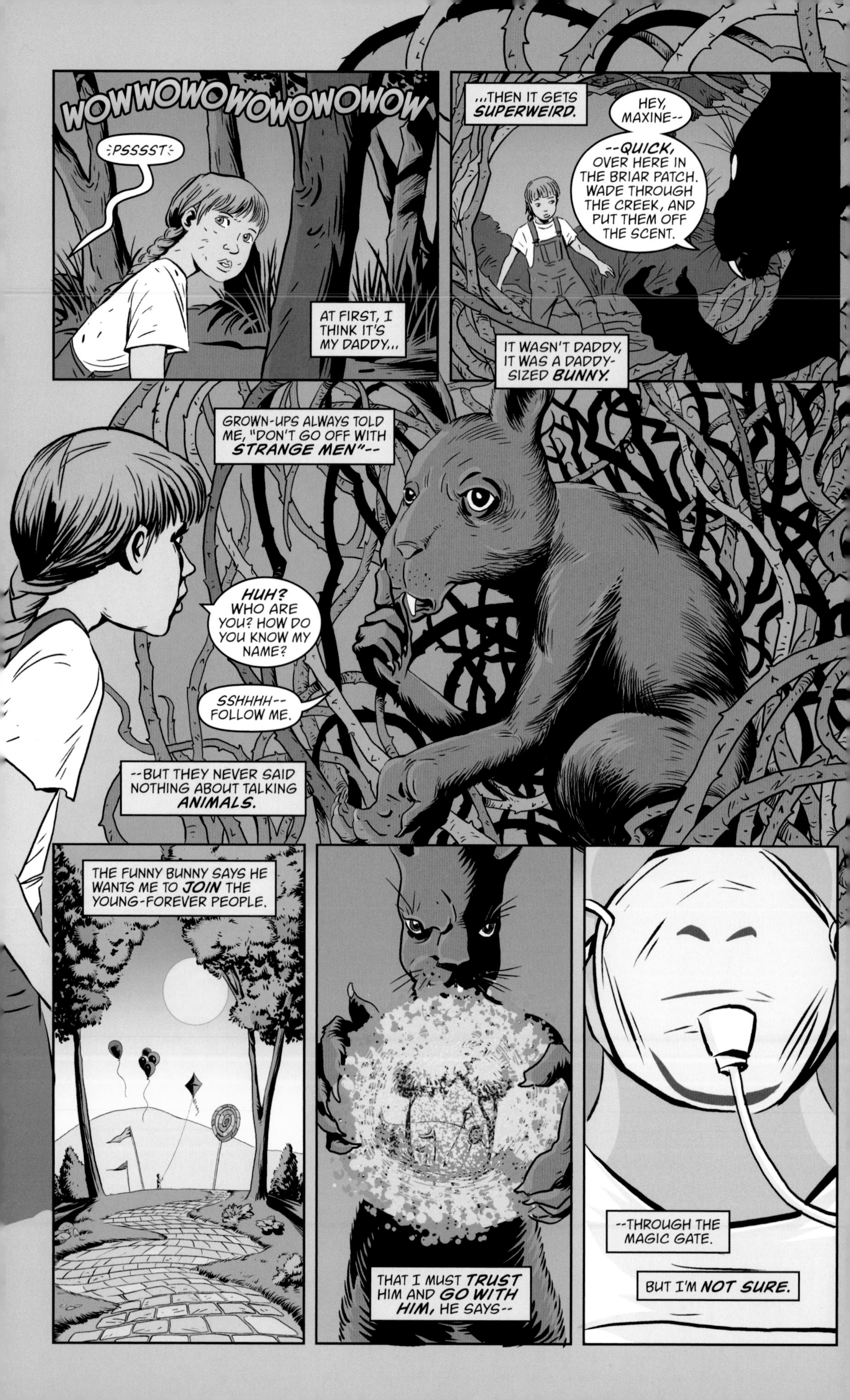
WOWWOWOWOWOWOWOWOW
PSSSST
AT FIRST, I THINK IT'S MY DADDY...
...THEN IT GETS SUPERWEIRD.
HEY, MAXINE--
--QUICK, OVER HERE IN THE BRIAR PATCH. WADE THROUGH THE CREEK, AND PUT THEM OFF THE SCENT.
IT WASN'T DADDY, IT WAS A DADDY-SIZED BUNNY.
GROWN-UPS ALWAYS TOLD ME, "DON'T GO OFF WITH STRANGE MEN"--
HUH? WHO ARE YOU? HOW DO YOU KNOW MY NAME?
SSHHHH-- FOLLOW ME.
--BUT THEY NEVER SAID NOTHING ABOUT TALKING ANIMALS.
THE FUNNY BUNNY SAYS HE WANTS ME TO JOIN THE YOUNG-FOREVER PEOPLE.
THAT I MUST TRUST HIM AND GO WITH HIM, HE SAYS--
--THROUGH THE MAGIC GATE.
BUT I'M NOT SURE.

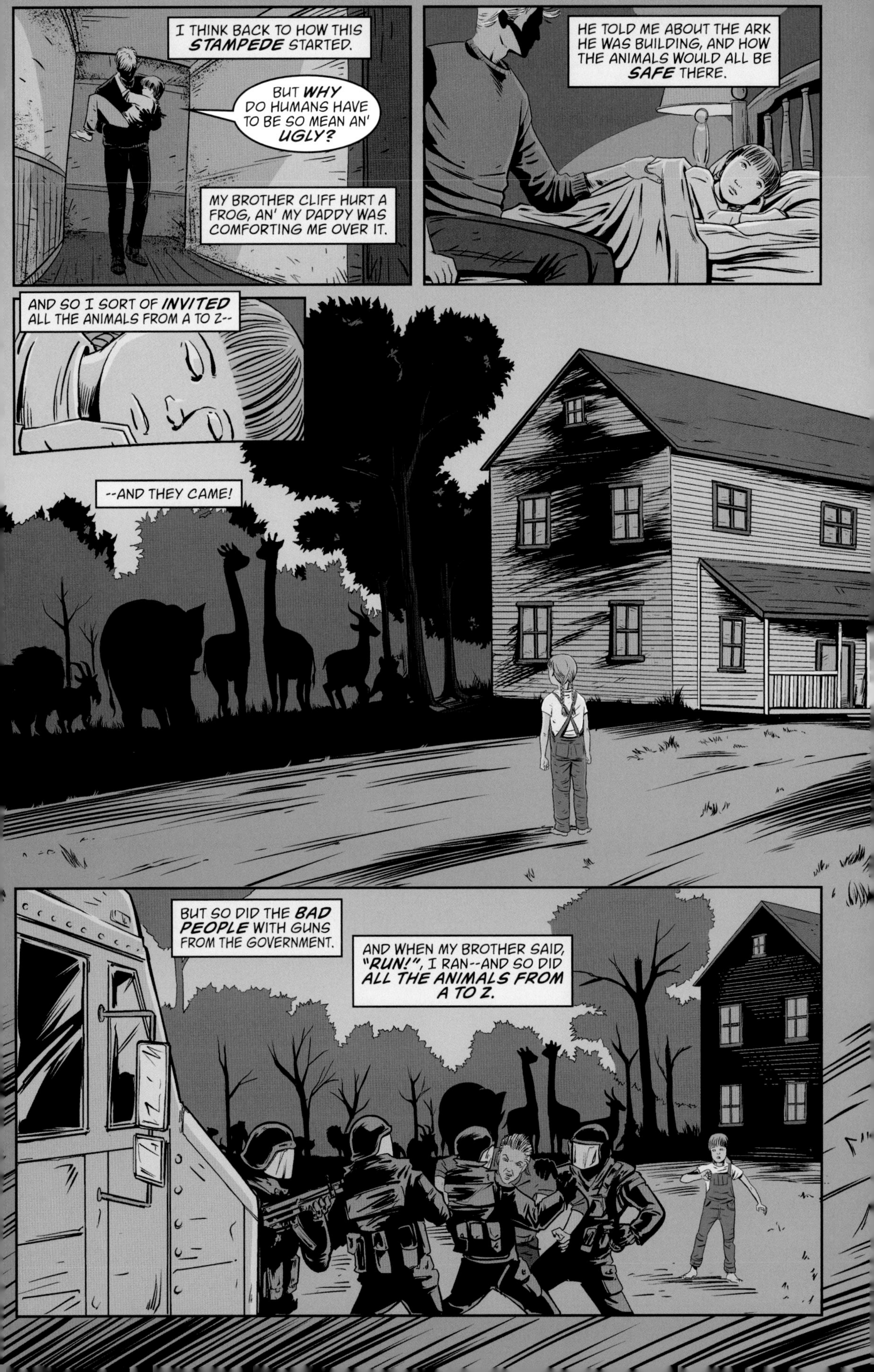
I THINK BACK TO HOW THIS STAMPEDE STARTED.
BUT WHY DO HUMANS HAVE TO BE SO MEAN AN' UGLY?
MY BROTHER CLIFF HURT A FROG, AN' MY DADDY WAS COMFORTING ME OVER IT.
HE TOLD ME ABOUT THE ARK HE WAS BUILDING, AND HOW THE ANIMALS WOULD ALL BE SAFE THERE.
AND SO I SORT OF INVITED ALL THE ANIMALS FROM A TO Z--
--AND THEY CAME!
BUT SO DID THE BAD PEOPLE WITH GUNS FROM THE GOVERNMENT.
AND WHEN MY BROTHER SAID, "RUN!", I RAN--AND SO DID ALL THE ANIMALS FROM A TO Z.

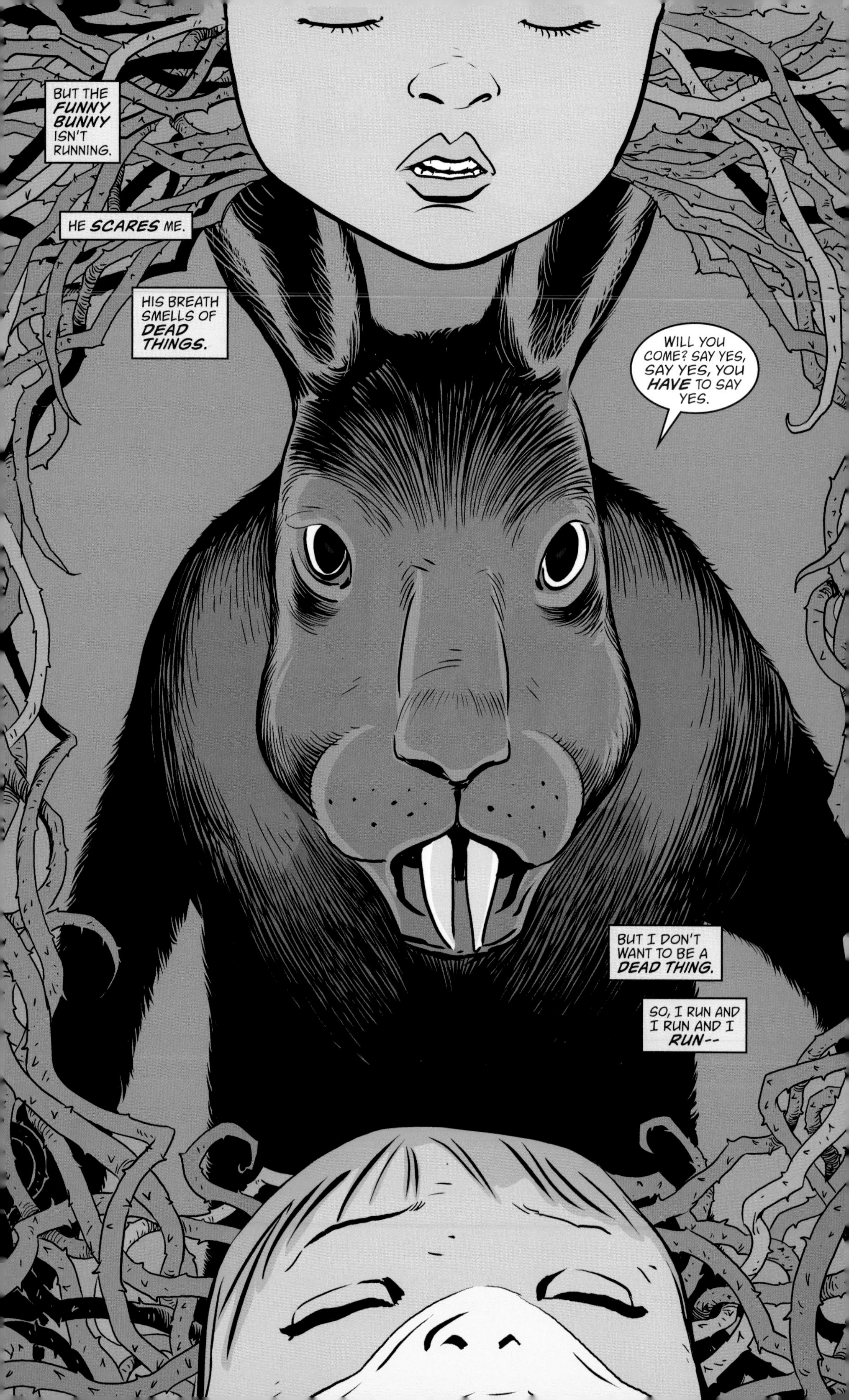
BUT THE FUNNY BUNNY ISN'T RUNNING.
HE SCARES ME.
HIS BREATH SMELLS OF DEAD THINGS.
WILL YOU COME? SAY YES, SAY YES, YOU HAVE TO SAY YES.
BUT I DON'T WANT TO BE A DEAD THING.
SO, I RUN AND I RUN AND I RUN--

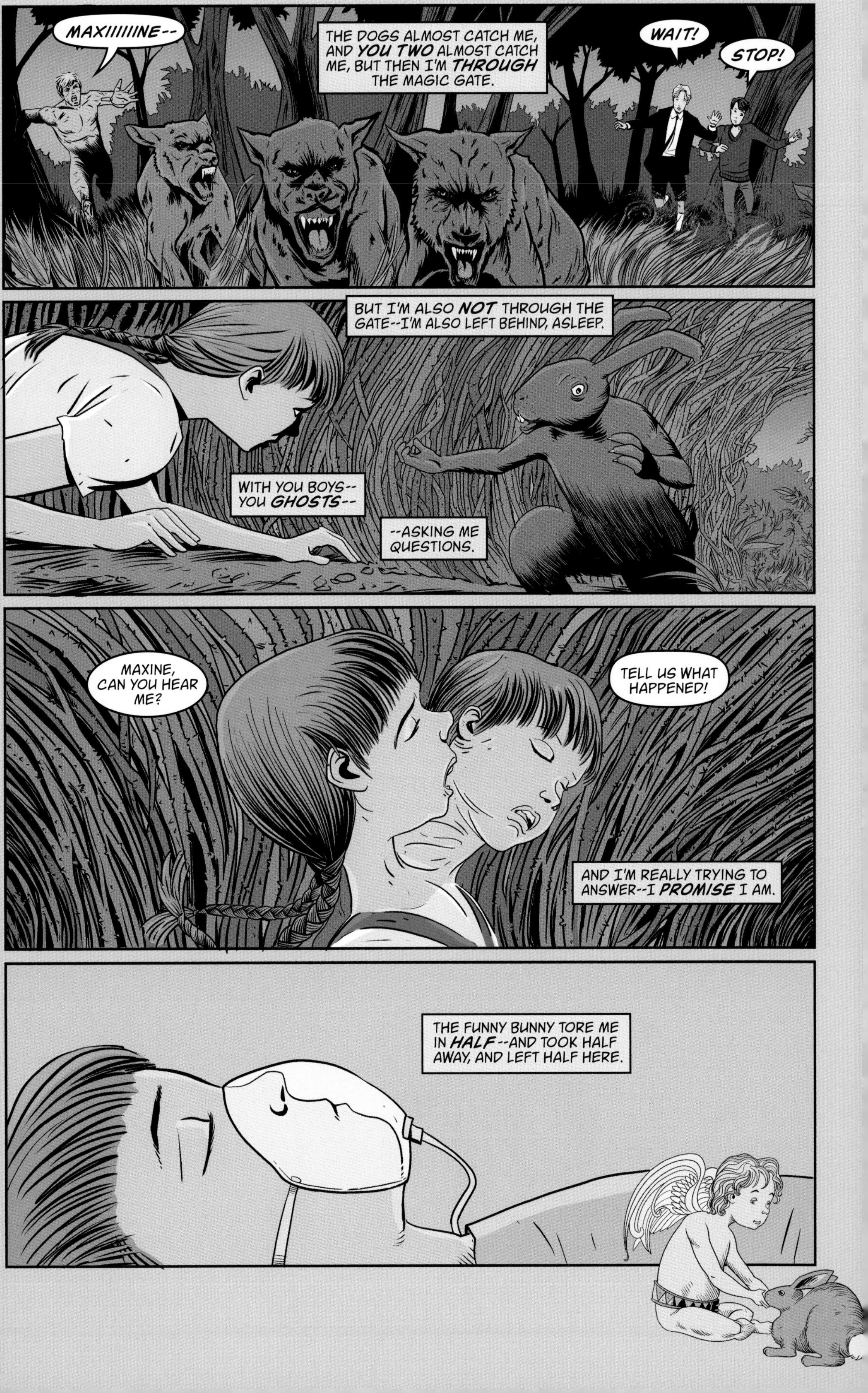
MAXIIIIIINE--
THE DOGS ALMOST CATCH ME, AND YOU TWO ALMOST CATCH ME, BUT THEN I'M THROUGH THE MAGIC GATE.
WAIT!
STOP!
BUT I'M ALSO NOT THROUGH THE GATE--I'M ALSO LEFT BEHIND, ASLEEP.
WITH YOU BOYS-- YOU GHOSTS--
--ASKING ME QUESTIONS.
MAXINE, CAN YOU HEAR ME?
TELL US WHAT HAPPENED!
AND I'M REALLY TRYING TO ANSWER--I PROMISE I AM.
THE FUNNY BUNNY TORE ME IN HALF--AND TOOK HALF AWAY, AND LEFT HALF HERE.

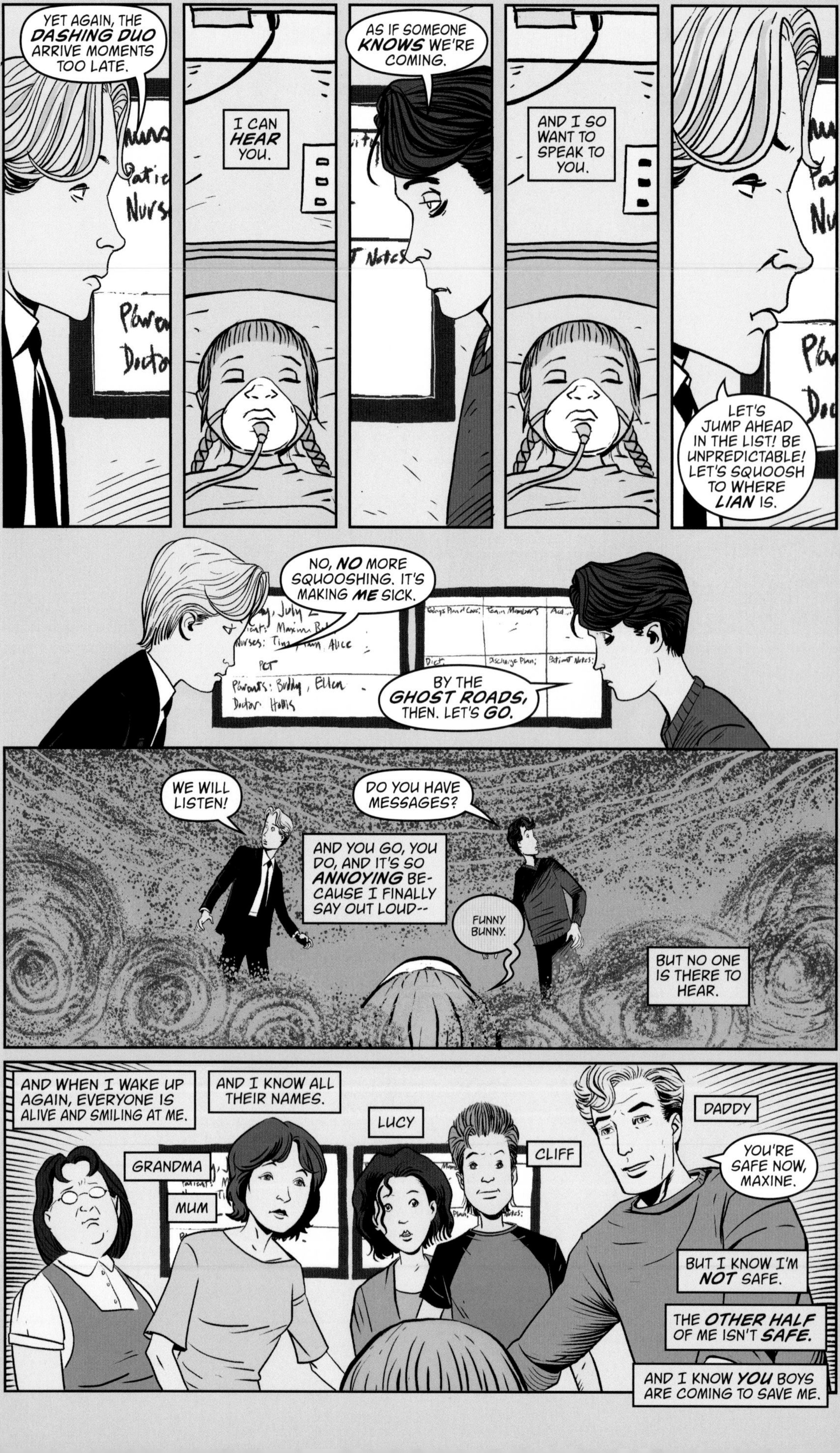
YET AGAIN, THE DASHING DUO ARRIVE MOMENTS TOO LATE.
I CAN HEAR YOU.
AS IF SOMEONE KNOWS WE'RE COMING.
AND I SO WANT TO SPEAK TO YOU.
LET'S JUMP AHEAD IN THE LIST! BE UNPREDICTABLE! LET'S SQUOOSH TO WHERE LIAN IS.
NO, NO MORE SQUOOSHING. IT'S MAKING ME SICK.
BY THE GHOST ROADS, THEN. LET'S GO.
WE WILL LISTEN!
DO YOU HAVE MESSAGES?
AND YOU GO, YOU DO, AND IT'S SO ANNOYING BE-CAUSE I FINALLY SAY OUT LOUD--
FUNNY BUNNY.
BUT NO ONE IS THERE TO HEAR.
AND WHEN I WAKE UP AGAIN, EVERYONE IS ALIVE AND SMILING AT ME.
AND I KNOW ALL THEIR NAMES.
GRANDMA
MUM
LUCY
CLIFF
DADDY
YOU'RE SAFE NOW, MAXINE.
BUT I KNOW I'M NOT SAFE.
THE OTHER HALF OF ME ISN'T SAFE.
AND I KNOW YOU BOYS ARE COMING TO SAVE ME.

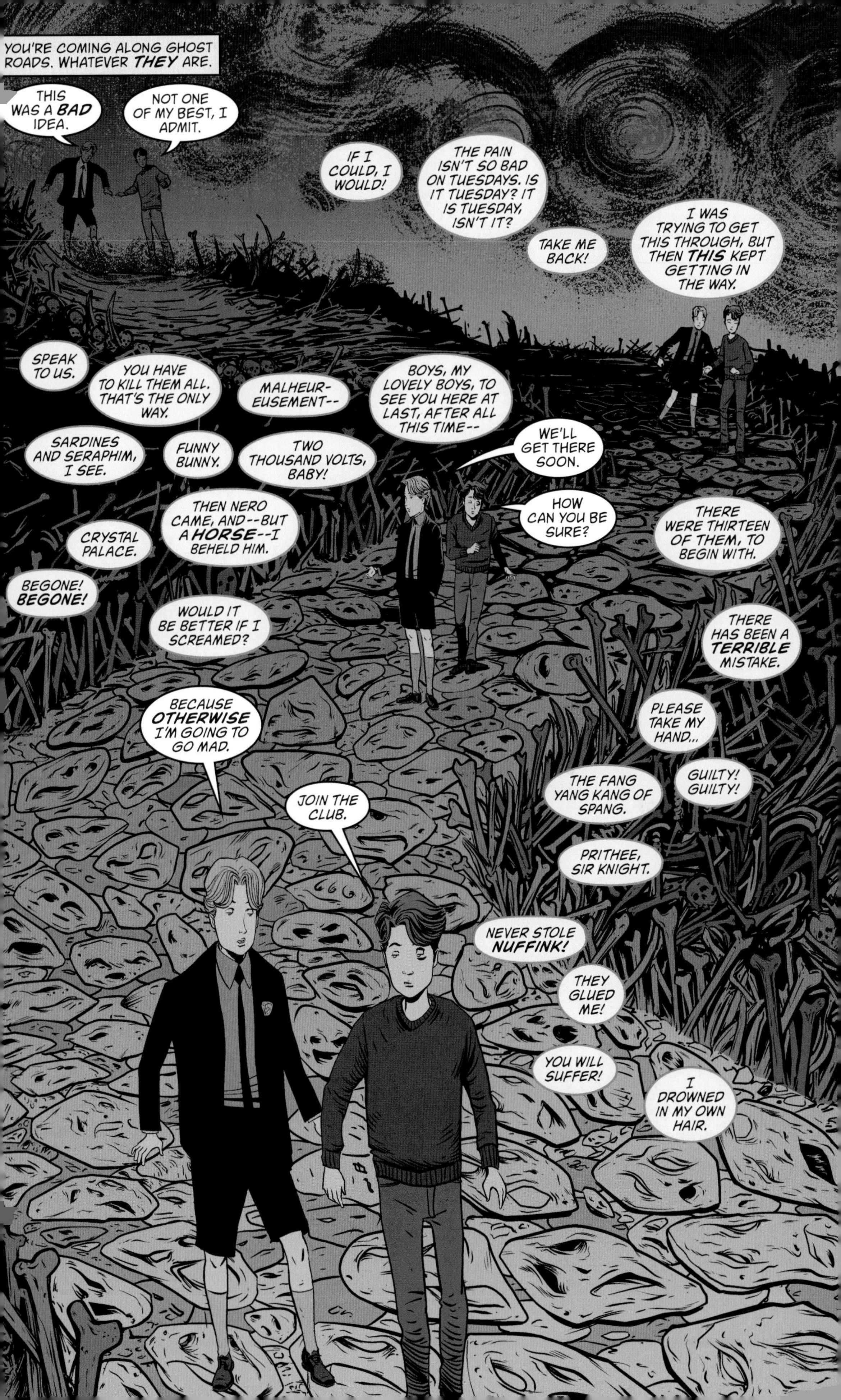

YOU'RE COMING ALONG GHOST ROADS. WHATEVER THEY ARE.
THIS WAS A BAD IDEA.
NOT ONE OF MY BEST, I ADMIT.
IF I COULD, I WOULD!
THE PAIN ISN'T SO BAD ON TUESDAYS. IS IT TUESDAY? IT IS TUESDAY, ISN'T IT?
TAKE ME BACK!
I WAS TRYING TO GET THIS THROUGH, BUT THEN THIS KEPT GETTING IN THE WAY.
SPEAK TO US.
YOU HAVE TO KILL THEM ALL. THAT'S THE ONLY WAY.
MALHEUR-EUSEMENT--
BOYS, MY LOVELY BOYS, TO SEE YOU HERE AT LAST, AFTER ALL THIS TIME--
SARDINES AND SERAPHIM, I SEE.
FUNNY BUNNY.
TWO THOUSAND VOLTS, BABY!
WE'LL GET THERE SOON.
HOW CAN YOU BE SURE?
THEN NERO CAME, AND--BUT A HORSE--I BEHELD HIM.
CRYSTAL PALACE.
THERE WERE THIRTEEN OF THEM, TO BEGIN WITH.
BEGONE! BEGONE!
WOULD IT BE BETTER IF I SCREAMED?
THERE HAS BEEN A TERRIBLE MISTAKE.
BECAUSE OTHERWISE I'M GOING TO GO MAD.
PLEASE TAKE MY HAND...
JOIN THE CLUB.
THE FANG YANG KANG OF SPANG.
GUILTY! GUILTY!
PRITHEE, SIR KNIGHT.
NEVER STOLE NUFFINK!
THEY GLUED ME!
YOU WILL SUFFER!
I DROWNED IN MY OWN HAIR.

CHAPTER SEVEN: JUST WHO ARE THE CHILDREN OF POWER?

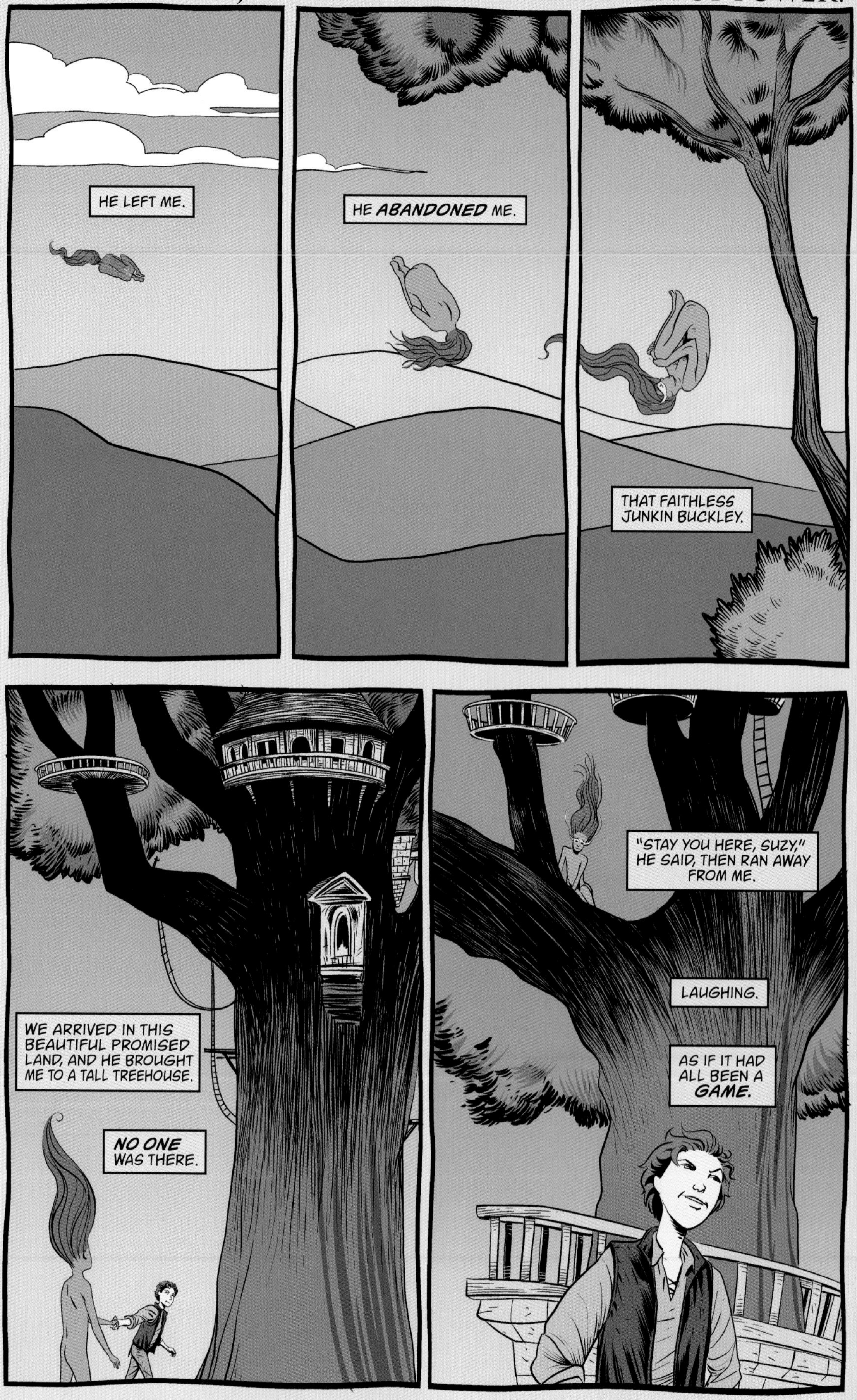
HE LEFT ME.
HE *ABANDONED* ME.
THAT FAITHLESS JUNKIN BUCKLEY.
WE ARRIVED IN THIS BEAUTIFUL PROMISED LAND, AND HE BROUGHT ME TO A TALL TREEHOUSE.
NO ONE WAS THERE.
"STAY YOU HERE, SUZY," HE SAID, THEN RAN AWAY FROM ME.
LAUGHING.
AS IF IT HAD ALL BEEN A *GAME*.

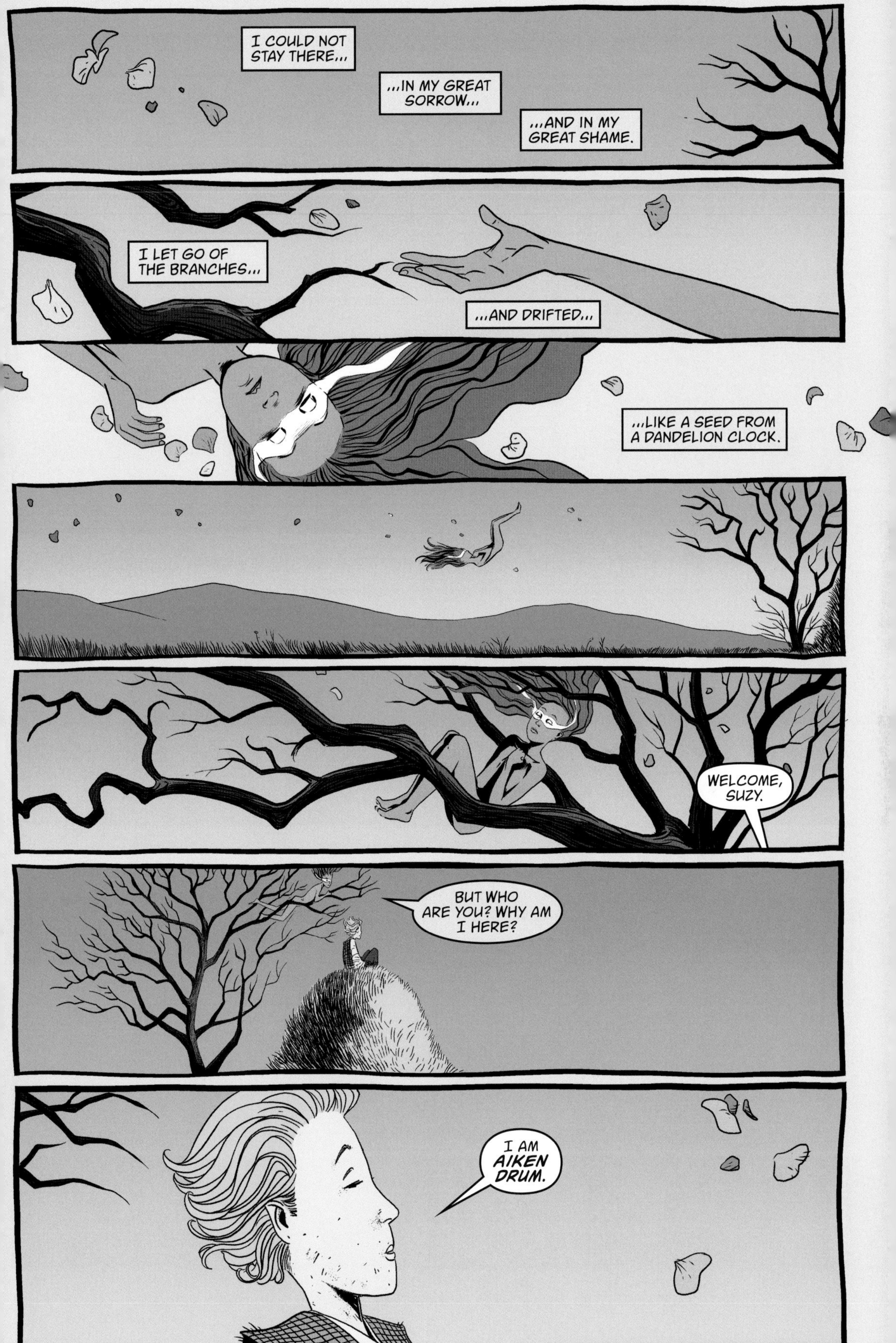
I COULD NOT STAY THERE...
...IN MY GREAT SORROW...
...AND IN MY GREAT SHAME.
I LET GO OF THE BRANCHES...
...AND DRIFTED...
...LIKE A SEED FROM A DANDELION CLOCK.
WELCOME, SUZY.
BUT WHO ARE YOU? WHY AM I HERE?
I AM AIKEN DRUM.

"ATTEND AND BE STILL, IF YOU WOULD LISTEN, IF YOU WOULD LEARN.

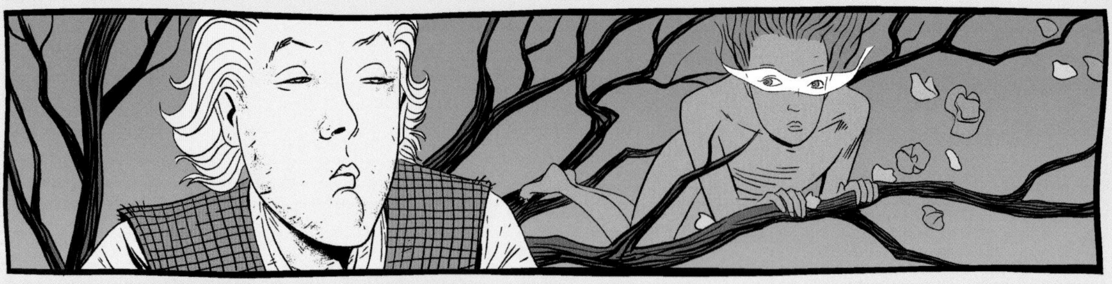

"YOU, SUZY, ARE A ***CHILD OF POWER***--OF WHICH THERE ARE ANOTHER FOUR.

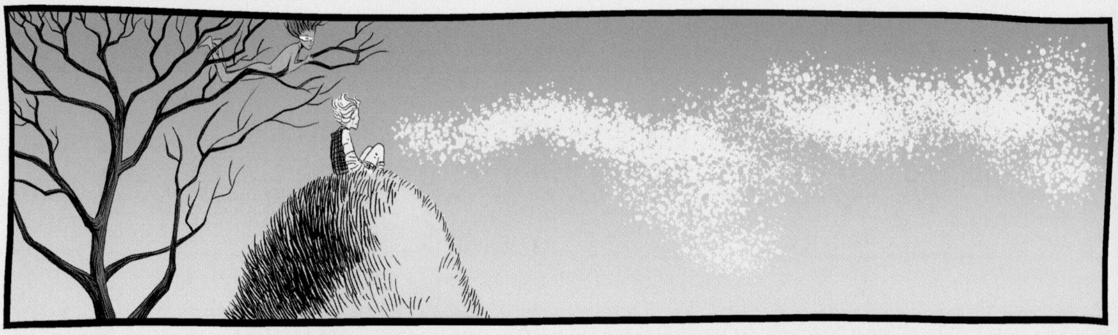

"BEFORE THIS WORLD WAS ***HERE*** THERE WAS NO LIKE WORLD, THERE WAS BUT AN IDEA.

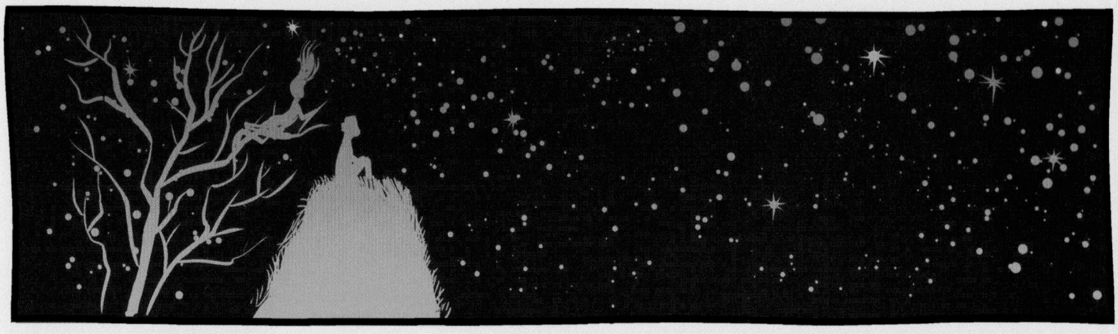

"TO MAKE A WORLD, TO MAKE A ***WHERE*** FROM AN IDEA, REQUIRES EXTRAORDINARY ENERGY.

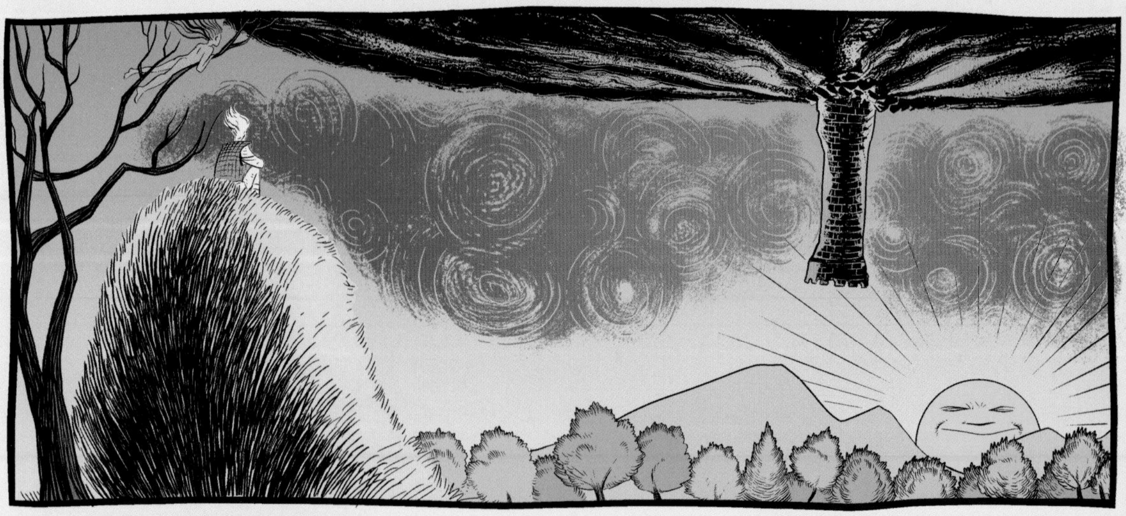

"BUT TO ***EXTEND*** THAT WORLD TAKES NOT JUST ***ENERGY***--IT TAKES PURE ***POWER.***"

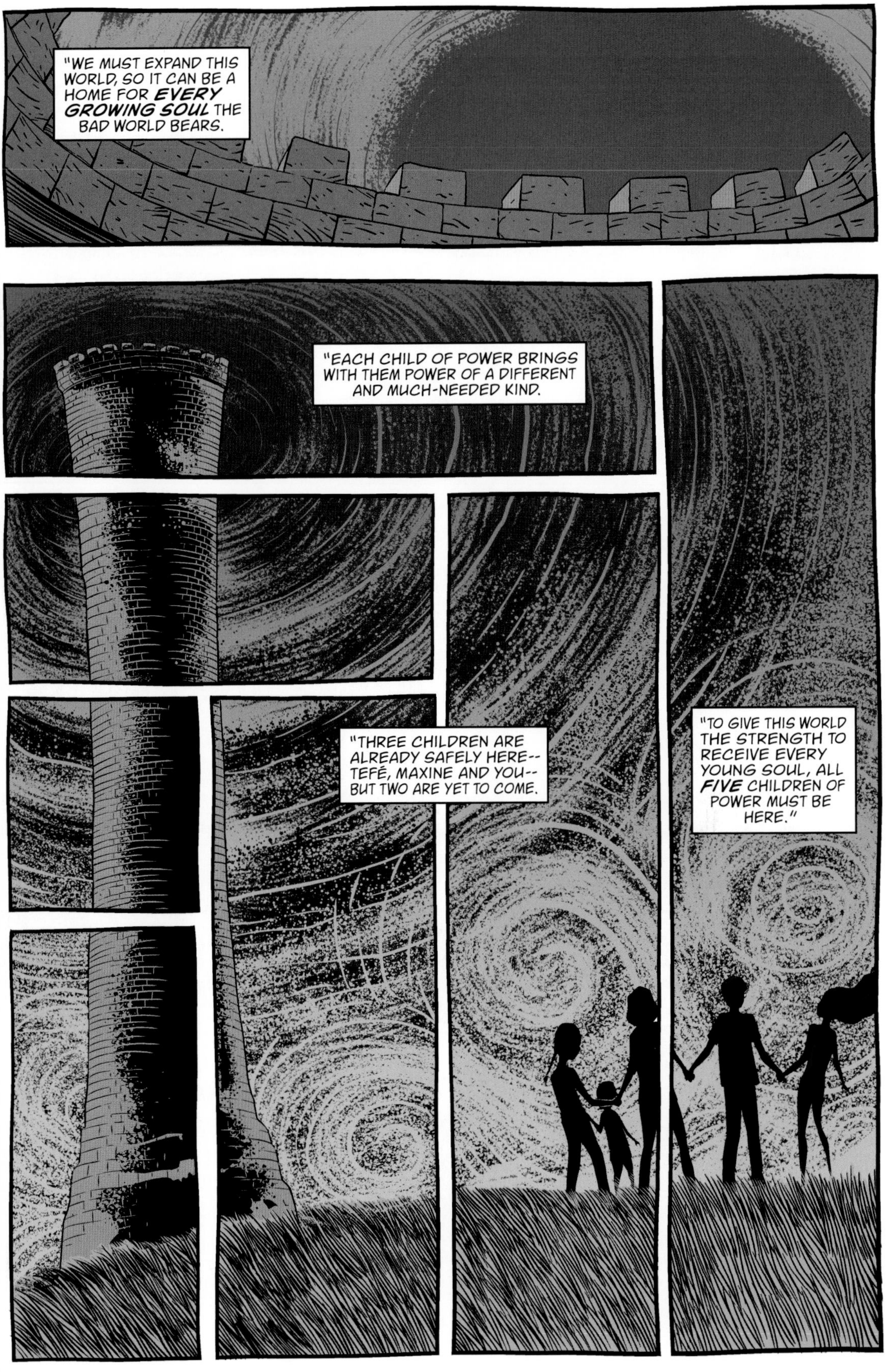
"WE MUST EXPAND THIS WORLD, SO IT CAN BE A HOME FOR EVERY GROWING SOUL THE BAD WORLD BEARS.
"EACH CHILD OF POWER BRINGS WITH THEM POWER OF A DIFFERENT AND MUCH-NEEDED KIND.
"THREE CHILDREN ARE ALREADY SAFELY HERE-- TEFÉ, MAXINE AND YOU-- BUT TWO ARE YET TO COME.
"TO GIVE THIS WORLD THE STRENGTH TO RECEIVE EVERY YOUNG SOUL, ALL FIVE CHILDREN OF POWER MUST BE HERE."

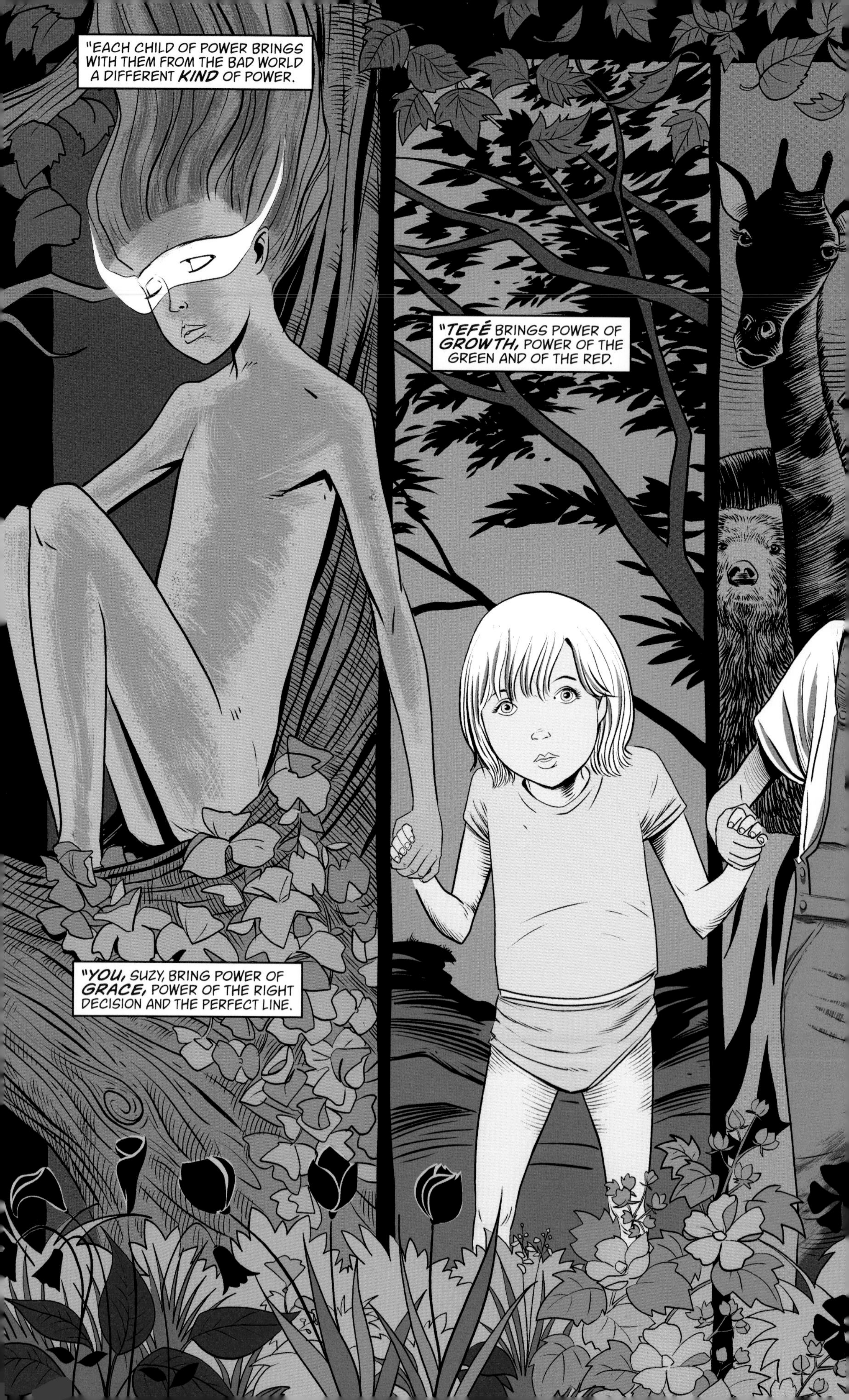
"EACH CHILD OF POWER BRINGS WITH THEM FROM THE BAD WORLD A DIFFERENT KIND OF POWER.
"TEFÉ BRINGS POWER OF GROWTH, POWER OF THE GREEN AND OF THE RED.
"YOU, SUZY, BRING POWER OF GRACE, POWER OF THE RIGHT DECISION AND THE PERFECT LINE.

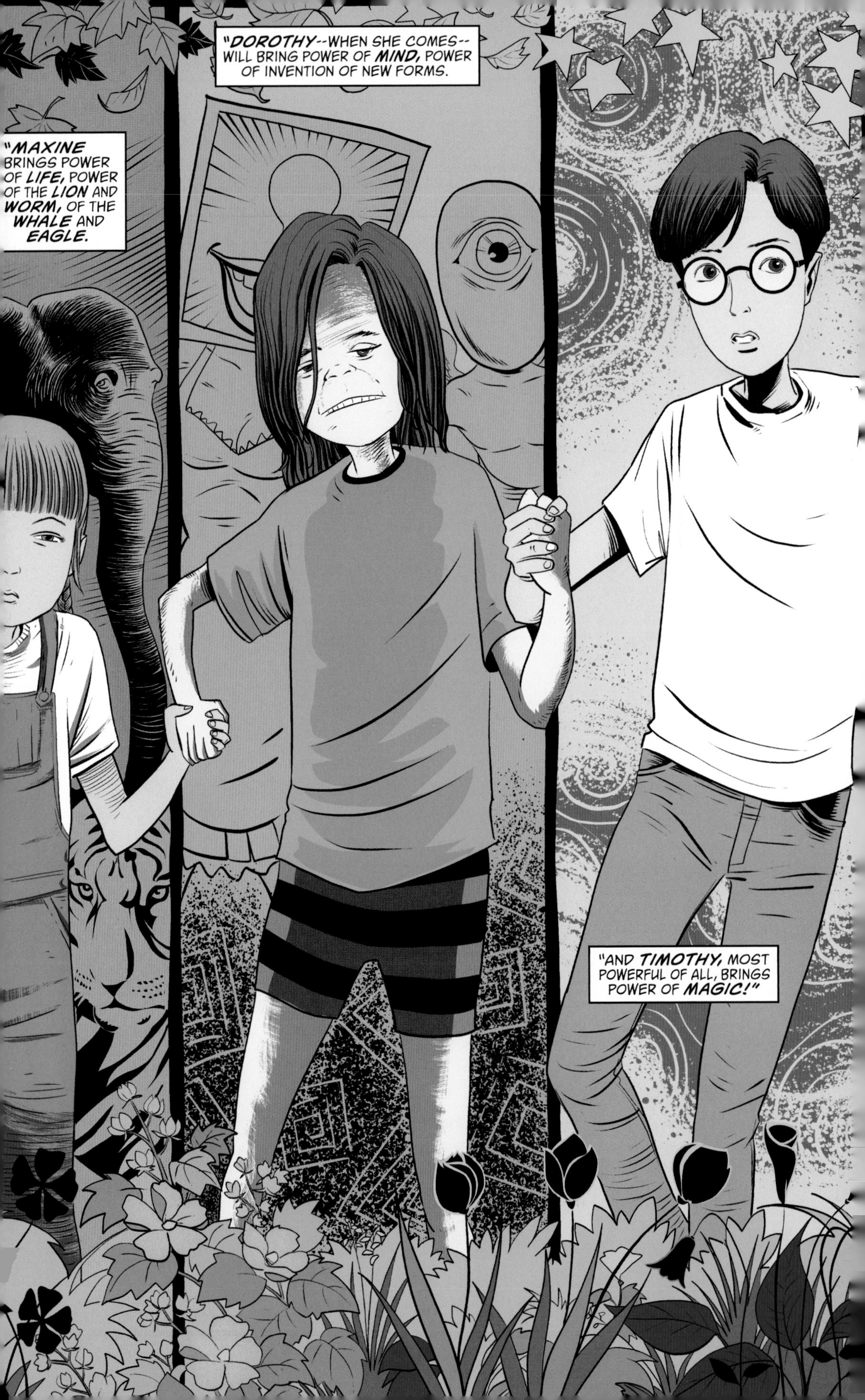
"MAXINE BRINGS POWER OF LIFE, POWER OF THE LION AND WORM, OF THE WHALE AND EAGLE.
"DOROTHY--WHEN SHE COMES--WILL BRING POWER OF MIND, POWER OF INVENTION OF NEW FORMS.
"AND TIMOTHY, MOST POWERFUL OF ALL, BRINGS POWER OF MAGIC!"

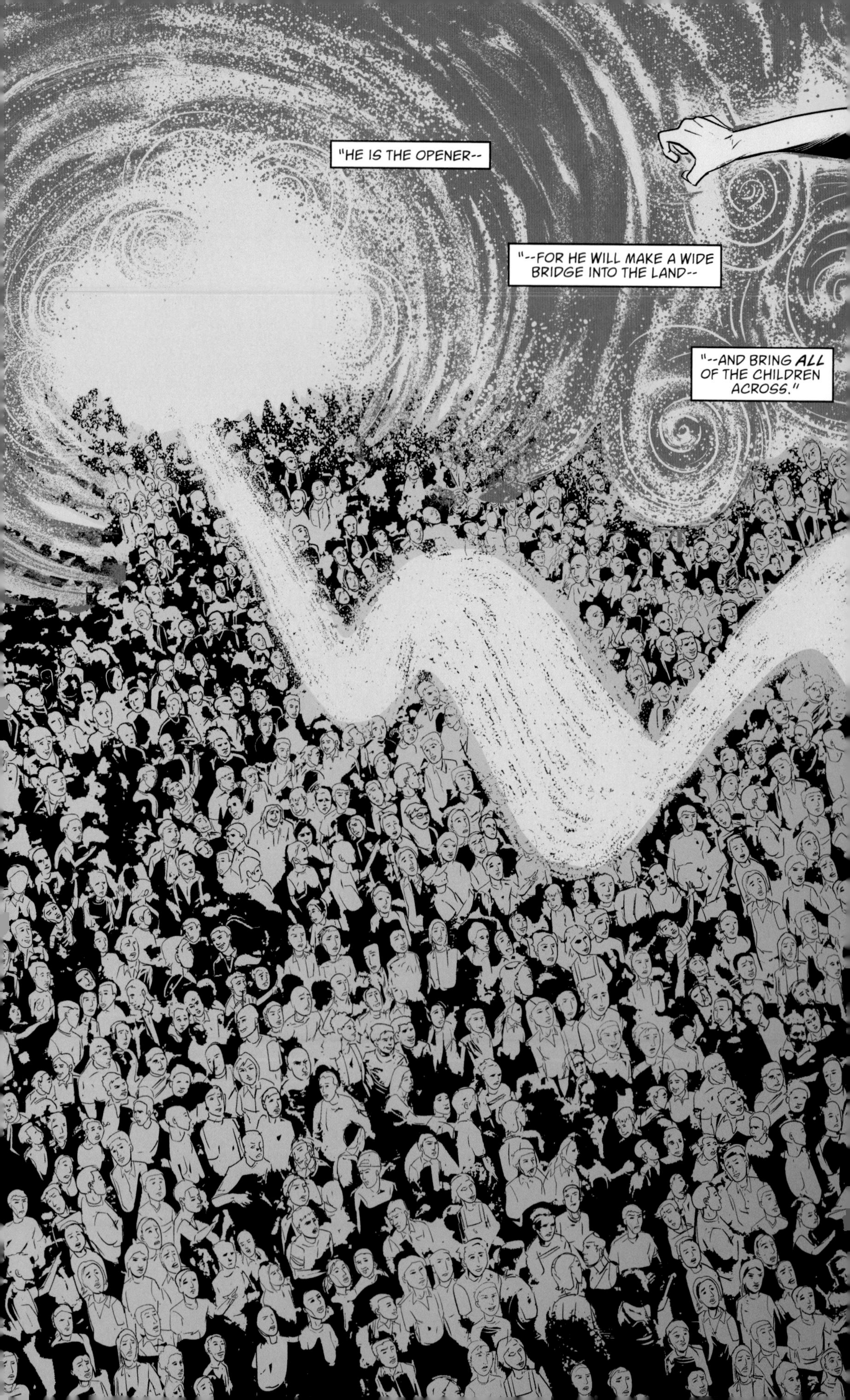
"HE IS THE OPENER--
"--FOR HE WILL MAKE A WIDE BRIDGE INTO THE LAND--
"--AND BRING ALL OF THE CHILDREN ACROSS."

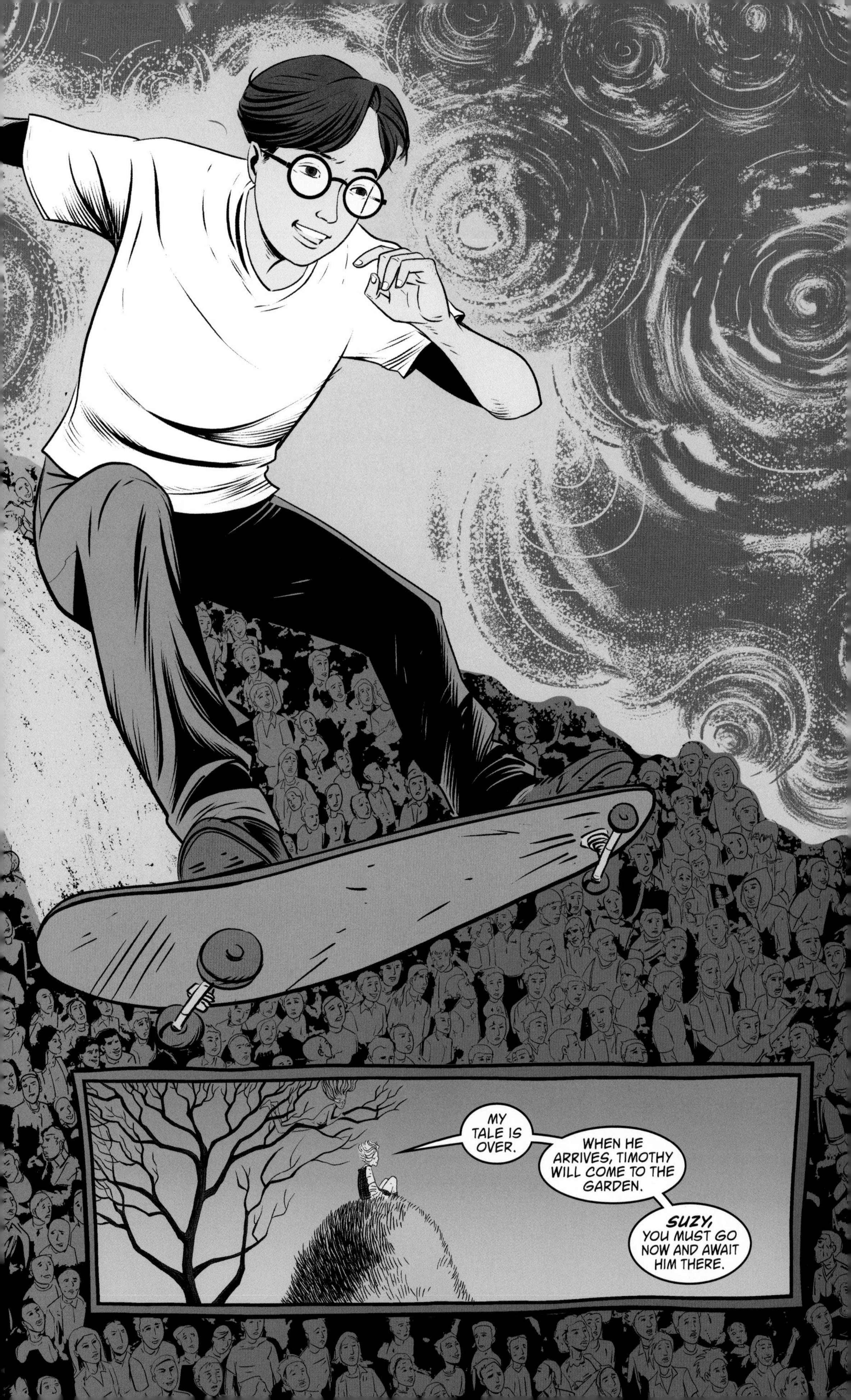
MY TALE IS OVER.
WHEN HE ARRIVES, TIMOTHY WILL COME TO THE GARDEN.
SUZY, YOU MUST GO NOW AND AWAIT HIM THERE.

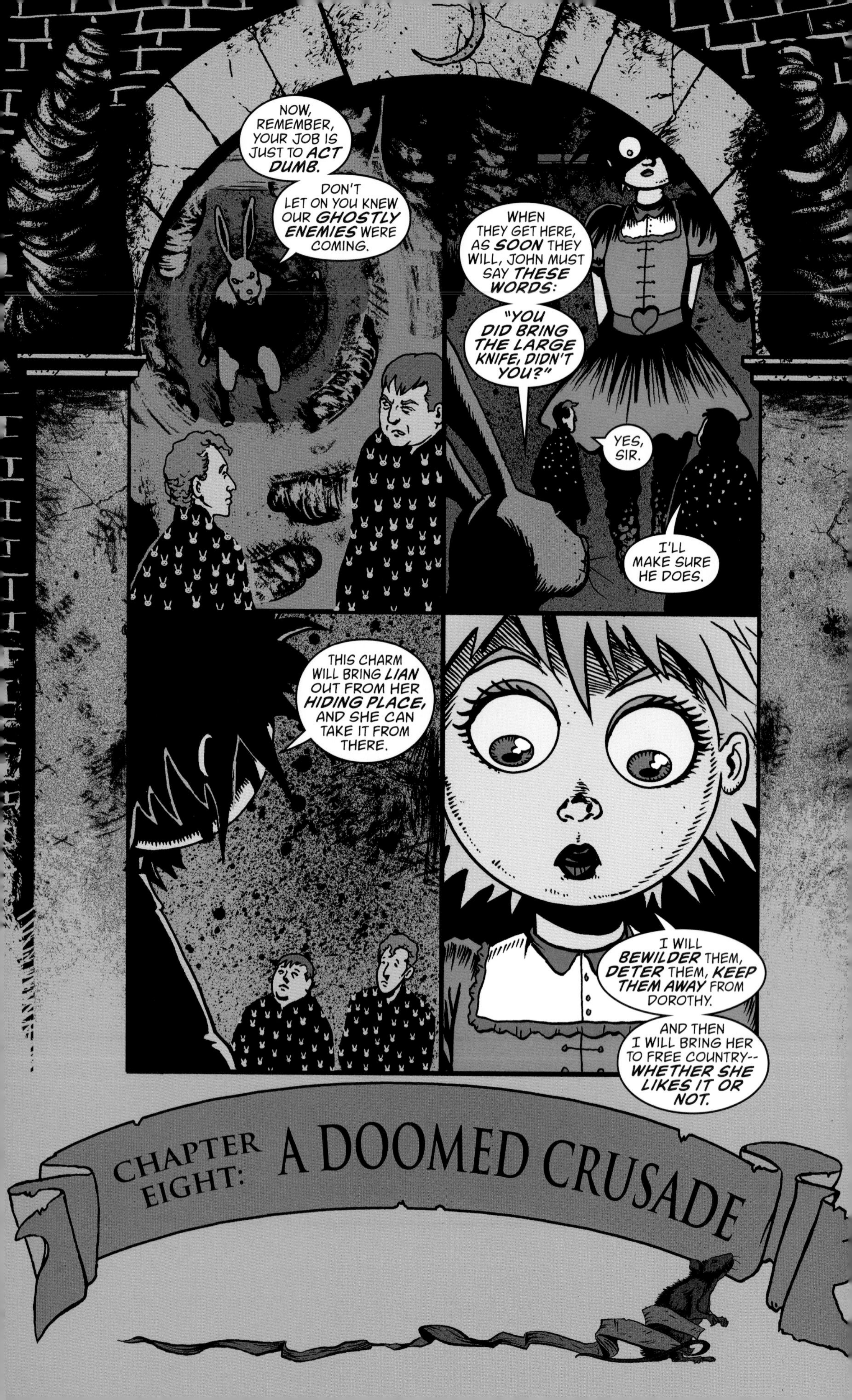

NOW, REMEMBER, YOUR JOB IS JUST TO ACT DUMB.
DON'T LET ON YOU KNEW OUR GHOSTLY ENEMIES WERE COMING.
WHEN THEY GET HERE, AS SOON THEY WILL, JOHN MUST SAY THESE WORDS:
"YOU DID BRING THE LARGE KNIFE, DIDN'T YOU?"
YES, SIR.
I'LL MAKE SURE HE DOES.
THIS CHARM WILL BRING LIAN OUT FROM HER HIDING PLACE, AND SHE CAN TAKE IT FROM THERE.
I WILL BEWILDER THEM, DETER THEM, KEEP THEM AWAY FROM DOROTHY.
AND THEN I WILL BRING HER TO FREE COUNTRY-- WHETHER SHE LIKES IT OR NOT.

CHAPTER EIGHT: A DOOMED CRUSADE

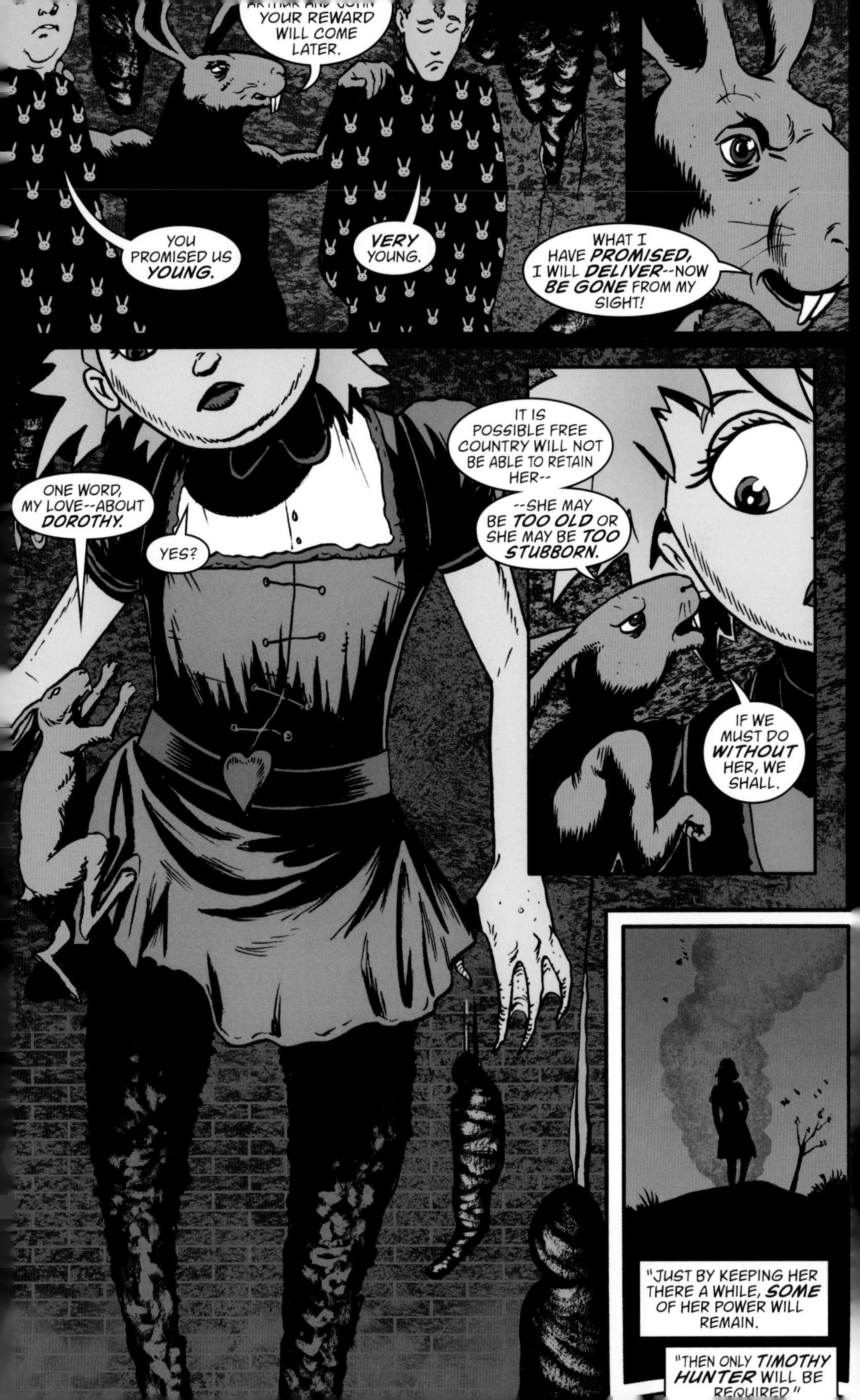

YOUR REWARD WILL COME LATER.
YOU PROMISED US *YOUNG.*
VERY YOUNG.
WHAT I HAVE ***PROMISED,*** I WILL ***DELIVER***--NOW ***BE GONE*** FROM MY SIGHT!
ONE WORD, MY LOVE--ABOUT *DOROTHY.*
YES?
IT IS POSSIBLE FREE COUNTRY WILL NOT BE ABLE TO RETAIN HER--
--SHE MAY BE ***TOO OLD*** OR SHE MAY BE ***TOO STUBBORN.***
IF WE MUST DO ***WITHOUT*** HER, WE SHALL.
"JUST BY KEEPING HER THERE A WHILE, ***SOME*** OF HER POWER WILL REMAIN.
"THEN ONLY ***TIMOTHY HUNTER*** WILL BE REQUIRED."

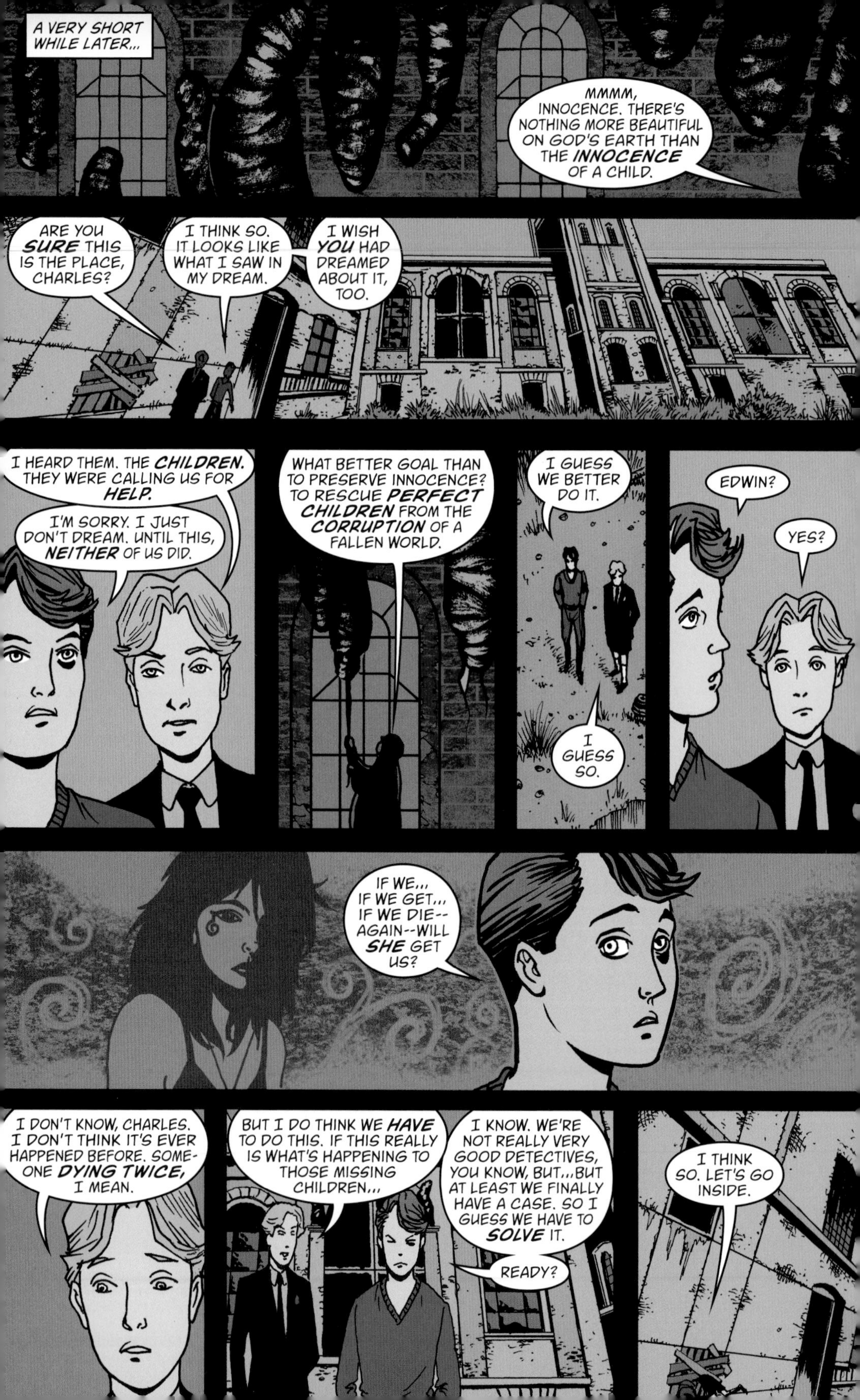
A VERY SHORT WHILE LATER...
MMMM, INNOCENCE. THERE'S NOTHING MORE BEAUTIFUL ON GOD'S EARTH THAN THE INNOCENCE OF A CHILD.
ARE YOU SURE THIS IS THE PLACE, CHARLES?
I THINK SO. IT LOOKS LIKE WHAT I SAW IN MY DREAM.
I WISH YOU HAD DREAMED ABOUT IT, TOO.
I HEARD THEM. THE CHILDREN. THEY WERE CALLING US FOR HELP.
I'M SORRY. I JUST DON'T DREAM. UNTIL THIS, NEITHER OF US DID.
WHAT BETTER GOAL THAN TO PRESERVE INNOCENCE? TO RESCUE PERFECT CHILDREN FROM THE CORRUPTION OF A FALLEN WORLD.
I GUESS WE BETTER DO IT.
I GUESS SO.
EDWIN?
YES?
IF WE... IF WE GET... IF WE DIE--AGAIN--WILL SHE GET US?
I DON'T KNOW, CHARLES. I DON'T THINK IT'S EVER HAPPENED BEFORE. SOME-ONE DYING TWICE, I MEAN.
BUT I DO THINK WE HAVE TO DO THIS. IF THIS REALLY IS WHAT'S HAPPENING TO THOSE MISSING CHILDREN...
I KNOW. WE'RE NOT REALLY VERY GOOD DETECTIVES, YOU KNOW, BUT...BUT AT LEAST WE FINALLY HAVE A CASE. SO I GUESS WE HAVE TO SOLVE IT.
READY?
I THINK SO. LET'S GO INSIDE.

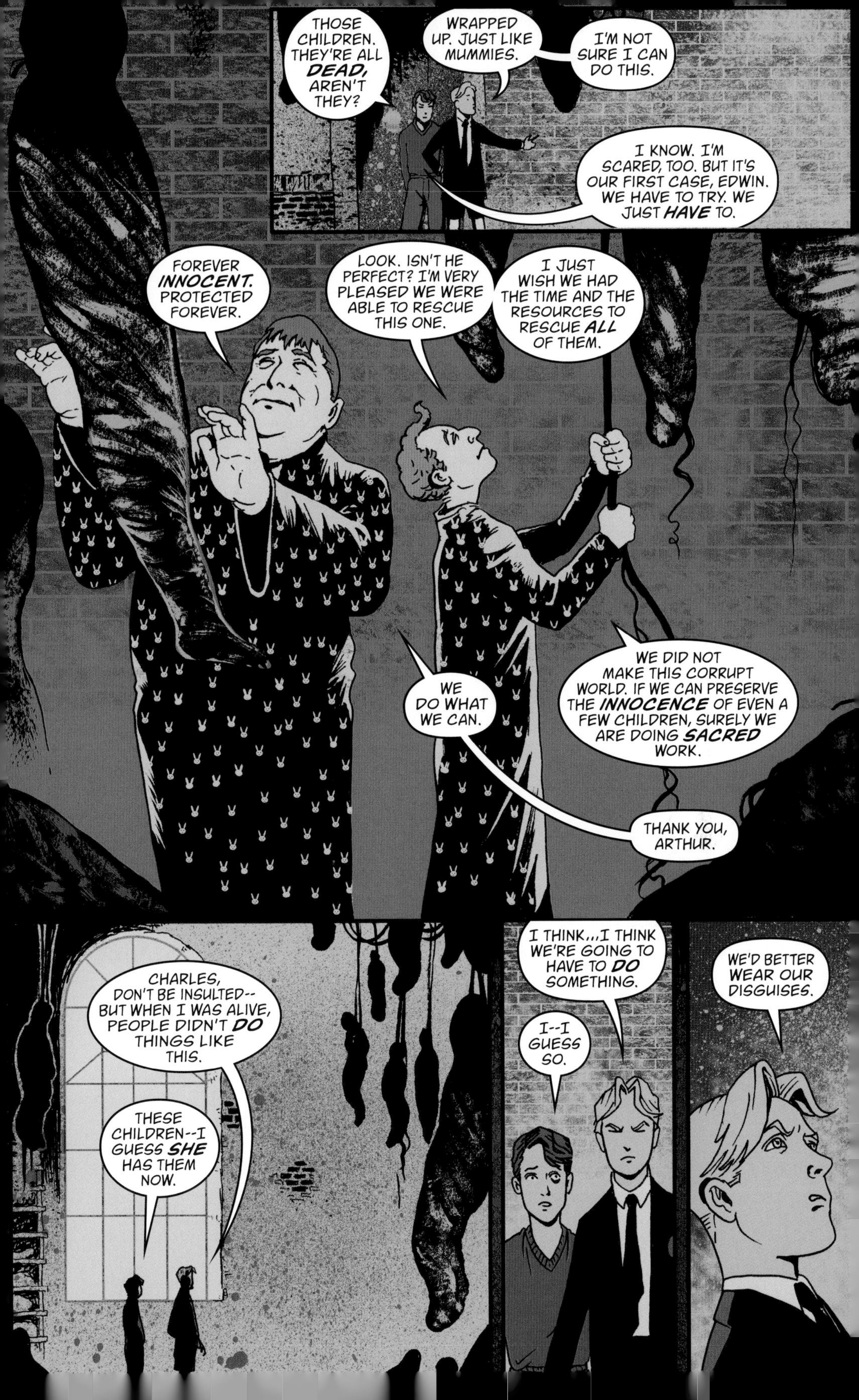
THOSE CHILDREN. THEY'RE ALL DEAD, AREN'T THEY?
WRAPPED UP. JUST LIKE MUMMIES.
I'M NOT SURE I CAN DO THIS.
I KNOW. I'M SCARED, TOO. BUT IT'S OUR FIRST CASE, EDWIN. WE HAVE TO TRY. WE JUST HAVE TO.
FOREVER INNOCENT. PROTECTED FOREVER.
LOOK. ISN'T HE PERFECT? I'M VERY PLEASED WE WERE ABLE TO RESCUE THIS ONE.
I JUST WISH WE HAD THE TIME AND THE RESOURCES TO RESCUE ALL OF THEM.
WE DO WHAT WE CAN.
WE DID NOT MAKE THIS CORRUPT WORLD. IF WE CAN PRESERVE THE INNOCENCE OF EVEN A FEW CHILDREN, SURELY WE ARE DOING SACRED WORK.
THANK YOU, ARTHUR.
CHARLES, DON'T BE INSULTED-- BUT WHEN I WAS ALIVE, PEOPLE DIDN'T DO THINGS LIKE THIS.
THESE CHILDREN--I GUESS SHE HAS THEM NOW.
I THINK...I THINK WE'RE GOING TO HAVE TO DO SOMETHING.
I--I GUESS SO.
WE'D BETTER WEAR OUR DISGUISES.

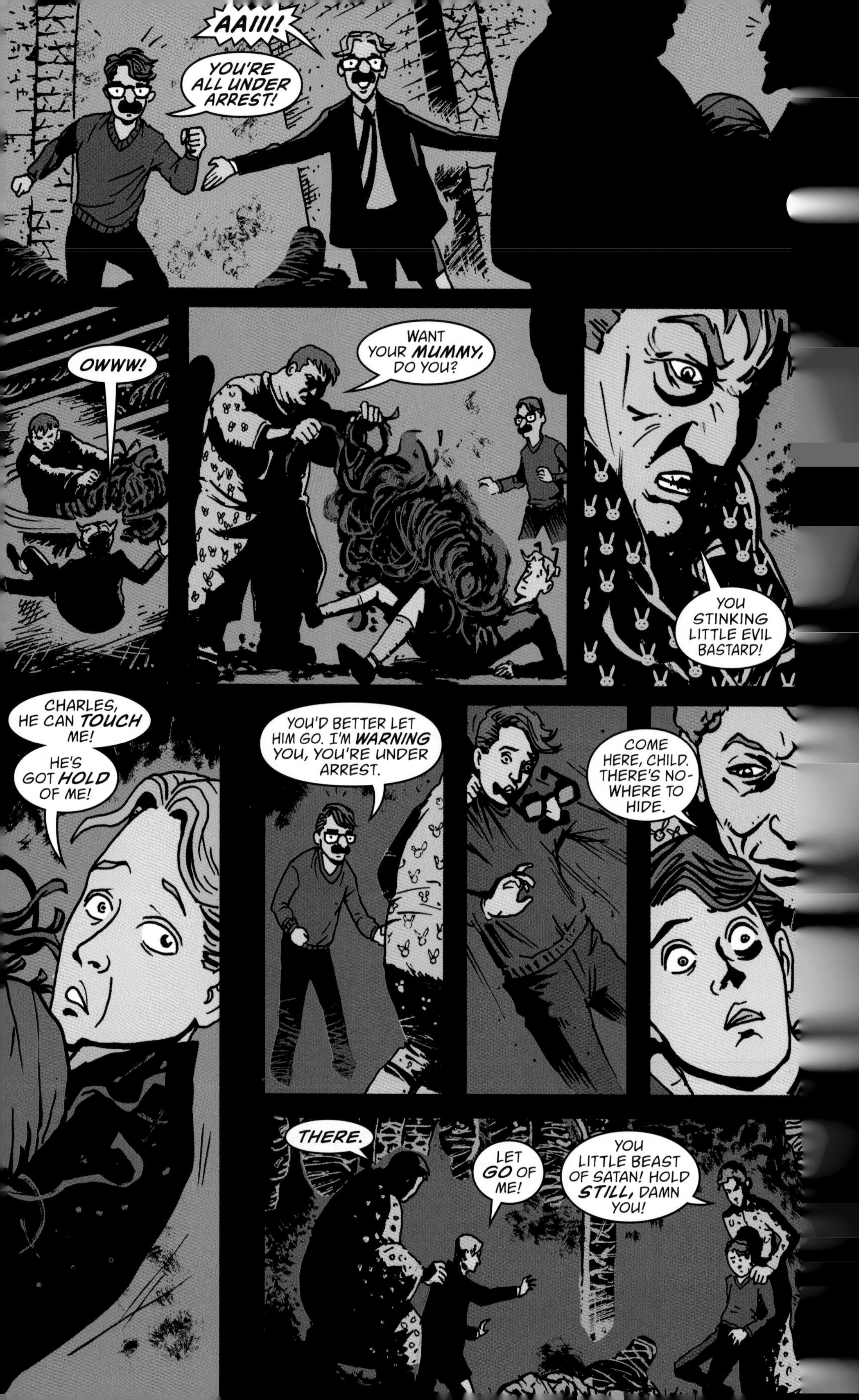
AAIII!
YOU'RE ALL UNDER ARREST!
OWWW!
WANT YOUR MUMMY, DO YOU?
YOU STINKING LITTLE EVIL BASTARD!
CHARLES, HE CAN TOUCH ME!
HE'S GOT HOLD OF ME!
YOU'D BETTER LET HIM GO. I'M WARNING YOU, YOU'RE UNDER ARREST.
COME HERE, CHILD. THERE'S NO-WHERE TO HIDE.
THERE.
LET GO OF ME!
YOU LITTLE BEAST OF SATAN! HOLD STILL, DAMN YOU!

YOU KNOW, ARTHUR...IT'S REALLY VERY SAD. SO YOUNG AND ALREADY CORRUPTED. I WISH WE COULD PRESERVE THEM, BUT *CLEARLY* IT'S TOO LATE.

WE CAN ONLY SEND THEM TO *HELL.* WHERE THEY BELONG.

YOU *DID* BRING THE LARGE KNIFE, DIDN'T YOU?

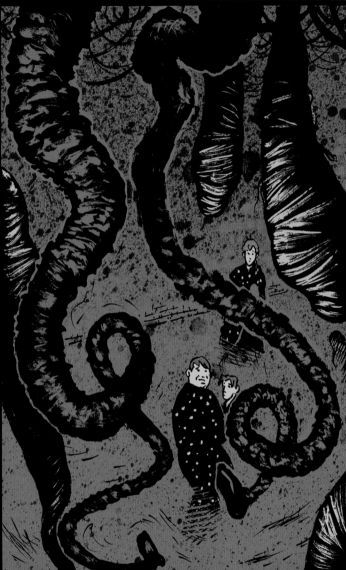

NO!

UNNNHH!

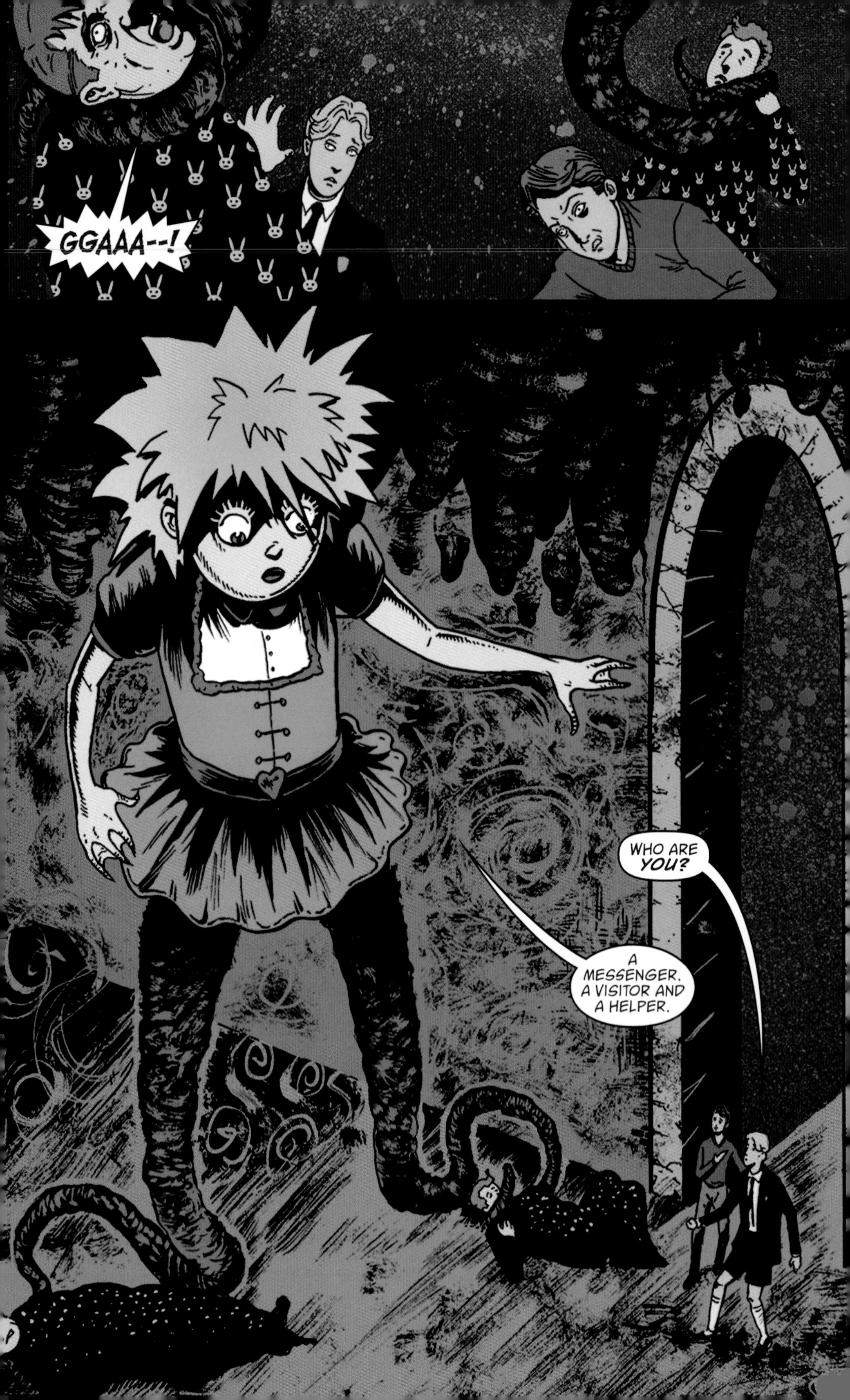
GGAAA--!
WHO ARE YOU?
A MESSENGER. A VISITOR AND A HELPER.

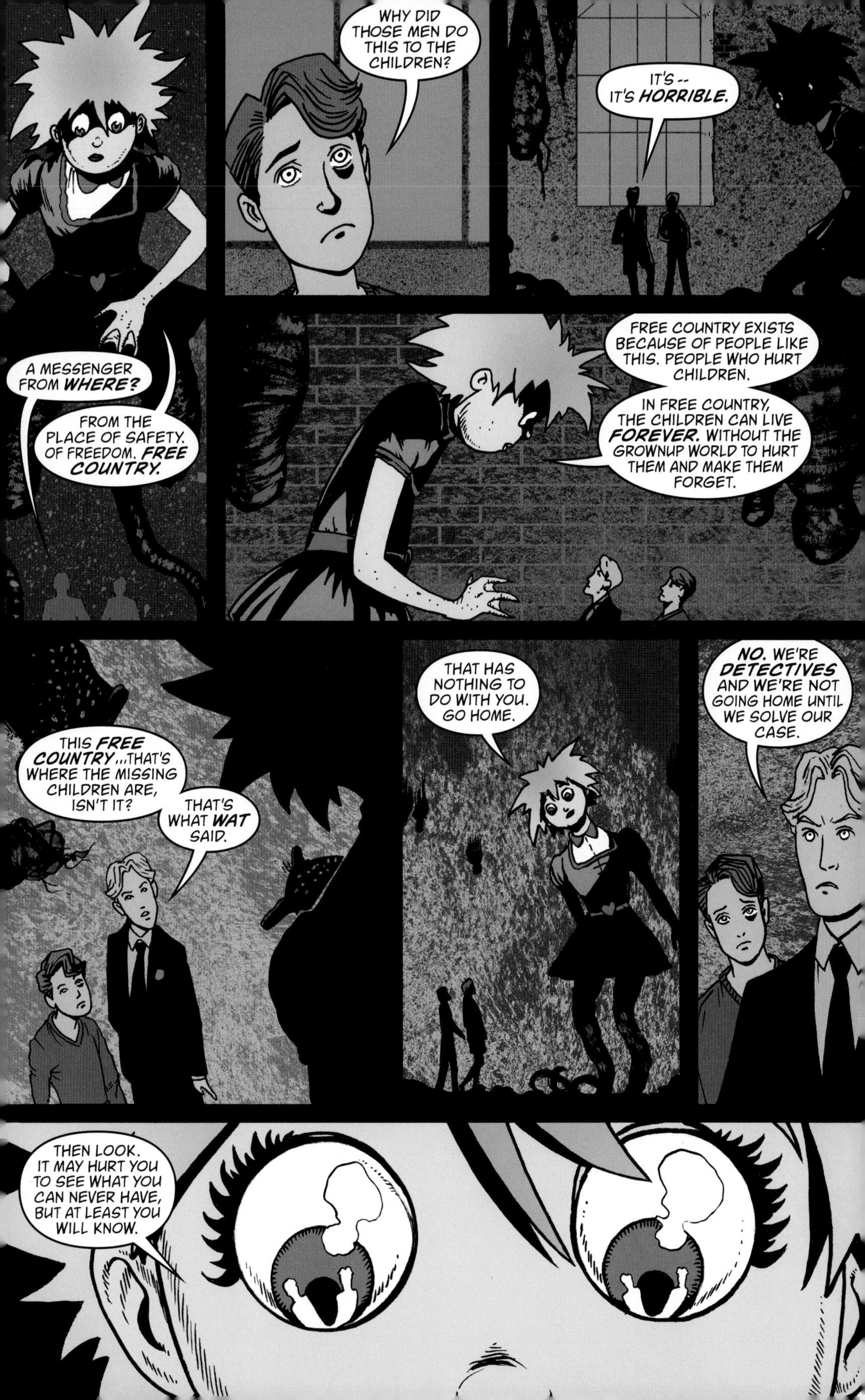
WHY DID THOSE MEN DO THIS TO THE CHILDREN?
IT'S -- IT'S HORRIBLE.
A MESSENGER FROM WHERE?
FROM THE PLACE OF SAFETY. OF FREEDOM. FREE COUNTRY.
FREE COUNTRY EXISTS BECAUSE OF PEOPLE LIKE THIS. PEOPLE WHO HURT CHILDREN.
IN FREE COUNTRY, THE CHILDREN CAN LIVE FOREVER. WITHOUT THE GROWNUP WORLD TO HURT THEM AND MAKE THEM FORGET.
THIS FREE COUNTRY...THAT'S WHERE THE MISSING CHILDREN ARE, ISN'T IT?
THAT'S WHAT WAT SAID.
THAT HAS NOTHING TO DO WITH YOU. GO HOME.
NO. WE'RE DETECTIVES AND WE'RE NOT GOING HOME UNTIL WE SOLVE OUR CASE.
THEN LOOK. IT MAY HURT YOU TO SEE WHAT YOU CAN NEVER HAVE, BUT AT LEAST YOU WILL KNOW.

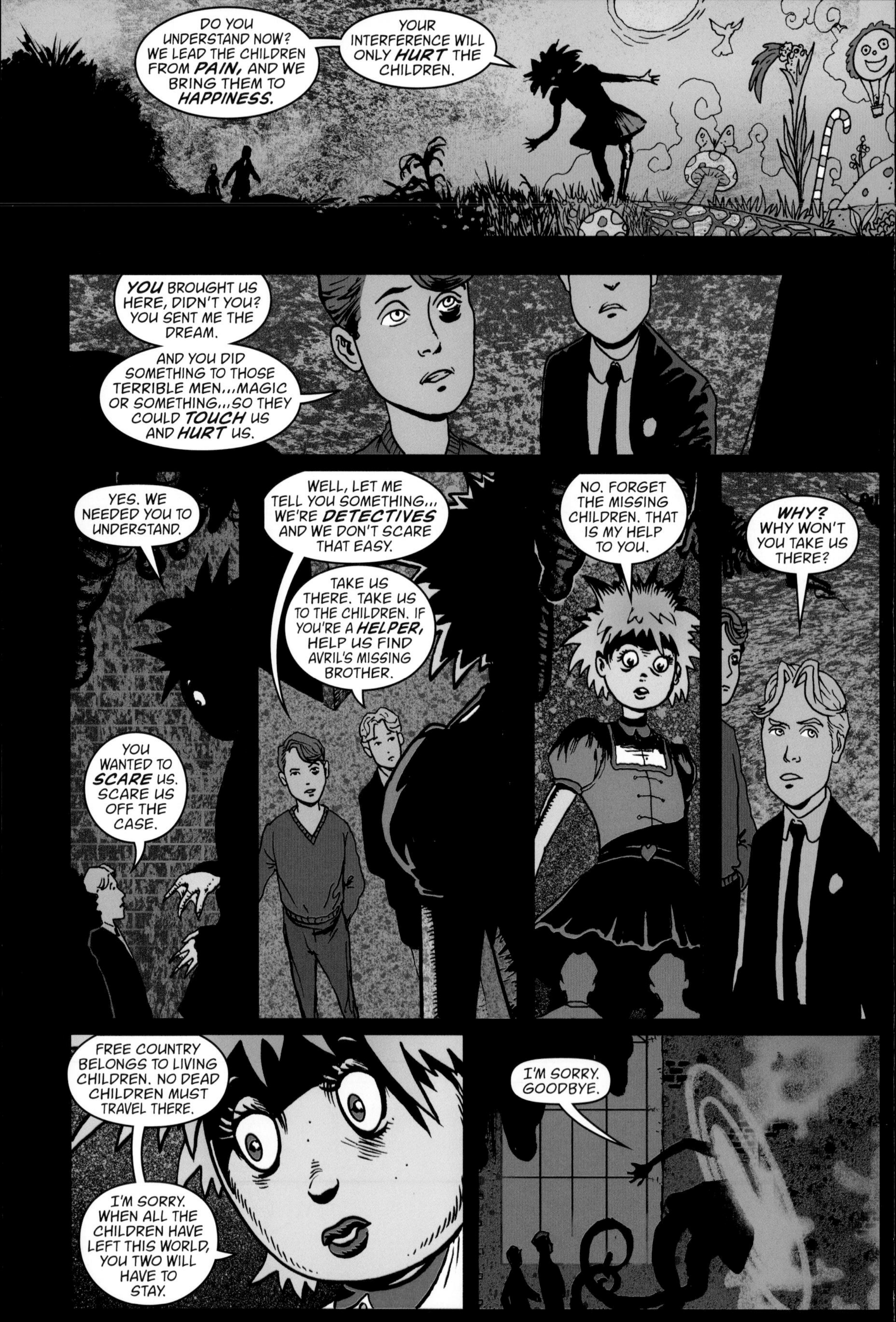

DO YOU UNDERSTAND NOW? WE LEAD THE CHILDREN FROM PAIN, AND WE BRING THEM TO HAPPINESS.
YOUR INTERFERENCE WILL ONLY HURT THE CHILDREN.
YOU BROUGHT US HERE, DIDN'T YOU? YOU SENT ME THE DREAM.
AND YOU DID SOMETHING TO THOSE TERRIBLE MEN...MAGIC OR SOMETHING...SO THEY COULD TOUCH US AND HURT US.
YES. WE NEEDED YOU TO UNDERSTAND.
YOU WANTED TO SCARE US. SCARE US OFF THE CASE.
WELL, LET ME TELL YOU SOMETHING... WE'RE DETECTIVES AND WE DON'T SCARE THAT EASY.
TAKE US THERE. TAKE US TO THE CHILDREN. IF YOU'RE A HELPER, HELP US FIND AVRIL'S MISSING BROTHER.
NO. FORGET THE MISSING CHILDREN. THAT IS MY HELP TO YOU.
WHY? WHY WON'T YOU TAKE US THERE?
FREE COUNTRY BELONGS TO LIVING CHILDREN. NO DEAD CHILDREN MUST TRAVEL THERE.
I'M SORRY. WHEN ALL THE CHILDREN HAVE LEFT THIS WORLD, YOU TWO WILL HAVE TO STAY.
I'M SORRY. GOODBYE.

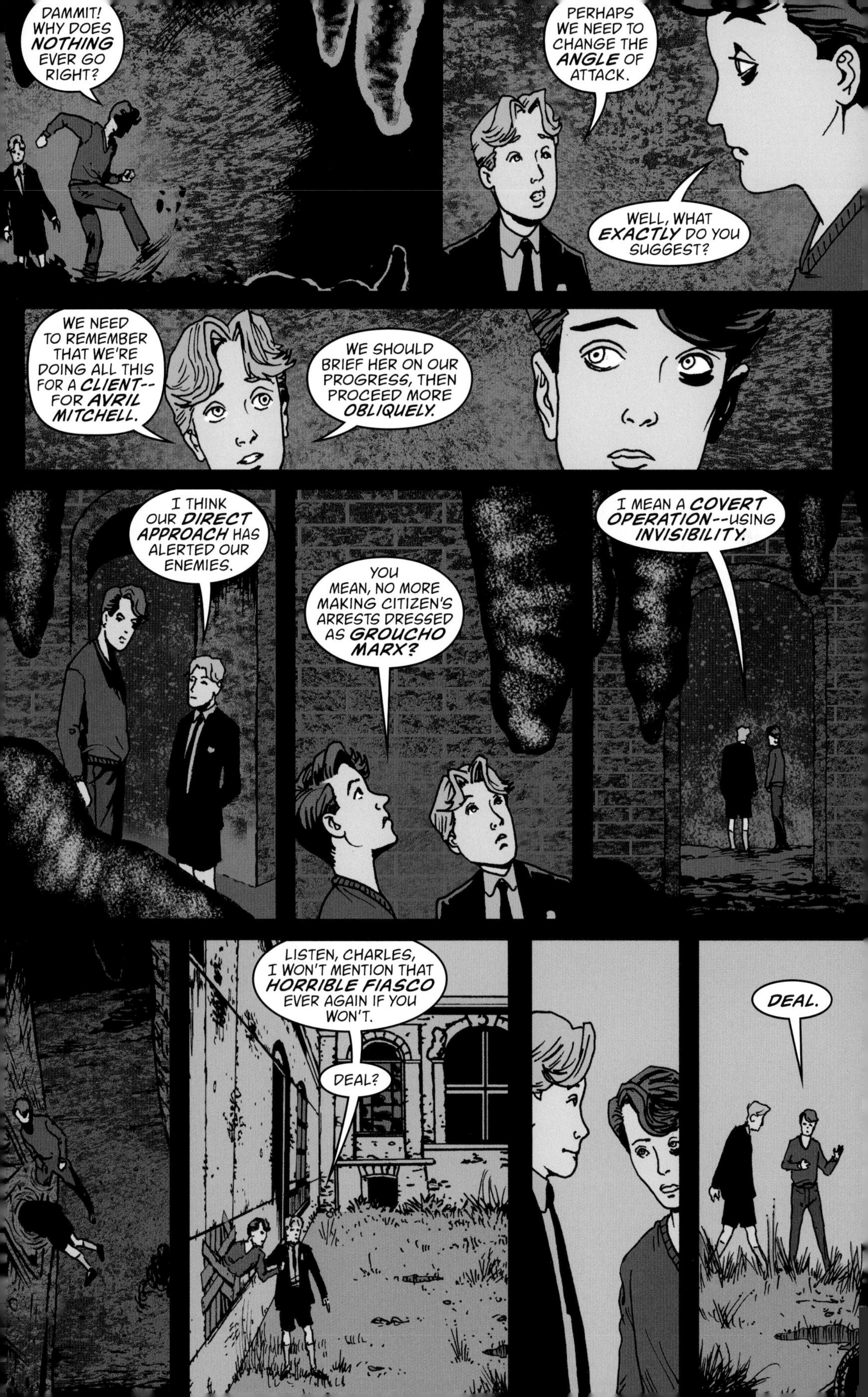
DAMMIT! WHY DOES NOTHING EVER GO RIGHT?
PERHAPS WE NEED TO CHANGE THE ANGLE OF ATTACK.
WELL, WHAT EXACTLY DO YOU SUGGEST?
WE NEED TO REMEMBER THAT WE'RE DOING ALL THIS FOR A CLIENT-- FOR AVRIL MITCHELL.
WE SHOULD BRIEF HER ON OUR PROGRESS, THEN PROCEED MORE OBLIQUELY.
I THINK OUR DIRECT APPROACH HAS ALERTED OUR ENEMIES.
YOU MEAN, NO MORE MAKING CITIZEN'S ARRESTS DRESSED AS GROUCHO MARX?
I MEAN A COVERT OPERATION--USING INVISIBILITY.
LISTEN, CHARLES, I WON'T MENTION THAT HORRIBLE FIASCO EVER AGAIN IF YOU WON'T.
DEAL?
DEAL.

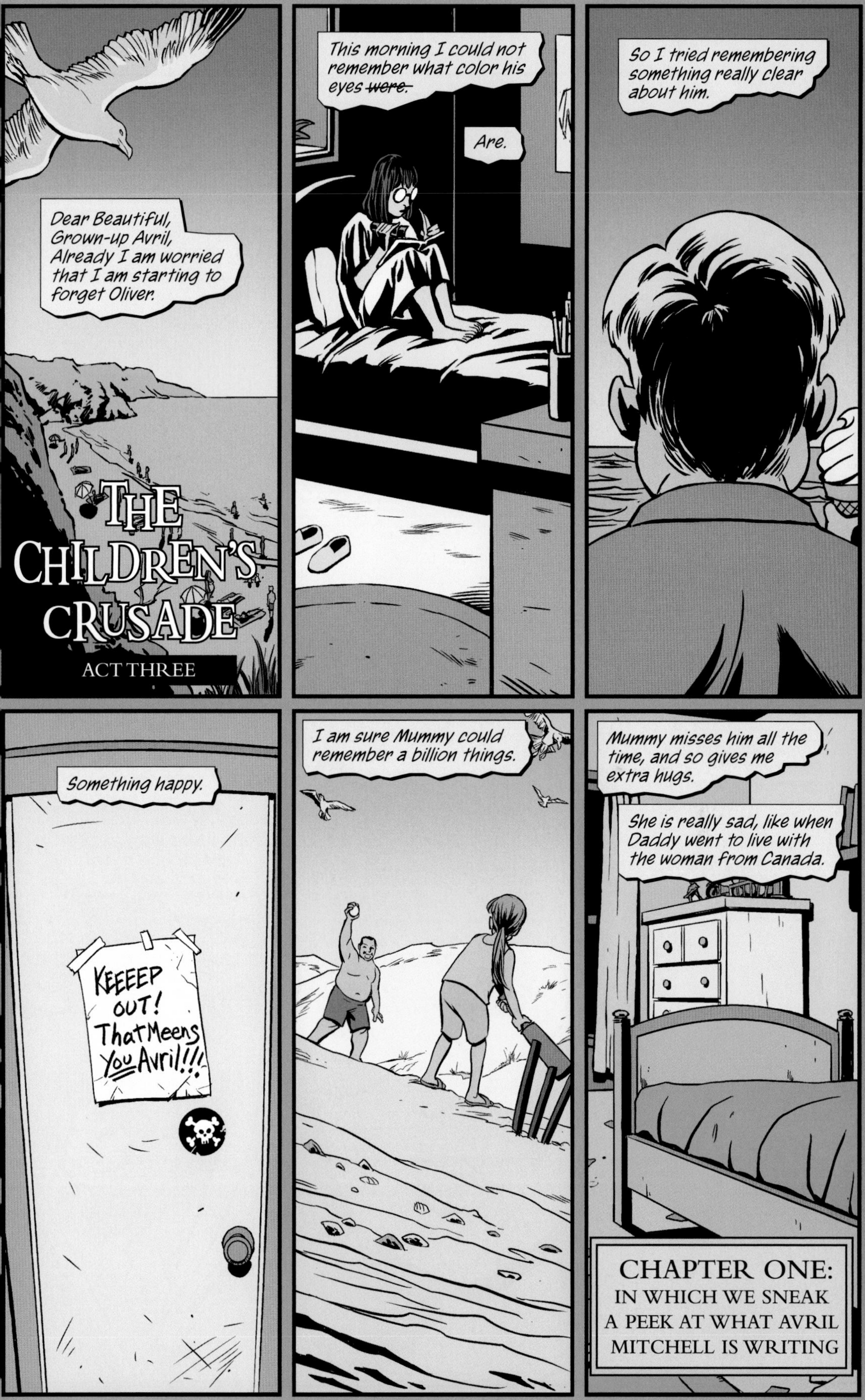
Dear Beautiful, Grown-up Avril, Already I am worried that I am starting to forget Oliver.
THE CHILDREN'S CRUSADE
ACT THREE
This morning I could not remember what color his eyes ~~were~~.
Are.
So I tried remembering something really clear about him.
Something happy.
KEEEEP OUT! ThatMeens You Avril!!!
I am sure Mummy could remember a billion things.
Mummy misses him all the time, and so gives me extra hugs.
She is really sad, like when Daddy went to live with the woman from Canada.
CHAPTER ONE:
IN WHICH WE SNEAK A PEEK AT WHAT AVRIL MITCHELL IS WRITING

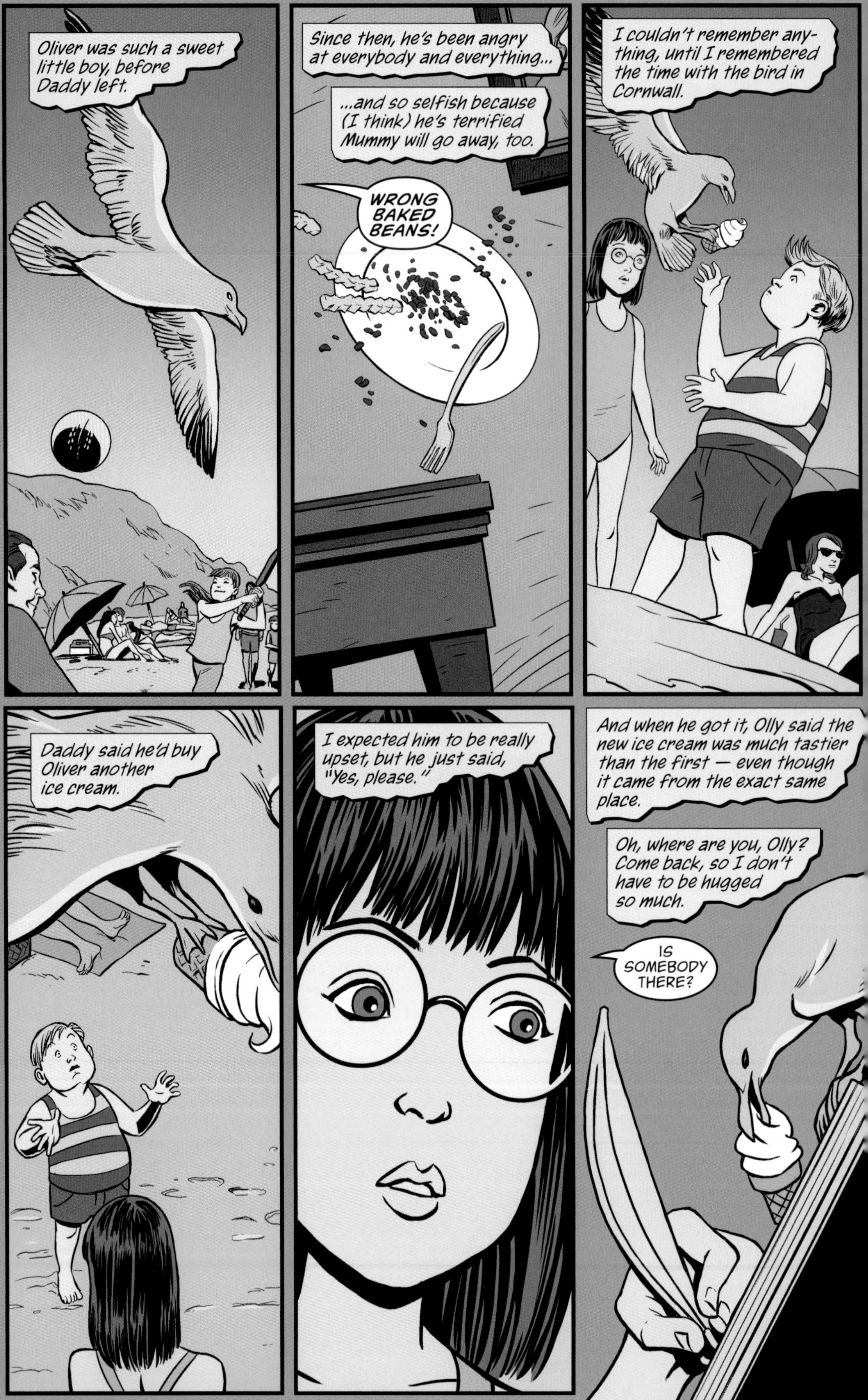
Oliver was such a sweet little boy, before Daddy left.
Since then, he's been angry at everybody and everything...
...and so selfish because (I think) he's terrified Mummy will go away, too.
WRONG BAKED BEANS!
I couldn't remember anything, until I remembered the time with the bird in Cornwall.
Daddy said he'd buy Oliver another ice cream.
I expected him to be really upset, but he just said, "Yes, please."
And when he got it, Olly said the new ice cream was much tastier than the first — even though it came from the exact same place.
Oh, where are you, Olly? Come back, so I don't have to be hugged so much.
IS SOMEBODY THERE?

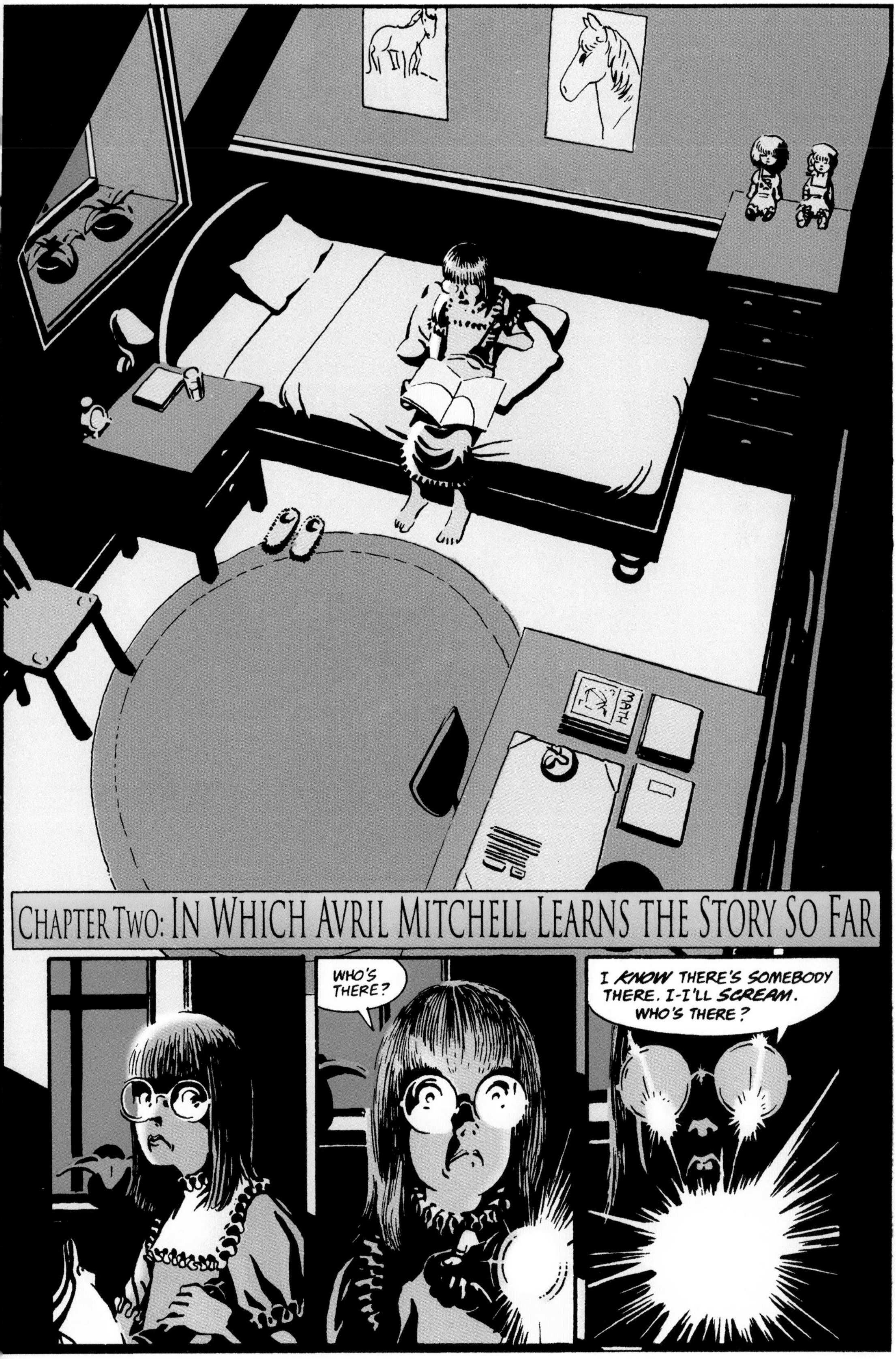

CHAPTER TWO: IN WHICH AVRIL MITCHELL LEARNS THE STORY SO FAR
WHO'S THERE?
I KNOW THERE'S SOMEBODY THERE. I-I'LL SCREAM. WHO'S THERE?

PLEASE. DON'T SCREAM. IT'S ONLY US.

YOUR DETECTIVES.

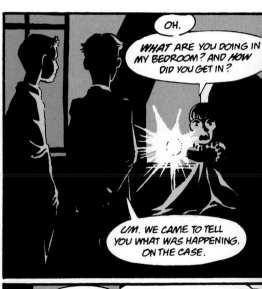

OH. *WHAT* ARE YOU DOING IN MY BEDROOM? AND *HOW* DID YOU GET IN?

UM. WE CAME TO TELL YOU WHAT WAS HAPPENING. ON THE CASE.

CASE?

YOUR BROTHER. OLIVER. THE MISSING PERSON.

OH. *HIM.* HAVE YOU *FOUND* HIM YET?

NO.

BUT WE KNOW WHERE HE IS.

WELL? WHERE *IS* HE? I BET THE LITTLE CREEP'S IN DISNEYLAND OR SOMEWHERE.

THERE WAS A THING ON *TELLY* THIS EVENING ABOUT RUNAWAY KIDS SELLING THEIR BODIES ON THE STREETS OF LONDON, AND MUMMY STARTED CRYING AND I SAID DON'T BE *SILLY,* OLIVER'S NOT GOING TO BE DOING *THAT.*

I SAID, NO ONE IN THEIR RIGHT MIND'S GOING TO PAY FOR *OLIVER'S* COMPANY.

AND MUMMY STOPPED CRYING.

AND *THEN* I SAID THAT ALL OLIVER HAD TO BE SCARED OF WAS A PORK BUTCHER WITH A SHORTAGE OF PIE-FILLING, AND MUMMY STARTED CRYING AGAIN.

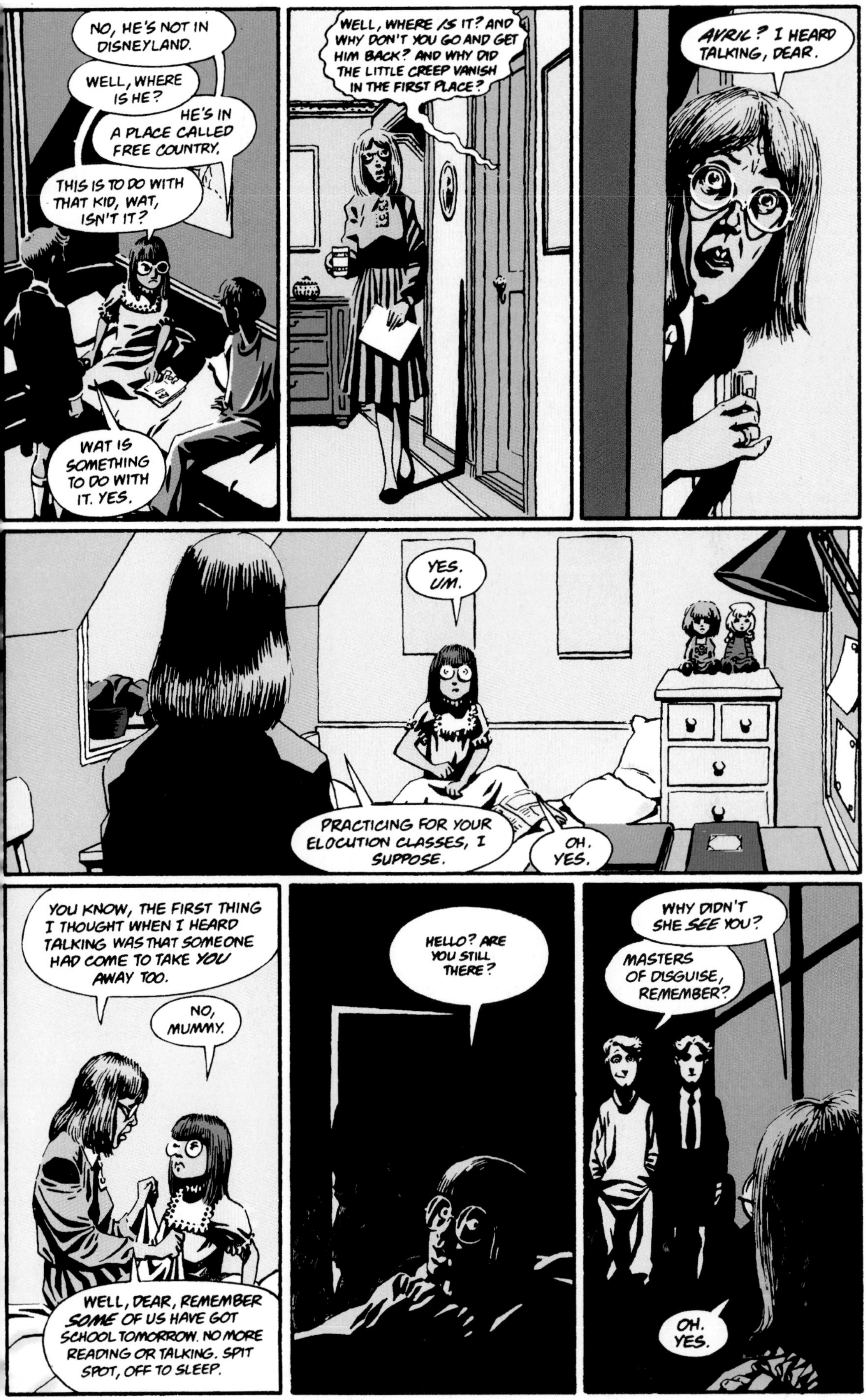
NO, HE'S NOT IN DISNEYLAND.
WELL, WHERE IS HE?
HE'S IN A PLACE CALLED FREE COUNTRY.
THIS IS TO DO WITH THAT KID, WAT, ISN'T IT?
WAT IS SOMETHING TO DO WITH IT. YES.
WELL, WHERE IS IT? AND WHY DON'T YOU GO AND GET HIM BACK? AND WHY DID THE LITTLE CREEP VANISH IN THE FIRST PLACE?
AVRIL? I HEARD TALKING, DEAR.
YES. UM.
PRACTICING FOR YOUR ELOCUTION CLASSES, I SUPPOSE.
OH. YES.
YOU KNOW, THE FIRST THING I THOUGHT WHEN I HEARD TALKING WAS THAT SOMEONE HAD COME TO TAKE YOU AWAY TOO.
NO, MUMMY.
WELL, DEAR, REMEMBER SOME OF US HAVE GOT SCHOOL TOMORROW. NO MORE READING OR TALKING. SPIT SPOT, OFF TO SLEEP.
HELLO? ARE YOU STILL THERE?
WHY DIDN'T SHE SEE YOU?
MASTERS OF DISGUISE, REMEMBER?
OH. YES.

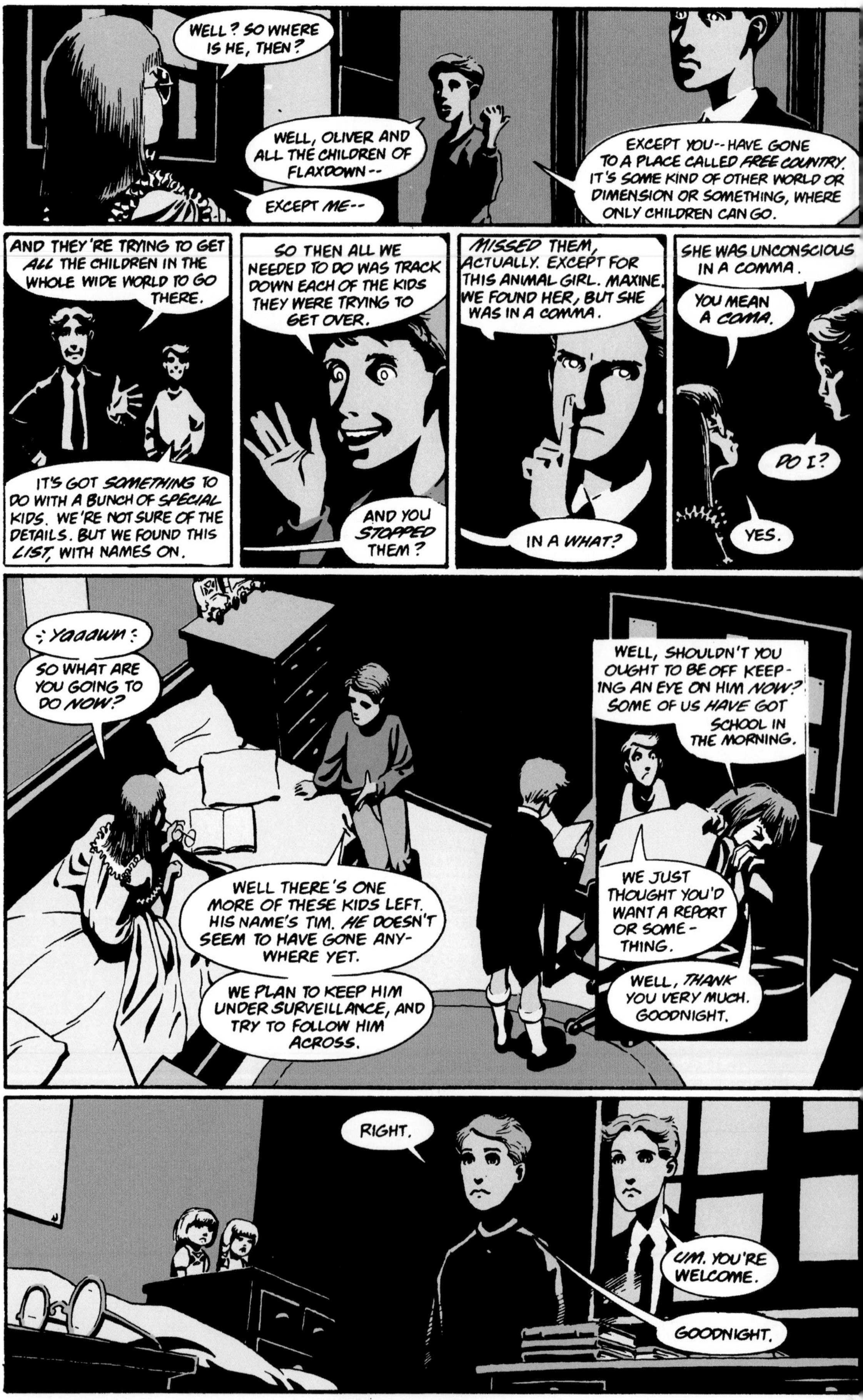
WELL? SO WHERE IS HE, THEN?
WELL, OLIVER AND ALL THE CHILDREN OF FLAXDOWN--
EXCEPT ME--
EXCEPT YOU--HAVE GONE TO A PLACE CALLED FREE COUNTRY. IT'S SOME KIND OF OTHER WORLD OR DIMENSION OR SOMETHING, WHERE ONLY CHILDREN CAN GO.
AND THEY'RE TRYING TO GET ALL THE CHILDREN IN THE WHOLE WIDE WORLD TO GO THERE.
IT'S GOT SOMETHING TO DO WITH A BUNCH OF SPECIAL KIDS. WE'RE NOT SURE OF THE DETAILS. BUT WE FOUND THIS LIST, WITH NAMES ON.
SO THEN ALL WE NEEDED TO DO WAS TRACK DOWN EACH OF THE KIDS THEY WERE TRYING TO GET OVER.
AND YOU STOPPED THEM?
MISSED THEM, ACTUALLY. EXCEPT FOR THIS ANIMAL GIRL. MAXINE. WE FOUND HER, BUT SHE WAS IN A COMMA.
IN A WHAT?
SHE WAS UNCONSCIOUS IN A COMMA.
YOU MEAN A COMA.
DO I?
YES.
:YAAAWN:
SO WHAT ARE YOU GOING TO DO NOW?
WELL THERE'S ONE MORE OF THESE KIDS LEFT. HIS NAME'S TIM. HE DOESN'T SEEM TO HAVE GONE ANYWHERE YET.
WE PLAN TO KEEP HIM UNDER SURVEILLANCE, AND TRY TO FOLLOW HIM ACROSS.
WELL, SHOULDN'T YOU OUGHT TO BE OFF KEEPING AN EYE ON HIM NOW? SOME OF US HAVE GOT SCHOOL IN THE MORNING.
WE JUST THOUGHT YOU'D WANT A REPORT OR SOMETHING.
WELL, THANK YOU VERY MUCH. GOODNIGHT.
RIGHT.
UM. YOU'RE WELCOME.
GOODNIGHT.

ChapterThree: In Which the High Council Does Not Reveal Its Secret Plan

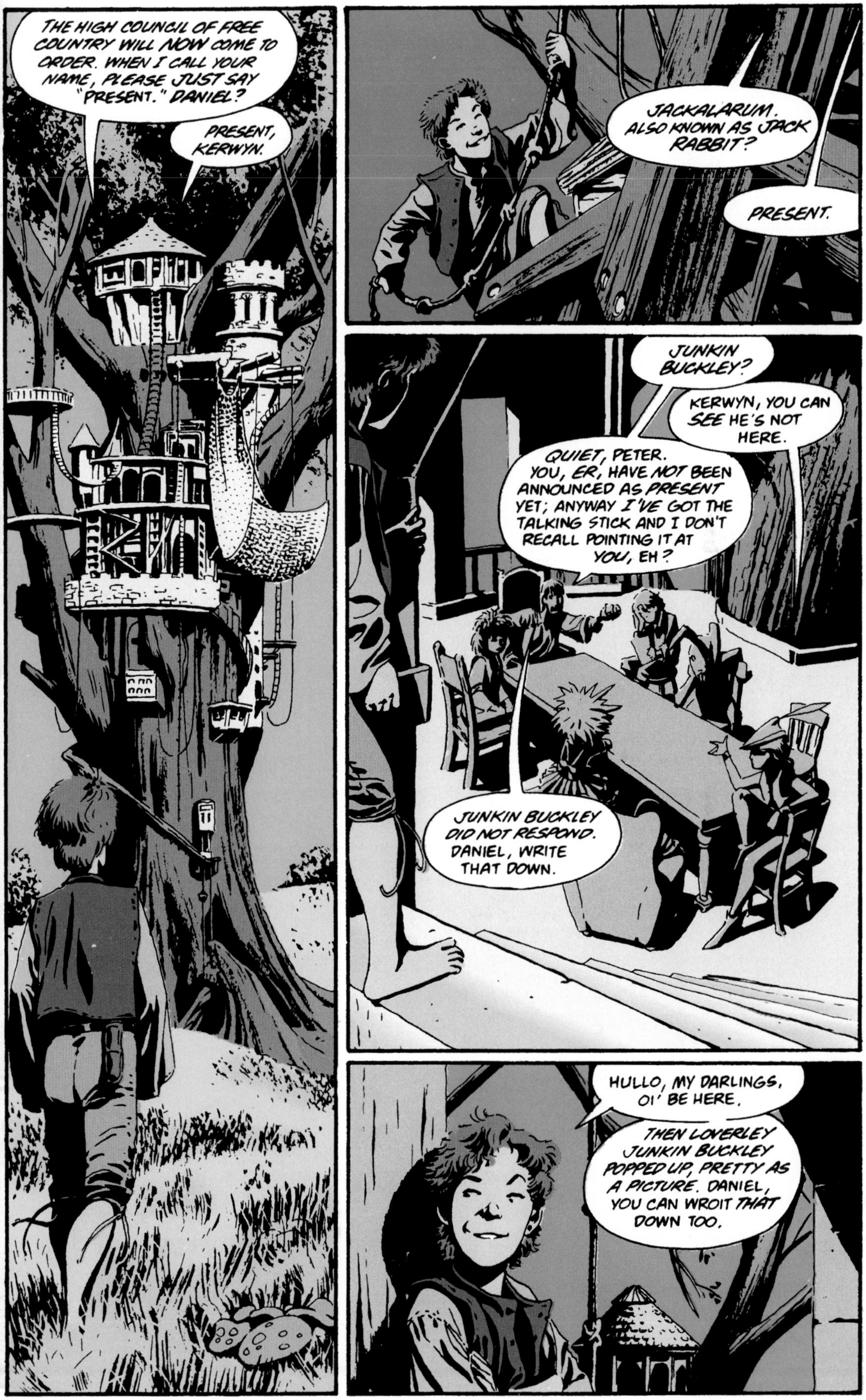
THE HIGH COUNCIL OF FREE COUNTRY WILL NOW COME TO ORDER. WHEN I CALL YOUR NAME, PLEASE JUST SAY "PRESENT." DANIEL?
PRESENT, KERWYN.
JACKALARUM. ALSO KNOWN AS JACK RABBIT?
PRESENT.
JUNKIN BUCKLEY?
KERWYN, YOU CAN SEE HE'S NOT HERE.
QUIET, PETER. YOU, ER, HAVE NOT BEEN ANNOUNCED AS PRESENT YET; ANYWAY I'VE GOT THE TALKING STICK AND I DON'T RECALL POINTING IT AT YOU, EH?
JUNKIN BUCKLEY DID NOT RESPOND. DANIEL, WRITE THAT DOWN.
HULLO, MY DARLINGS, OI' BE HERE.
THEN LOVERLEY JUNKIN BUCKLEY POPPED UP, PRETTY AS A PICTURE. DANIEL, YOU CAN WROIT THAT DOWN TOO.

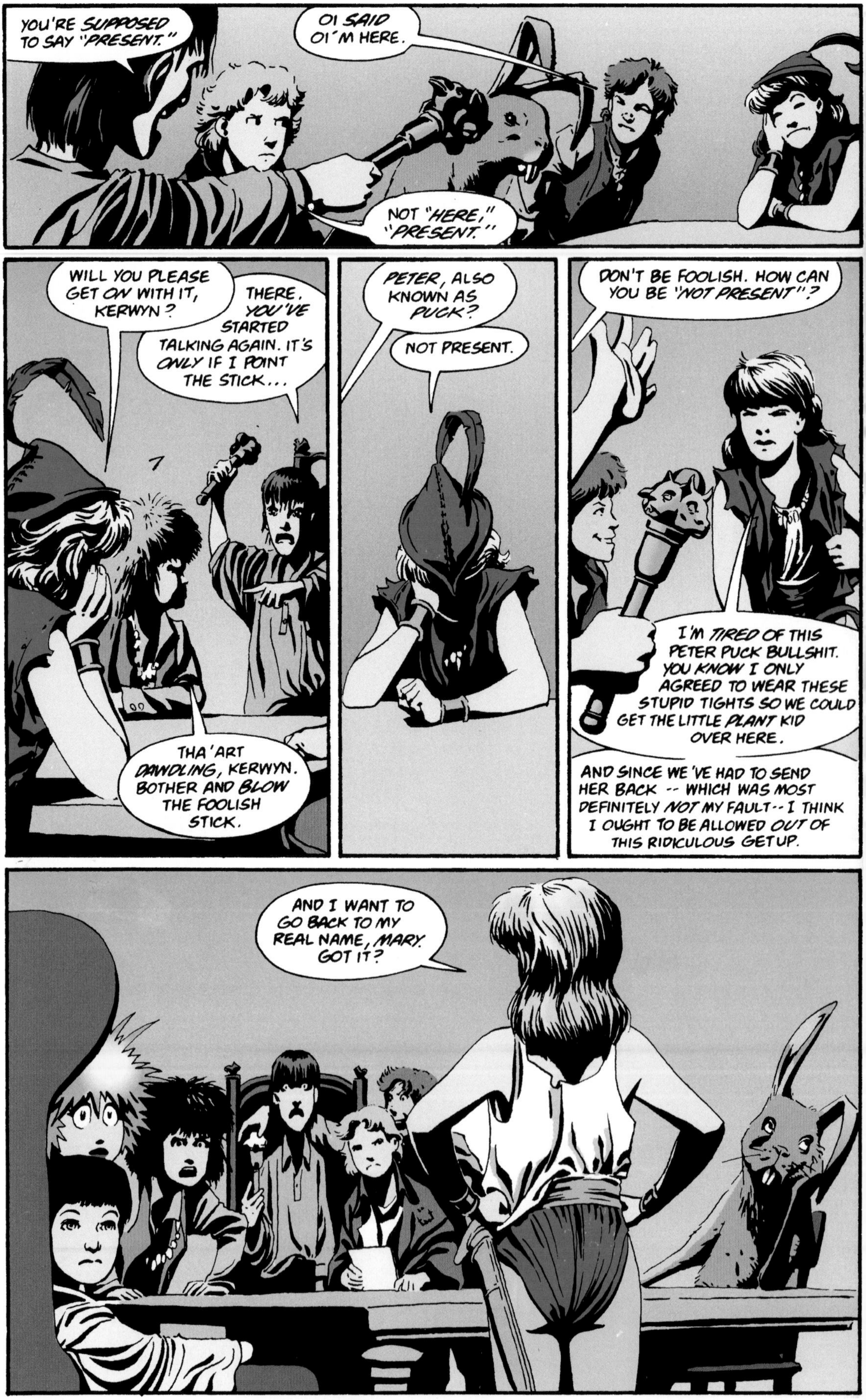
YOU'RE SUPPOSED TO SAY "PRESENT."
OI SAID OI'M HERE.
NOT "HERE," "PRESENT."
WILL YOU PLEASE GET ON WITH IT, KERWYN?
THERE. YOU'VE STARTED TALKING AGAIN. IT'S ONLY IF I POINT THE STICK...
THA'ART DAWDLING, KERWYN. BOTHER AND BLOW THE FOOLISH STICK.
PETER, ALSO KNOWN AS PUCK?
NOT PRESENT.
DON'T BE FOOLISH. HOW CAN YOU BE "NOT PRESENT"?
I'M TIRED OF THIS PETER PUCK BULLSHIT. YOU KNOW I ONLY AGREED TO WEAR THESE STUPID TIGHTS SO WE COULD GET THE LITTLE PLANT KID OVER HERE.
AND SINCE WE'VE HAD TO SEND HER BACK -- WHICH WAS MOST DEFINITELY NOT MY FAULT -- I THINK I OUGHT TO BE ALLOWED OUT OF THIS RIDICULOUS GETUP.
AND I WANT TO GO BACK TO MY REAL NAME, MARY. GOT IT?

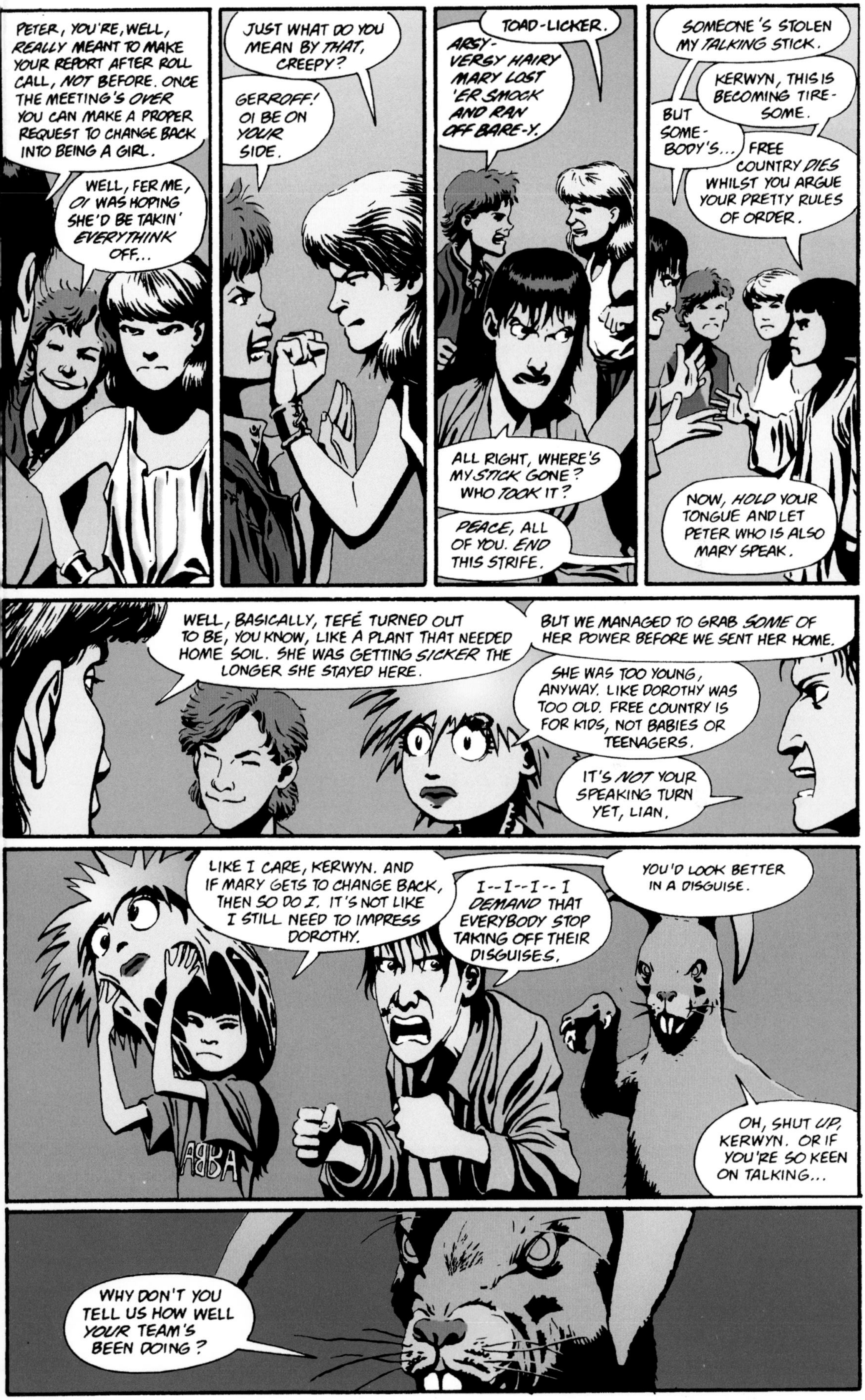
PETER, YOU'RE, WELL, REALLY MEANT TO MAKE YOUR REPORT AFTER ROLL CALL, NOT BEFORE. ONCE THE MEETING'S OVER YOU CAN MAKE A PROPER REQUEST TO CHANGE BACK INTO BEING A GIRL.
WELL, FER ME, OI WAS HOPING SHE'D BE TAKIN' EVERYTHINK OFF...
JUST WHAT DO YOU MEAN BY THAT, CREEPY?
GERROFF! OI BE ON YOUR SIDE.
TOAD-LICKER.
ARSY-VERSY HAIRY MARY LOST 'ER SMOCK AND RAN OFF BARE-Y.
ALL RIGHT, WHERE'S MY STICK GONE? WHO TOOK IT?
PEACE, ALL OF YOU. END THIS STRIFE.
SOMEONE'S STOLEN MY TALKING STICK.
KERWYN, THIS IS BECOMING TIRE-SOME.
BUT SOME-BODY'S...
FREE COUNTRY DIES WHILST YOU ARGUE YOUR PRETTY RULES OF ORDER.
NOW, HOLD YOUR TONGUE AND LET PETER WHO IS ALSO MARY SPEAK.
WELL, BASICALLY, TEFÉ TURNED OUT TO BE, YOU KNOW, LIKE A PLANT THAT NEEDED HOME SOIL. SHE WAS GETTING SICKER THE LONGER SHE STAYED HERE.
BUT WE MANAGED TO GRAB SOME OF HER POWER BEFORE WE SENT HER HOME.
SHE WAS TOO YOUNG, ANYWAY. LIKE DOROTHY WAS TOO OLD. FREE COUNTRY IS FOR KIDS, NOT BABIES OR TEENAGERS.
IT'S NOT YOUR SPEAKING TURN YET, LIAN.
LIKE I CARE, KERWYN. AND IF MARY GETS TO CHANGE BACK, THEN SO DO I. IT'S NOT LIKE I STILL NEED TO IMPRESS DOROTHY.
I--I--I--I DEMAND THAT EVERYBODY STOP TAKING OFF THEIR DISGUISES.
YOU'D LOOK BETTER IN A DISGUISE.
ABBA
OH, SHUT UP, KERWYN. OR IF YOU'RE SO KEEN ON TALKING...
WHY DON'T YOU TELL US HOW WELL YOUR TEAM'S BEEN DOING?

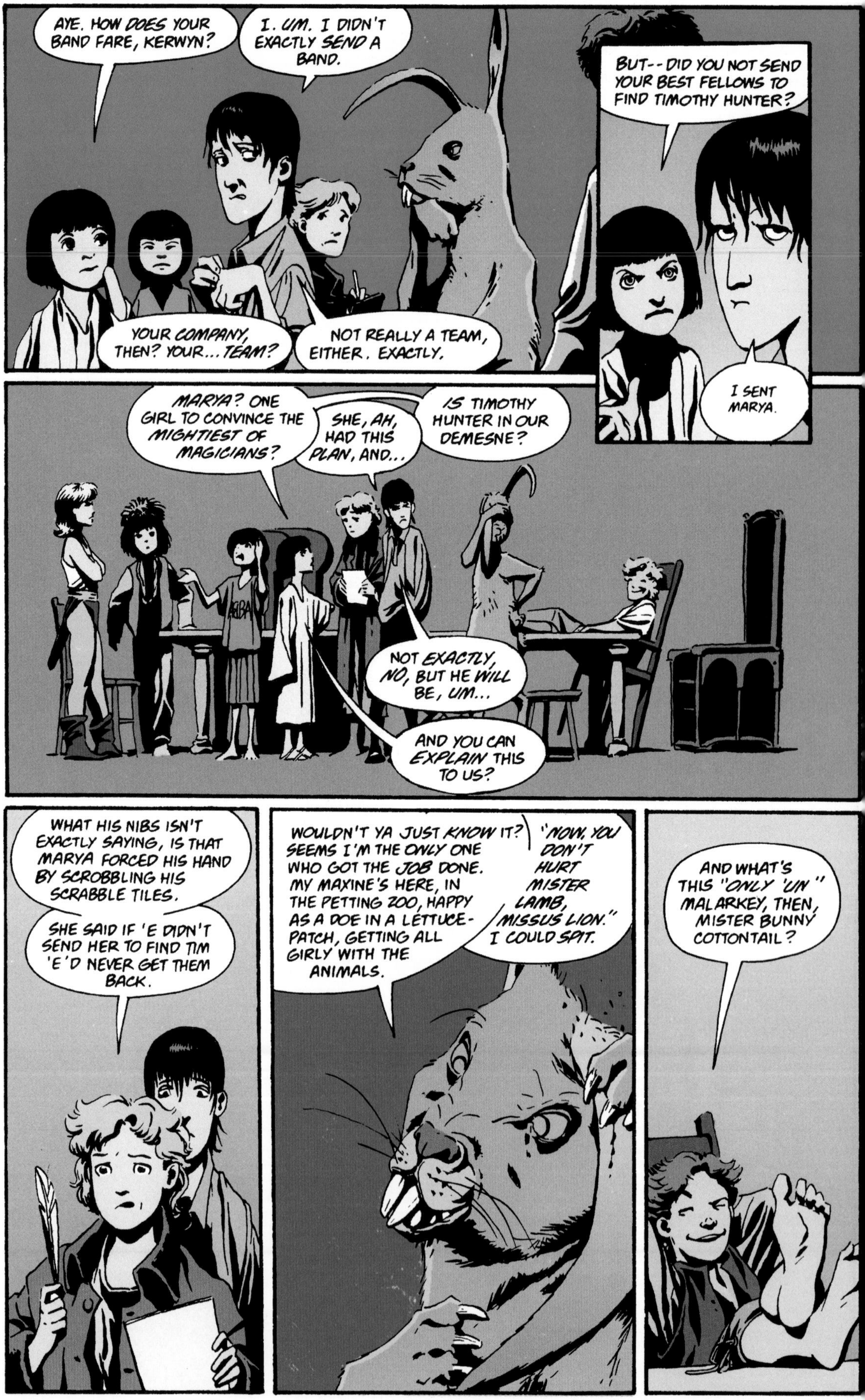

AYE. HOW DOES YOUR BAND FARE, KERWYN?
I. UM. I DIDN'T EXACTLY SEND A BAND.
YOUR COMPANY, THEN? YOUR... TEAM?
NOT REALLY A TEAM, EITHER. EXACTLY.
BUT-- DID YOU NOT SEND YOUR BEST FELLOWS TO FIND TIMOTHY HUNTER?
I SENT MARYA.
MARYA? ONE GIRL TO CONVINCE THE MIGHTIEST OF MAGICIANS?
SHE, AH, HAD THIS PLAN, AND...
IS TIMOTHY HUNTER IN OUR DEMESNE?
NOT EXACTLY, NO, BUT HE WILL BE, UM...
AND YOU CAN EXPLAIN THIS TO US?
WHAT HIS NIBS ISN'T EXACTLY SAYING, IS THAT MARYA FORCED HIS HAND BY SCROBBLING HIS SCRABBLE TILES.
SHE SAID IF 'E DIDN'T SEND HER TO FIND TIM 'E'D NEVER GET THEM BACK.
WOULDN'T YA JUST KNOW IT? SEEMS I'M THE ONLY ONE WHO GOT THE JOB DONE. MY MAXINE'S HERE, IN THE PETTING ZOO, HAPPY AS A DOE IN A LETTUCE-PATCH, GETTING ALL GIRLY WITH THE ANIMALS.
"NOW, YOU DON'T HURT MISTER LAMB, MISSUS LION." I COULD SPIT.
AND WHAT'S THIS "ONLY 'UN" MALARKEY, THEN, MISTER BUNNY COTTONTAIL?

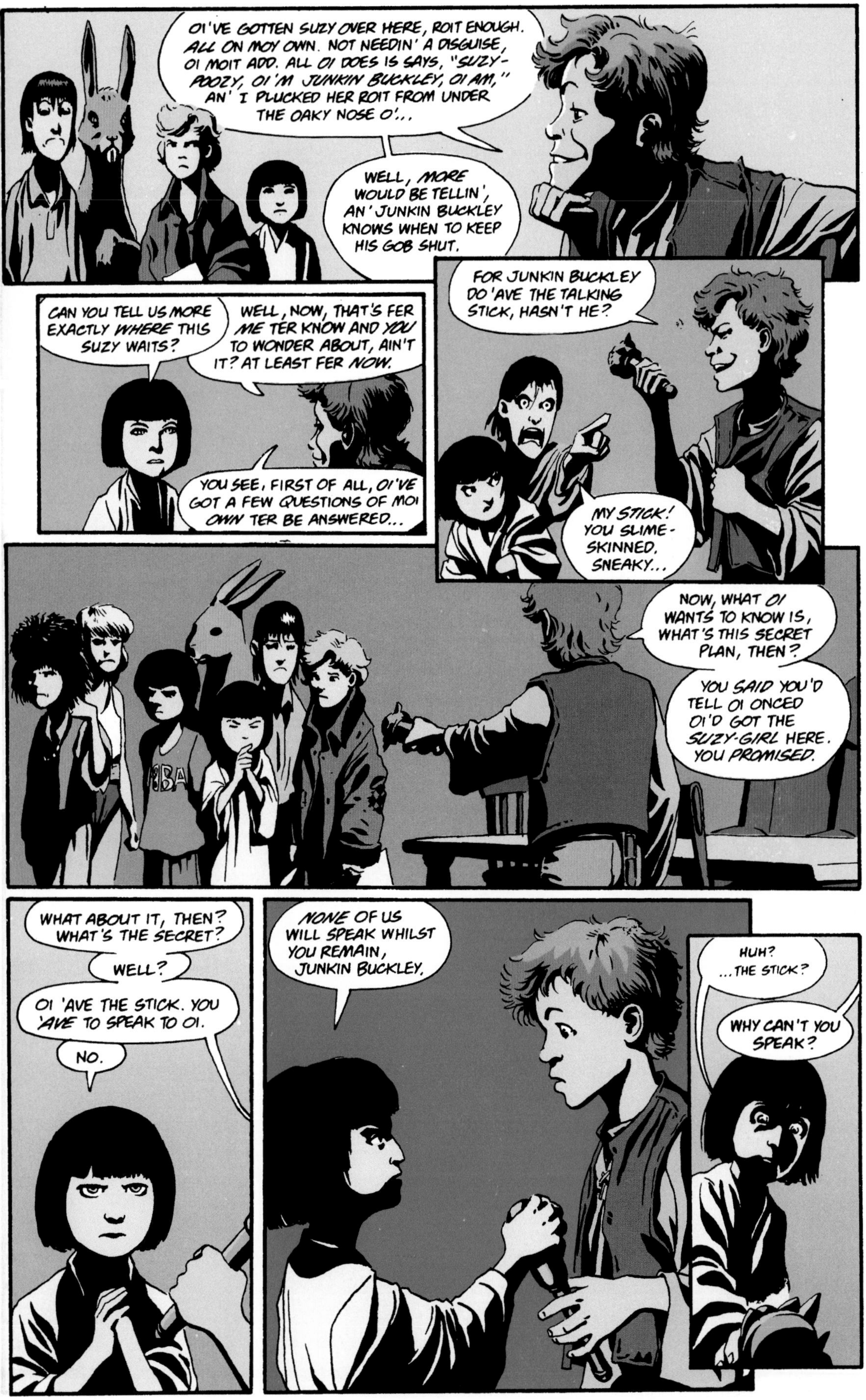
OI'VE GOTTEN SUZY OVER HERE, ROIT ENOUGH. ALL ON MOY OWN. NOT NEEDIN' A DISGUISE, OI MOIT ADD. ALL OI DOES IS SAYS, "SUZY-POOZY, OI'M JUNKIN BUCKLEY, OI AM," AN' I PLUCKED HER ROIT FROM UNDER THE OAKY NOSE O'...
WELL, MORE WOULD BE TELLIN', AN' JUNKIN BUCKLEY KNOWS WHEN TO KEEP HIS GOB SHUT.
CAN YOU TELL US MORE EXACTLY WHERE THIS SUZY WAITS?
WELL, NOW, THAT'S FER ME TER KNOW AND YOU TO WONDER ABOUT, AIN'T IT? AT LEAST FER NOW.
YOU SEE, FIRST OF ALL, OI'VE GOT A FEW QUESTIONS OF MOI OWN TER BE ANSWERED...
FOR JUNKIN BUCKLEY DO 'AVE THE TALKING STICK, HASN'T HE?
MY STICK! YOU SLIME-SKINNED, SNEAKY...
NOW, WHAT OI WANTS TO KNOW IS, WHAT'S THIS SECRET PLAN, THEN?
YOU SAID YOU'D TELL OI ONCED OI'D GOT THE SUZY-GIRL HERE. YOU PROMISED.
WHAT ABOUT IT, THEN? WHAT'S THE SECRET?
WELL?
OI 'AVE THE STICK. YOU 'AVE TO SPEAK TO OI.
NO.
NONE OF US WILL SPEAK WHILST YOU REMAIN, JUNKIN BUCKLEY.
HUH? ...THE STICK?
WHY CAN'T YOU SPEAK?

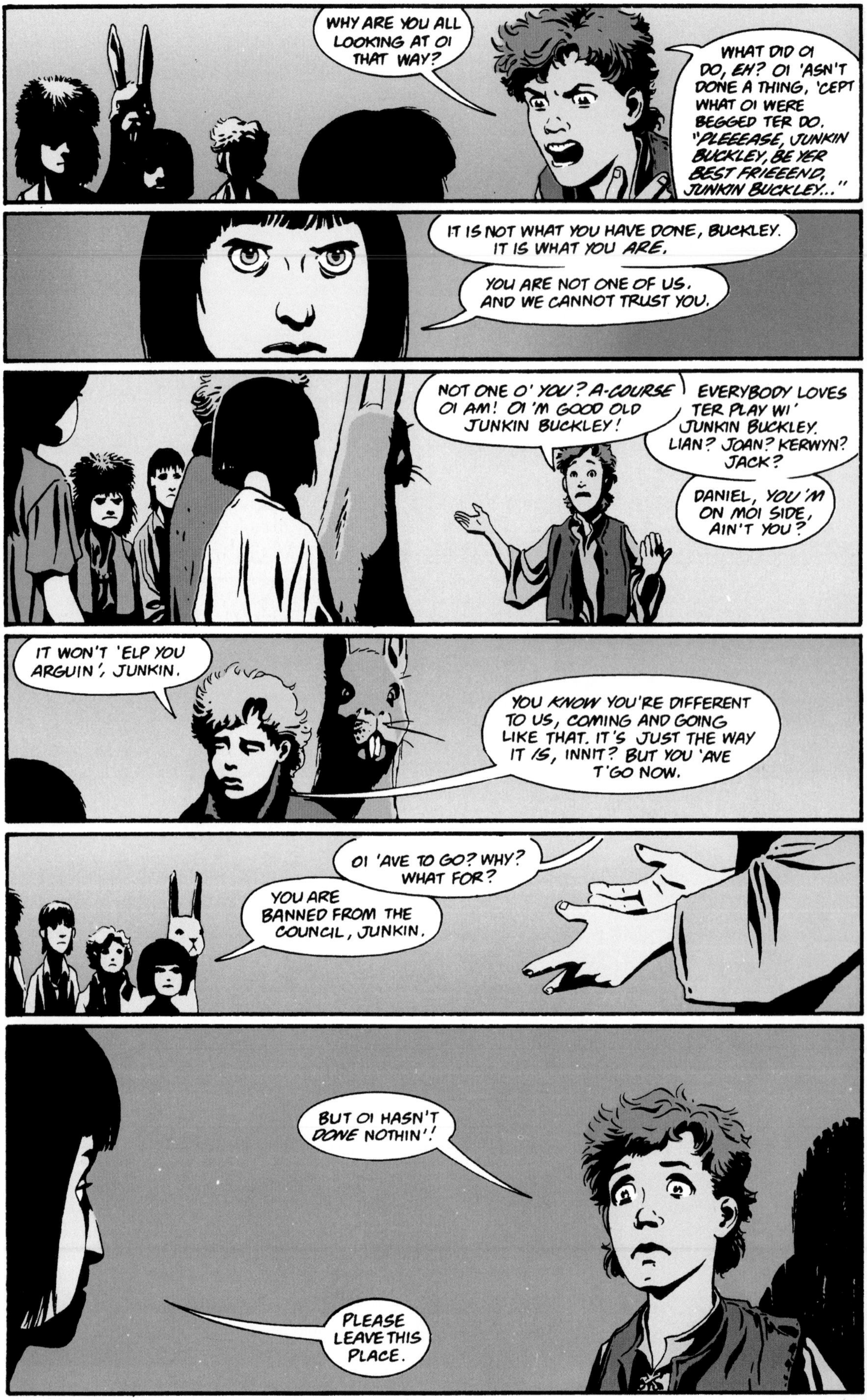
WHY ARE YOU ALL LOOKING AT OI THAT WAY?
WHAT DID OI DO, EH? OI 'ASN'T DONE A THING, 'CEPT WHAT OI WERE BEGGED TER DO. "PLEEEASE, JUNKIN BUCKLEY, BE YER BEST FRIEEEND, JUNKIN BUCKLEY..."
IT IS NOT WHAT YOU HAVE DONE, BUCKLEY. IT IS WHAT YOU ARE.
YOU ARE NOT ONE OF US. AND WE CANNOT TRUST YOU.
NOT ONE O' YOU? A-COURSE OI AM! OI 'M GOOD OLD JUNKIN BUCKLEY!
EVERYBODY LOVES TER PLAY WI' JUNKIN BUCKLEY. LIAN? JOAN? KERWYN? JACK?
DANIEL, YOU'M ON MOI SIDE, AIN'T YOU?
IT WON'T 'ELP YOU ARGUIN', JUNKIN.
YOU KNOW YOU'RE DIFFERENT TO US, COMING AND GOING LIKE THAT. IT'S JUST THE WAY IT IS, INNIT? BUT YOU 'AVE T'GO NOW.
OI 'AVE TO GO? WHY? WHAT FOR?
YOU ARE BANNED FROM THE COUNCIL, JUNKIN.
BUT OI HASN'T DONE NOTHIN'!
PLEASE LEAVE THIS PLACE.

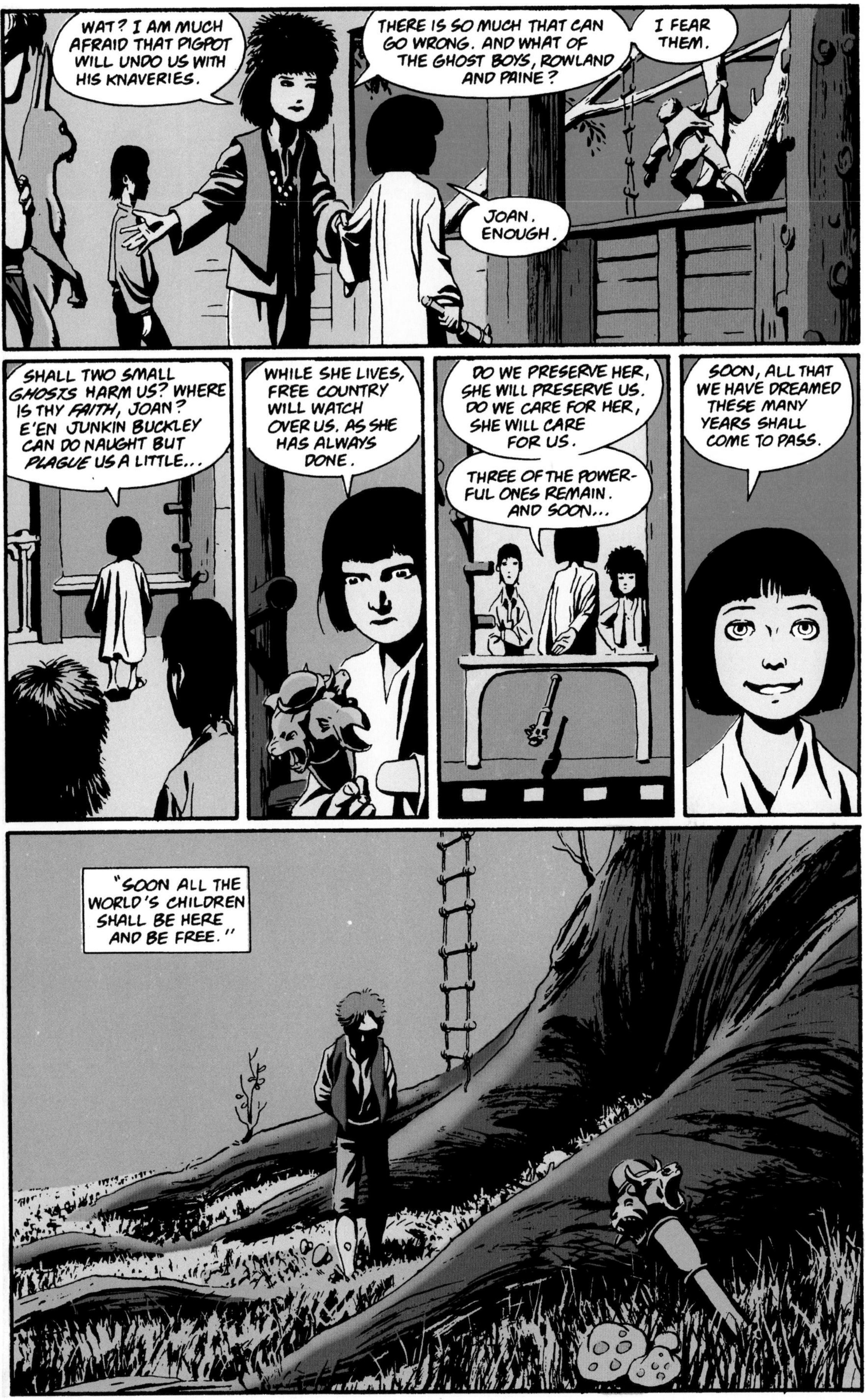
WAT? I AM MUCH AFRAID THAT PIGPOT WILL UNDO US WITH HIS KNAVERIES.
THERE IS SO MUCH THAT CAN GO WRONG. AND WHAT OF THE GHOST BOYS, ROWLAND AND PAINE?
I FEAR THEM.
JOAN. ENOUGH.
SHALL TWO SMALL GHOSTS HARM US? WHERE IS THY FAITH, JOAN? E'EN JUNKIN BUCKLEY CAN DO NAUGHT BUT PLAGUE US A LITTLE...
WHILE SHE LIVES, FREE COUNTRY WILL WATCH OVER US. AS SHE HAS ALWAYS DONE.
DO WE PRESERVE HER, SHE WILL PRESERVE US. DO WE CARE FOR HER, SHE WILL CARE FOR US.
THREE OF THE POWERFUL ONES REMAIN. AND SOON...
SOON, ALL THAT WE HAVE DREAMED THESE MANY YEARS SHALL COME TO PASS.
"SOON ALL THE WORLD'S CHILDREN SHALL BE HERE AND BE FREE."

Chapter Four: In Which Timothy Hunter Is Formally Welcomed to Free Country

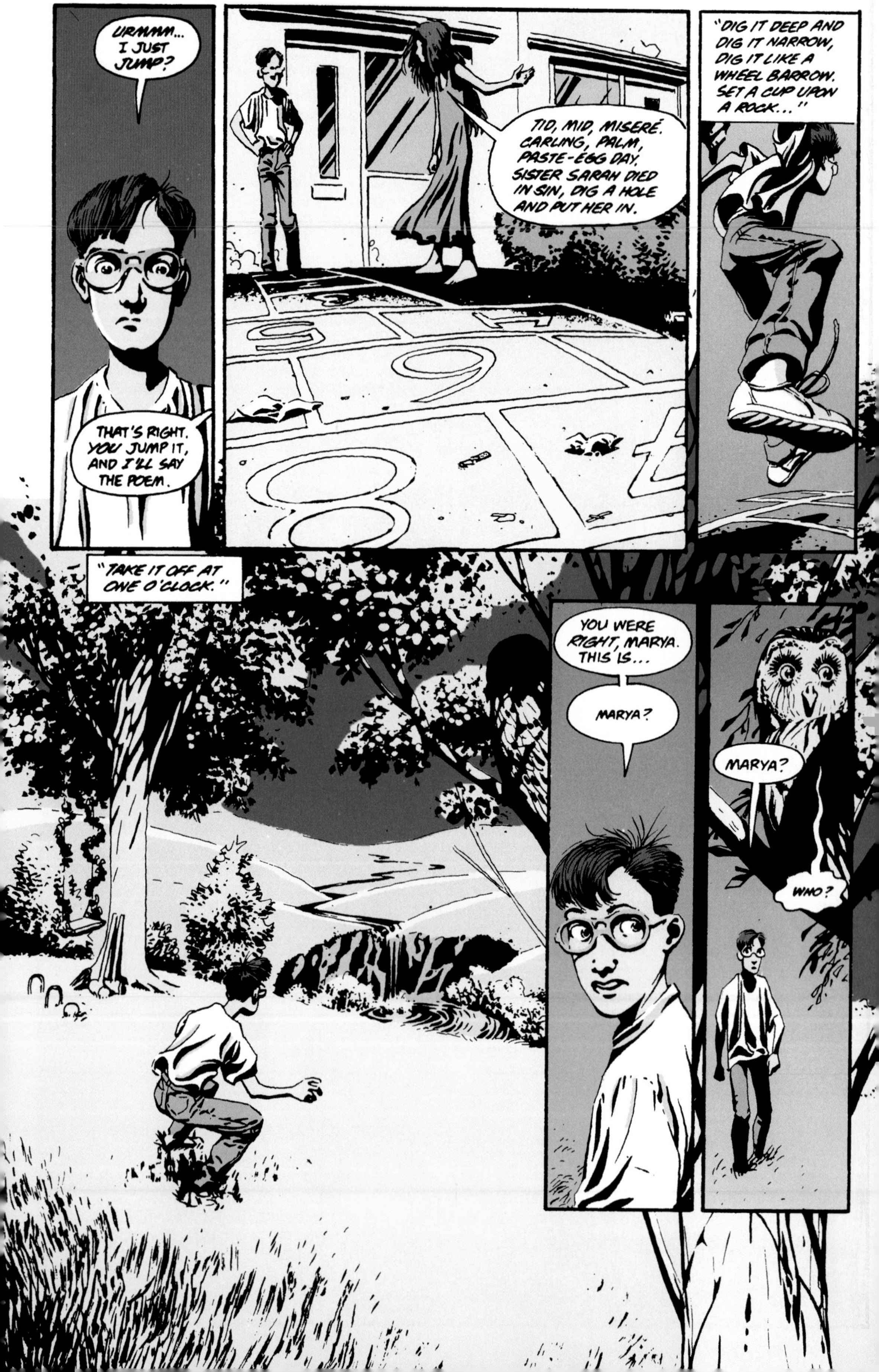
URMMM... I JUST JUMP?
THAT'S RIGHT. YOU JUMP IT, AND I'LL SAY THE POEM.
TID, MID, MISERÉ. CARLING, PALM, PASTE-EGG DAY. SISTER SARAH DIED IN SIN, DIG A HOLE AND PUT HER IN.
"DIG IT DEEP AND DIG IT NARROW, DIG IT LIKE A WHEEL BARROW. SET A CUP UPON A ROCK..."
"TAKE IT OFF AT ONE O'CLOCK."
YOU WERE RIGHT, MARYA. THIS IS...
MARYA?
MARYA?
WHO?

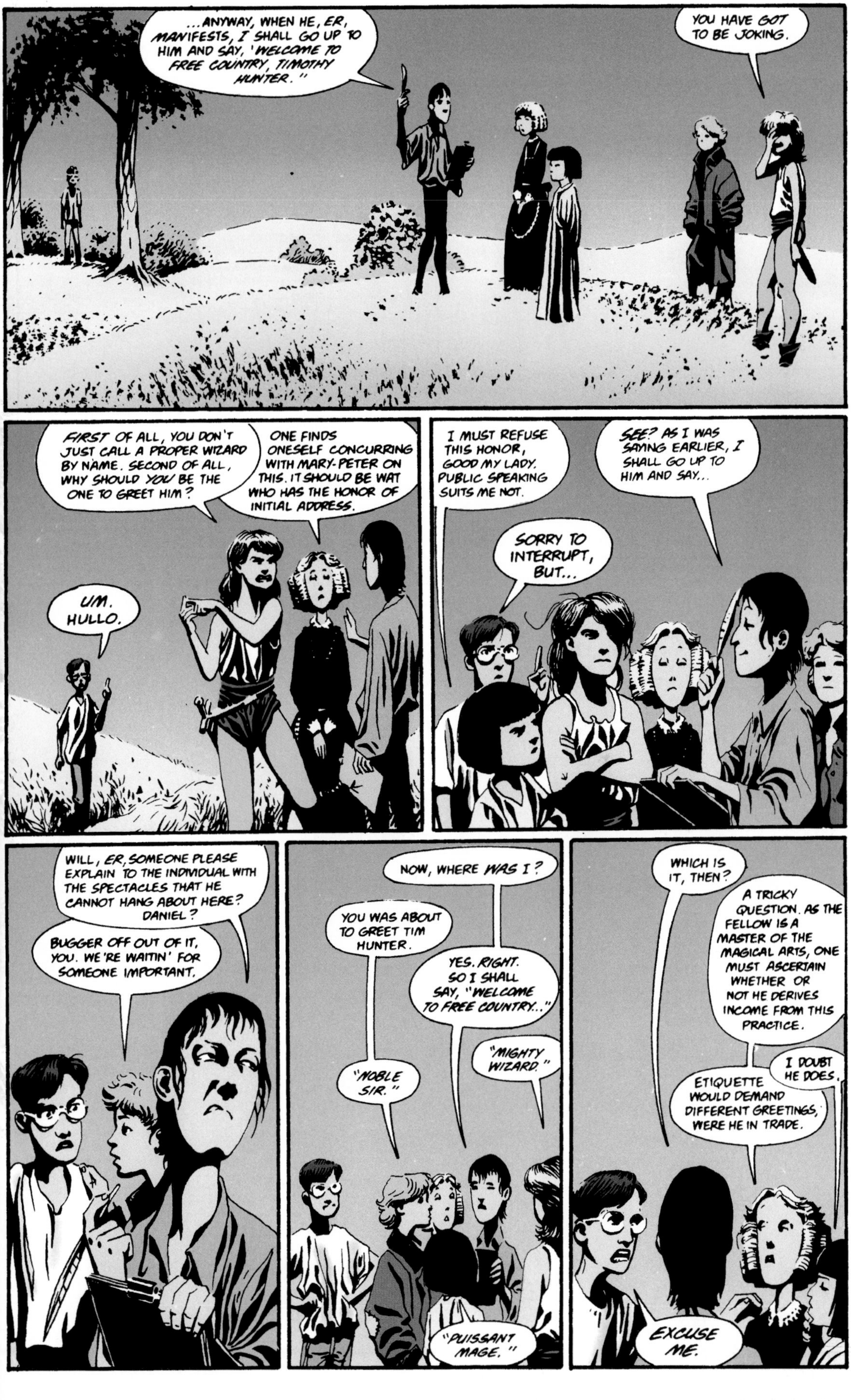
...ANYWAY, WHEN HE, ER, MANIFESTS, I SHALL GO UP TO HIM AND SAY, 'WELCOME TO FREE COUNTRY, TIMOTHY HUNTER.'
YOU HAVE GOT TO BE JOKING.
FIRST OF ALL, YOU DON'T JUST CALL A PROPER WIZARD BY NAME. SECOND OF ALL, WHY SHOULD YOU BE THE ONE TO GREET HIM?
ONE FINDS ONESELF CONCURRING WITH MARY-PETER ON THIS. IT SHOULD BE WAT WHO HAS THE HONOR OF INITIAL ADDRESS.
UM. HULLO.
I MUST REFUSE THIS HONOR, GOOD MY LADY. PUBLIC SPEAKING SUITS ME NOT.
SEE? AS I WAS SAYING EARLIER, I SHALL GO UP TO HIM AND SAY...
SORRY TO INTERRUPT, BUT...
WILL, ER, SOMEONE PLEASE EXPLAIN TO THE INDIVIDUAL WITH THE SPECTACLES THAT HE CANNOT HANG ABOUT HERE? DANIEL?
BUGGER OFF OUT OF IT, YOU. WE'RE WAITIN' FOR SOMEONE IMPORTANT.
NOW, WHERE WAS I?
YOU WAS ABOUT TO GREET TIM HUNTER.
YES. RIGHT. SO I SHALL SAY, "WELCOME TO FREE COUNTRY..."
"NOBLE SIR."
"MIGHTY WIZARD."
"PUISSANT MAGE."
WHICH IS IT, THEN?
A TRICKY QUESTION. AS THE FELLOW IS A MASTER OF THE MAGICAL ARTS, ONE MUST ASCERTAIN WHETHER OR NOT HE DERIVES INCOME FROM THIS PRACTICE.
ETIQUETTE WOULD DEMAND DIFFERENT GREETINGS, WERE HE IN TRADE.
I DOUBT HE DOES.
EXCUSE ME.

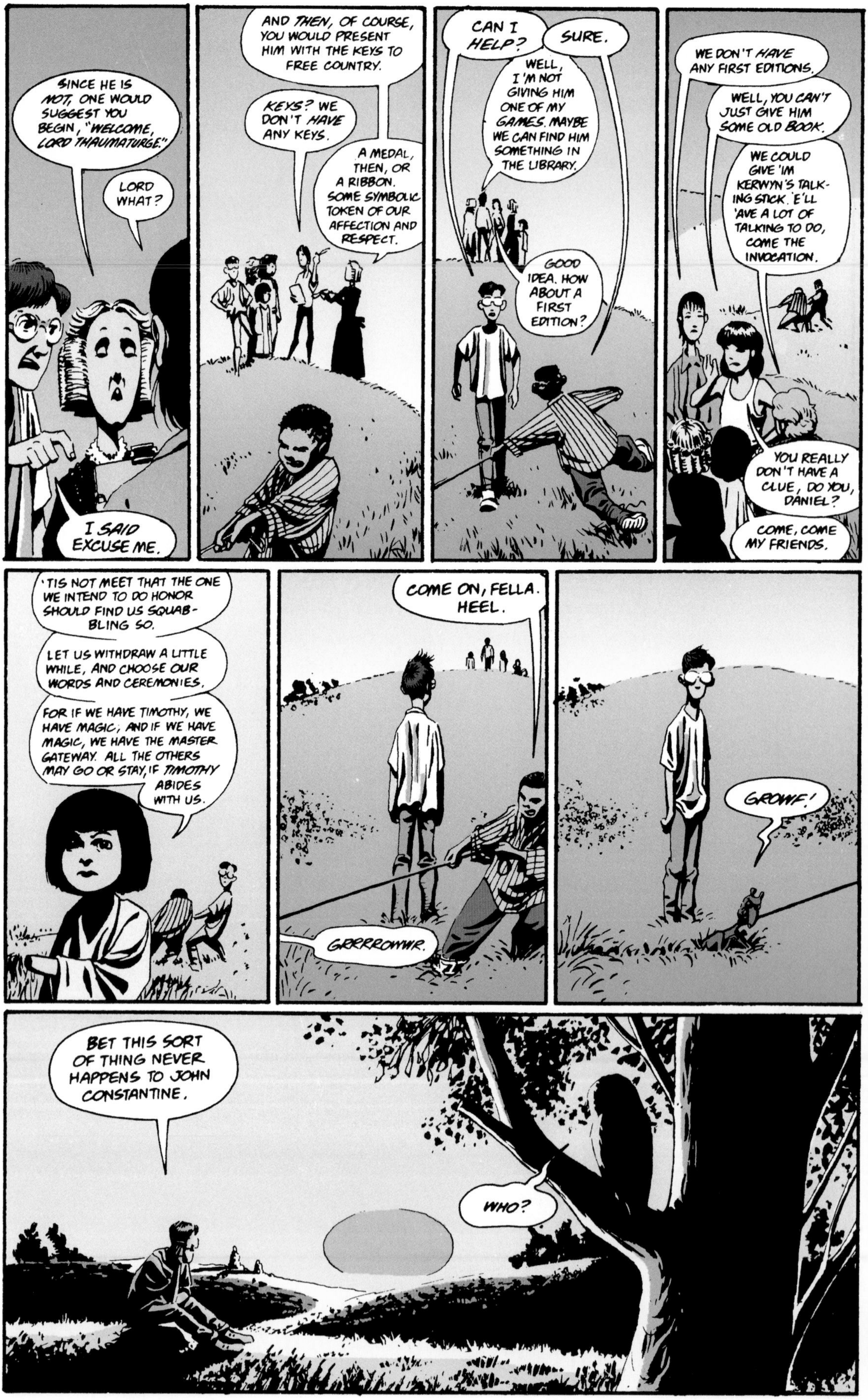

SINCE HE IS NOT, ONE WOULD SUGGEST YOU BEGIN, "WELCOME, LORD THAUMATURGE."
LORD WHAT?
I SAID EXCUSE ME.
AND THEN, OF COURSE, YOU WOULD PRESENT HIM WITH THE KEYS TO FREE COUNTRY.
KEYS? WE DON'T HAVE ANY KEYS.
A MEDAL, THEN, OR A RIBBON. SOME SYMBOLIC TOKEN OF OUR AFFECTION AND RESPECT.
CAN I HELP?
SURE.
WELL, I'M NOT GIVING HIM ONE OF MY GAMES. MAYBE WE CAN FIND HIM SOMETHING IN THE LIBRARY.
GOOD IDEA. HOW ABOUT A FIRST EDITION?
WE DON'T HAVE ANY FIRST EDITIONS.
WELL, YOU CAN'T JUST GIVE HIM SOME OLD BOOK.
WE COULD GIVE 'IM KERWYN'S TALKING STICK. 'E'LL 'AVE A LOT OF TALKING TO DO, COME THE INVOCATION.
YOU REALLY DON'T HAVE A CLUE, DO YOU, DANIEL?
COME, COME MY FRIENDS.
'TIS NOT MEET THAT THE ONE WE INTEND TO DO HONOR SHOULD FIND US SQUABBLING SO.
LET US WITHDRAW A LITTLE WHILE, AND CHOOSE OUR WORDS AND CEREMONIES.
FOR IF WE HAVE TIMOTHY, WE HAVE MAGIC; AND IF WE HAVE MAGIC, WE HAVE THE MASTER GATEWAY. ALL THE OTHERS MAY GO OR STAY, IF TIMOTHY ABIDES WITH US.
COME ON, FELLA. HEEL.
GRRRROWWR.
GROWF!
BET THIS SORT OF THING NEVER HAPPENS TO JOHN CONSTANTINE.
WHO?

Chapter Five: In Which We Visit the Beach

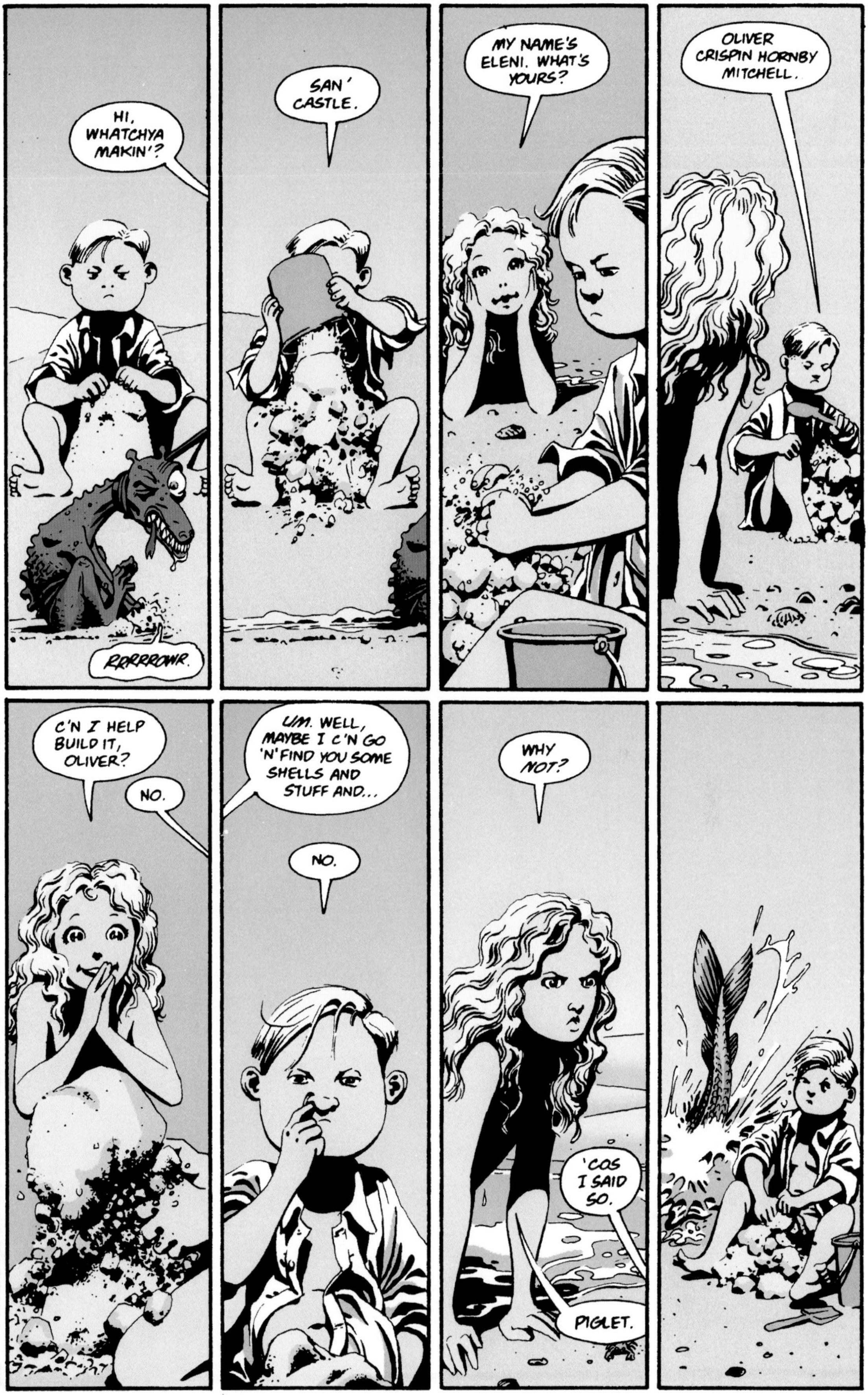
HI, WHATCHYA MAKIN'?
RRRRROWR.
SAN' CASTLE.
MY NAME'S ELENI. WHAT'S YOURS?
OLIVER CRISPIN HORNBY MITCHELL.
C'N I HELP BUILD IT, OLIVER?
NO.
UM. WELL, MAYBE I C'N GO 'N' FIND YOU SOME SHELLS AND STUFF AND...
NO.
WHY NOT?
'COS I SAID SO.
PIGLET.

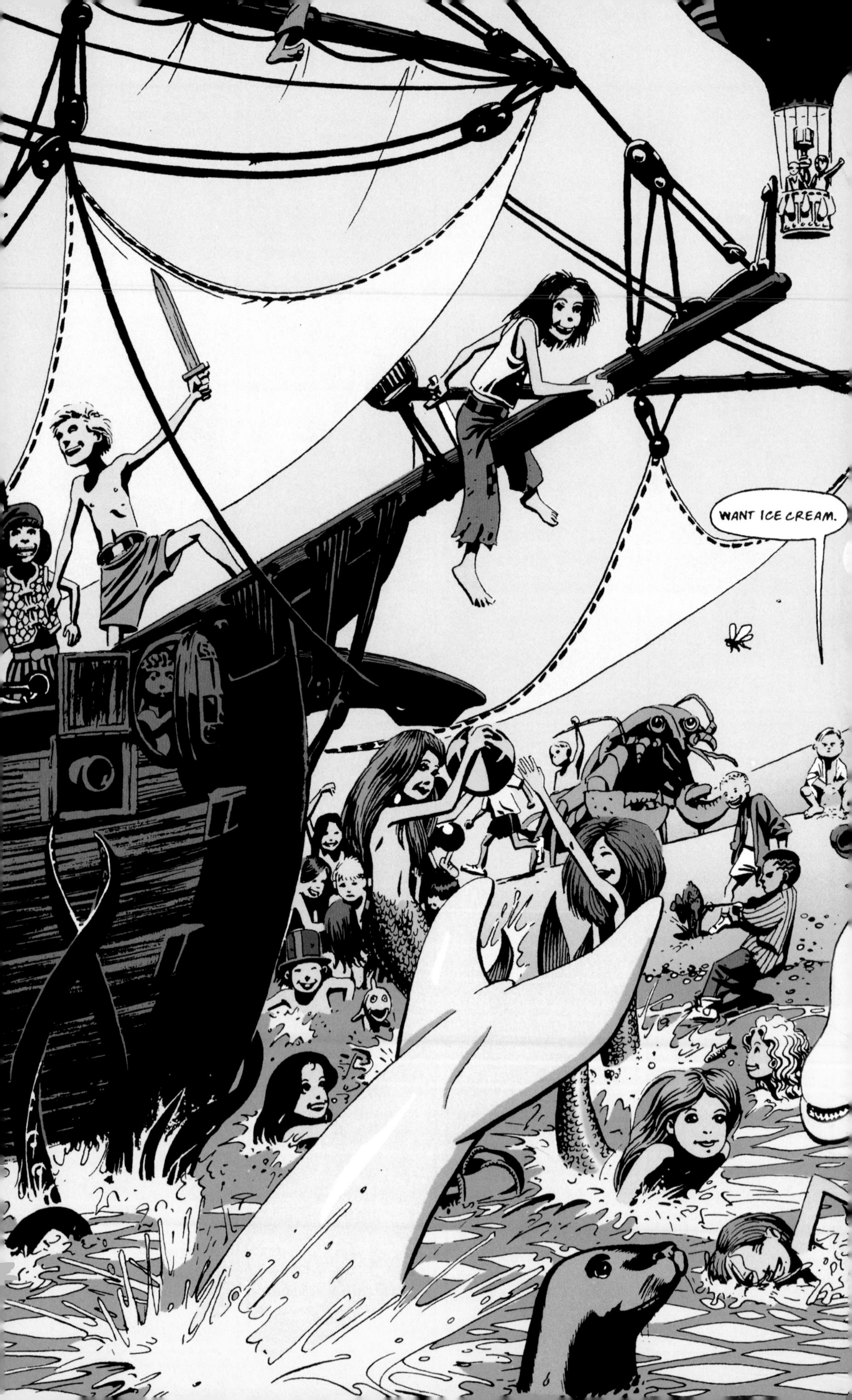
WANT ICE CREAM.

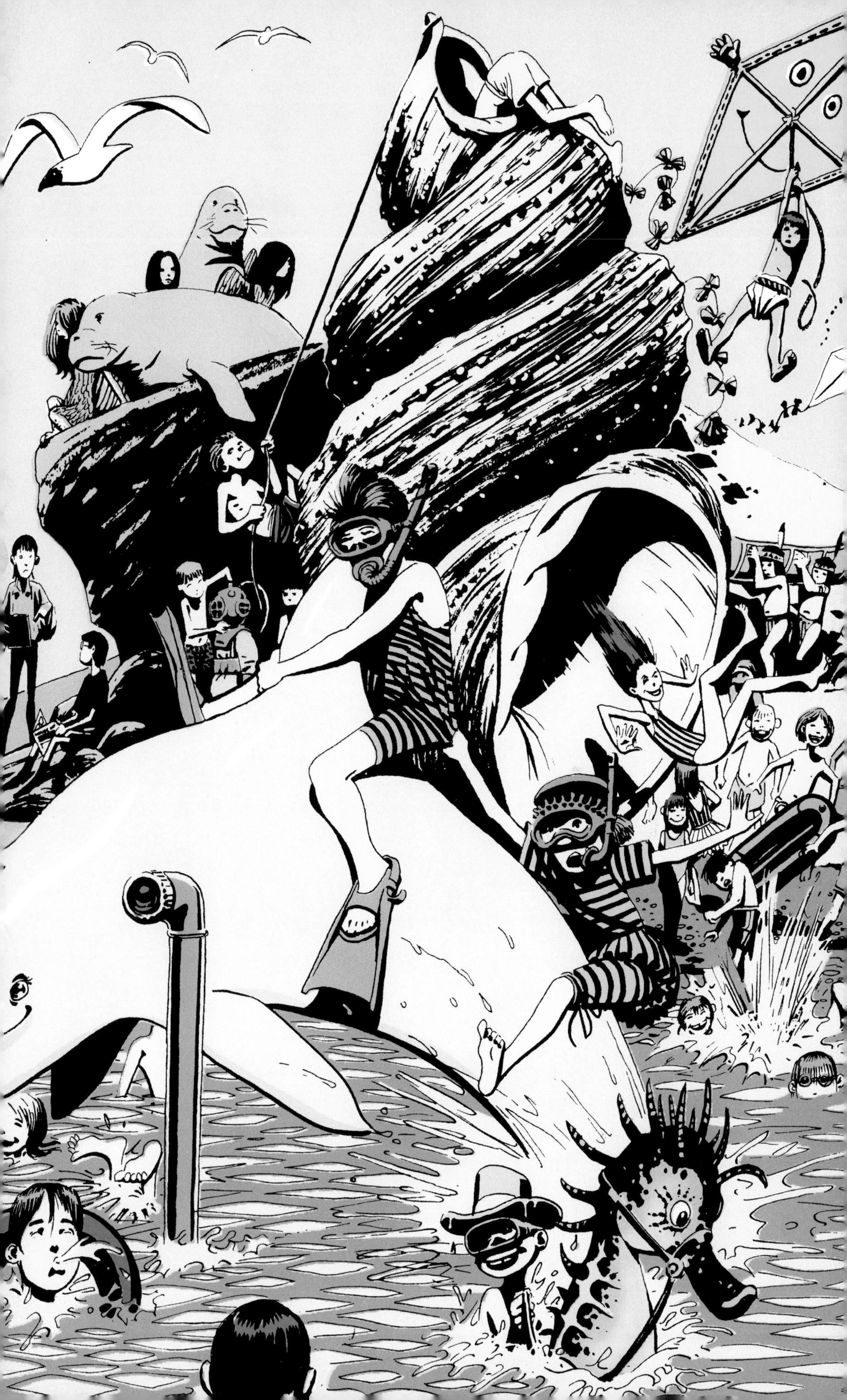

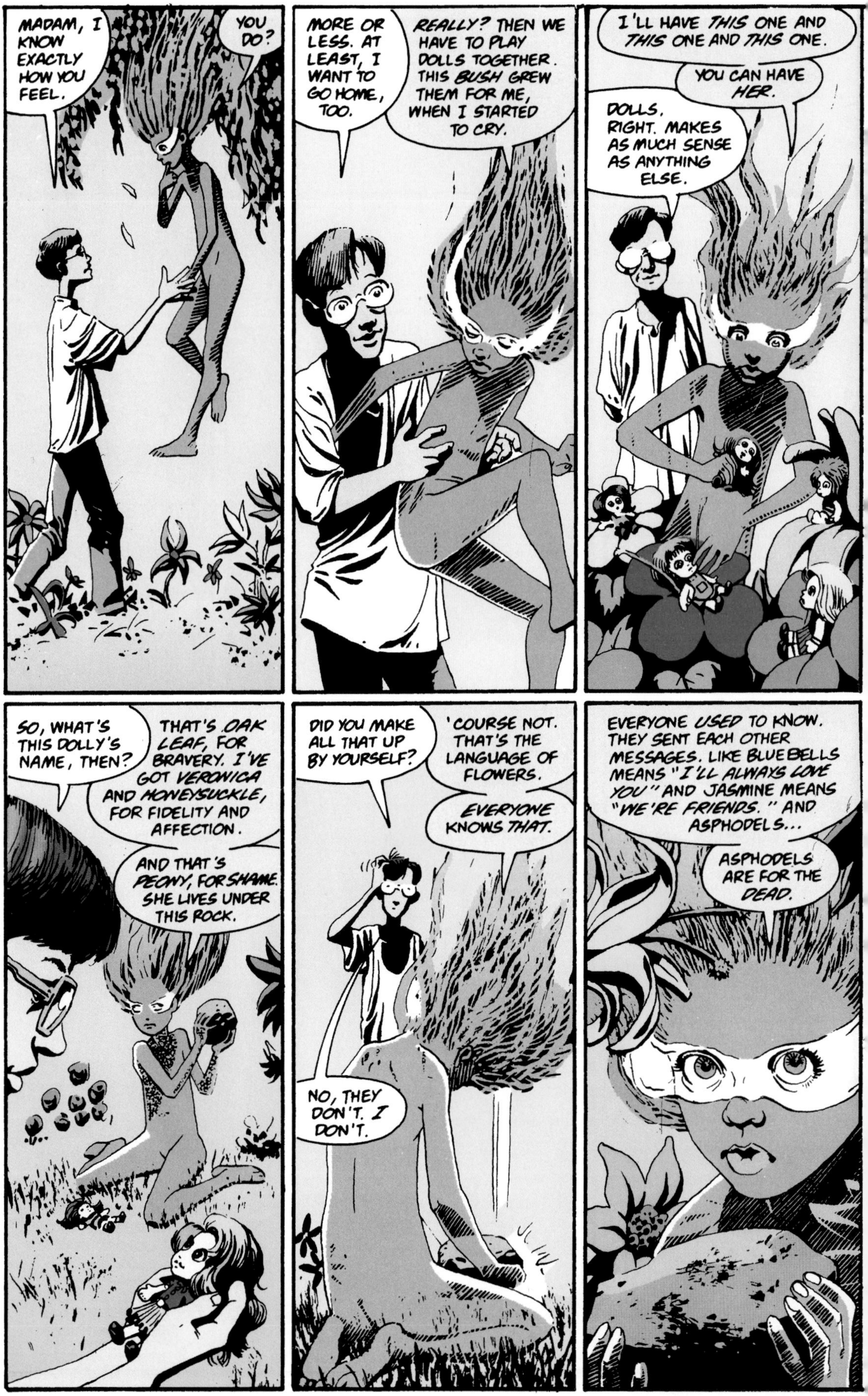
MADAM, I KNOW EXACTLY HOW YOU FEEL.
YOU DO?
MORE OR LESS. AT LEAST, I WANT TO GO HOME, TOO.
REALLY? THEN WE HAVE TO PLAY DOLLS TOGETHER. THIS *BUSH* GREW THEM FOR ME, WHEN I STARTED TO CRY.
I'LL HAVE *THIS* ONE AND *THIS* ONE AND *THIS* ONE.
YOU CAN HAVE *HER*.
DOLLS. RIGHT. MAKES AS MUCH SENSE AS ANYTHING ELSE.
SO, WHAT'S THIS DOLLY'S NAME, THEN?
THAT'S *OAK LEAF*, FOR BRAVERY. *I'VE* GOT *VERONICA* AND *HONEYSUCKLE*, FOR FIDELITY AND AFFECTION.
AND THAT'S *PEONY*, FOR *SHAME*. SHE LIVES UNDER THIS ROCK.
DID YOU MAKE ALL THAT UP BY YOURSELF?
'COURSE NOT. THAT'S THE LANGUAGE OF FLOWERS.
EVERYONE KNOWS *THAT*.
NO, THEY DON'T. *I* DON'T.
EVERYONE *USED* TO KNOW. THEY SENT EACH OTHER MESSAGES. LIKE BLUEBELLS MEANS "*I'LL ALWAYS LOVE YOU*" AND JASMINE MEANS "*WE'RE FRIENDS.*" AND ASPHODELS...
ASPHODELS ARE FOR THE *DEAD*.

Chapter Six: In Which We Learn Something of the Language of Flowers

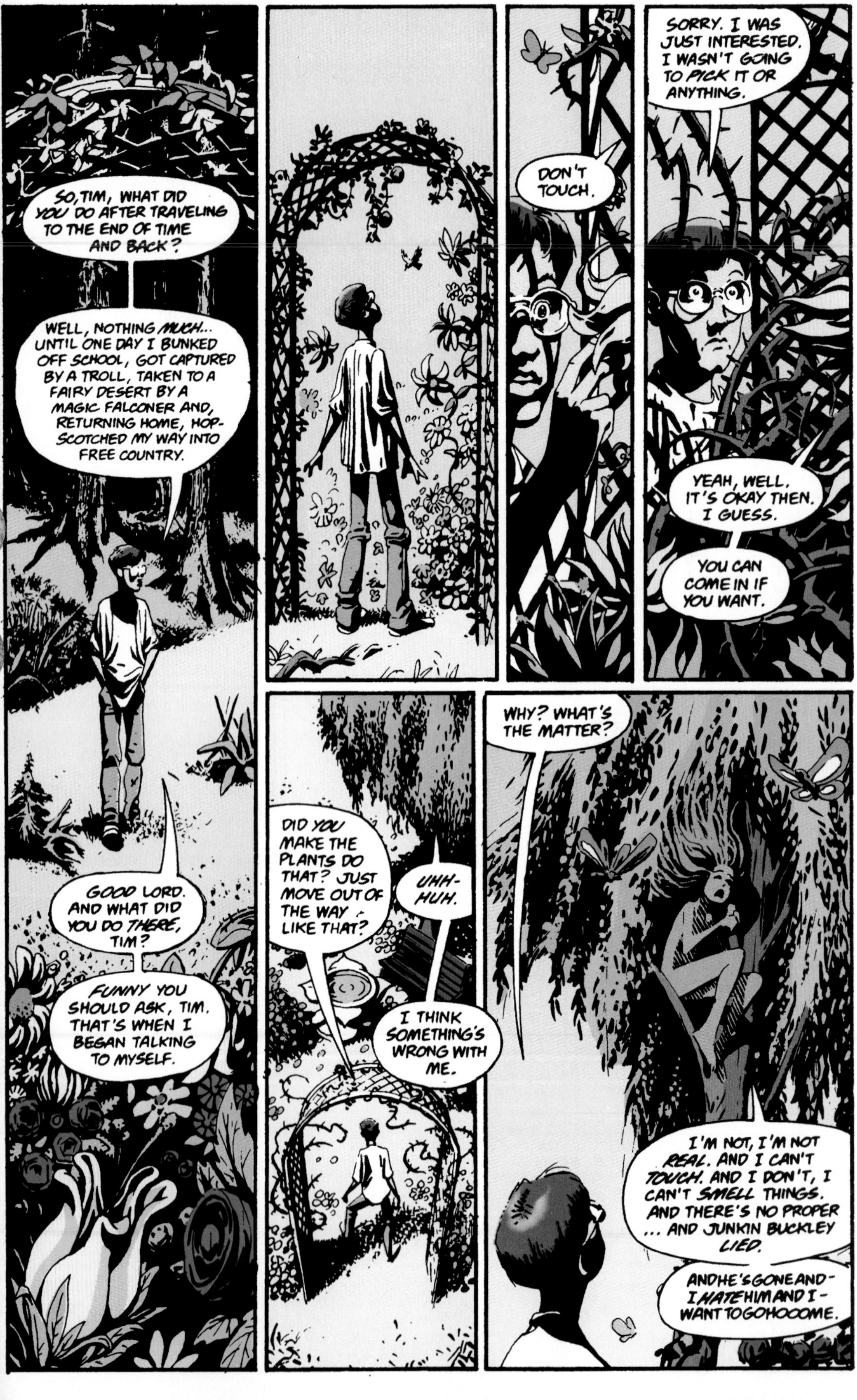

SO, TIM, WHAT DID YOU DO AFTER TRAVELING TO THE END OF TIME AND BACK?
WELL, NOTHING MUCH... UNTIL ONE DAY I BUNKED OFF SCHOOL, GOT CAPTURED BY A TROLL, TAKEN TO A FAIRY DESERT BY A MAGIC FALCONER AND, RETURNING HOME, HOP-SCOTCHED MY WAY INTO FREE COUNTRY.
GOOD LORD. AND WHAT DID YOU DO THERE, TIM?
FUNNY YOU SHOULD ASK, TIM. THAT'S WHEN I BEGAN TALKING TO MYSELF.
DON'T TOUCH.
SORRY. I WAS JUST INTERESTED. I WASN'T GOING TO PICK IT OR ANYTHING.
YEAH, WELL, IT'S OKAY THEN. I GUESS.
YOU CAN COME IN IF YOU WANT.
DID YOU MAKE THE PLANTS DO THAT? JUST MOVE OUT OF THE WAY LIKE THAT?
UHH-HUH.
I THINK SOMETHING'S WRONG WITH ME.
WHY? WHAT'S THE MATTER?
I'M NOT, I'M NOT REAL. AND I CAN'T TOUCH. AND I DON'T, I CAN'T SMELL THINGS. AND THERE'S NO PROPER ... AND JUNKIN BUCKLEY LIED.
ANDHE'SGONEAND- I HATEHIMAND I- WANTTOGOHOOOME.

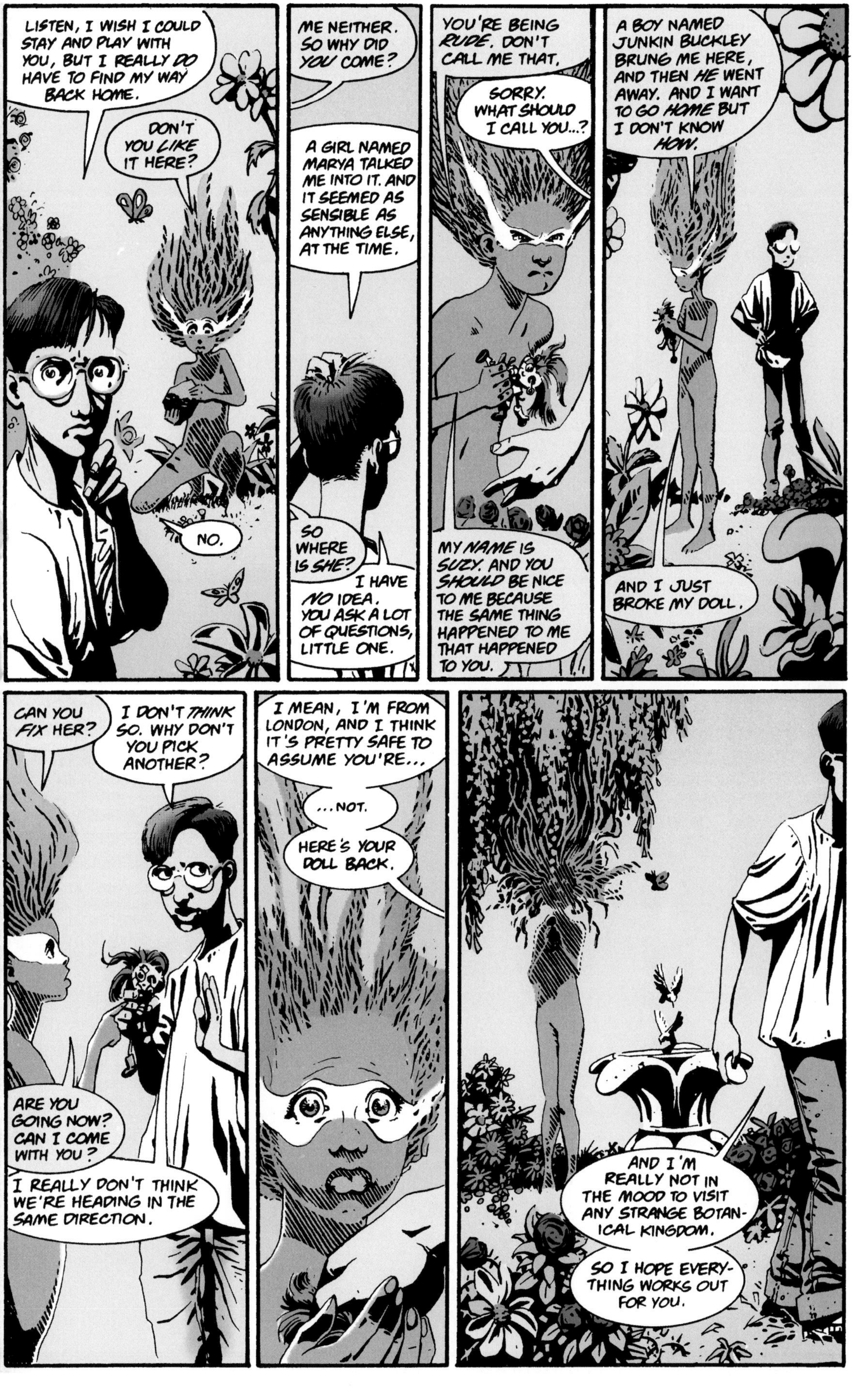
LISTEN, I WISH I COULD STAY AND PLAY WITH YOU, BUT I REALLY DO HAVE TO FIND MY WAY BACK HOME.
DON'T YOU LIKE IT HERE?
NO.
ME NEITHER. SO WHY DID YOU COME?
A GIRL NAMED MARYA TALKED ME INTO IT. AND IT SEEMED AS SENSIBLE AS ANYTHING ELSE, AT THE TIME.
SO WHERE IS SHE?
I HAVE NO IDEA. YOU ASK A LOT OF QUESTIONS, LITTLE ONE.
YOU'RE BEING RUDE. DON'T CALL ME THAT.
SORRY. WHAT SHOULD I CALL YOU...?
MY NAME IS SUZY. AND YOU SHOULD BE NICE TO ME BECAUSE THE SAME THING HAPPENED TO ME THAT HAPPENED TO YOU.
A BOY NAMED JUNKIN BUCKLEY BRUNG ME HERE, AND THEN HE WENT AWAY. AND I WANT TO GO HOME BUT I DON'T KNOW HOW.
AND I JUST BROKE MY DOLL.
CAN YOU FIX HER?
I DON'T THINK SO. WHY DON'T YOU PICK ANOTHER?
ARE YOU GOING NOW? CAN I COME WITH YOU?
I REALLY DON'T THINK WE'RE HEADING IN THE SAME DIRECTION.
I MEAN, I'M FROM LONDON, AND I THINK IT'S PRETTY SAFE TO ASSUME YOU'RE...
...NOT.
HERE'S YOUR DOLL BACK.
AND I'M REALLY NOT IN THE MOOD TO VISIT ANY STRANGE BOTANICAL KINGDOM.
SO I HOPE EVERYTHING WORKS OUT FOR YOU.

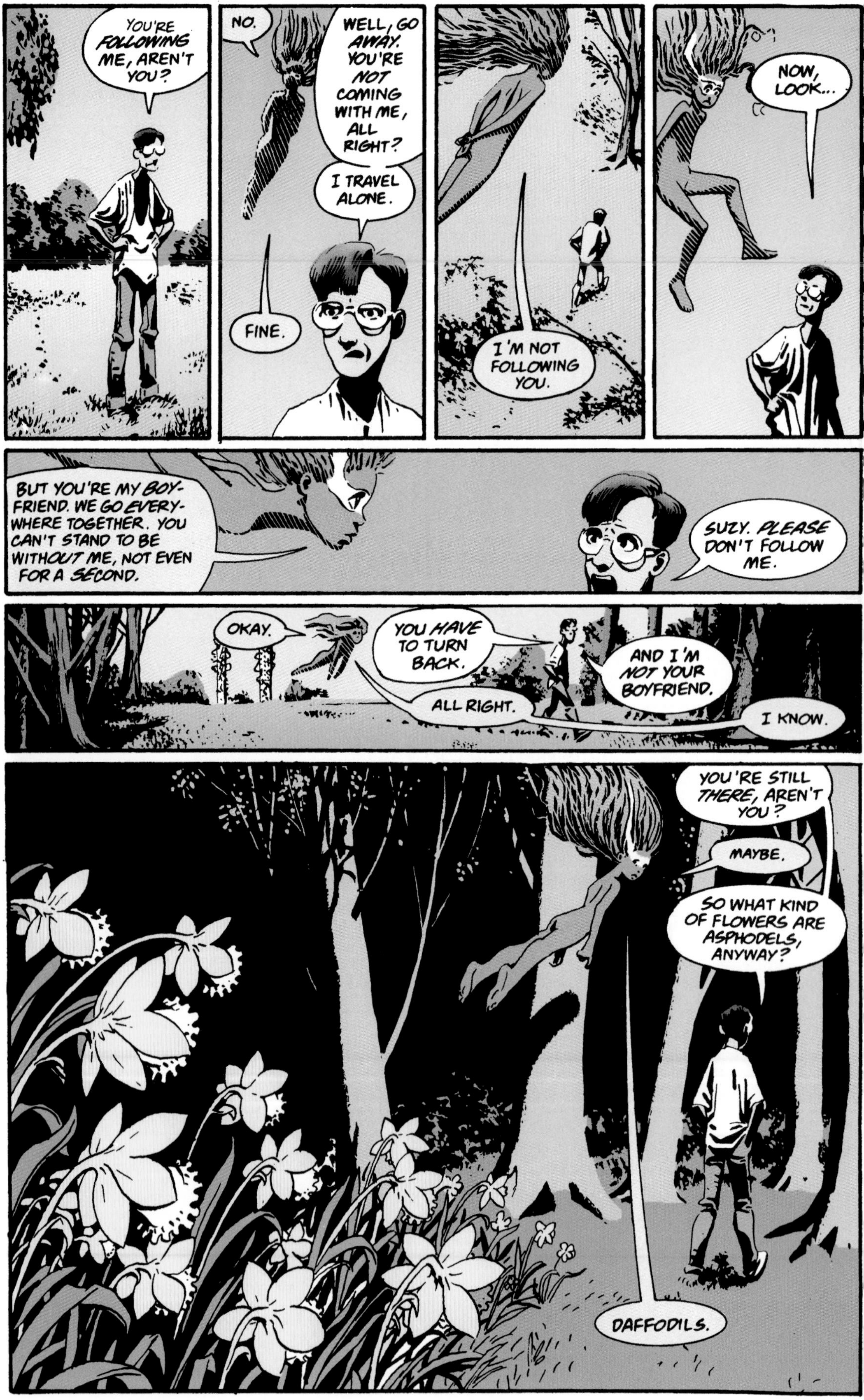
YOU'RE FOLLOWING ME, AREN'T YOU?
NO.
WELL, GO AWAY. YOU'RE NOT COMING WITH ME, ALL RIGHT?
I TRAVEL ALONE.
FINE.
I'M NOT FOLLOWING YOU.
NOW, LOOK...
BUT YOU'RE MY BOY-FRIEND. WE GO EVERY-WHERE TOGETHER. YOU CAN'T STAND TO BE WITHOUT ME, NOT EVEN FOR A SECOND.
SUZY. PLEASE DON'T FOLLOW ME.
OKAY.
YOU HAVE TO TURN BACK.
ALL RIGHT.
AND I'M NOT YOUR BOYFRIEND.
I KNOW.
YOU'RE STILL THERE, AREN'T YOU?
MAYBE.
SO WHAT KIND OF FLOWERS ARE ASPHODELS, ANYWAY?
DAFFODILS.

Chapter Seven: In Which the Pigeon Is Taken

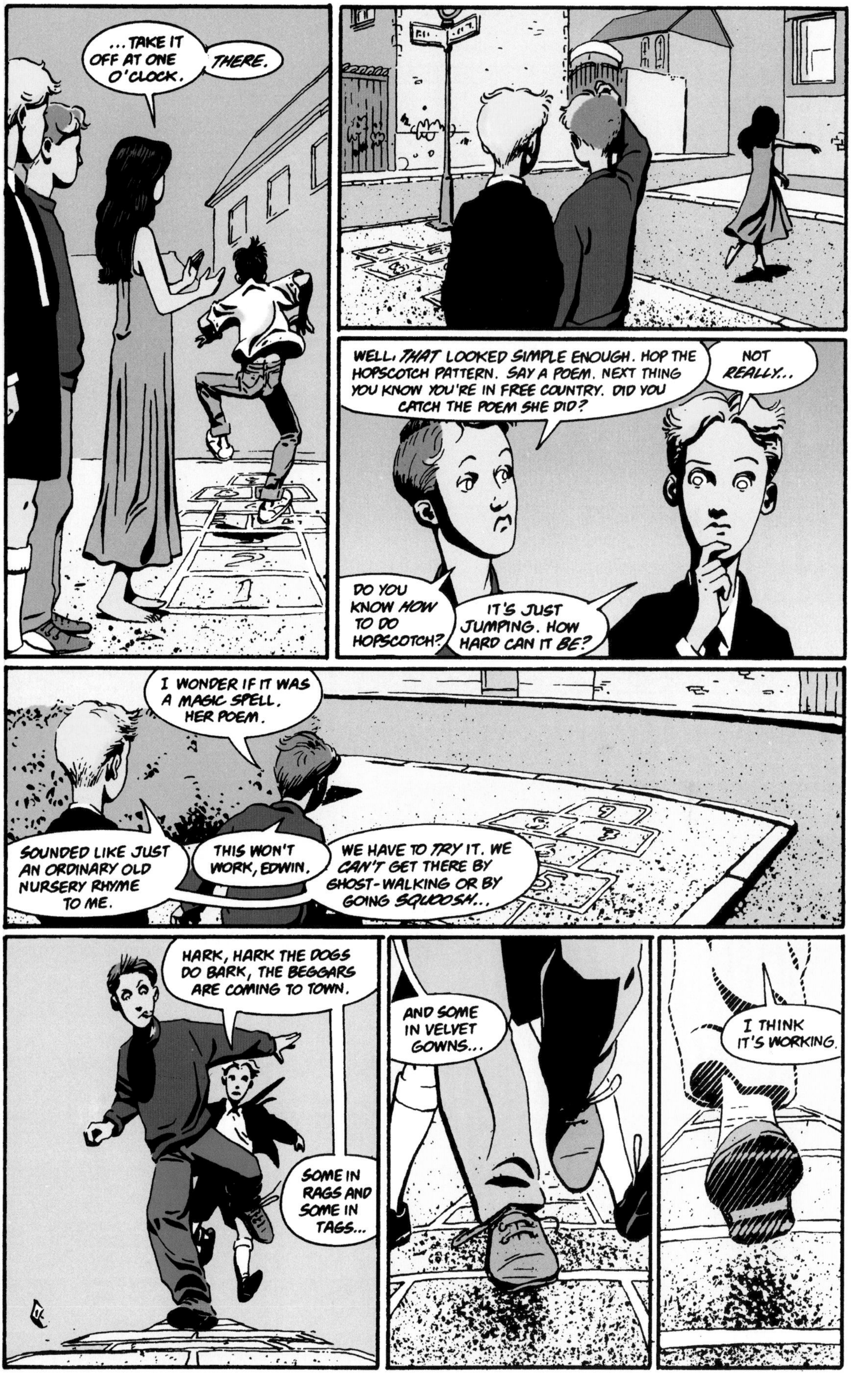

...TAKE IT OFF AT ONE O'CLOCK.
THERE.
WELL, THAT LOOKED SIMPLE ENOUGH. HOP THE HOPSCOTCH PATTERN. SAY A POEM. NEXT THING YOU KNOW YOU'RE IN FREE COUNTRY. DID YOU CATCH THE POEM SHE DID?
NOT REALLY...
DO YOU KNOW HOW TO DO HOPSCOTCH?
IT'S JUST JUMPING. HOW HARD CAN IT BE?
I WONDER IF IT WAS A MAGIC SPELL. HER POEM.
SOUNDED LIKE JUST AN ORDINARY OLD NURSERY RHYME TO ME.
THIS WON'T WORK, EDWIN.
WE HAVE TO TRY IT. WE CAN'T GET THERE BY GHOST-WALKING OR BY GOING SQUOOSH...
HARK, HARK THE DOGS DO BARK, THE BEGGARS ARE COMING TO TOWN.
SOME IN RAGS AND SOME IN TAGS...
AND SOME IN VELVET GOWNS...
I THINK IT'S WORKING.

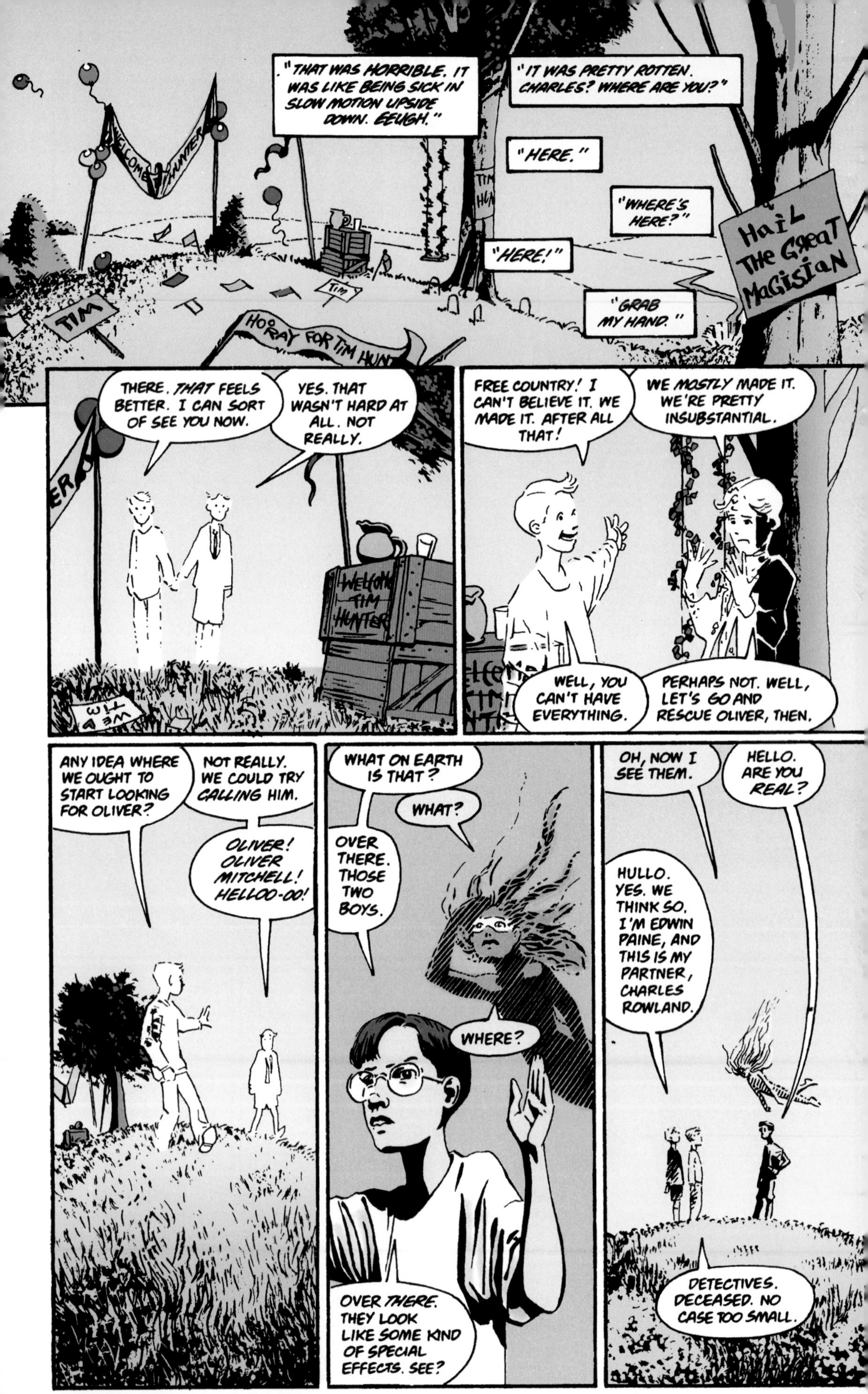
WELCOME HUNTER
"THAT WAS HORRIBLE. IT WAS LIKE BEING SICK IN SLOW MOTION UPSIDE DOWN. EEUGH."
"IT WAS PRETTY ROTTEN. CHARLES? WHERE ARE YOU?"
"HERE."
"WHERE'S HERE?"
"HERE!"
"GRAB MY HAND."
TIM HUNTER
HAIL THE GREAT MAGISIAN
TIM
TIM
HOORAY FOR TIM HUNTER
THERE. THAT FEELS BETTER. I CAN SORT OF SEE YOU NOW.
YES. THAT WASN'T HARD AT ALL. NOT REALLY.
WELCOME TIM HUNTER
FREE COUNTRY! I CAN'T BELIEVE IT. WE MADE IT. AFTER ALL THAT!
WE MOSTLY MADE IT. WE'RE PRETTY INSUBSTANTIAL.
WELL, YOU CAN'T HAVE EVERYTHING.
PERHAPS NOT. WELL, LET'S GO AND RESCUE OLIVER, THEN.
ANY IDEA WHERE WE OUGHT TO START LOOKING FOR OLIVER?
NOT REALLY. WE COULD TRY CALLING HIM.
OLIVER! OLIVER MITCHELL! HELLOO-OO!
WHAT ON EARTH IS THAT?
WHAT?
OVER THERE. THOSE TWO BOYS.
WHERE?
OVER THERE. THEY LOOK LIKE SOME KIND OF SPECIAL EFFECTS. SEE?
OH, NOW I SEE THEM.
HELLO. ARE YOU REAL?
HULLO. YES. WE THINK SO. I'M EDWIN PAINE, AND THIS IS MY PARTNER, CHARLES ROWLAND.
DETECTIVES. DECEASED. NO CASE TOO SMALL.

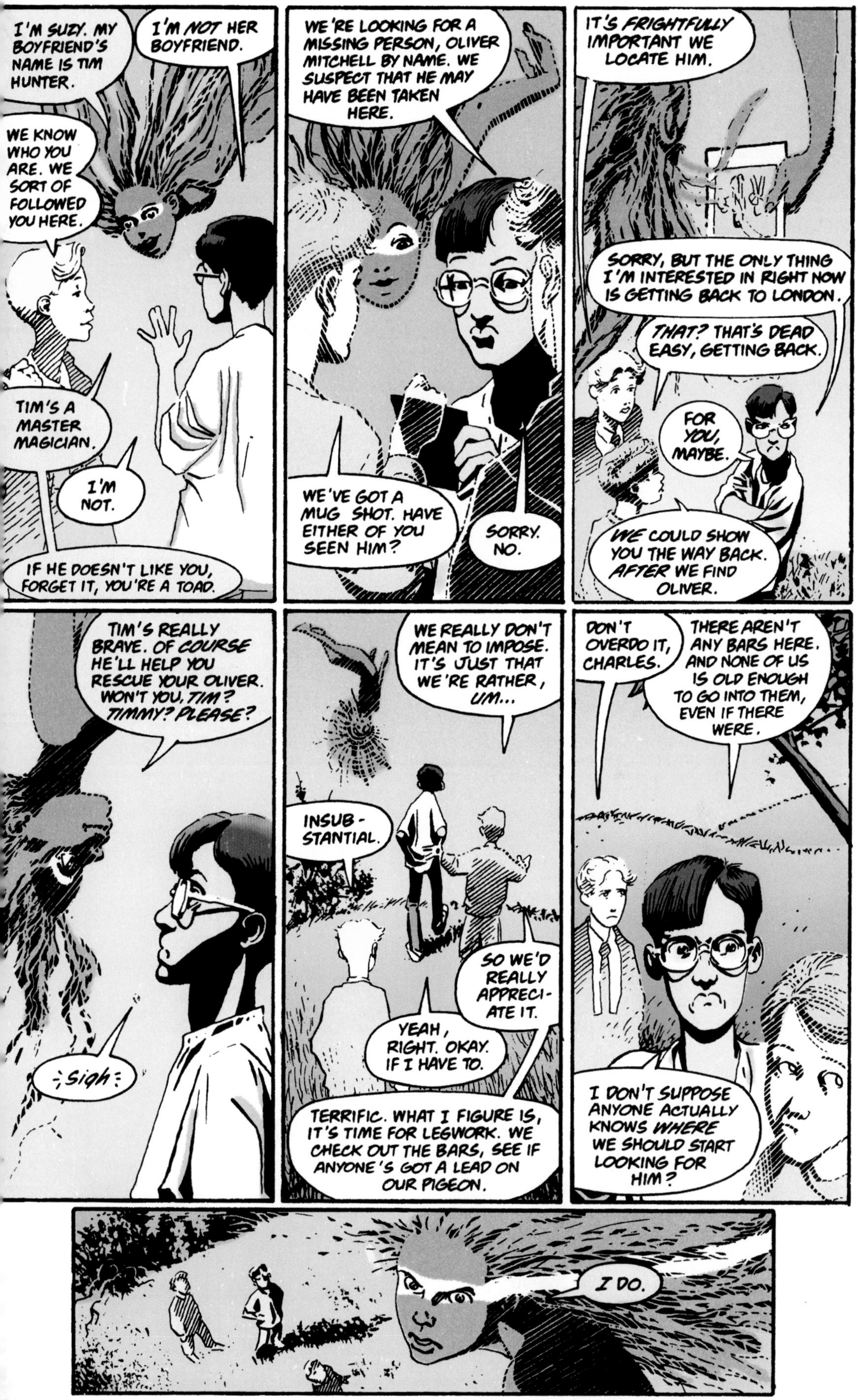
I'M SUZY. MY BOYFRIEND'S NAME IS TIM HUNTER.
I'M NOT HER BOYFRIEND.
WE KNOW WHO YOU ARE. WE SORT OF FOLLOWED YOU HERE.
TIM'S A MASTER MAGICIAN.
I'M NOT.
IF HE DOESN'T LIKE YOU, FORGET IT, YOU'RE A TOAD.
WE'RE LOOKING FOR A MISSING PERSON, OLIVER MITCHELL BY NAME. WE SUSPECT THAT HE MAY HAVE BEEN TAKEN HERE.
WE'VE GOT A MUG SHOT. HAVE EITHER OF YOU SEEN HIM?
SORRY. NO.
IT'S FRIGHTFULLY IMPORTANT WE LOCATE HIM.
SORRY, BUT THE ONLY THING I'M INTERESTED IN RIGHT NOW IS GETTING BACK TO LONDON.
THAT? THAT'S DEAD EASY, GETTING BACK.
FOR YOU, MAYBE.
WE COULD SHOW YOU THE WAY BACK. AFTER WE FIND OLIVER.
TIM'S REALLY BRAVE. OF COURSE HE'LL HELP YOU RESCUE YOUR OLIVER. WON'T YOU, TIM? TIMMY? PLEASE?
:SIGH:
WE REALLY DON'T MEAN TO IMPOSE. IT'S JUST THAT WE'RE RATHER, UM...
INSUB-STANTIAL.
SO WE'D REALLY APPRECI-ATE IT.
YEAH, RIGHT. OKAY. IF I HAVE TO.
TERRIFIC. WHAT I FIGURE IS, IT'S TIME FOR LEGWORK. WE CHECK OUT THE BARS, SEE IF ANYONE'S GOT A LEAD ON OUR PIGEON.
DON'T OVERDO IT, CHARLES.
THERE AREN'T ANY BARS HERE. AND NONE OF US IS OLD ENOUGH TO GO INTO THEM, EVEN IF THERE WERE.
I DON'T SUPPOSE ANYONE ACTUALLY KNOWS WHERE WE SHOULD START LOOKING FOR HIM?
I DO.

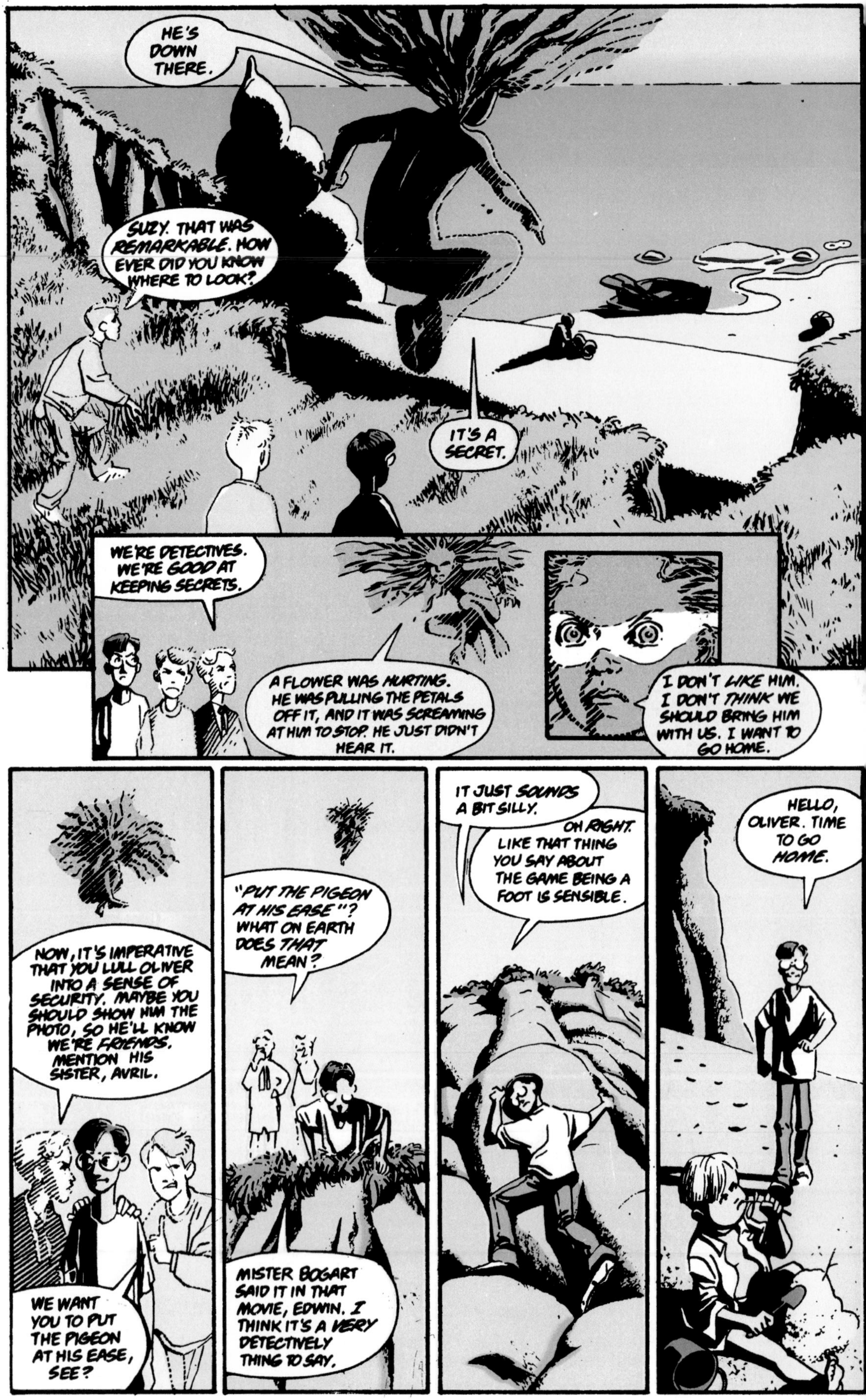
HE'S DOWN THERE.
SUZY. THAT WAS REMARKABLE. HOW EVER DID YOU KNOW WHERE TO LOOK?
IT'S A SECRET.
WE'RE DETECTIVES. WE'RE GOOD AT KEEPING SECRETS.
A FLOWER WAS HURTING. HE WAS PULLING THE PETALS OFF IT, AND IT WAS SCREAMING AT HIM TO STOP. HE JUST DIDN'T HEAR IT.
I DON'T LIKE HIM. I DON'T THINK WE SHOULD BRING HIM WITH US. I WANT TO GO HOME.
NOW, IT'S IMPERATIVE THAT YOU LULL OLIVER INTO A SENSE OF SECURITY. MAYBE YOU SHOULD SHOW HIM THE PHOTO, SO HE'LL KNOW WE'RE FRIENDS. MENTION HIS SISTER, AVRIL.
WE WANT YOU TO PUT THE PIGEON AT HIS EASE, SEE?
"PUT THE PIGEON AT HIS EASE"? WHAT ON EARTH DOES THAT MEAN?
MISTER BOGART SAID IT IN THAT MOVIE, EDWIN. I THINK IT'S A VERY DETECTIVELY THING TO SAY.
IT JUST SOUNDS A BIT SILLY.
OH RIGHT. LIKE THAT THING YOU SAY ABOUT THE GAME BEING A FOOT IS SENSIBLE.
HELLO, OLIVER. TIME TO GO HOME.

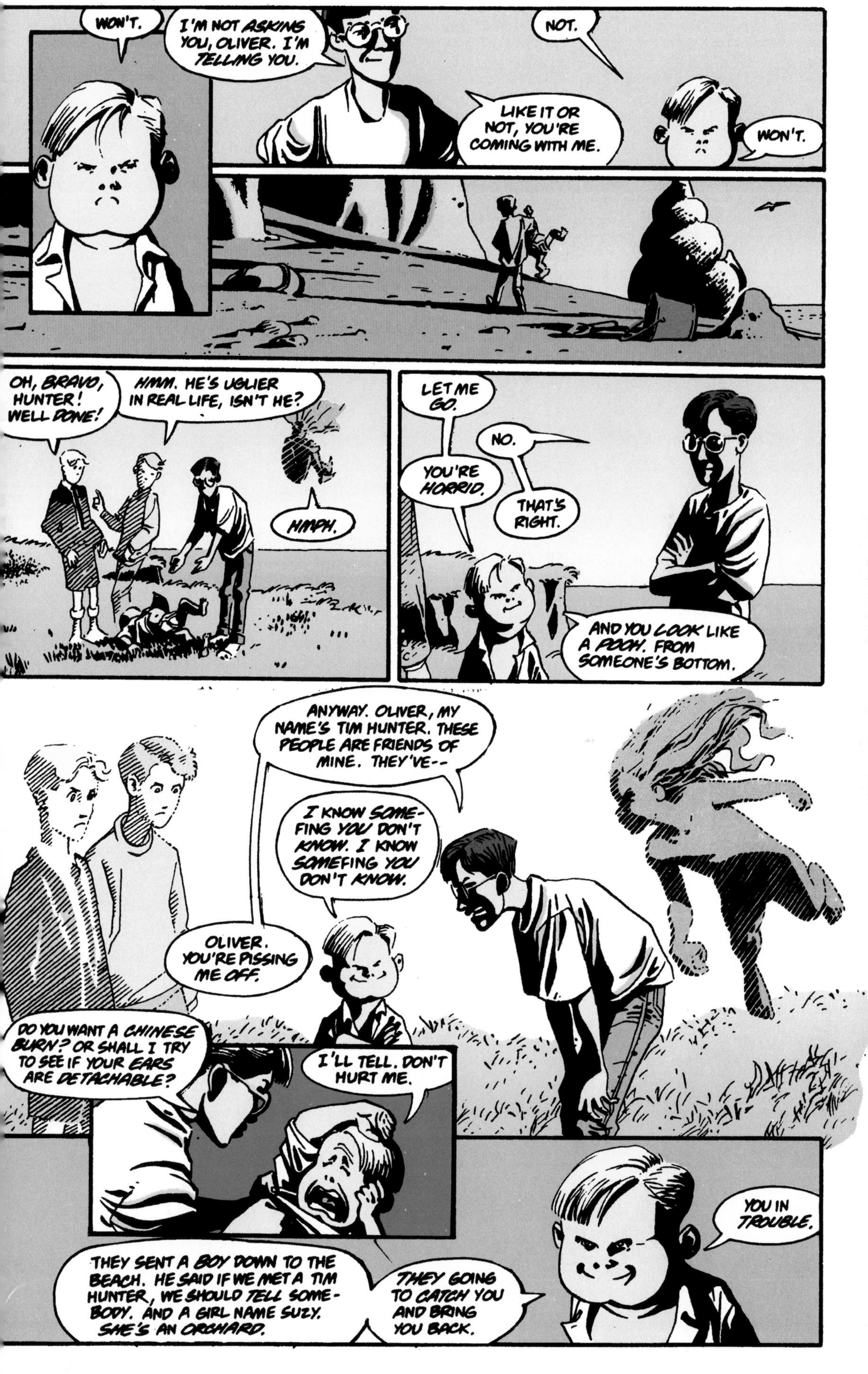
WON'T.
I'M NOT ASKING YOU, OLIVER. I'M TELLING YOU.
NOT.
LIKE IT OR NOT, YOU'RE COMING WITH ME.
WON'T.
OH, BRAVO, HUNTER! WELL DONE!
HMM. HE'S UGLIER IN REAL LIFE, ISN'T HE?
HMPH.
LET ME GO.
YOU'RE HORRID.
NO.
THAT'S RIGHT.
AND YOU LOOK LIKE A POOH. FROM SOMEONE'S BOTTOM.
ANYWAY. OLIVER, MY NAME'S TIM HUNTER. THESE PEOPLE ARE FRIENDS OF MINE. THEY'VE--
I KNOW SOMEFING YOU DON'T KNOW. I KNOW SOMEFING YOU DON'T KNOW.
OLIVER. YOU'RE PISSING ME OFF.
DO YOU WANT A CHINESE BURN? OR SHALL I TRY TO SEE IF YOUR EARS ARE DETACHABLE?
I'LL TELL. DON'T HURT ME.
THEY SENT A BOY DOWN TO THE BEACH. HE SAID IF WE MET A TIM HUNTER, WE SHOULD TELL SOMEBODY. AND A GIRL NAME SUZY. SHE'S AN ORCHARD.
THEY GOING TO CATCH YOU AND BRING YOU BACK.
YOU IN TROUBLE.

CHAPTER EIGHT: IN WHICH THE PLOT THICKENS

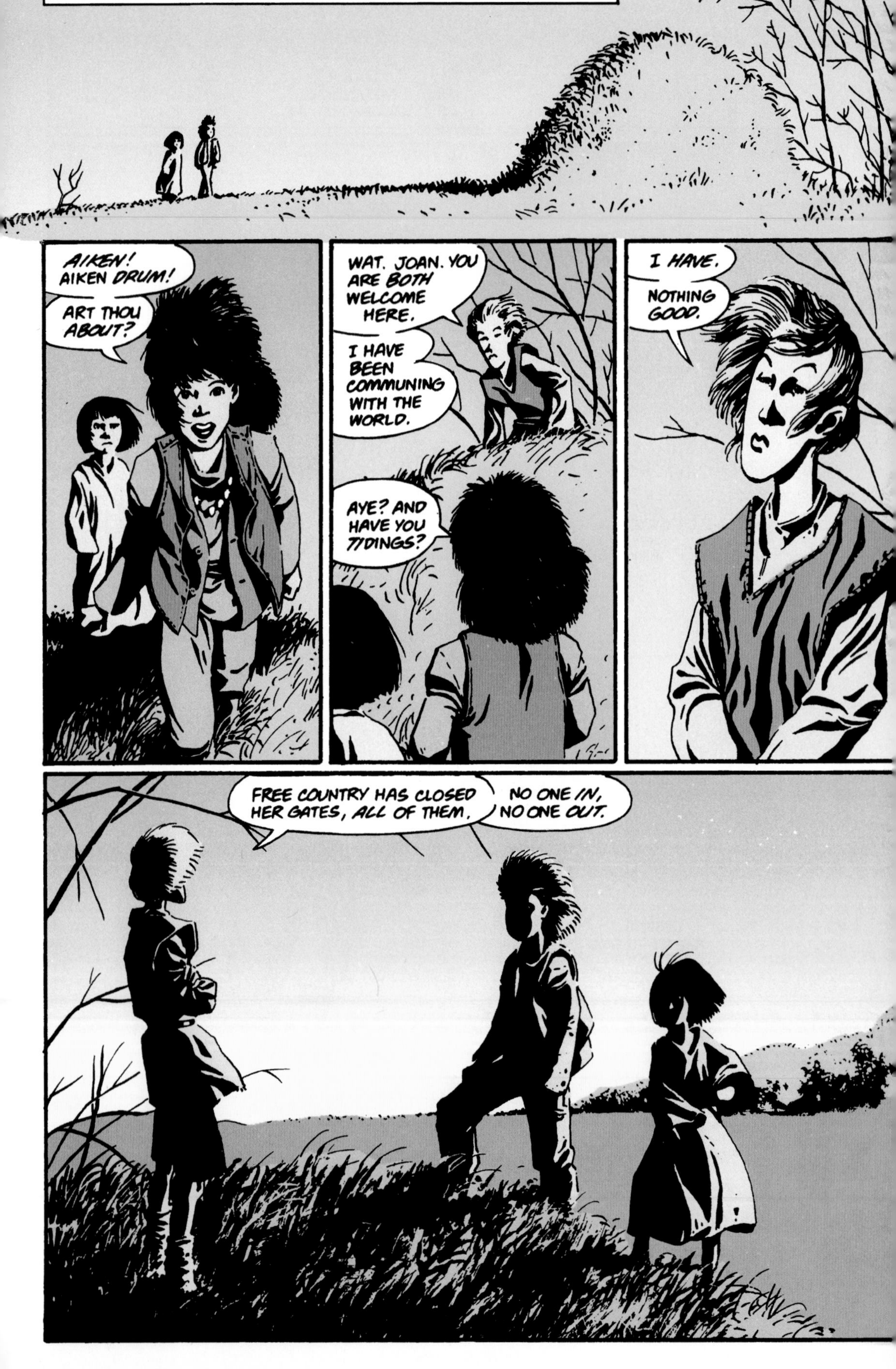
AIKEN! AIKEN DRUM!
ART THOU ABOUT?
WAT. JOAN. YOU ARE BOTH WELCOME HERE.
I HAVE BEEN COMMUNING WITH THE WORLD.
AYE? AND HAVE YOU TIDINGS?
I HAVE.
NOTHING GOOD.
FREE COUNTRY HAS CLOSED HER GATES, ALL OF THEM.
NO ONE IN, NO ONE OUT.

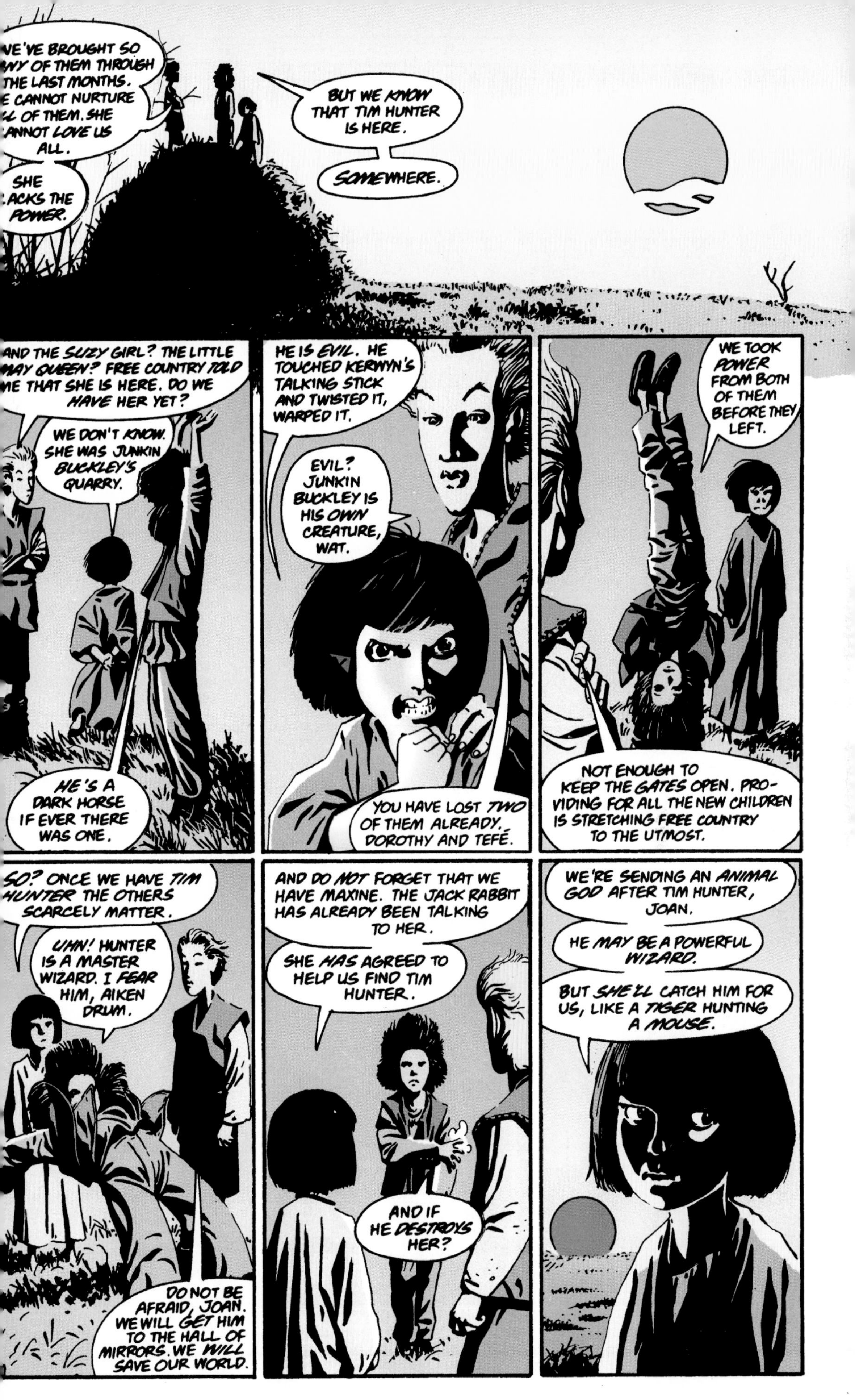

VE'VE BROUGHT SO
WY OF THEM THROUGH
THE LAST MONTHS.
E CANNOT NURTURE
L OF THEM. SHE
ANNOT LOVE US
ALL.
SHE
ACKS THE
POWER.
BUT WE KNOW THAT TIM HUNTER IS HERE.
SOMEWHERE.
AND THE SUZY GIRL? THE LITTLE MAY QUEEN? FREE COUNTRY TOLD ME THAT SHE IS HERE. DO WE HAVE HER YET?
WE DON'T KNOW. SHE WAS JUNKIN BUCKLEY'S QUARRY.
HE'S A DARK HORSE IF EVER THERE WAS ONE.
HE IS EVIL. HE TOUCHED KERWYN'S TALKING STICK AND TWISTED IT, WARPED IT.
EVIL? JUNKIN BUCKLEY IS HIS OWN CREATURE, WAT.
YOU HAVE LOST TWO OF THEM ALREADY. DOROTHY AND TEFÉ.
WE TOOK POWER FROM BOTH OF THEM BEFORE THEY LEFT.
NOT ENOUGH TO KEEP THE GATES OPEN. PROVIDING FOR ALL THE NEW CHILDREN IS STRETCHING FREE COUNTRY TO THE UTMOST.
SO? ONCE WE HAVE TIM HUNTER THE OTHERS SCARCELY MATTER.
UHN! HUNTER IS A MASTER WIZARD. I FEAR HIM, AIKEN DRUM.
DO NOT BE AFRAID, JOAN. WE WILL GET HIM TO THE HALL OF MIRRORS. WE WILL SAVE OUR WORLD.
AND DO NOT FORGET THAT WE HAVE MAXINE. THE JACK RABBIT HAS ALREADY BEEN TALKING TO HER.
SHE HAS AGREED TO HELP US FIND TIM HUNTER.
AND IF HE DESTROYS HER?
WE'RE SENDING AN ANIMAL GOD AFTER TIM HUNTER, JOAN.
HE MAY BE A POWERFUL WIZARD.
BUT SHE'LL CATCH HIM FOR US, LIKE A TIGER HUNTING A MOUSE.

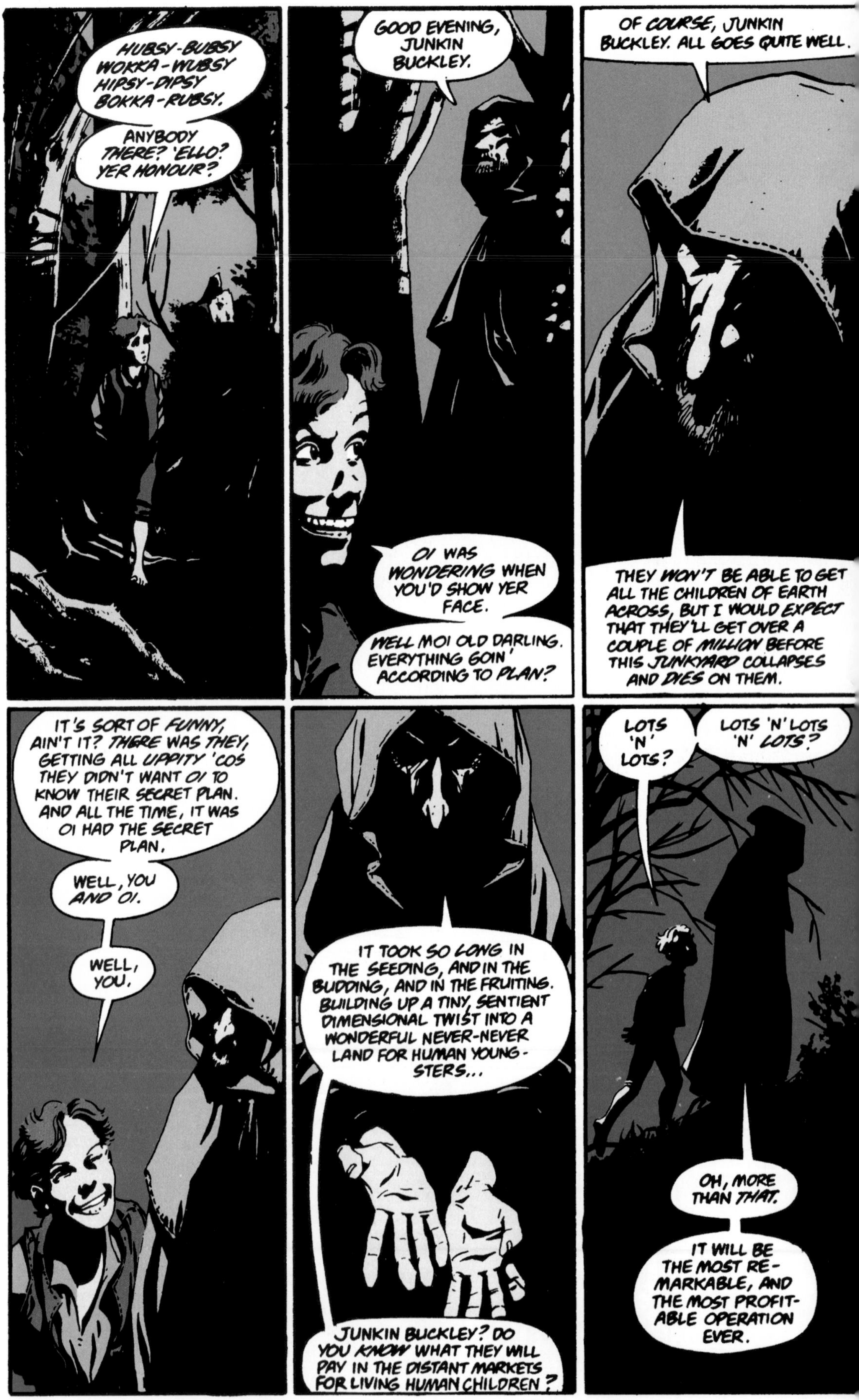
HUBSY-BUBSY WOKKA-WUBSY HIPSY-DIPSY BOKKA-RUBSY.
ANYBODY THERE? 'ELLO? YER HONOUR?
GOOD EVENING, JUNKIN BUCKLEY.
OI WAS WONDERING WHEN YOU'D SHOW YER FACE.
WELL MOI OLD DARLING. EVERYTHING GOIN' ACCORDING TO PLAN?
OF COURSE, JUNKIN BUCKLEY. ALL GOES QUITE WELL.
THEY WON'T BE ABLE TO GET ALL THE CHILDREN OF EARTH ACROSS, BUT I WOULD EXPECT THAT THEY'LL GET OVER A COUPLE OF MILLION BEFORE THIS JUNKYARD COLLAPSES AND DIES ON THEM.
IT'S SORT OF FUNNY, AIN'T IT? THERE WAS THEY, GETTING ALL UPPITY 'COS THEY DIDN'T WANT OI TO KNOW THEIR SECRET PLAN. AND ALL THE TIME, IT WAS OI HAD THE SECRET PLAN.
WELL, YOU AND OI.
WELL, YOU.
IT TOOK SO LONG IN THE SEEDING, AND IN THE BUDDING, AND IN THE FRUITING. BUILDING UP A TINY, SENTIENT DIMENSIONAL TWIST INTO A WONDERFUL NEVER-NEVER LAND FOR HUMAN YOUNG-STERS...
JUNKIN BUCKLEY? DO YOU KNOW WHAT THEY WILL PAY IN THE DISTANT MARKETS FOR LIVING HUMAN CHILDREN?
LOTS 'N' LOTS?
LOTS 'N' LOTS 'N' LOTS?
OH, MORE THAN THAT.
IT WILL BE THE MOST RE-MARKABLE, AND THE MOST PROFIT-ABLE OPERATION EVER.

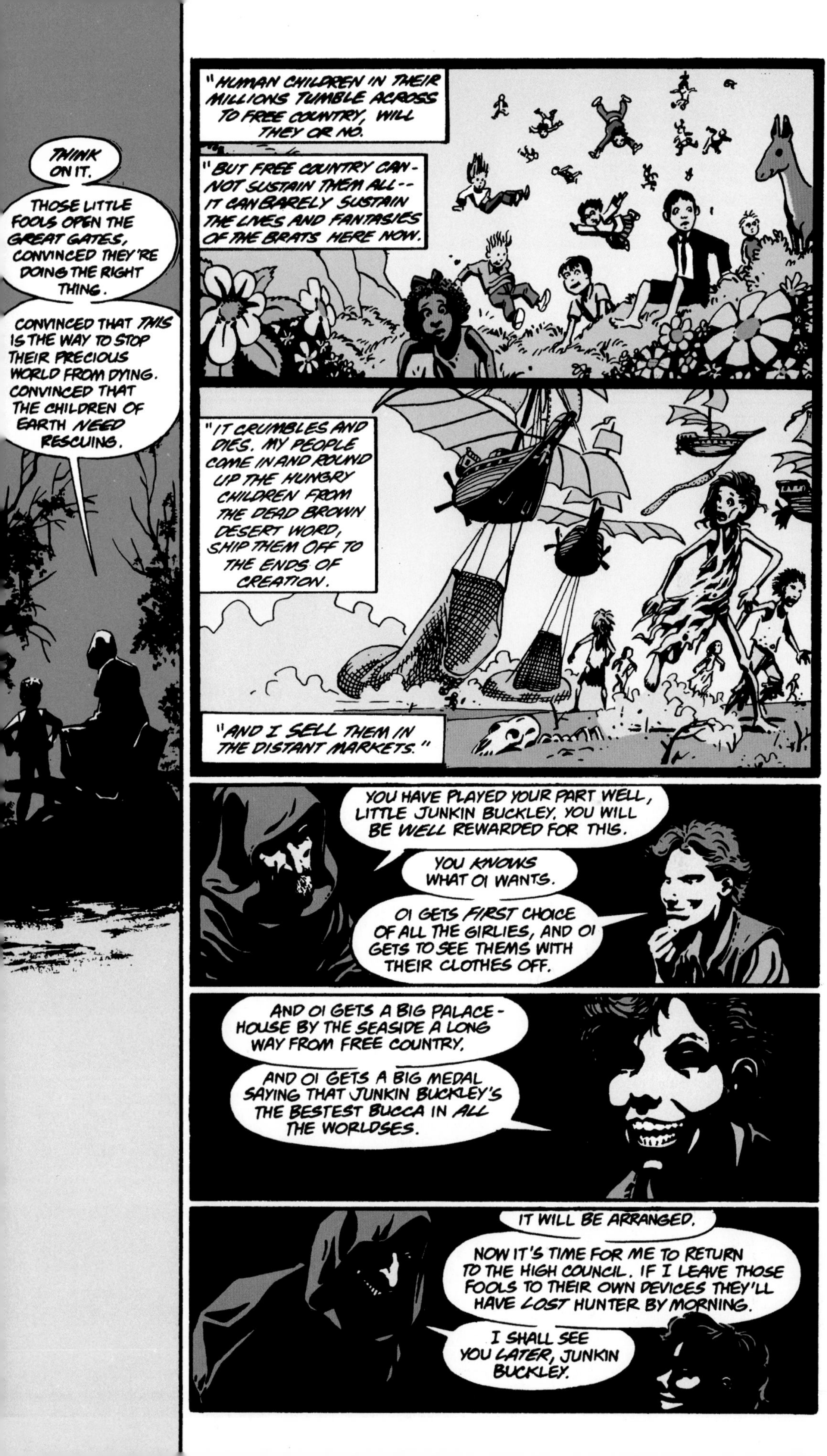
THINK ON IT.
THOSE LITTLE FOOLS OPEN THE GREAT GATES, CONVINCED THEY'RE DOING THE RIGHT THING.
CONVINCED THAT THIS IS THE WAY TO STOP THEIR PRECIOUS WORLD FROM DYING. CONVINCED THAT THE CHILDREN OF EARTH NEED RESCUING.
"HUMAN CHILDREN IN THEIR MILLIONS TUMBLE ACROSS TO FREE COUNTRY, WILL THEY OR NO.
"BUT FREE COUNTRY CANNOT SUSTAIN THEM ALL-- IT CAN BARELY SUSTAIN THE LIVES AND FANTASIES OF THE BRATS HERE NOW.
"IT CRUMBLES AND DIES. MY PEOPLE COME IN AND ROUND UP THE HUNGRY CHILDREN FROM THE DEAD BROWN DESERT WORD, SHIP THEM OFF TO THE ENDS OF CREATION.
"AND I SELL THEM IN THE DISTANT MARKETS."
YOU HAVE PLAYED YOUR PART WELL, LITTLE JUNKIN BUCKLEY. YOU WILL BE WELL REWARDED FOR THIS.
YOU KNOWS WHAT OI WANTS.
OI GETS FIRST CHOICE OF ALL THE GIRLIES, AND OI GETS TO SEE THEMS WITH THEIR CLOTHES OFF.
AND OI GETS A BIG PALACE-HOUSE BY THE SEASIDE A LONG WAY FROM FREE COUNTRY.
AND OI GETS A BIG MEDAL SAYING THAT JUNKIN BUCKLEY'S THE BESTEST BUCCA IN ALL THE WORLDSES.
IT WILL BE ARRANGED.
NOW IT'S TIME FOR ME TO RETURN TO THE HIGH COUNCIL. IF I LEAVE THOSE FOOLS TO THEIR OWN DEVICES THEY'LL HAVE LOST HUNTER BY MORNING.
I SHALL SEE YOU LATER, JUNKIN BUCKLEY.

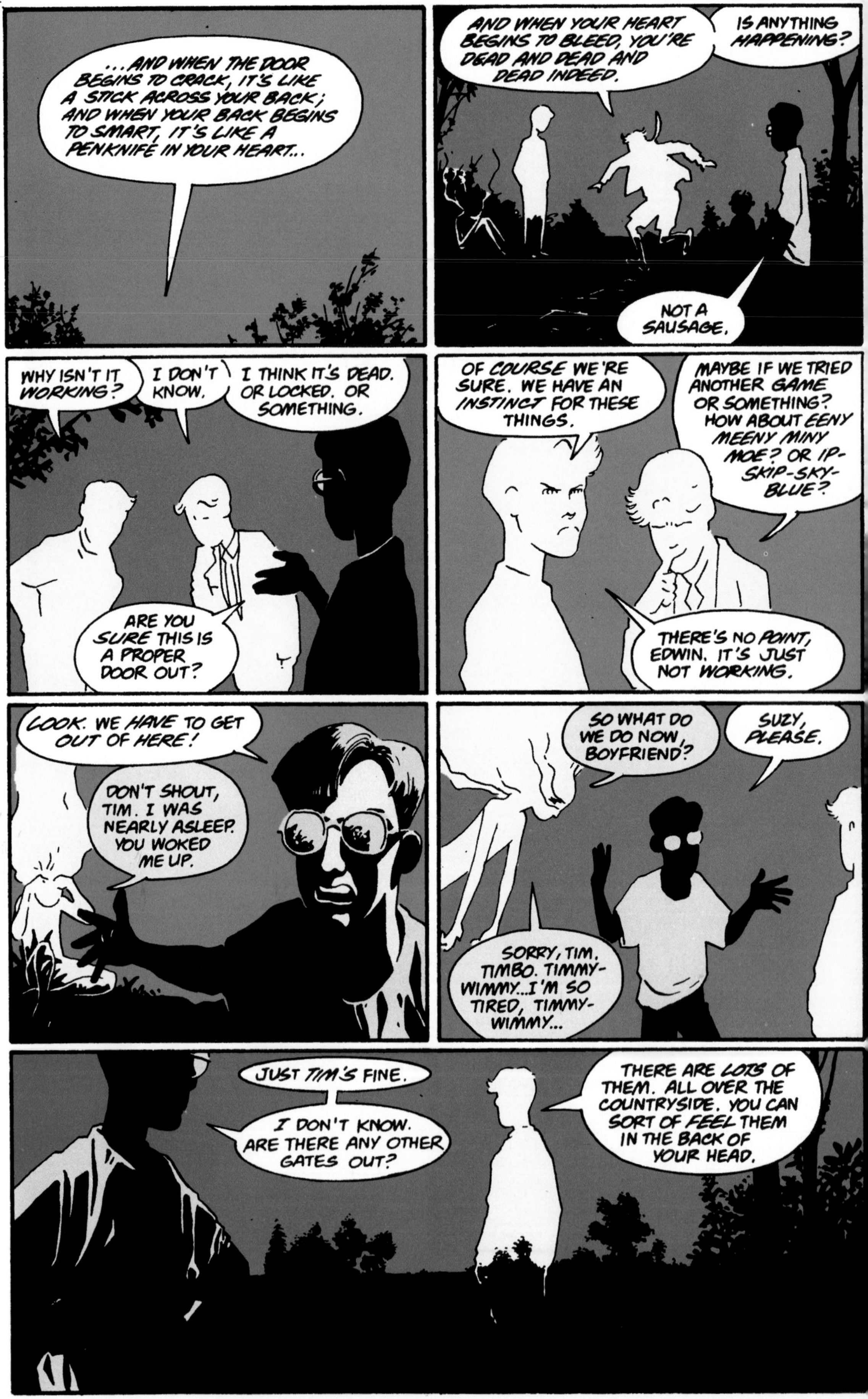
...AND WHEN THE DOOR BEGINS TO CRACK, IT'S LIKE A STICK ACROSS YOUR BACK; AND WHEN YOUR BACK BEGINS TO SMART, IT'S LIKE A PENKNIFE IN YOUR HEART...
AND WHEN YOUR HEART BEGINS TO BLEED, YOU'RE DEAD AND DEAD AND DEAD INDEED.
IS ANYTHING HAPPENING?
NOT A SAUSAGE.
WHY ISN'T IT WORKING?
I DON'T KNOW.
I THINK IT'S DEAD. OR LOCKED. OR SOMETHING.
ARE YOU SURE THIS IS A PROPER DOOR OUT?
OF COURSE WE'RE SURE. WE HAVE AN INSTINCT FOR THESE THINGS.
MAYBE IF WE TRIED ANOTHER GAME OR SOMETHING? HOW ABOUT EENY MEENY MINY MOE? OR IP-SKIP-SKY-BLUE?
THERE'S NO POINT, EDWIN. IT'S JUST NOT WORKING.
LOOK. WE HAVE TO GET OUT OF HERE!
DON'T SHOUT, TIM. I WAS NEARLY ASLEEP. YOU WOKED ME UP.
SO WHAT DO WE DO NOW, BOYFRIEND?
SUZY, PLEASE.
SORRY, TIM. TIMBO. TIMMY-WIMMY...I'M SO TIRED, TIMMY-WIMMY...
JUST TIM'S FINE.
I DON'T KNOW. ARE THERE ANY OTHER GATES OUT?
THERE ARE LOTS OF THEM. ALL OVER THE COUNTRYSIDE. YOU CAN SORT OF FEEL THEM IN THE BACK OF YOUR HEAD.

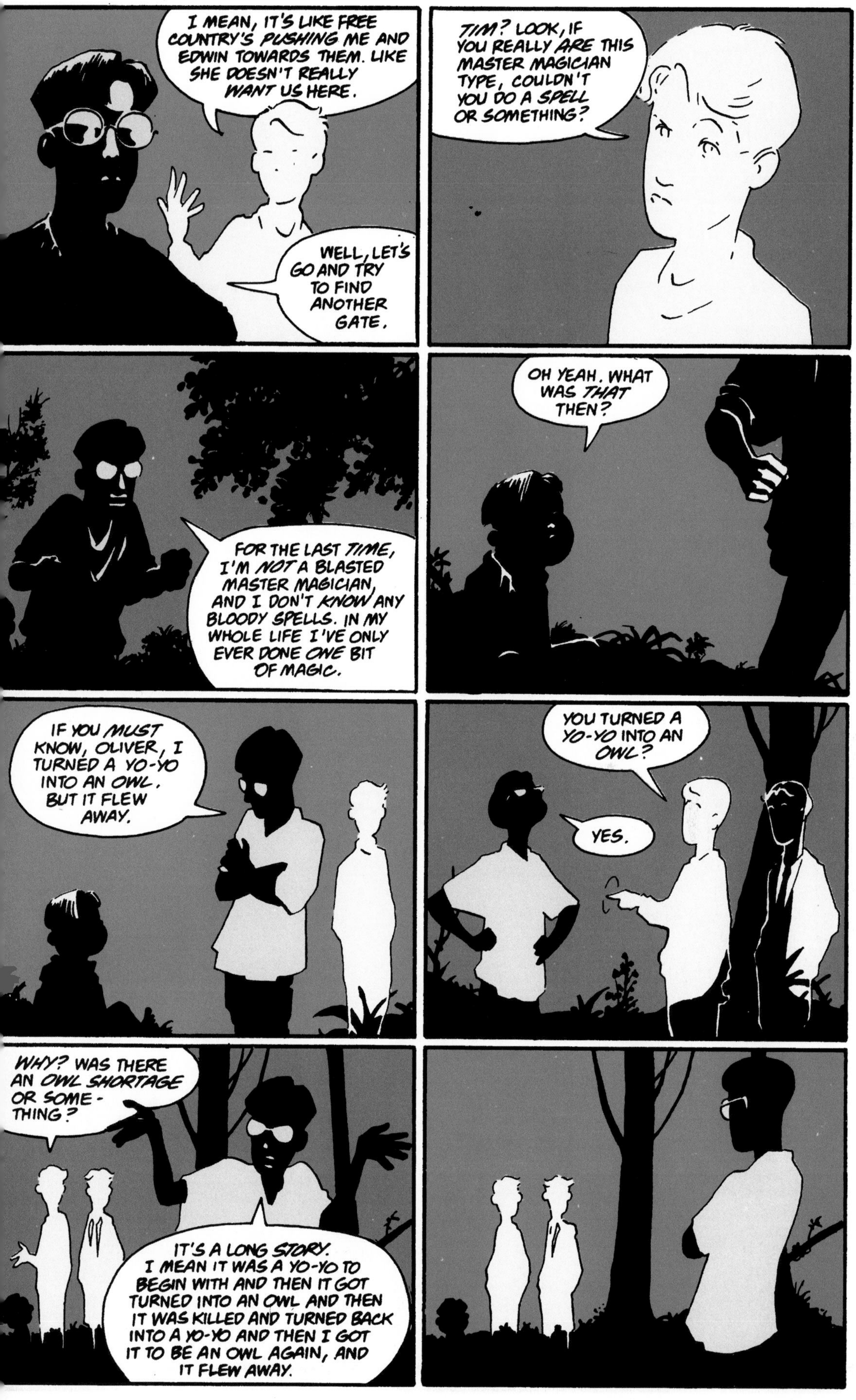
I MEAN, IT'S LIKE FREE COUNTRY'S PUSHING ME AND EDWIN TOWARDS THEM. LIKE SHE DOESN'T REALLY WANT US HERE.
WELL, LET'S GO AND TRY TO FIND ANOTHER GATE.
TIM? LOOK, IF YOU REALLY ARE THIS MASTER MAGICIAN TYPE, COULDN'T YOU DO A SPELL OR SOMETHING?
FOR THE LAST TIME, I'M NOT A BLASTED MASTER MAGICIAN, AND I DON'T KNOW ANY BLOODY SPELLS. IN MY WHOLE LIFE I'VE ONLY EVER DONE ONE BIT OF MAGIC.
OH YEAH. WHAT WAS THAT THEN?
IF YOU MUST KNOW, OLIVER, I TURNED A YO-YO INTO AN OWL. BUT IT FLEW AWAY.
YOU TURNED A YO-YO INTO AN OWL?
YES.
WHY? WAS THERE AN OWL SHORTAGE OR SOME-THING?
IT'S A LONG STORY. I MEAN IT WAS A YO-YO TO BEGIN WITH AND THEN IT GOT TURNED INTO AN OWL AND THEN IT WAS KILLED AND TURNED BACK INTO A YO-YO AND THEN I GOT IT TO BE AN OWL AGAIN, AND IT FLEW AWAY.

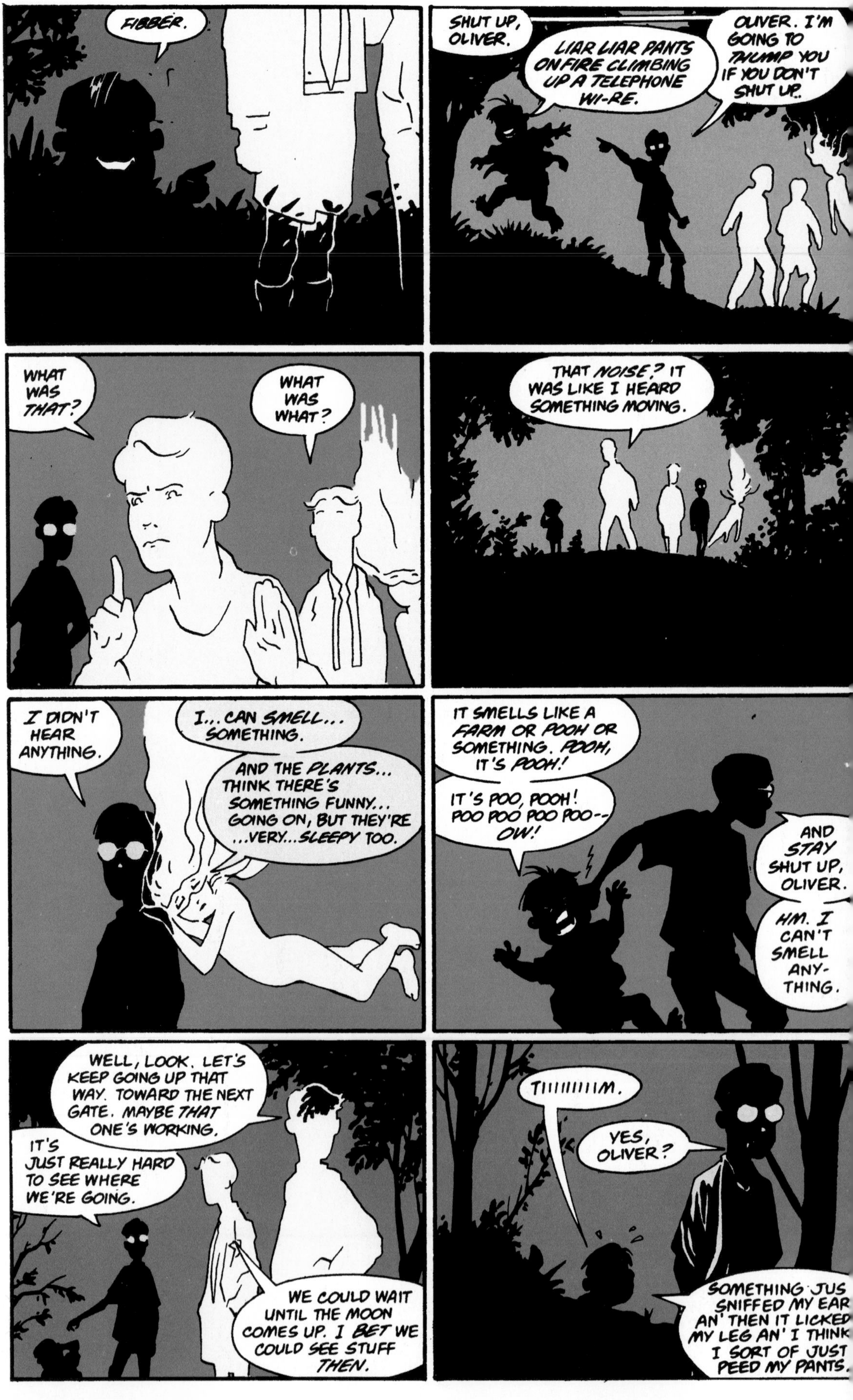
FIBBER.
SHUT UP, OLIVER.
LIAR LIAR PANTS ON FIRE CLIMBING UP A TELEPHONE WI-RE.
OLIVER. I'M GOING TO THUMP YOU IF YOU DON'T SHUT UP.
WHAT WAS THAT?
WHAT WAS WHAT?
THAT NOISE? IT WAS LIKE I HEARD SOMETHING MOVING.
I DIDN'T HEAR ANYTHING.
I... CAN SMELL... SOMETHING.
AND THE PLANTS... THINK THERE'S SOMETHING FUNNY... GOING ON, BUT THEY'RE ...VERY...SLEEPY TOO.
IT SMELLS LIKE A FARM OR POOH OR SOMETHING. POOH, IT'S POOH!
IT'S POO, POOH! POO POO POO POO--OW!
AND STAY SHUT UP, OLIVER.
HM. I CAN'T SMELL ANY-THING.
WELL, LOOK. LET'S KEEP GOING UP THAT WAY. TOWARD THE NEXT GATE. MAYBE THAT ONE'S WORKING.
IT'S JUST REALLY HARD TO SEE WHERE WE'RE GOING.
WE COULD WAIT UNTIL THE MOON COMES UP. I BET WE COULD SEE STUFF THEN.
TIIIIIIIIIM.
YES, OLIVER?
SOMETHING JUS SNIFFED MY EAR AN' THEN IT LICKED MY LEG AN' I THINK I SORT OF JUST PEED MY PANTS.

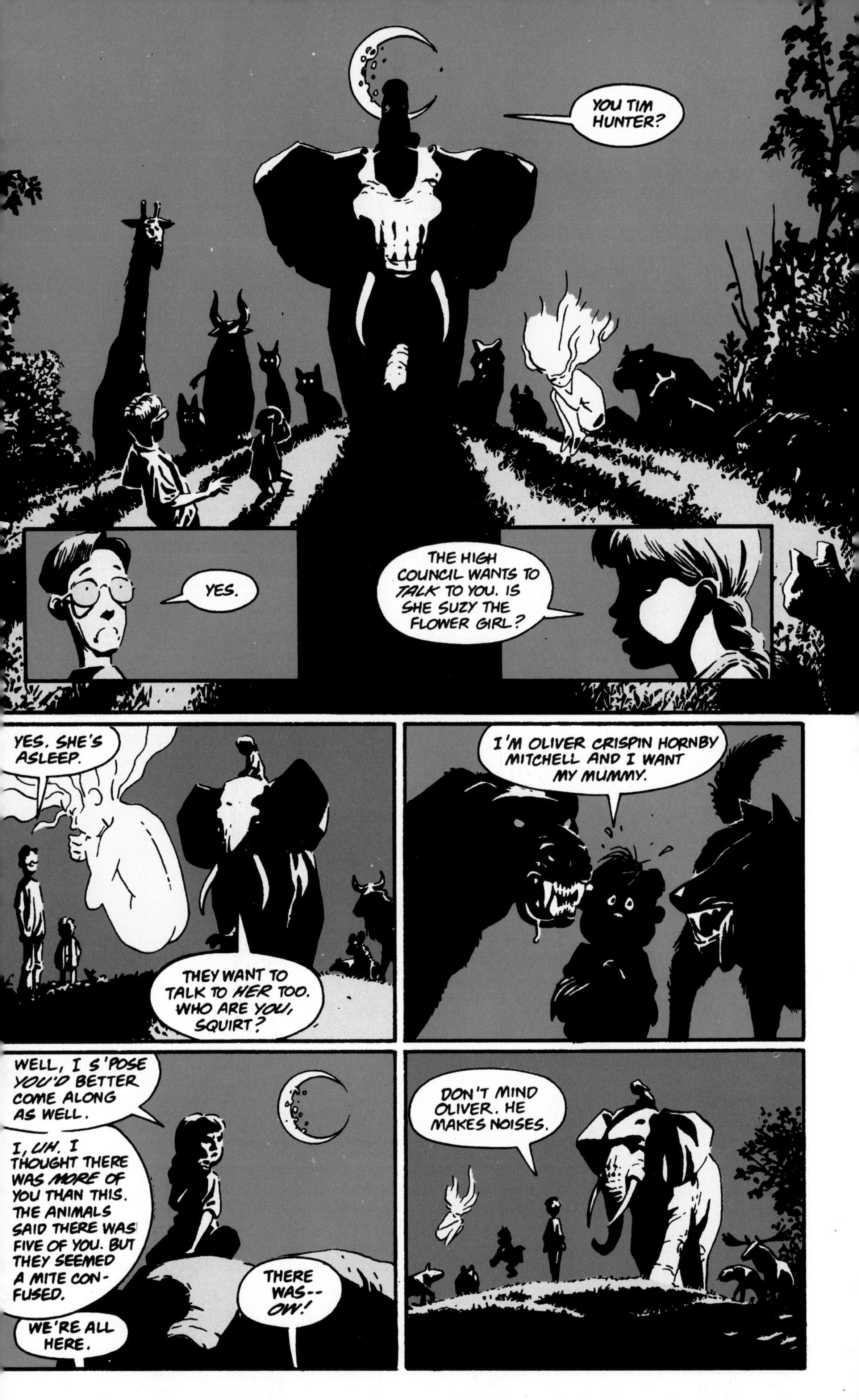
YOU TIM HUNTER?
YES.
THE HIGH COUNCIL WANTS TO TALK TO YOU. IS SHE SUZY THE FLOWER GIRL?
YES. SHE'S ASLEEP.
THEY WANT TO TALK TO HER TOO. WHO ARE YOU, SQUIRT?
I'M OLIVER CRISPIN HORNBY MITCHELL AND I WANT MY MUMMY.
WELL, I S'POSE YOU'D BETTER COME ALONG AS WELL.
I, UH. I THOUGHT THERE WAS MORE OF YOU THAN THIS. THE ANIMALS SAID THERE WAS FIVE OF YOU. BUT THEY SEEMED A MITE CON-FUSED.
WE'RE ALL HERE.
THERE WAS-- OW!
DON'T MIND OLIVER. HE MAKES NOISES.

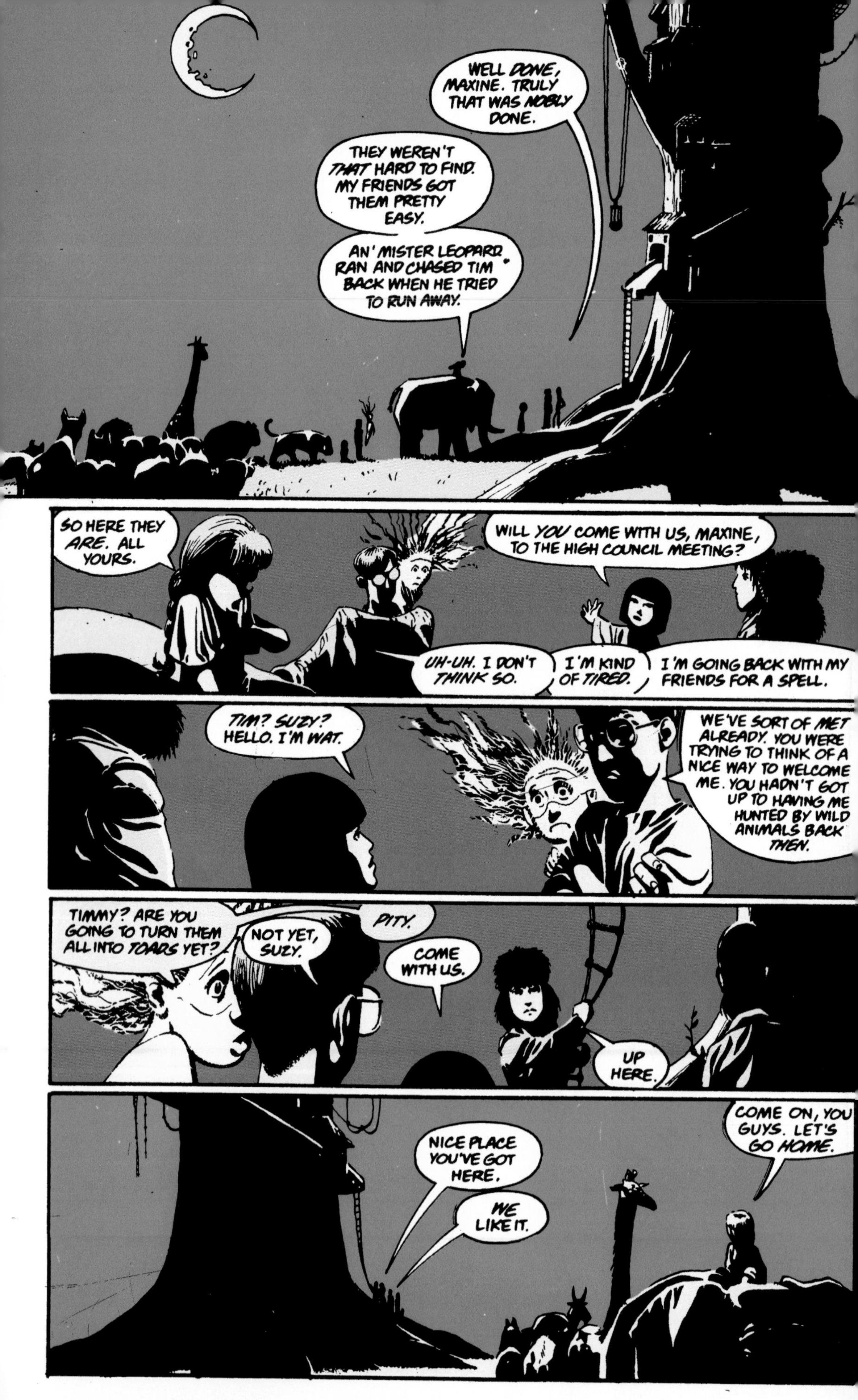
WELL DONE, MAXINE. TRULY THAT WAS NOBLY DONE.
THEY WEREN'T THAT HARD TO FIND. MY FRIENDS GOT THEM PRETTY EASY.
AN' MISTER LEOPARD RAN AND CHASED TIM BACK WHEN HE TRIED TO RUN AWAY.
SO HERE THEY ARE. ALL YOURS.
WILL YOU COME WITH US, MAXINE, TO THE HIGH COUNCIL MEETING?
UH-UH. I DON'T THINK SO.
I'M KIND OF TIRED.
I'M GOING BACK WITH MY FRIENDS FOR A SPELL.
TIM? SUZY? HELLO. I'M WAT.
WE'VE SORT OF MET ALREADY. YOU WERE TRYING TO THINK OF A NICE WAY TO WELCOME ME. YOU HADN'T GOT UP TO HAVING ME HUNTED BY WILD ANIMALS BACK THEN.
TIMMY? ARE YOU GOING TO TURN THEM ALL INTO TOADS YET?
NOT YET, SUZY.
PITY.
COME WITH US.
UP HERE.
NICE PLACE YOU'VE GOT HERE.
WE LIKE IT.
COME ON, YOU GUYS. LET'S GO HOME.

CHAPTER NINE: IN WHICH MAXINE PONDERS ON BUDDING

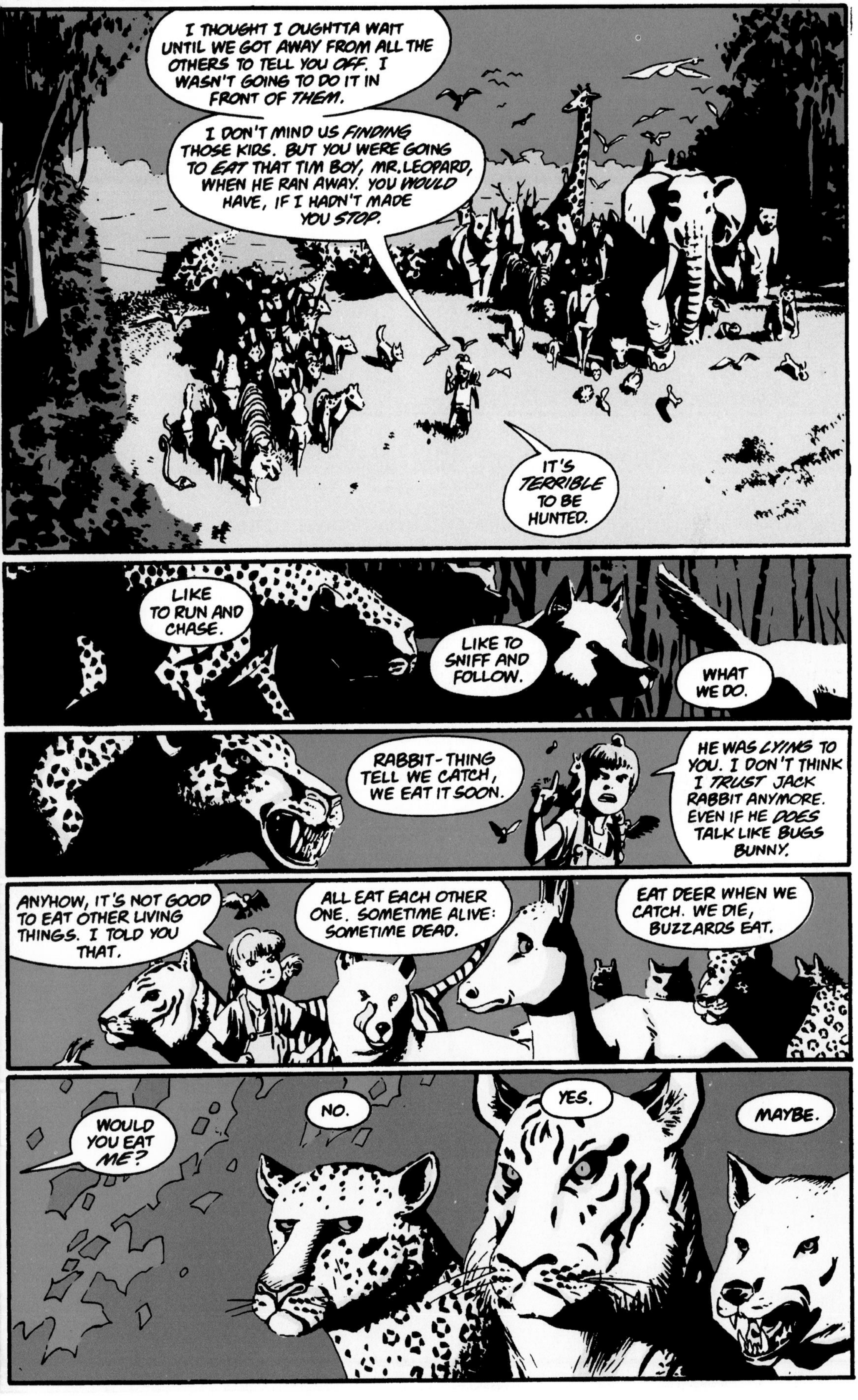
I THOUGHT I OUGHTTA WAIT UNTIL WE GOT AWAY FROM ALL THE OTHERS TO TELL YOU OFF. I WASN'T GOING TO DO IT IN FRONT OF THEM.
I DON'T MIND US FINDING THOSE KIDS. BUT YOU WERE GOING TO EAT THAT TIM BOY, MR. LEOPARD, WHEN HE RAN AWAY. YOU WOULD HAVE, IF I HADN'T MADE YOU STOP.
IT'S TERRIBLE TO BE HUNTED.
LIKE TO RUN AND CHASE.
LIKE TO SNIFF AND FOLLOW.
WHAT WE DO.
RABBIT-THING TELL WE CATCH, WE EAT IT SOON.
HE WAS LYING TO YOU. I DON'T THINK I TRUST JACK RABBIT ANYMORE. EVEN IF HE DOES TALK LIKE BUGS BUNNY.
ANYHOW, IT'S NOT GOOD TO EAT OTHER LIVING THINGS. I TOLD YOU THAT.
ALL EAT EACH OTHER ONE. SOMETIME ALIVE: SOMETIME DEAD.
EAT DEER WHEN WE CATCH. WE DIE, BUZZARDS EAT.
WOULD YOU EAT ME?
NO.
YES.
MAYBE.

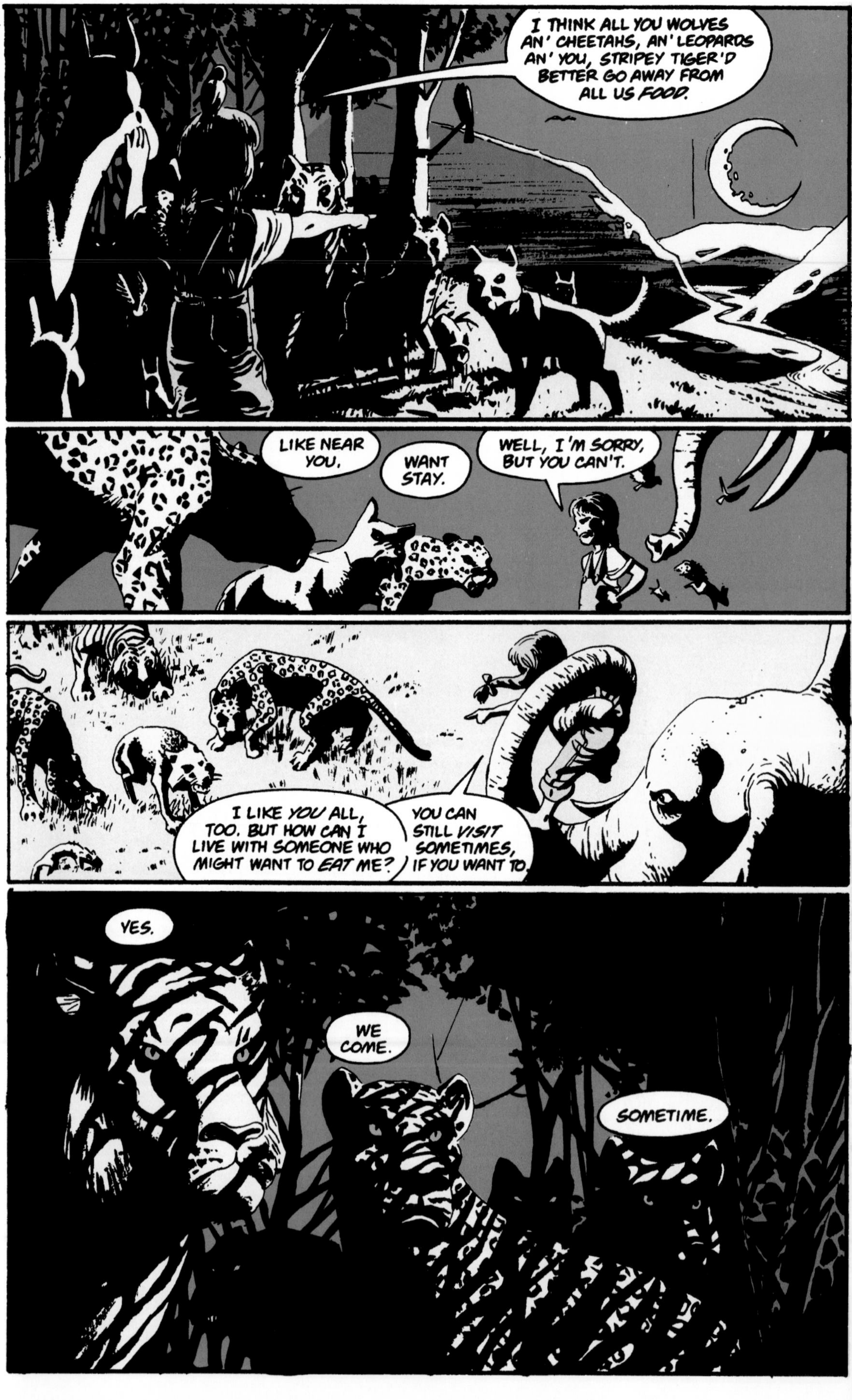
I THINK ALL YOU WOLVES AN' CHEETAHS, AN' LEOPARDS AN' YOU, STRIPEY TIGER'D BETTER GO AWAY FROM ALL US FOOD.
LIKE NEAR YOU.
WANT STAY.
WELL, I'M SORRY, BUT YOU CAN'T.
I LIKE YOU ALL, TOO. BUT HOW CAN I LIVE WITH SOMEONE WHO MIGHT WANT TO EAT ME?
YOU CAN STILL VISIT SOMETIMES, IF YOU WANT TO.
YES.
WE COME.
SOMETIME.

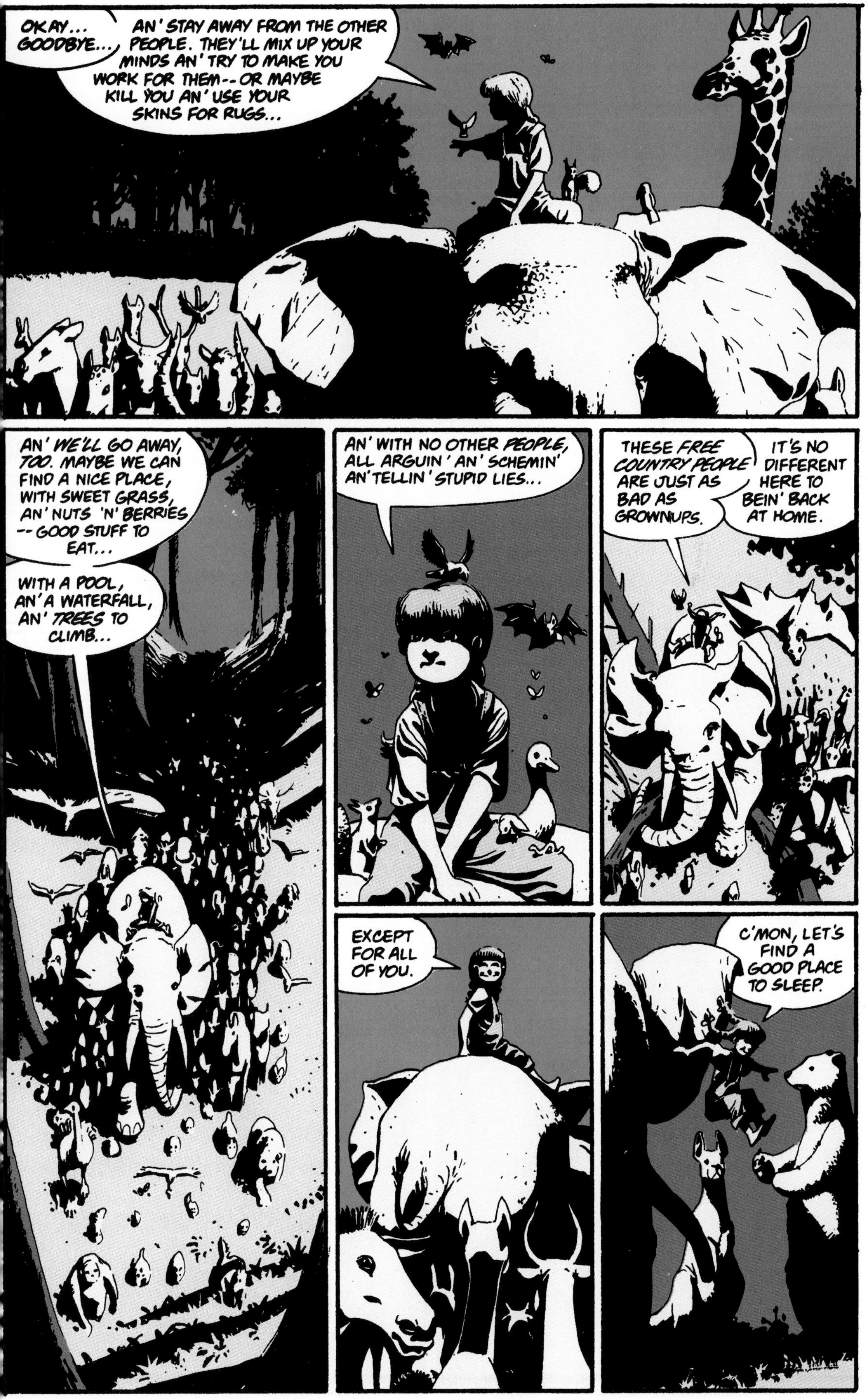
OKAY... GOODBYE...
AN' STAY AWAY FROM THE OTHER PEOPLE. THEY'LL MIX UP YOUR MINDS AN' TRY TO MAKE YOU WORK FOR THEM-- OR MAYBE KILL YOU AN' USE YOUR SKINS FOR RUGS...
AN' WE'LL GO AWAY, TOO. MAYBE WE CAN FIND A NICE PLACE, WITH SWEET GRASS, AN' NUTS 'N' BERRIES -- GOOD STUFF TO EAT...
WITH A POOL, AN' A WATERFALL, AN' TREES TO CLIMB...
AN' WITH NO OTHER PEOPLE, ALL ARGUIN' AN' SCHEMIN' AN' TELLIN' STUPID LIES...
THESE FREE COUNTRY PEOPLE ARE JUST AS BAD AS GROWNUPS.
IT'S NO DIFFERENT HERE TO BEIN' BACK AT HOME.
EXCEPT FOR ALL OF YOU.
C'MON, LET'S FIND A GOOD PLACE TO SLEEP.

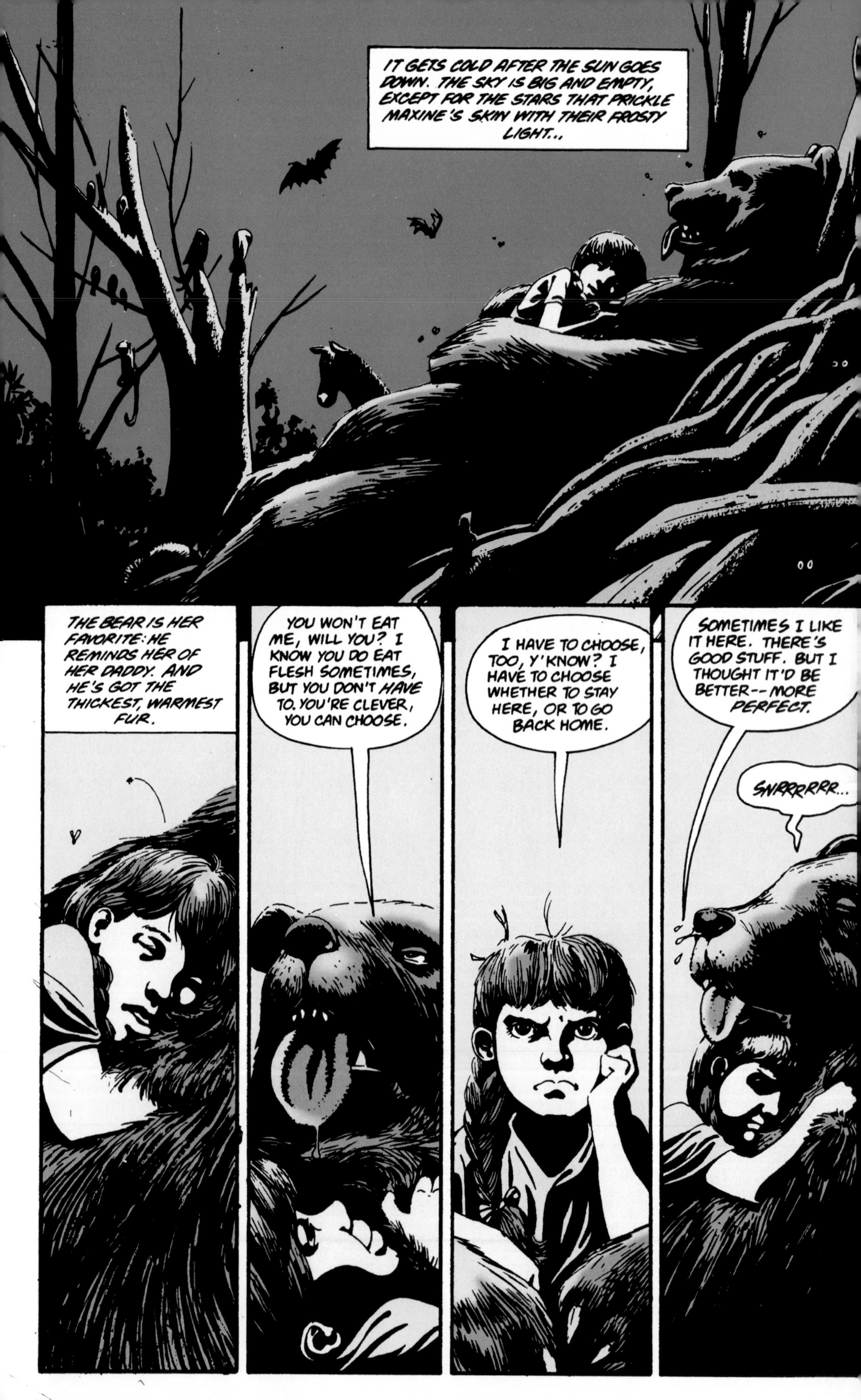
IT GETS COLD AFTER THE SUN GOES DOWN. THE SKY IS BIG AND EMPTY, EXCEPT FOR THE STARS THAT PRICKLE MAXINE'S SKIN WITH THEIR FROSTY LIGHT...
THE BEAR IS HER FAVORITE: HE REMINDS HER OF HER DADDY. AND HE'S GOT THE THICKEST, WARMEST FUR.
YOU WON'T EAT ME, WILL YOU? I KNOW YOU DO EAT FLESH SOMETIMES, BUT YOU DON'T HAVE TO. YOU'RE CLEVER, YOU CAN CHOOSE.
I HAVE TO CHOOSE, TOO, Y'KNOW? I HAVE TO CHOOSE WHETHER TO STAY HERE, OR TO GO BACK HOME.
SOMETIMES I LIKE IT HERE. THERE'S GOOD STUFF. BUT I THOUGHT IT'D BE BETTER-- MORE PERFECT.
SNRRRRRR...

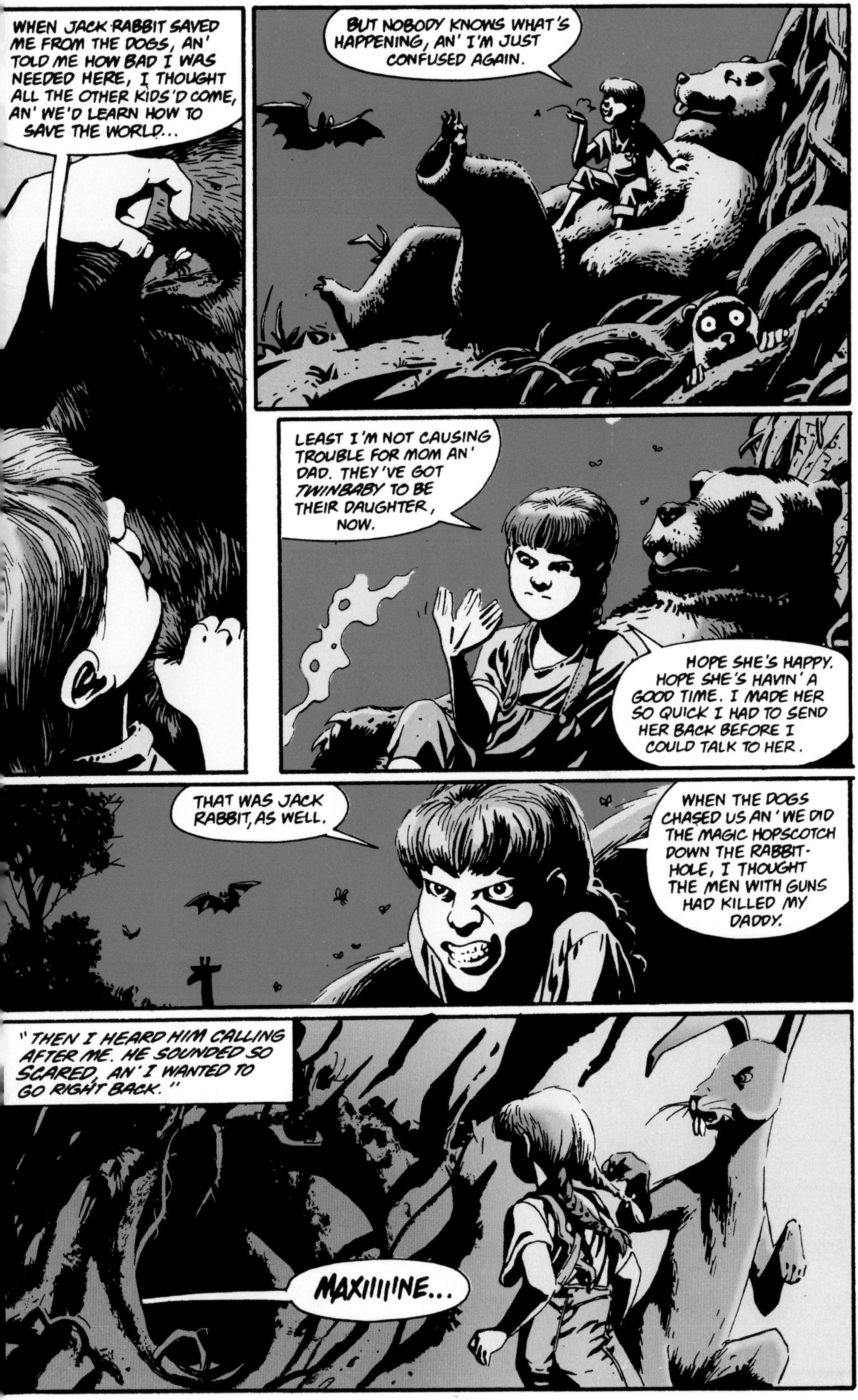
WHEN JACK RABBIT SAVED ME FROM THE DOGS, AN' TOLD ME HOW BAD I WAS NEEDED HERE, I THOUGHT ALL THE OTHER KIDS'D COME, AN' WE'D LEARN HOW TO SAVE THE WORLD...
BUT NOBODY KNOWS WHAT'S HAPPENING, AN' I'M JUST CONFUSED AGAIN.
LEAST I'M NOT CAUSING TROUBLE FOR MOM AN' DAD. THEY'VE GOT TWINBABY TO BE THEIR DAUGHTER, NOW.
HOPE SHE'S HAPPY. HOPE SHE'S HAVIN' A GOOD TIME. I MADE HER SO QUICK I HAD TO SEND HER BACK BEFORE I COULD TALK TO HER.
THAT WAS JACK RABBIT, AS WELL.
WHEN THE DOGS CHASED US AN' WE DID THE MAGIC HOPSCOTCH DOWN THE RABBIT-HOLE, I THOUGHT THE MEN WITH GUNS HAD KILLED MY DADDY.
"THEN I HEARD HIM CALLING AFTER ME. HE SOUNDED SO SCARED, AN' I WANTED TO GO RIGHT BACK."
MAXIIIIINE...

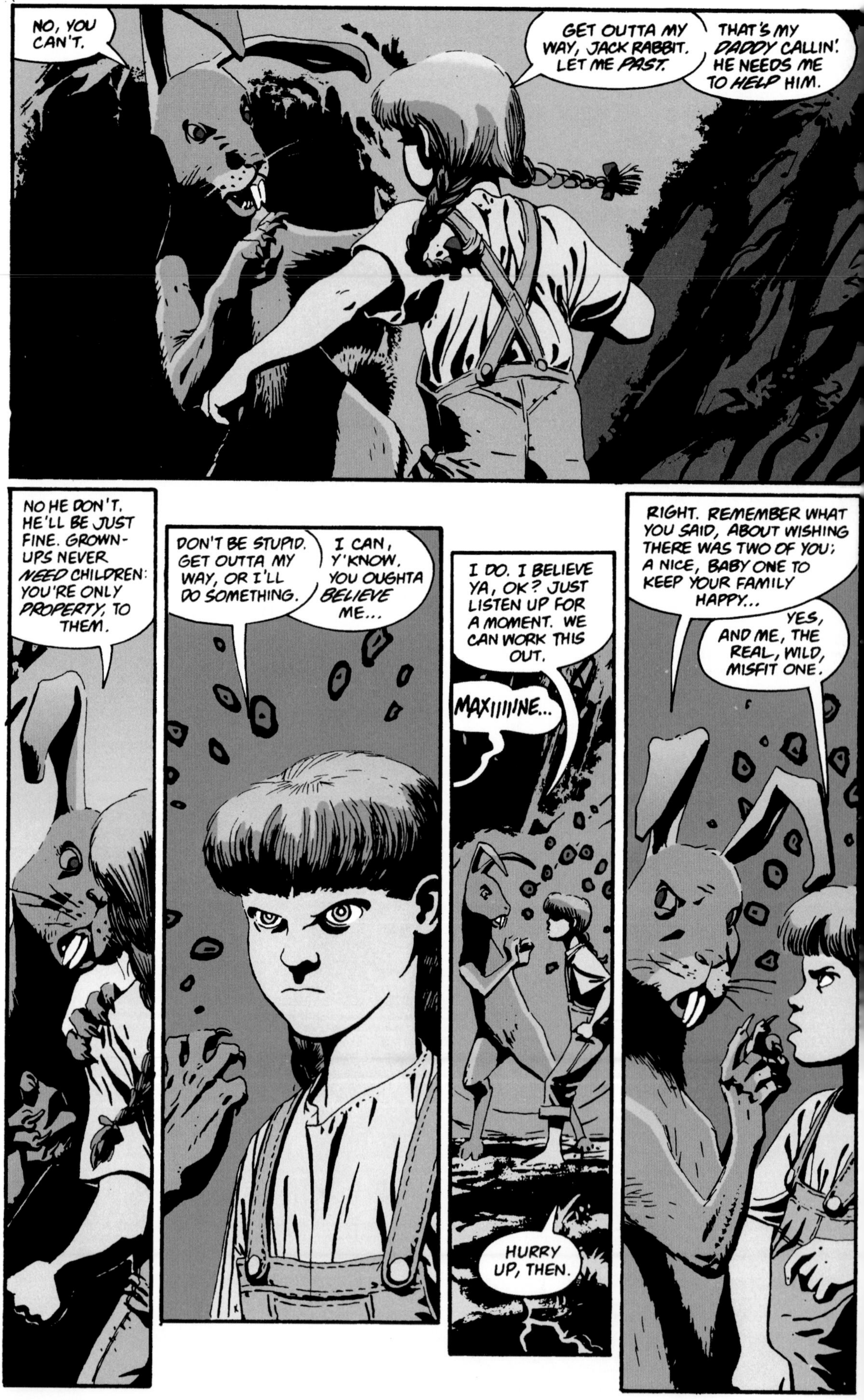
NO, YOU CAN'T.
GET OUTTA MY WAY, JACK RABBIT. LET ME PAST.
THAT'S MY DADDY CALLIN'. HE NEEDS ME TO HELP HIM.
NO HE DON'T. HE'LL BE JUST FINE. GROWN-UPS NEVER NEED CHILDREN: YOU'RE ONLY PROPERTY, TO THEM.
DON'T BE STUPID. GET OUTTA MY WAY, OR I'LL DO SOMETHING.
I CAN, Y'KNOW. YOU OUGHTA BELIEVE ME...
I DO. I BELIEVE YA, OK? JUST LISTEN UP FOR A MOMENT. WE CAN WORK THIS OUT.
MAXIIIIINE...
HURRY UP, THEN.
RIGHT. REMEMBER WHAT YOU SAID, ABOUT WISHING THERE WAS TWO OF YOU; A NICE, BABY ONE TO KEEP YOUR FAMILY HAPPY...
YES, AND ME, THE REAL, WILD, MISFIT ONE.

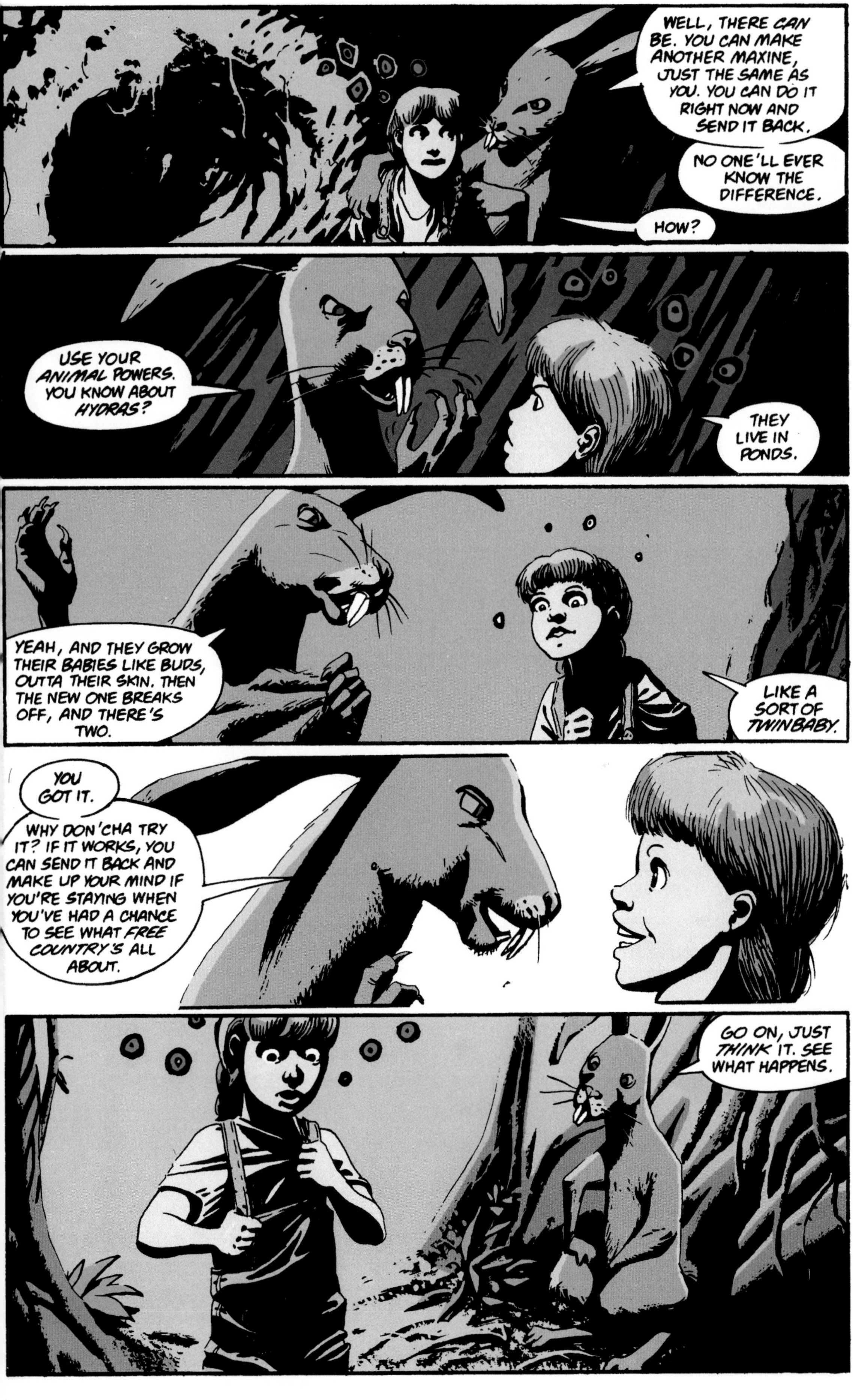

WELL, THERE CAN BE. YOU CAN MAKE ANOTHER MAXINE, JUST THE SAME AS YOU. YOU CAN DO IT RIGHT NOW AND SEND IT BACK.
NO ONE'LL EVER KNOW THE DIFFERENCE.
HOW?
USE YOUR ANIMAL POWERS. YOU KNOW ABOUT HYDRAS?
THEY LIVE IN PONDS.
YEAH, AND THEY GROW THEIR BABIES LIKE BUDS, OUTTA THEIR SKIN. THEN THE NEW ONE BREAKS OFF, AND THERE'S TWO.
LIKE A SORT OF TWINBABY.
YOU GOT IT.
WHY DON'CHA TRY IT? IF IT WORKS, YOU CAN SEND IT BACK AND MAKE UP YOUR MIND IF YOU'RE STAYING WHEN YOU'VE HAD A CHANCE TO SEE WHAT FREE COUNTRY'S ALL ABOUT.
GO ON, JUST THINK IT. SEE WHAT HAPPENS.

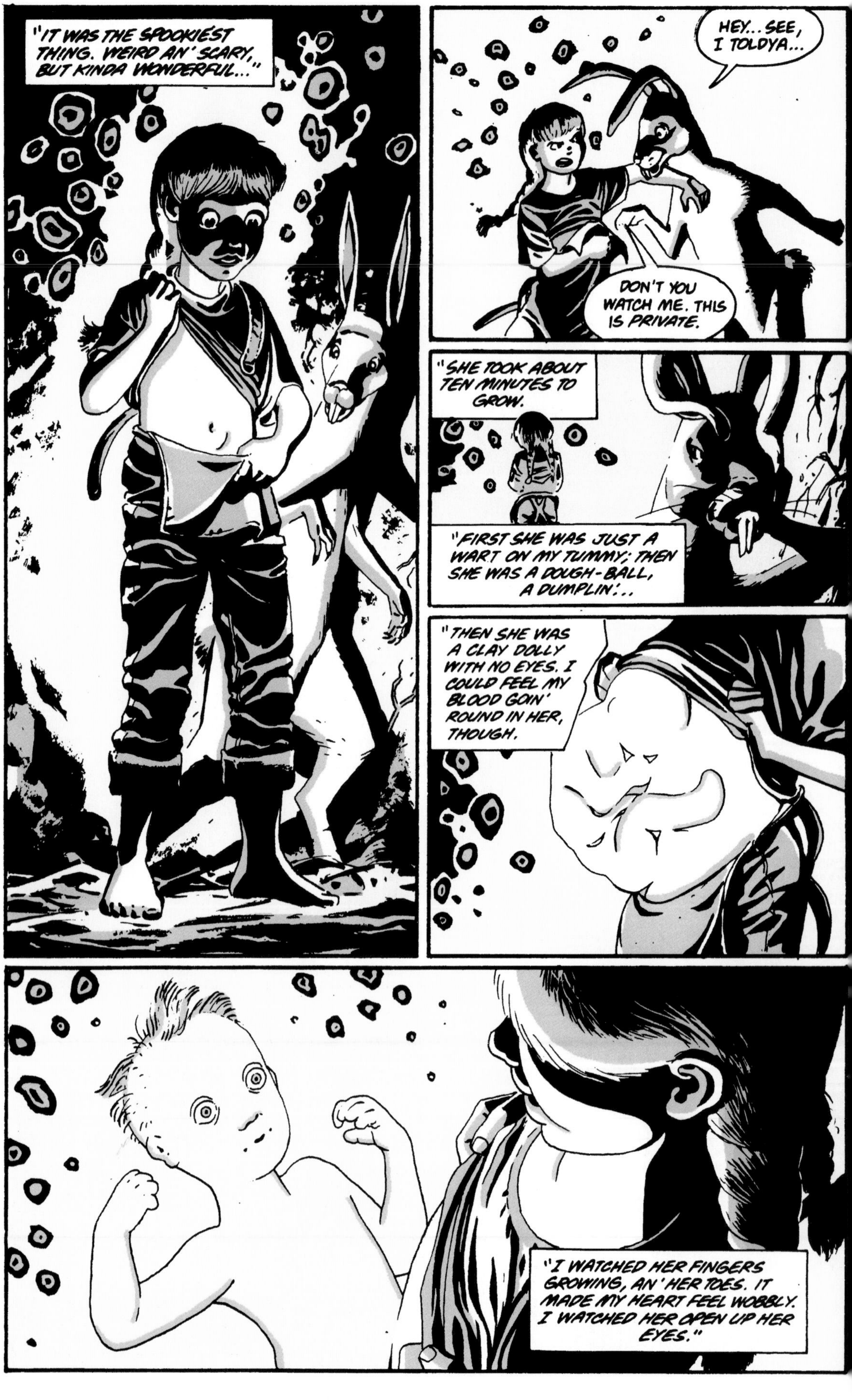
"IT WAS THE SPOOKIEST THING. WEIRD AN' SCARY, BUT KINDA WONDERFUL..."
HEY... SEE, I TOLDYA...
DON'T YOU WATCH ME. THIS IS PRIVATE.
"SHE TOOK ABOUT TEN MINUTES TO GROW.
"FIRST SHE WAS JUST A WART ON MY TUMMY; THEN SHE WAS A DOUGH-BALL, A DUMPLIN'...
"THEN SHE WAS A CLAY DOLLY WITH NO EYES. I COULD FEEL MY BLOOD GOIN' ROUND IN HER, THOUGH.
"I WATCHED HER FINGERS GROWING, AN' HER TOES. IT MADE MY HEART FEEL WOBBLY. I WATCHED HER OPEN UP HER EYES."

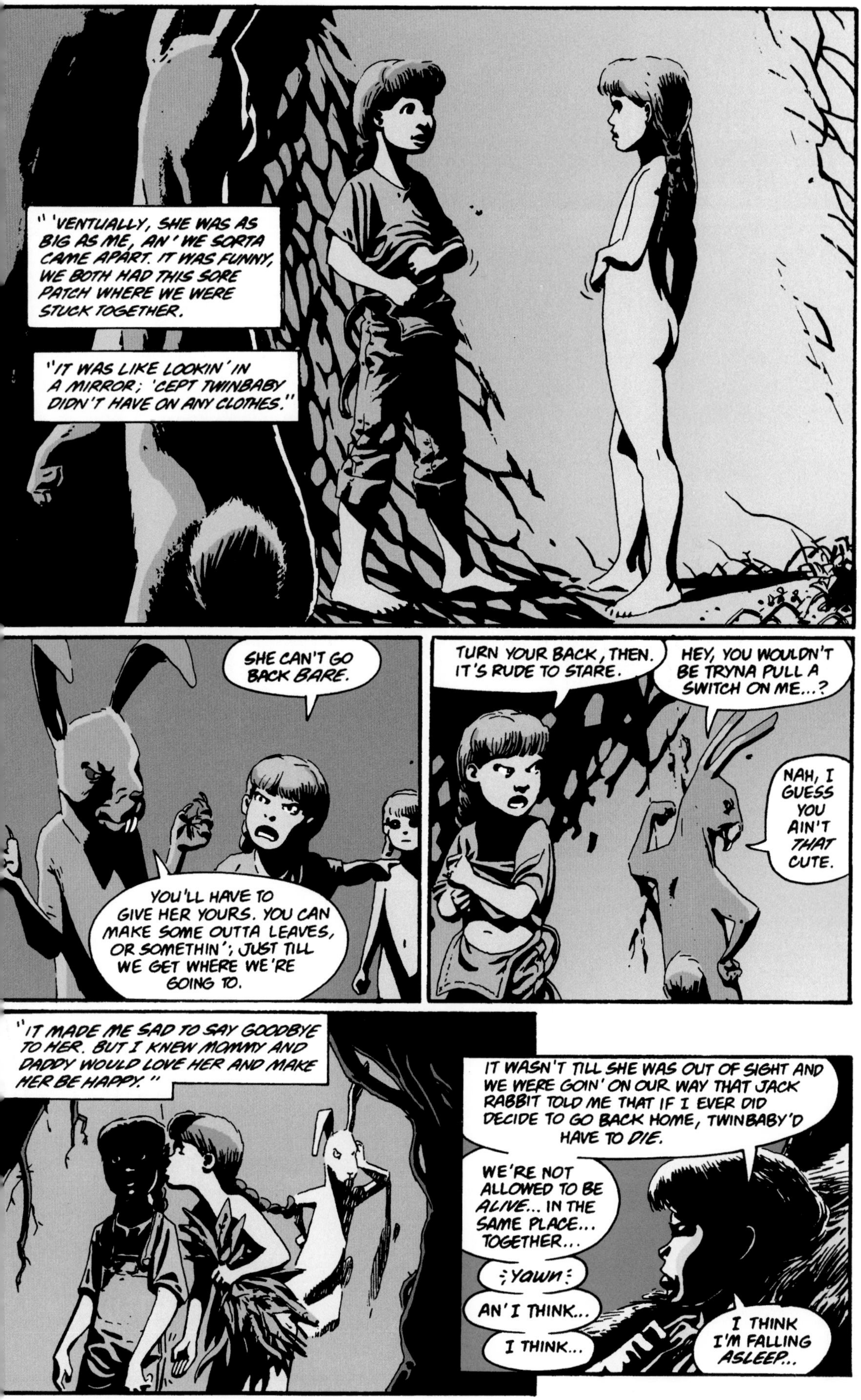
"'VENTUALLY, SHE WAS AS BIG AS ME, AN' WE SORTA CAME APART. IT WAS FUNNY, WE BOTH HAD THIS SORE PATCH WHERE WE WERE STUCK TOGETHER.
"IT WAS LIKE LOOKIN' IN A MIRROR; 'CEPT TWINBABY DIDN'T HAVE ON ANY CLOTHES."
SHE CAN'T GO BACK BARE.
YOU'LL HAVE TO GIVE HER YOURS. YOU CAN MAKE SOME OUTTA LEAVES, OR SOMETHIN'; JUST TILL WE GET WHERE WE'RE GOING TO.
TURN YOUR BACK, THEN. IT'S RUDE TO STARE.
HEY, YOU WOULDN'T BE TRYNA PULL A SWITCH ON ME...?
NAH, I GUESS YOU AIN'T THAT CUTE.
"IT MADE ME SAD TO SAY GOODBYE TO HER. BUT I KNEW MOMMY AND DADDY WOULD LOVE HER AND MAKE HER BE HAPPY."
IT WASN'T TILL SHE WAS OUT OF SIGHT AND WE WERE GOIN' ON OUR WAY THAT JACK RABBIT TOLD ME THAT IF I EVER DID DECIDE TO GO BACK HOME, TWINBABY'D HAVE TO DIE.
WE'RE NOT ALLOWED TO BE ALIVE... IN THE SAME PLACE... TOGETHER...
:YAWN:
AN' I THINK...
I THINK...
I THINK I'M FALLING ASLEEP...

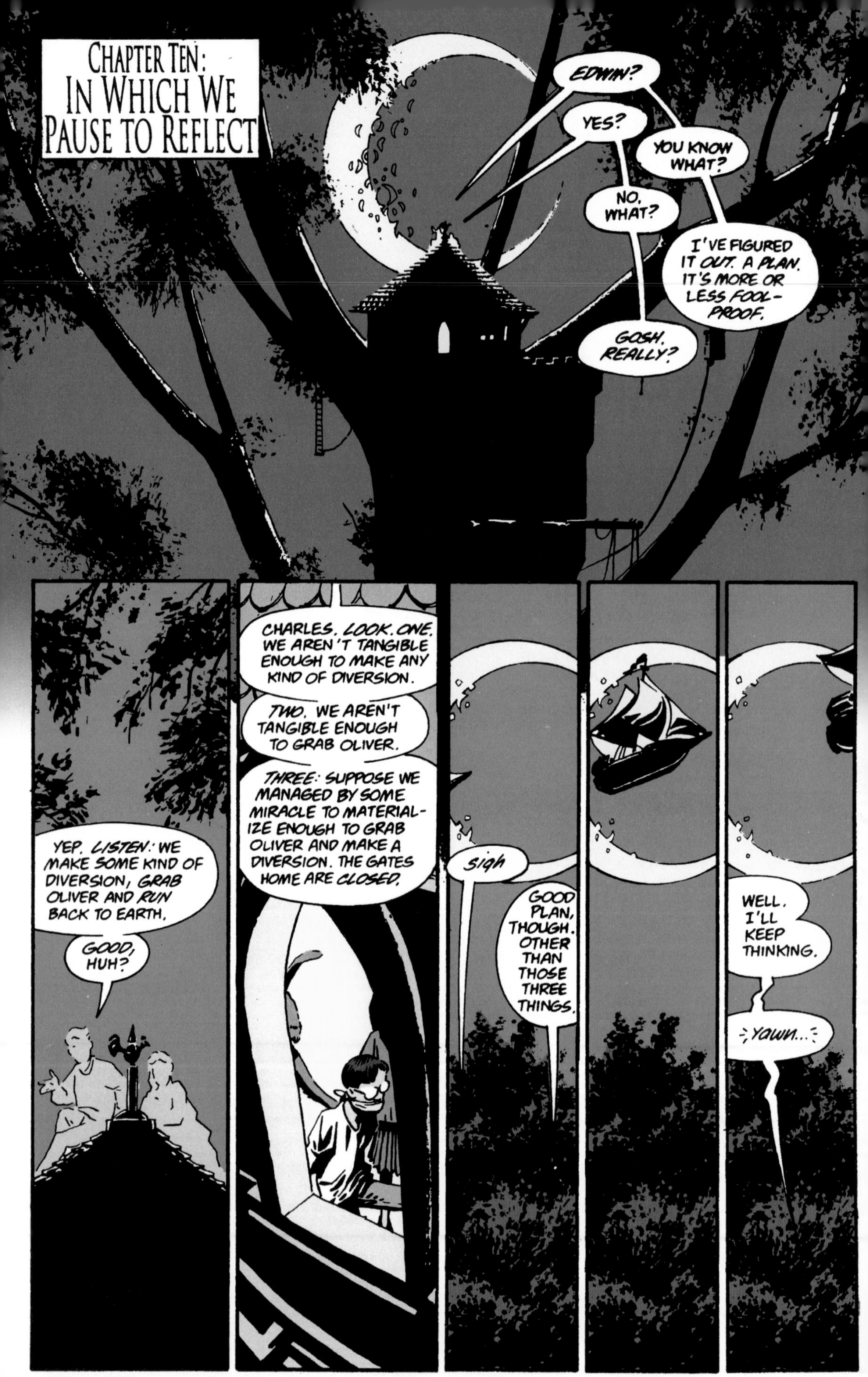
CHAPTER TEN:
IN WHICH WE PAUSE TO REFLECT
EDWIN?
YES?
YOU KNOW WHAT?
NO, WHAT?
I'VE FIGURED IT OUT. A PLAN. IT'S MORE OR LESS FOOL-PROOF.
GOSH. REALLY?
YEP. LISTEN: WE MAKE SOME KIND OF DIVERSION, GRAB OLIVER AND RUN BACK TO EARTH.
GOOD, HUH?
CHARLES. LOOK. ONE. WE AREN'T TANGIBLE ENOUGH TO MAKE ANY KIND OF DIVERSION.
TWO. WE AREN'T TANGIBLE ENOUGH TO GRAB OLIVER.
THREE: SUPPOSE WE MANAGED BY SOME MIRACLE TO MATERIAL-IZE ENOUGH TO GRAB OLIVER AND MAKE A DIVERSION. THE GATES HOME ARE CLOSED.
sigh
GOOD PLAN, THOUGH. OTHER THAN THOSE THREE THINGS.
WELL. I'LL KEEP THINKING.
yawn...

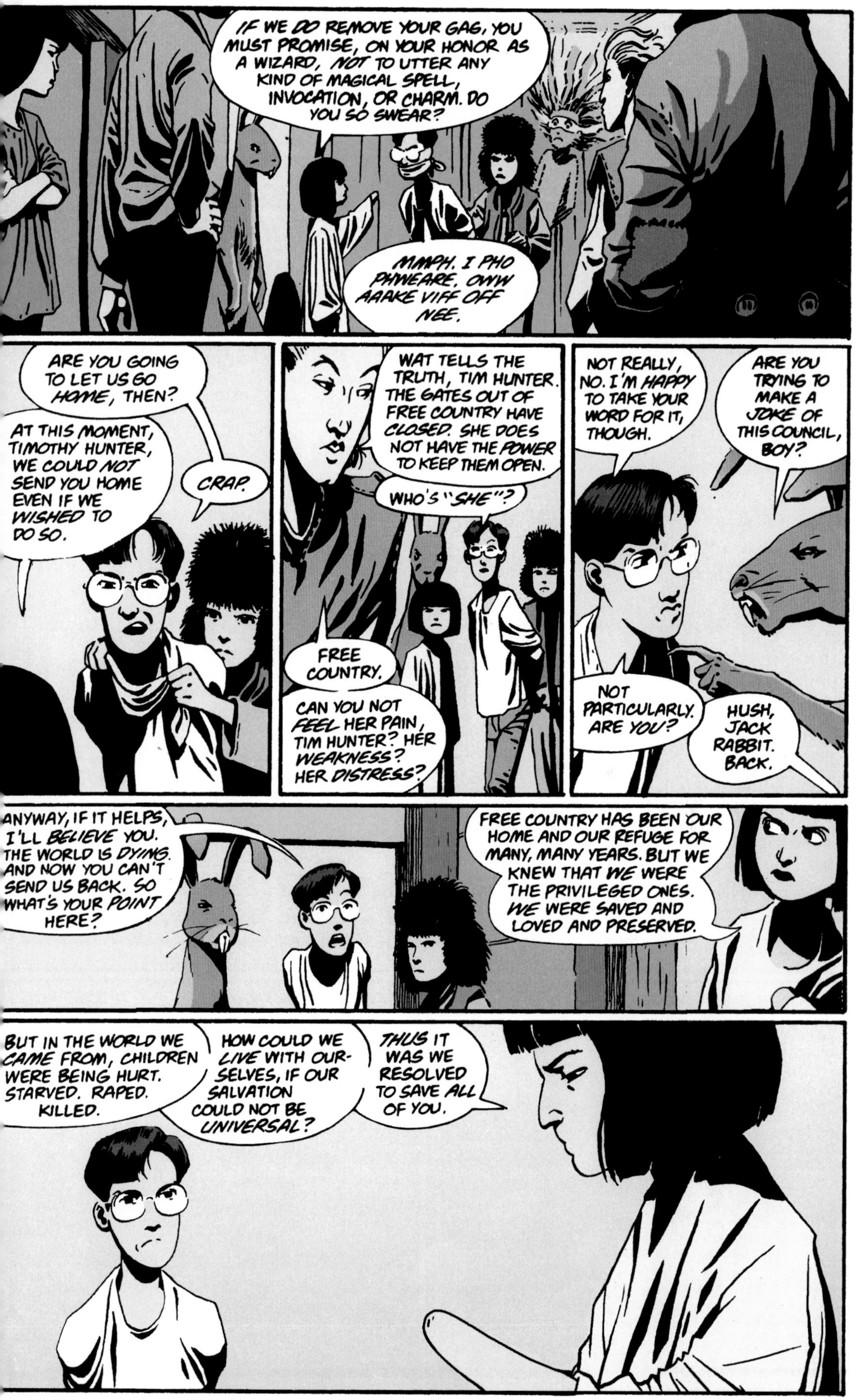
IF WE DO REMOVE YOUR GAG, YOU MUST PROMISE, ON YOUR HONOR AS A WIZARD, NOT TO UTTER ANY KIND OF MAGICAL SPELL, INVOCATION, OR CHARM. DO YOU SO SWEAR?
MMPH. I PHO PHWEARE. OWW AAAKE VIFF OFF NEE.
ARE YOU GOING TO LET US GO HOME, THEN?
AT THIS MOMENT, TIMOTHY HUNTER, WE COULD NOT SEND YOU HOME EVEN IF WE WISHED TO DO SO.
CRAP.
WAT TELLS THE TRUTH, TIM HUNTER. THE GATES OUT OF FREE COUNTRY HAVE CLOSED. SHE DOES NOT HAVE THE POWER TO KEEP THEM OPEN.
WHO'S "SHE"?
FREE COUNTRY.
CAN YOU NOT FEEL HER PAIN, TIM HUNTER? HER WEAKNESS? HER DISTRESS?
NOT REALLY, NO. I'M HAPPY TO TAKE YOUR WORD FOR IT, THOUGH.
ARE YOU TRYING TO MAKE A JOKE OF THIS COUNCIL, BOY?
NOT PARTICULARLY. ARE YOU?
HUSH, JACK RABBIT. BACK.
ANYWAY, IF IT HELPS, I'LL BELIEVE YOU. THE WORLD IS DYING. AND NOW YOU CAN'T SEND US BACK. SO WHAT'S YOUR POINT HERE?
FREE COUNTRY HAS BEEN OUR HOME AND OUR REFUGE FOR MANY, MANY YEARS. BUT WE KNEW THAT WE WERE THE PRIVILEGED ONES. WE WERE SAVED AND LOVED AND PRESERVED.
BUT IN THE WORLD WE CAME FROM, CHILDREN WERE BEING HURT. STARVED. RAPED. KILLED.
HOW COULD WE LIVE WITH OURSELVES, IF OUR SALVATION COULD NOT BE UNIVERSAL?
THUS IT WAS WE RESOLVED TO SAVE ALL OF YOU.

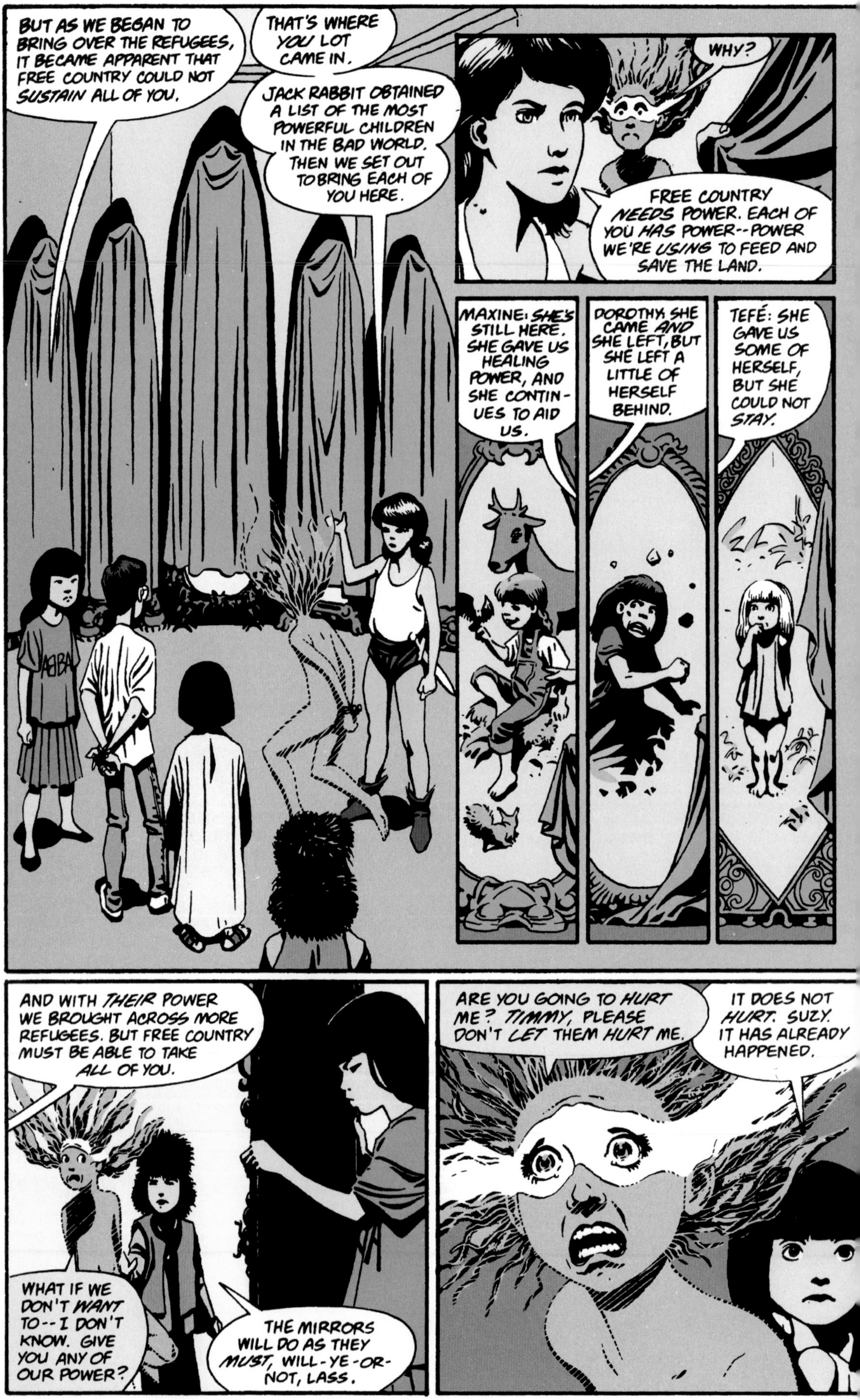
BUT AS WE BEGAN TO BRING OVER THE REFUGEES, IT BECAME APPARENT THAT FREE COUNTRY COULD NOT SUSTAIN ALL OF YOU.
THAT'S WHERE YOU LOT CAME IN.
JACK RABBIT OBTAINED A LIST OF THE MOST POWERFUL CHILDREN IN THE BAD WORLD. THEN WE SET OUT TO BRING EACH OF YOU HERE.
WHY?
FREE COUNTRY NEEDS POWER. EACH OF YOU HAS POWER--POWER WE'RE USING TO FEED AND SAVE THE LAND.
MAXINE: SHE'S STILL HERE. SHE GAVE US HEALING POWER, AND SHE CONTINUES TO AID US.
DOROTHY: SHE CAME AND SHE LEFT, BUT SHE LEFT A LITTLE OF HERSELF BEHIND.
TEFÉ: SHE GAVE US SOME OF HERSELF, BUT SHE COULD NOT STAY.
AND WITH THEIR POWER WE BROUGHT ACROSS MORE REFUGEES. BUT FREE COUNTRY MUST BE ABLE TO TAKE ALL OF YOU.
WHAT IF WE DON'T WANT TO--I DON'T KNOW. GIVE YOU ANY OF OUR POWER?
THE MIRRORS WILL DO AS THEY MUST, WILL-YE-OR-NOT, LASS.
ARE YOU GOING TO HURT ME? TIMMY, PLEASE DON'T LET THEM HURT ME.
IT DOES NOT HURT, SUZY. IT HAS ALREADY HAPPENED.

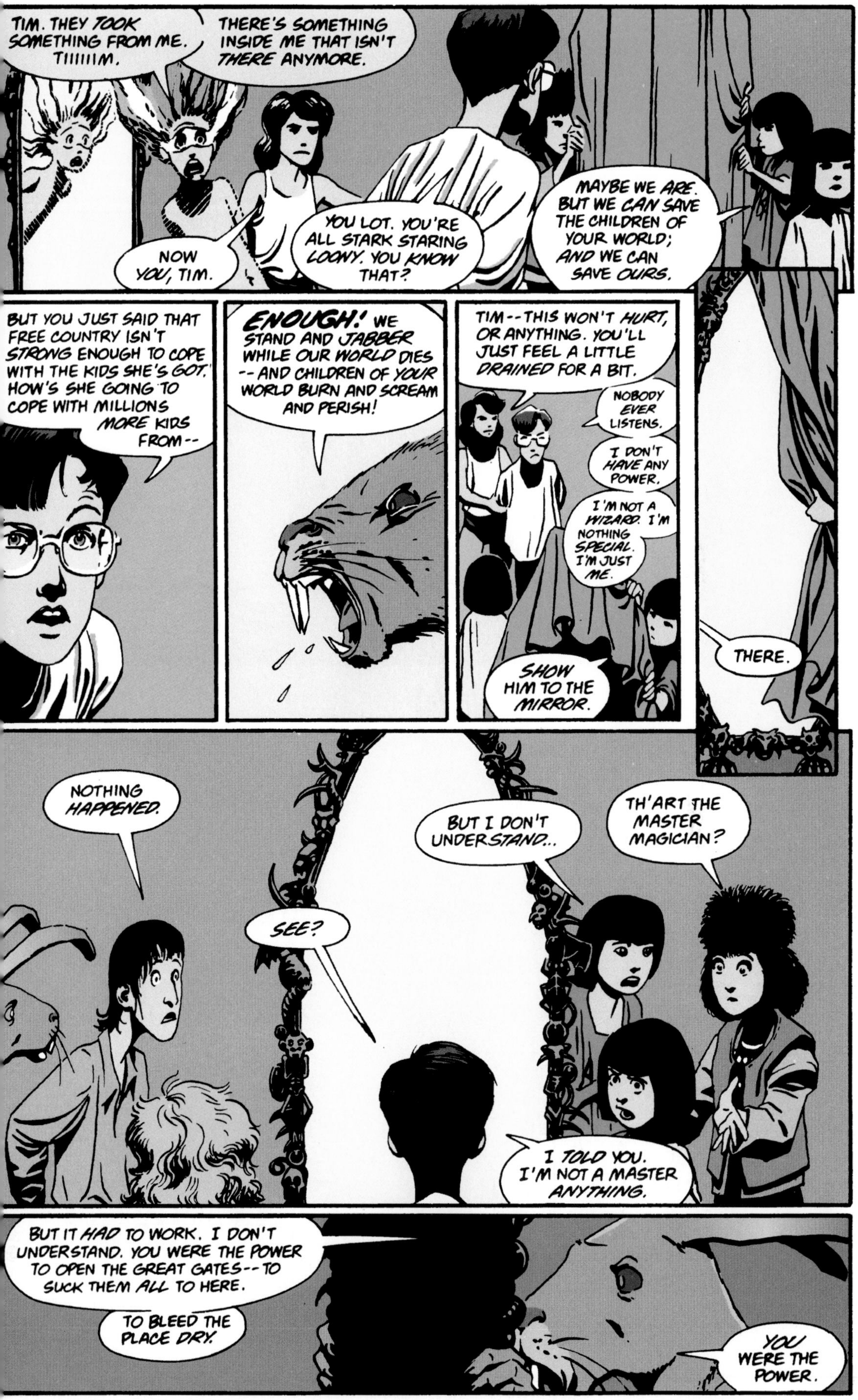
TIM. THEY TOOK SOMETHING FROM ME. TIIIIIIM.
THERE'S SOMETHING INSIDE ME THAT ISN'T THERE ANYMORE.
NOW YOU, TIM.
YOU LOT. YOU'RE ALL STARK STARING LOONY. YOU KNOW THAT?
MAYBE WE ARE. BUT WE CAN SAVE THE CHILDREN OF YOUR WORLD; AND WE CAN SAVE OURS.
BUT YOU JUST SAID THAT FREE COUNTRY ISN'T STRONG ENOUGH TO COPE WITH THE KIDS SHE'S GOT. HOW'S SHE GOING TO COPE WITH MILLIONS MORE KIDS FROM--
ENOUGH! WE STAND AND JABBER WHILE OUR WORLD DIES -- AND CHILDREN OF YOUR WORLD BURN AND SCREAM AND PERISH!
TIM--THIS WON'T HURT, OR ANYTHING. YOU'LL JUST FEEL A LITTLE DRAINED FOR A BIT.
NOBODY EVER LISTENS.
I DON'T HAVE ANY POWER.
I'M NOT A WIZARD. I'M NOTHING SPECIAL. I'M JUST ME.
SHOW HIM TO THE MIRROR.
THERE.
NOTHING HAPPENED.
SEE?
BUT I DON'T UNDERSTAND...
TH'ART THE MASTER MAGICIAN?
I TOLD YOU. I'M NOT A MASTER ANYTHING.
BUT IT HAD TO WORK. I DON'T UNDERSTAND. YOU WERE THE POWER TO OPEN THE GREAT GATES--TO SUCK THEM ALL TO HERE.
TO BLEED THE PLACE DRY.
YOU WERE THE POWER.

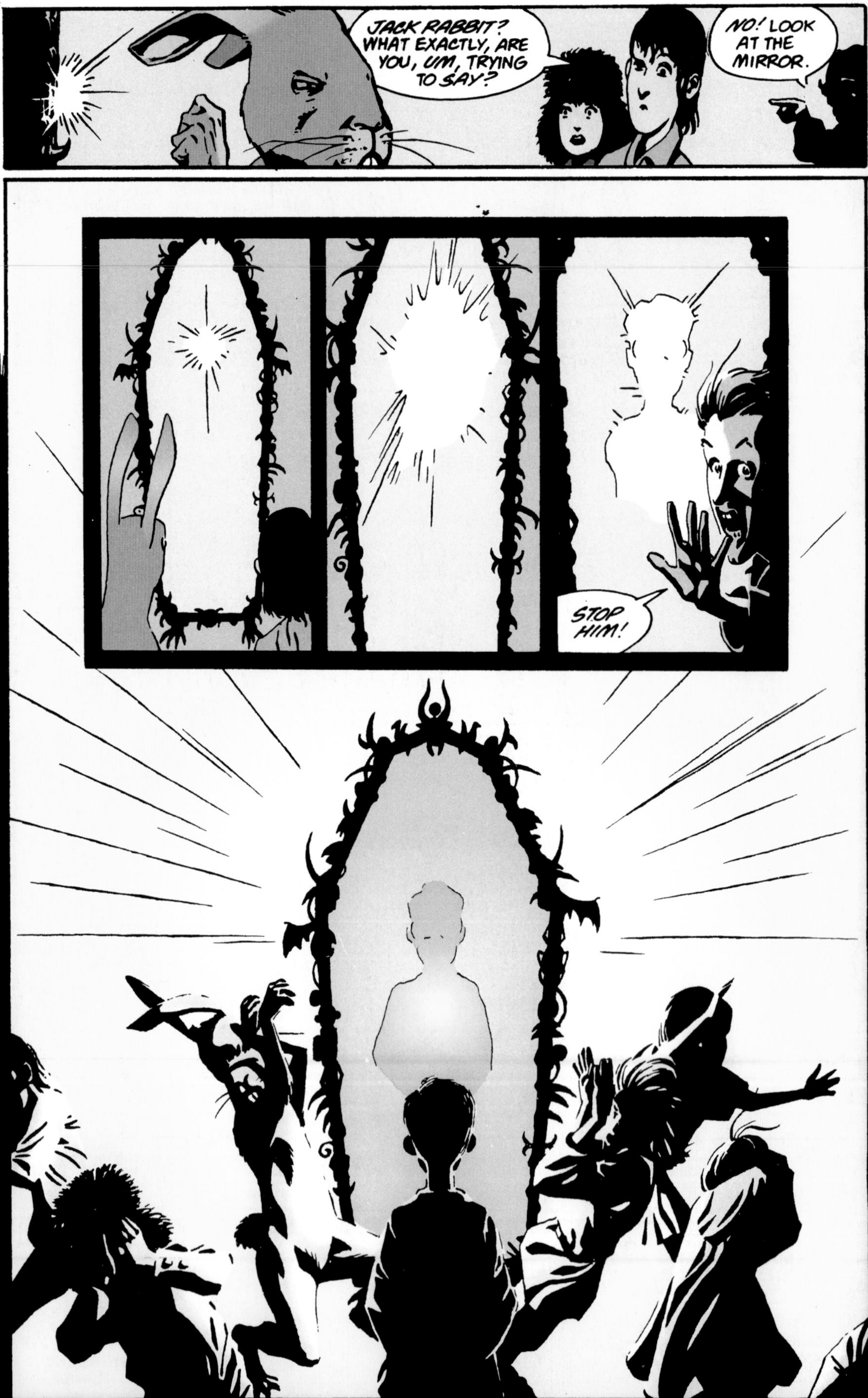
JACK RABBIT? WHAT EXACTLY, ARE YOU, UM, TRYING TO SAY?
NO! LOOK AT THE MIRROR.
STOP HIM!

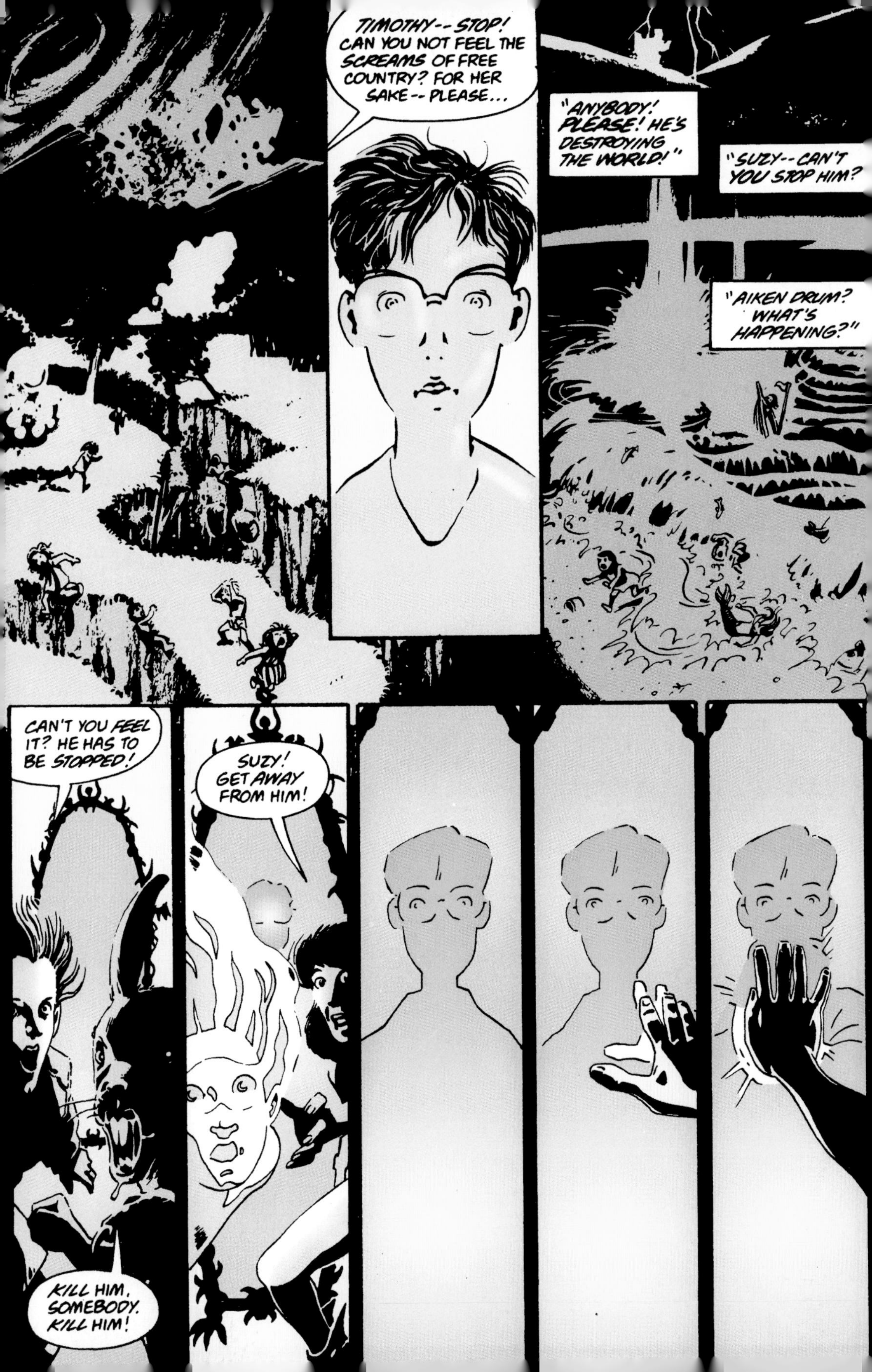
TIMOTHY-- STOP! CAN YOU NOT FEEL THE SCREAMS OF FREE COUNTRY? FOR HER SAKE-- PLEASE...
"ANYBODY! PLEASE! HE'S DESTROYING THE WORLD!"
"SUZY-- CAN'T YOU STOP HIM?
"AIKEN DRUM? WHAT'S HAPPENING?"
CAN'T YOU FEEL IT? HE HAS TO BE STOPPED!
KILL HIM, SOMEBODY. KILL HIM!
SUZY! GET AWAY FROM HIM!

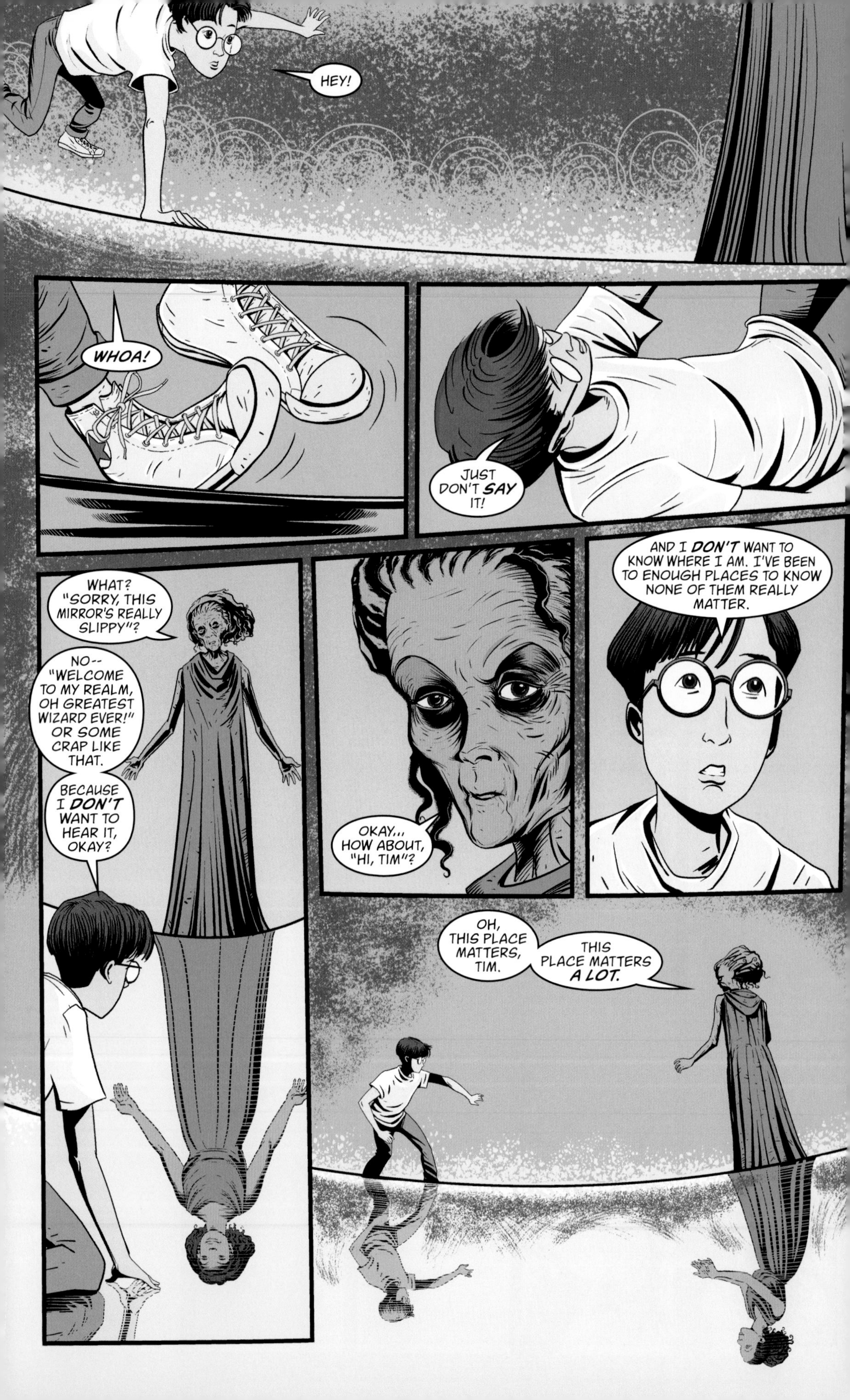
HEY!
WHOA!
JUST DON'T SAY IT!
WHAT? "SORRY, THIS MIRROR'S REALLY SLIPPY"?
NO-- "WELCOME TO MY REALM, OH GREATEST WIZARD EVER!" OR SOME CRAP LIKE THAT.
BECAUSE I DON'T WANT TO HEAR IT, OKAY?
OKAY... HOW ABOUT, "HI, TIM"?
AND I DON'T WANT TO KNOW WHERE I AM. I'VE BEEN TO ENOUGH PLACES TO KNOW NONE OF THEM REALLY MATTER.
OH, THIS PLACE MATTERS, TIM.
THIS PLACE MATTERS A LOT.

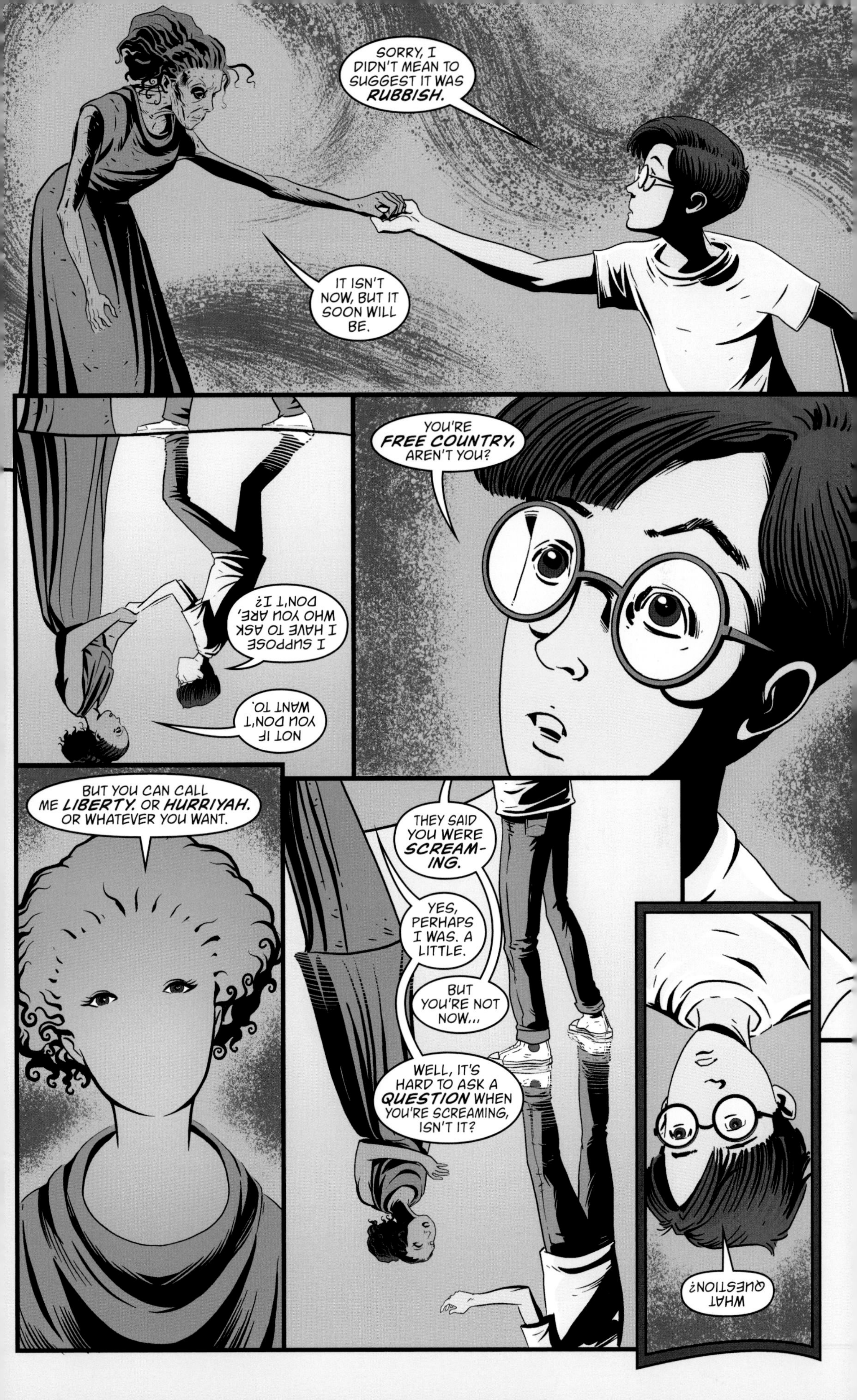
SORRY, I DIDN'T MEAN TO SUGGEST IT WAS RUBBISH.
IT ISN'T NOW, BUT IT SOON WILL BE.
I SUPPOSE I HAVE TO ASK WHO YOU ARE, DON'T I?
NOT IF YOU DON'T WANT TO.
YOU'RE FREE COUNTRY, AREN'T YOU?
BUT YOU CAN CALL ME LIBERTY. OR HURRIYAH. OR WHATEVER YOU WANT.
THEY SAID YOU WERE SCREAM-ING.
YES, PERHAPS I WAS. A LITTLE.
BUT YOU'RE NOT NOW...
WELL, IT'S HARD TO ASK A QUESTION WHEN YOU'RE SCREAMING, ISN'T IT?
WHAT QUESTION?

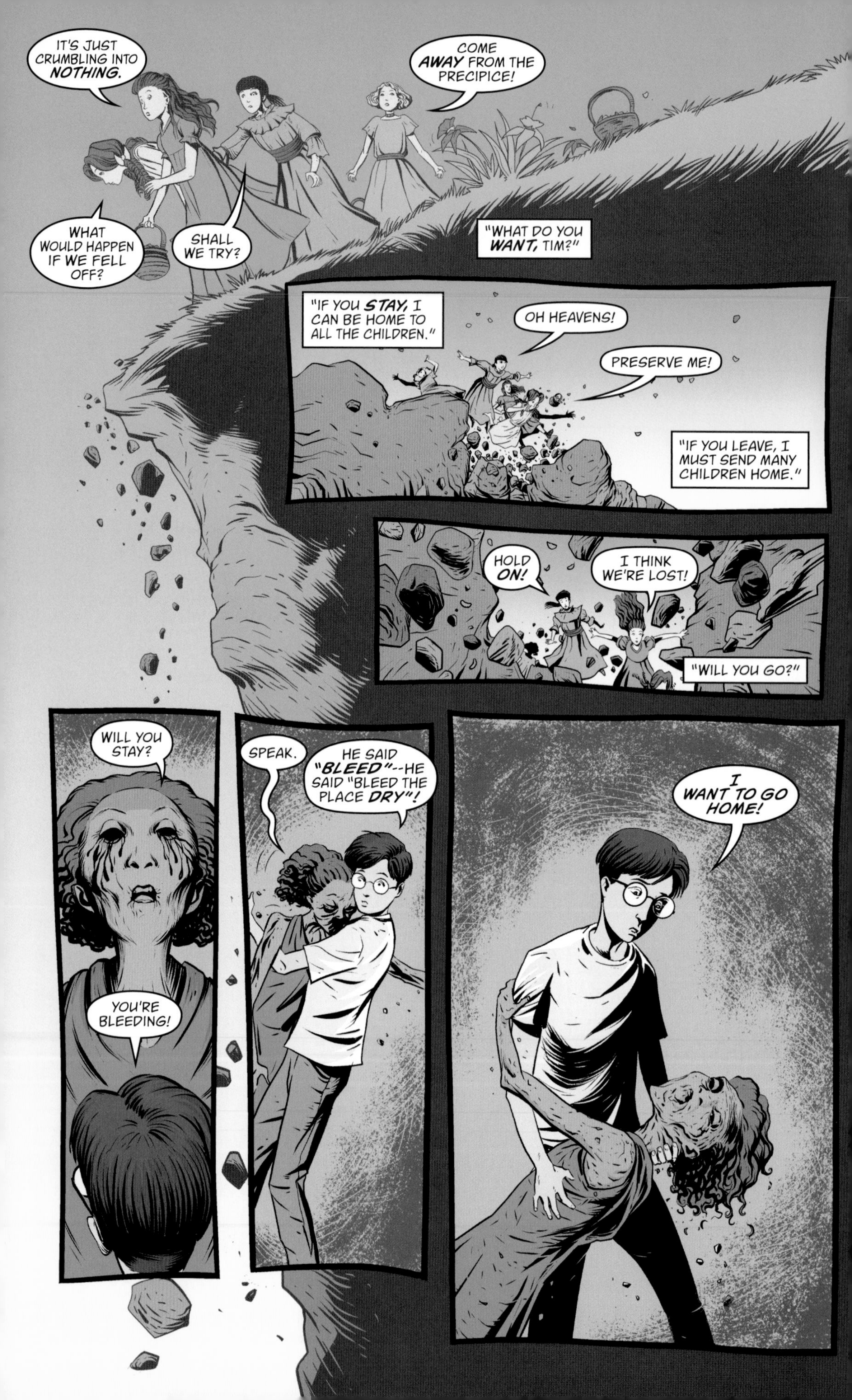
IT'S JUST CRUMBLING INTO NOTHING.
COME AWAY FROM THE PRECIPICE!
WHAT WOULD HAPPEN IF WE FELL OFF?
SHALL WE TRY?
"WHAT DO YOU WANT, TIM?"
"IF YOU STAY, I CAN BE HOME TO ALL THE CHILDREN."
OH HEAVENS!
PRESERVE ME!
"IF YOU LEAVE, I MUST SEND MANY CHILDREN HOME."
HOLD ON!
I THINK WE'RE LOST!
"WILL YOU GO?"
WILL YOU STAY?
YOU'RE BLEEDING!
SPEAK.
HE SAID "BLEED"--HE SAID "BLEED THE PLACE DRY"!
I WANT TO GO HOME!

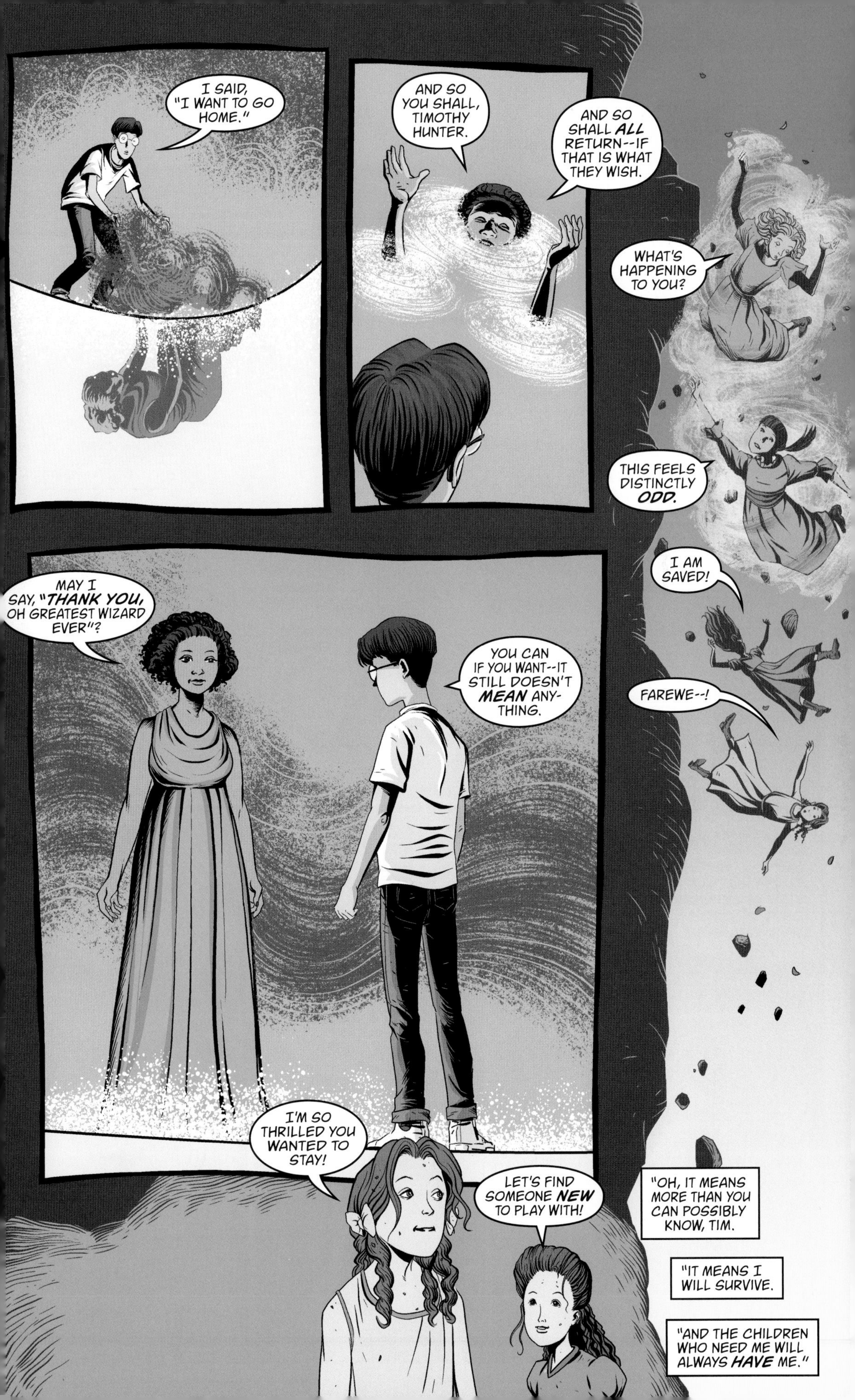
I SAID, "I WANT TO GO HOME."
AND SO YOU SHALL, TIMOTHY HUNTER.
AND SO SHALL ALL RETURN--IF THAT IS WHAT THEY WISH.
WHAT'S HAPPENING TO YOU?
THIS FEELS DISTINCTLY ODD.
I AM SAVED!
FAREWE--!
MAY I SAY, "THANK YOU, OH GREATEST WIZARD EVER"?
YOU CAN IF YOU WANT--IT STILL DOESN'T MEAN ANYTHING.
I'M SO THRILLED YOU WANTED TO STAY!
LET'S FIND SOMEONE NEW TO PLAY WITH!
"OH, IT MEANS MORE THAN YOU CAN POSSIBLY KNOW, TIM.
"IT MEANS I WILL SURVIVE.
"AND THE CHILDREN WHO NEED ME WILL ALWAYS HAVE ME."

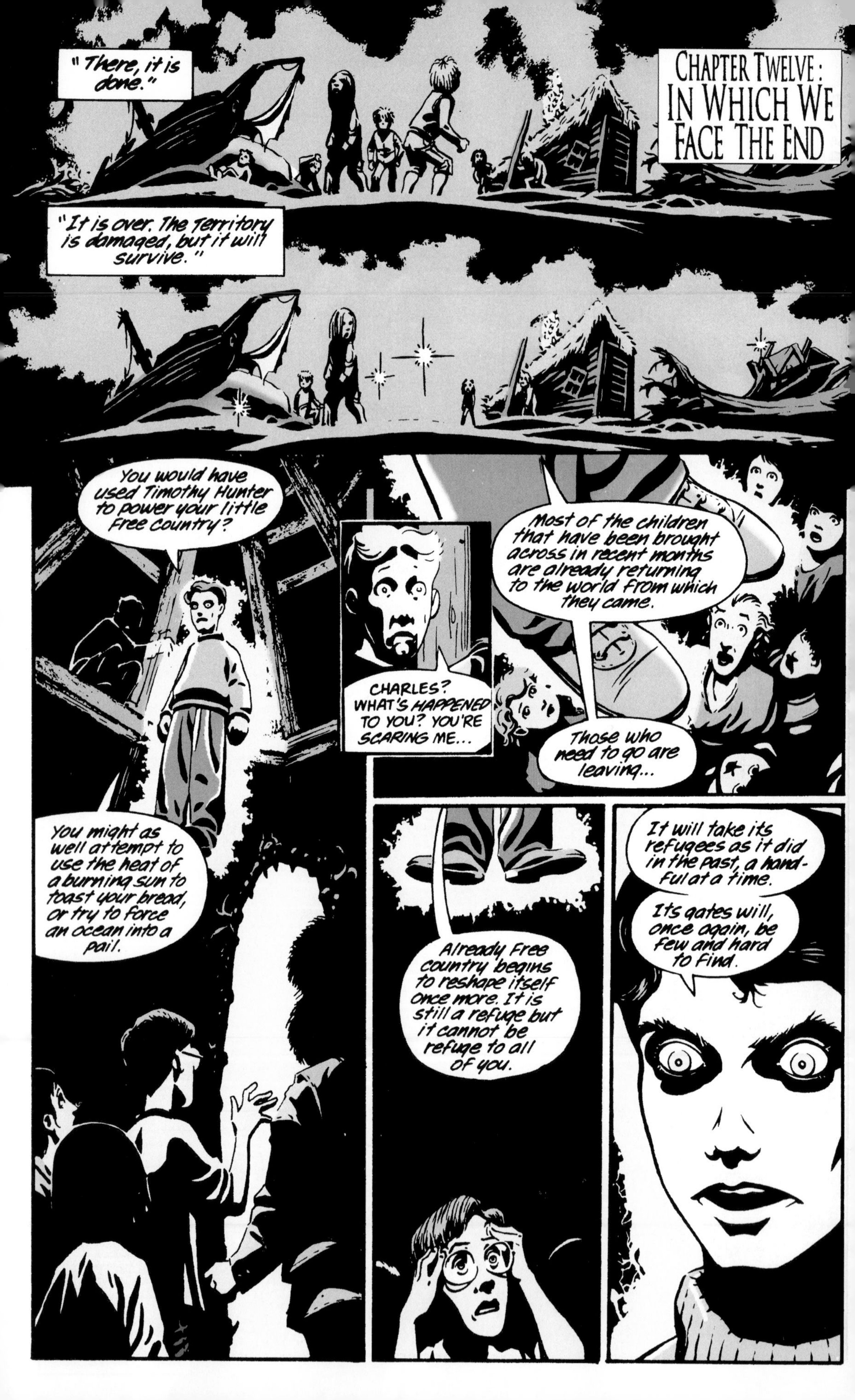

"There, it is done."
CHAPTER TWELVE: IN WHICH WE FACE THE END
"It is over. The Territory is damaged, but it will survive."
You would have used Timothy Hunter to power your little Free Country?
CHARLES? WHAT'S HAPPENED TO YOU? YOU'RE SCARING ME...
Most of the children that have been brought across in recent months are already returning to the world from which they came.
Those who need to go are leaving...
You might as well attempt to use the heat of a burning sun to toast your bread, or try to force an ocean into a pail.
Already Free Country begins to reshape itself once more. It is still a refuge but it cannot be refuge to all of you.
It will take its refugees as it did in the past, a handful at a time.
Its gates will, once again, be few and hard to find.

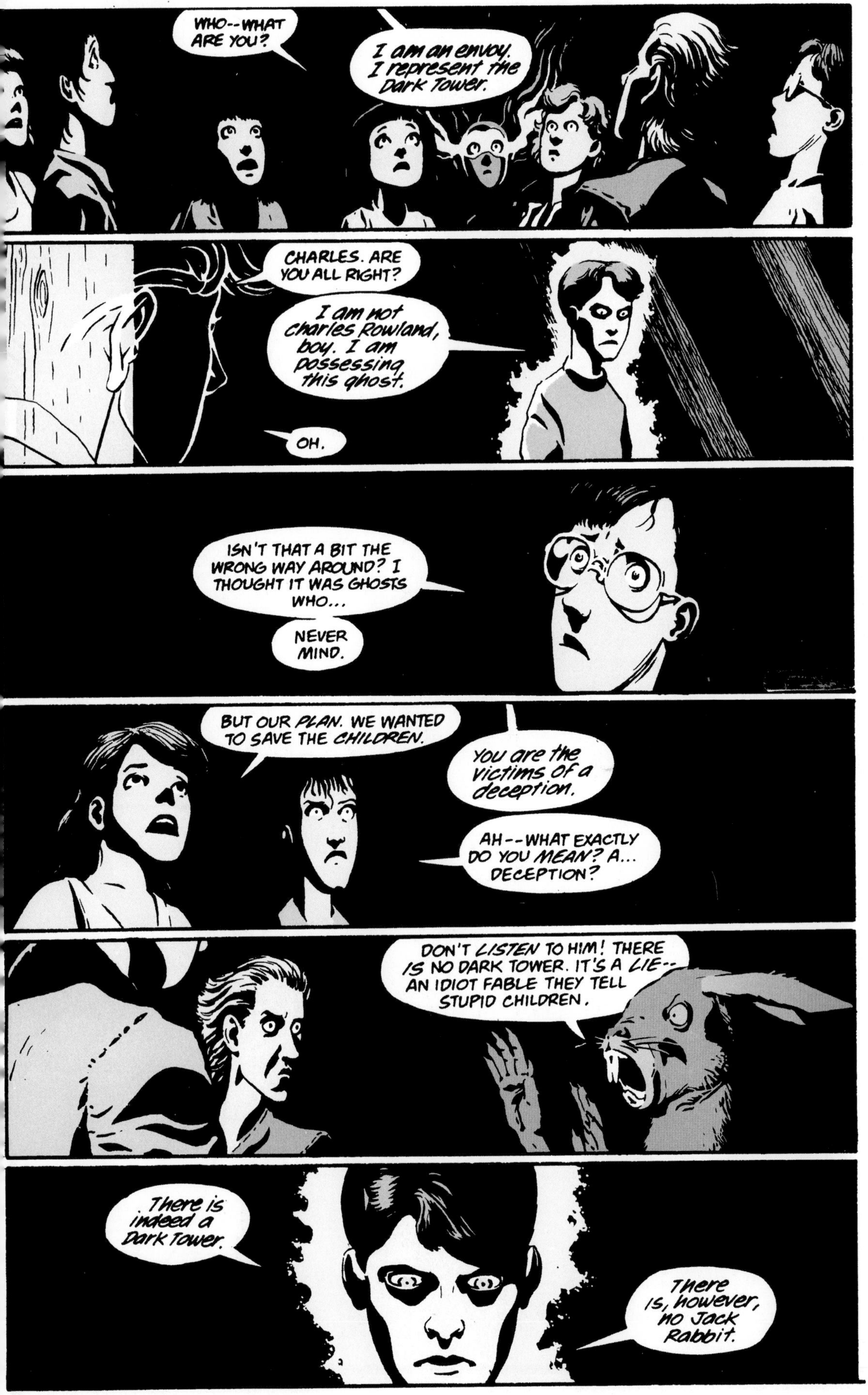
WHO--WHAT ARE YOU?
I am an envoy. I represent the Dark Tower.
CHARLES. ARE YOU ALL RIGHT?
I am not Charles Rowland, boy. I am possessing this ghost.
OH.
ISN'T THAT A BIT THE WRONG WAY AROUND? I THOUGHT IT WAS GHOSTS WHO...
NEVER MIND.
BUT OUR PLAN. WE WANTED TO SAVE THE CHILDREN.
You are the victims of a deception.
AH--WHAT EXACTLY DO YOU MEAN? A... DECEPTION?
DON'T LISTEN TO HIM! THERE IS NO DARK TOWER. IT'S A LIE--AN IDIOT FABLE THEY TELL STUPID CHILDREN.
There is indeed a Dark Tower.
There is, however, no Jack Rabbit.

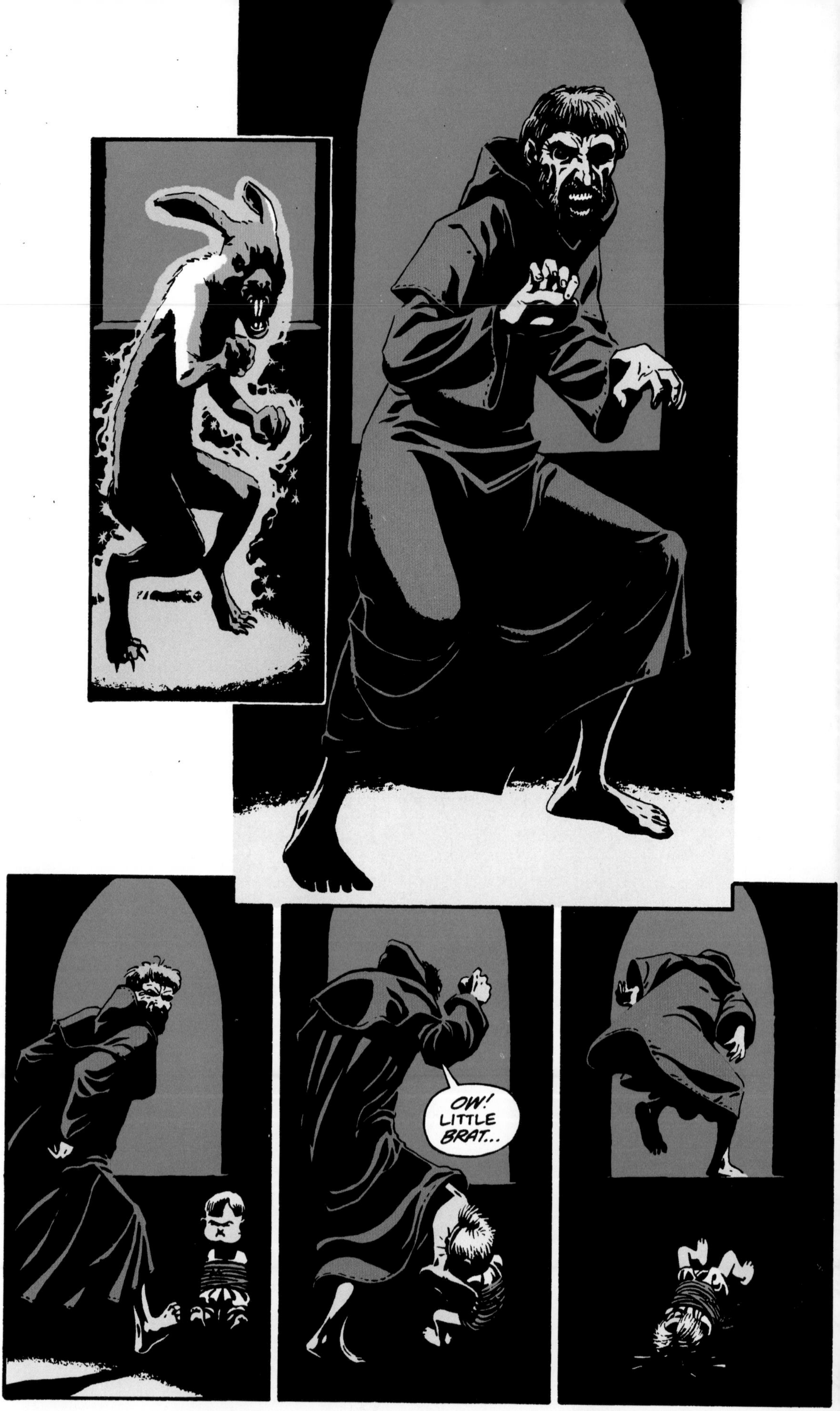
OW! LITTLE BRAT...

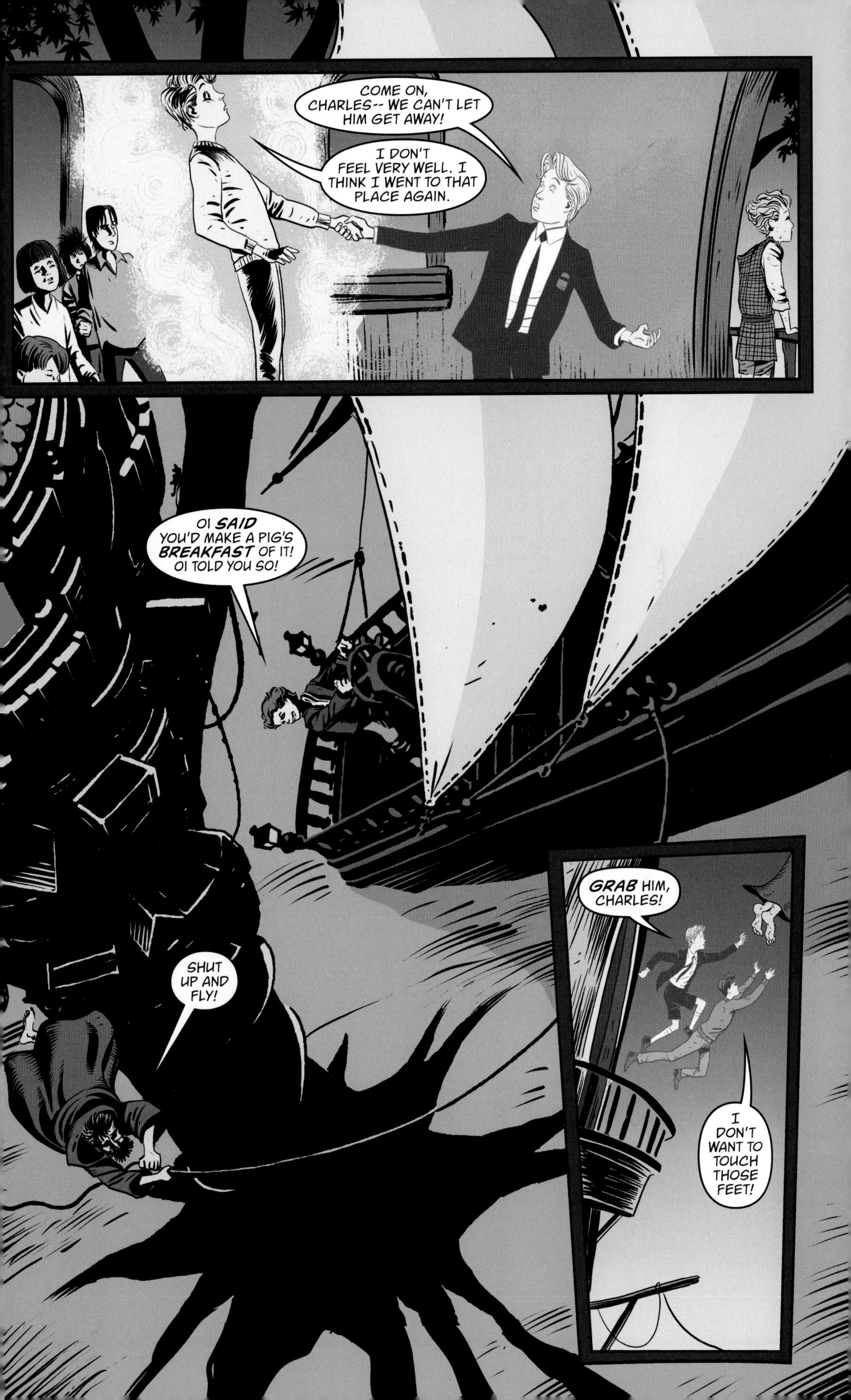
COME ON, CHARLES-- WE CAN'T LET HIM GET AWAY!
I DON'T FEEL VERY WELL. I THINK I WENT TO THAT PLACE AGAIN.
OI SAID YOU'D MAKE A PIG'S BREAKFAST OF IT! OI TOLD YOU SO!
SHUT UP AND FLY!
GRAB HIM, CHARLES!
I DON'T WANT TO TOUCH THOSE FEET!

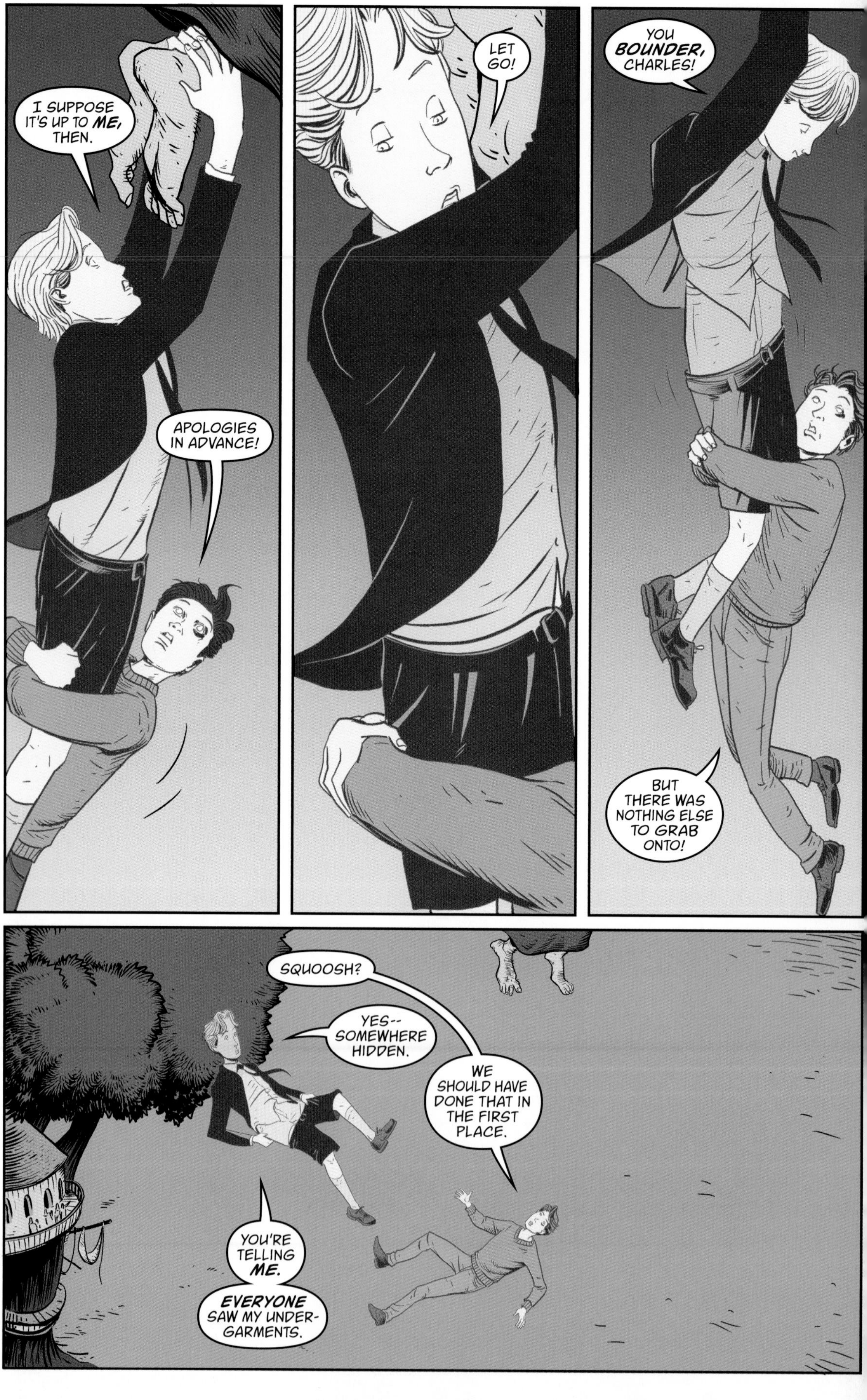
I SUPPOSE IT'S UP TO ME, THEN.
APOLOGIES IN ADVANCE!
LET GO!
YOU BOUNDER, CHARLES!
BUT THERE WAS NOTHING ELSE TO GRAB ONTO!
SQUOOSH?
YES-- SOMEWHERE HIDDEN.
WE SHOULD HAVE DONE THAT IN THE FIRST PLACE.
YOU'RE TELLING ME.
EVERYONE SAW MY UNDER-GARMENTS.

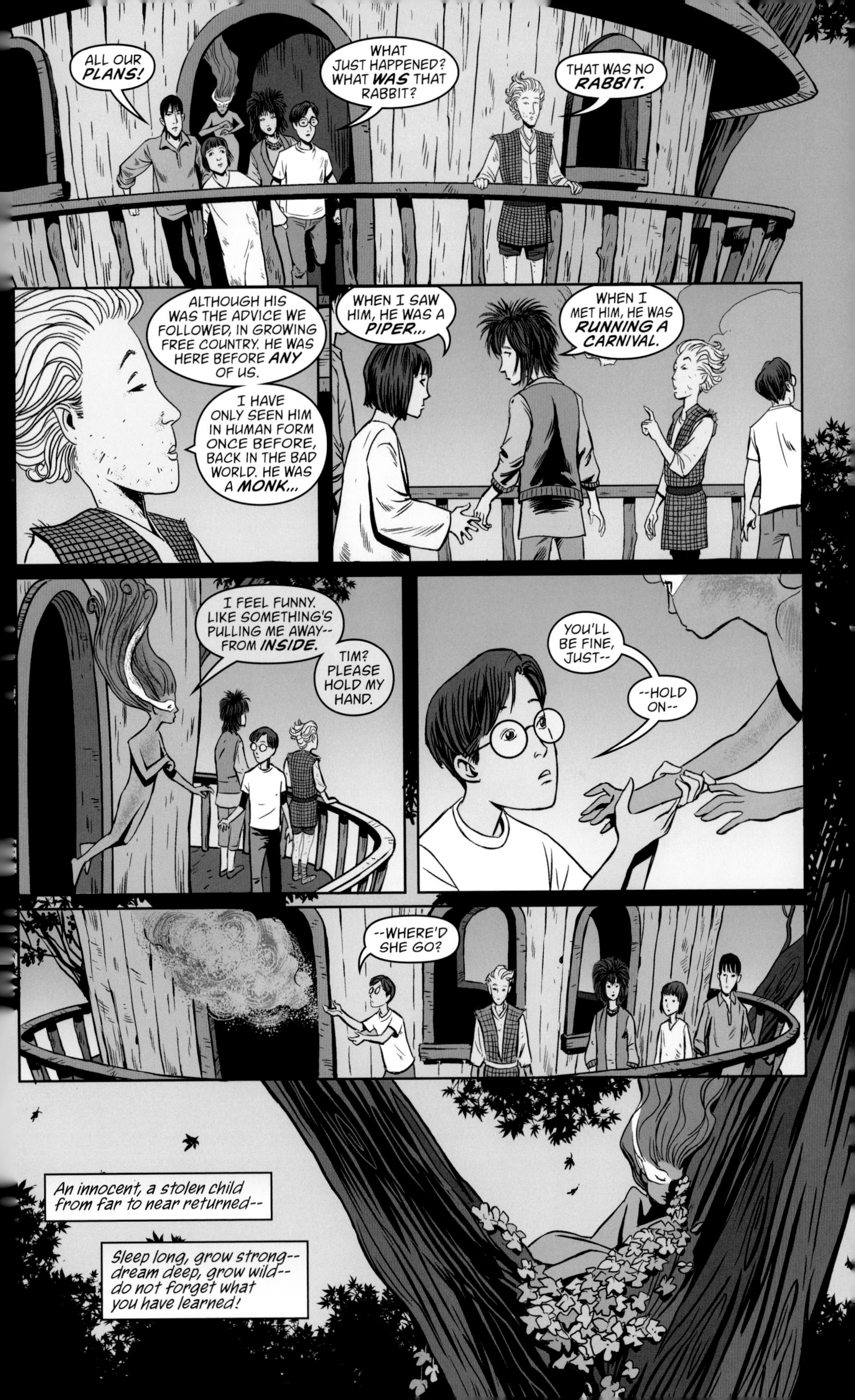
ALL OUR PLANS!
WHAT JUST HAPPENED? WHAT WAS THAT RABBIT?
THAT WAS NO RABBIT.
ALTHOUGH HIS WAS THE ADVICE WE FOLLOWED, IN GROWING FREE COUNTRY. HE WAS HERE BEFORE ANY OF US.
I HAVE ONLY SEEN HIM IN HUMAN FORM ONCE BEFORE, BACK IN THE BAD WORLD. HE WAS A MONK...
WHEN I SAW HIM, HE WAS A PIPER...
WHEN I MET HIM, HE WAS RUNNING A CARNIVAL.
I FEEL FUNNY. LIKE SOMETHING'S PULLING ME AWAY--FROM INSIDE.
TIM? PLEASE HOLD MY HAND.
YOU'LL BE FINE, JUST--
--HOLD ON--
--WHERE'D SHE GO?
An innocent, a stolen child from far to near returned--
Sleep long, grow strong--dream deep, grow wild--do not forget what you have learned!

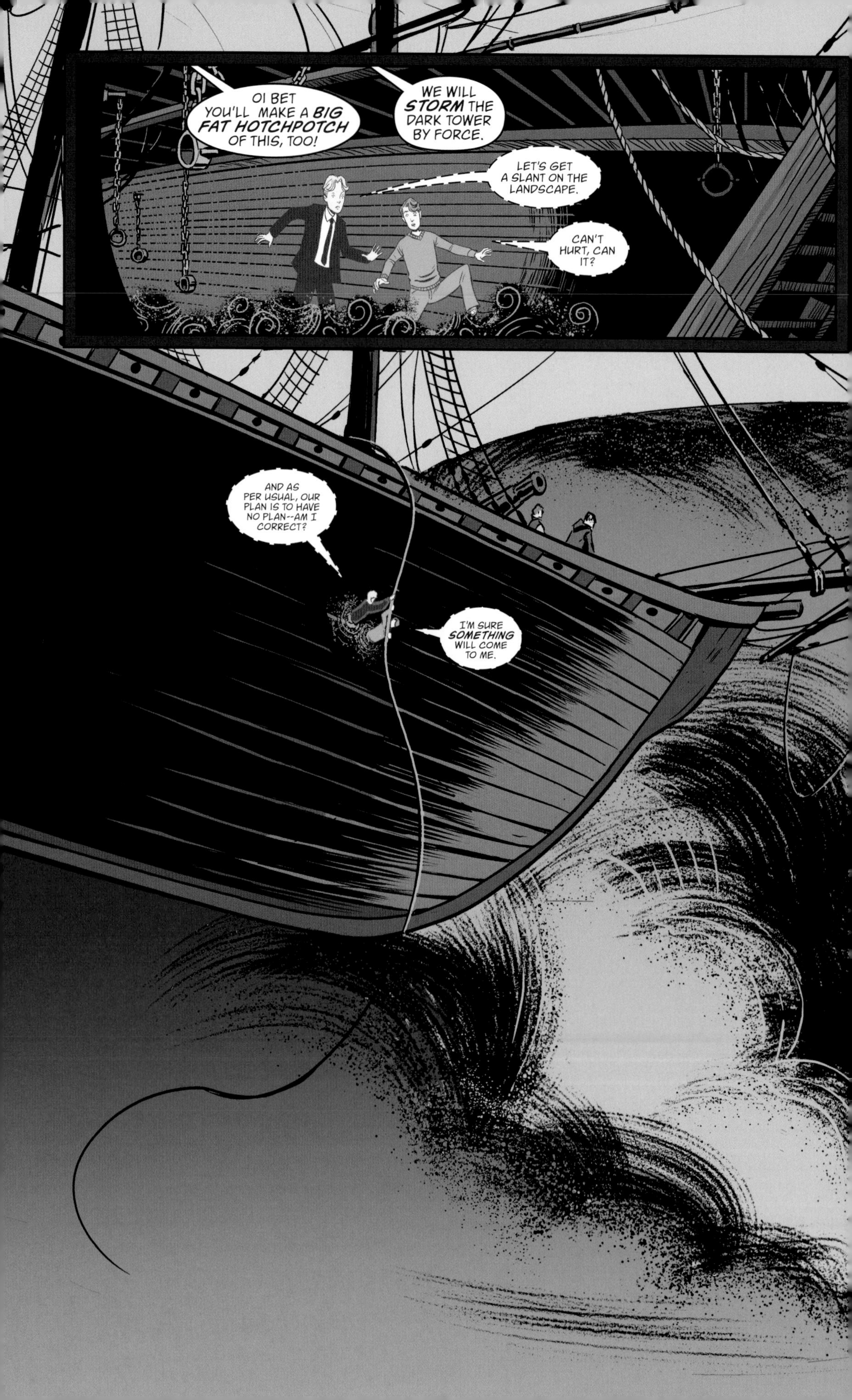
OI BET YOU'LL MAKE A BIG FAT HOTCHPOTCH OF THIS, TOO!
WE WILL STORM THE DARK TOWER BY FORCE.
LET'S GET A SLANT ON THE LANDSCAPE.
CAN'T HURT, CAN IT?
AND AS PER USUAL, OUR PLAN IS TO HAVE NO PLAN--AM I CORRECT?
I'M SURE SOMETHING WILL COME TO ME.

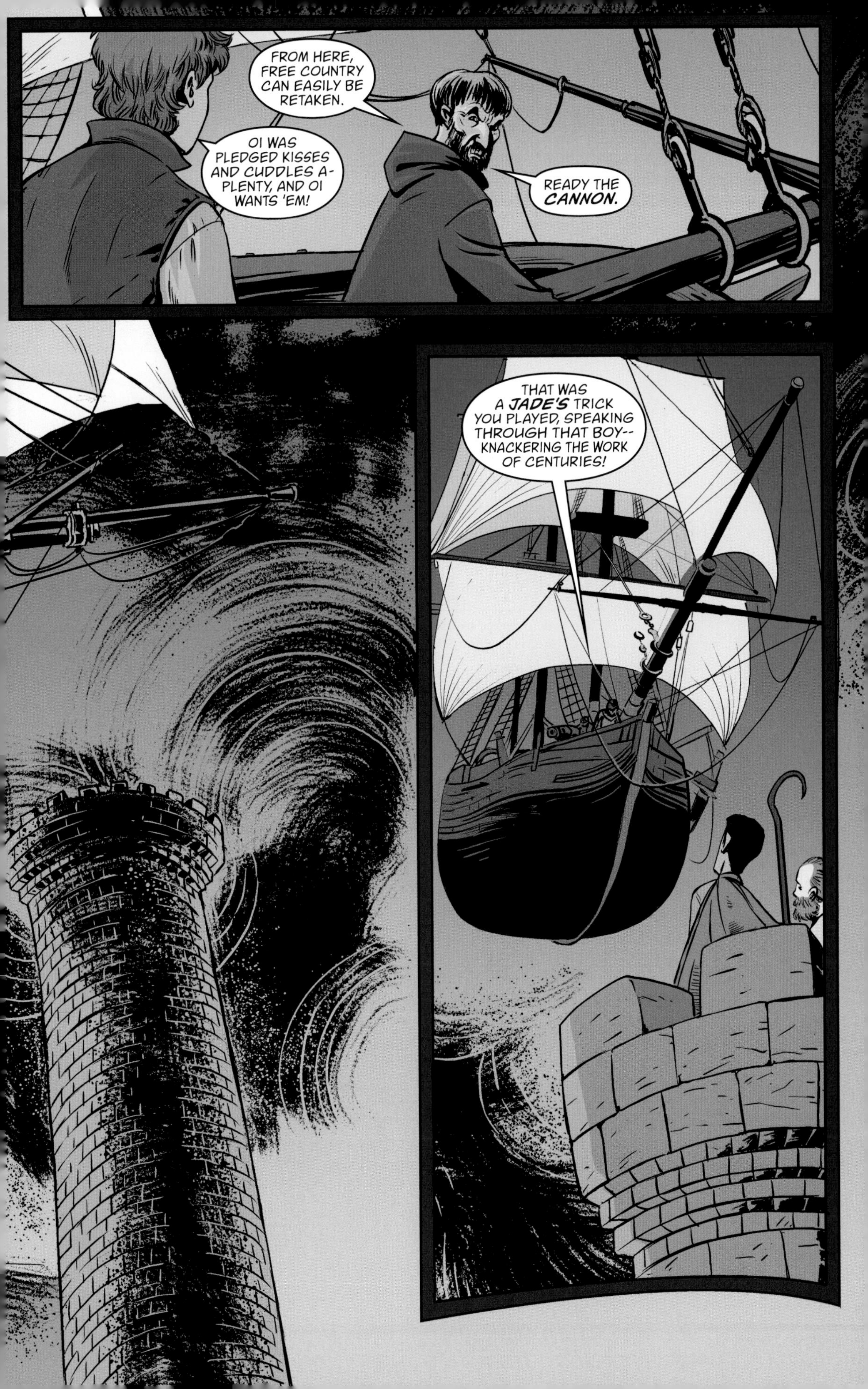
FROM HERE, FREE COUNTRY CAN EASILY BE RETAKEN.
OI WAS PLEDGED KISSES AND CUDDLES A-PLENTY, AND OI WANTS 'EM!
READY THE CANNON.
THAT WAS A JADE'S TRICK YOU PLAYED, SPEAKING THROUGH THAT BOY-- KNACKERING THE WORK OF CENTURIES!

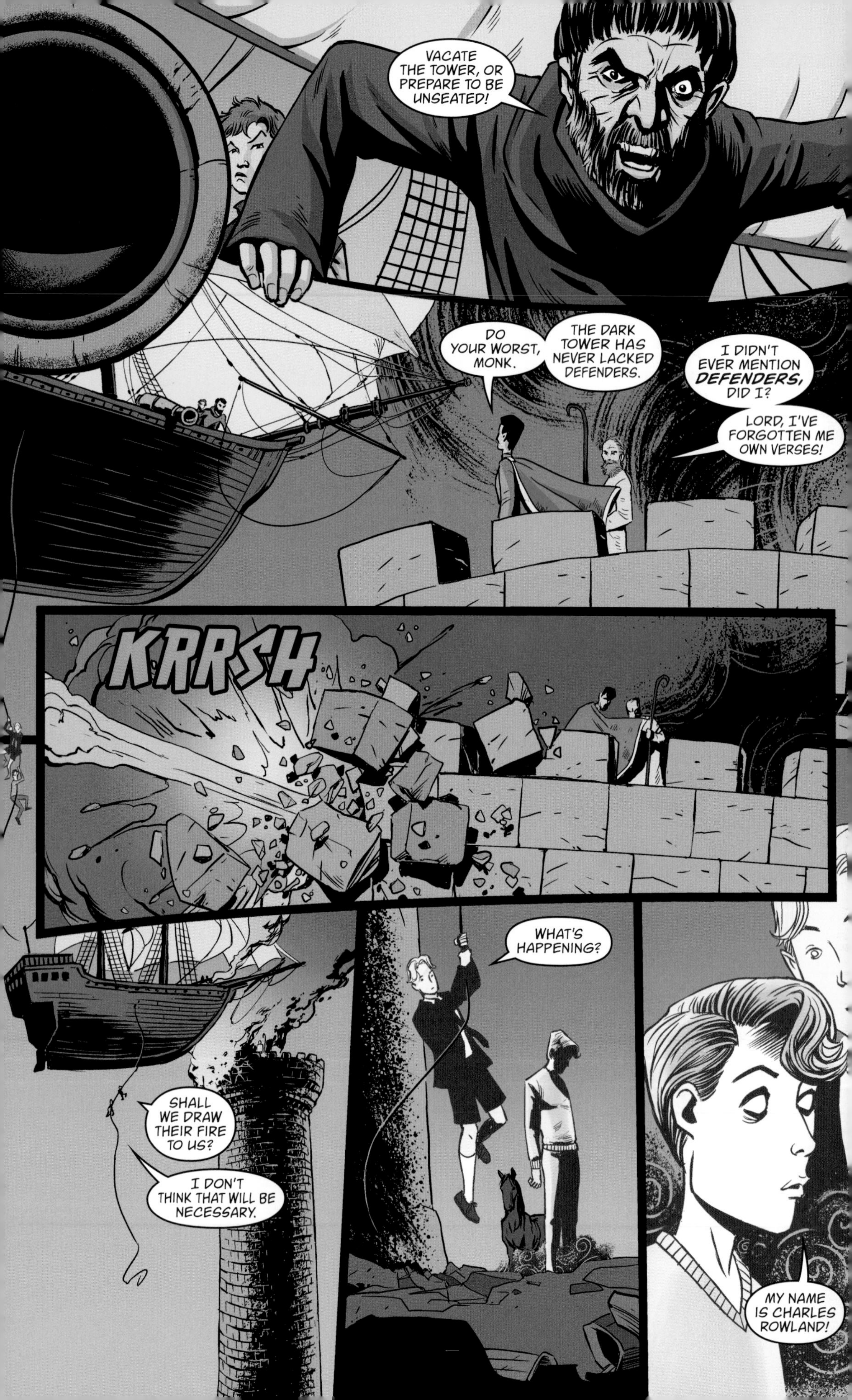
VACATE THE TOWER, OR PREPARE TO BE UNSEATED!
DO YOUR WORST, MONK.
THE DARK TOWER HAS NEVER LACKED DEFENDERS.
I DIDN'T EVER MENTION ***DEFENDERS,*** DID I?
LORD, I'VE FORGOTTEN ME OWN VERSES!
KRRSH
SHALL WE DRAW THEIR FIRE TO US?
I DON'T THINK THAT WILL BE NECESSARY.
WHAT'S HAPPENING?
MY NAME IS CHARLES ROWLAND!

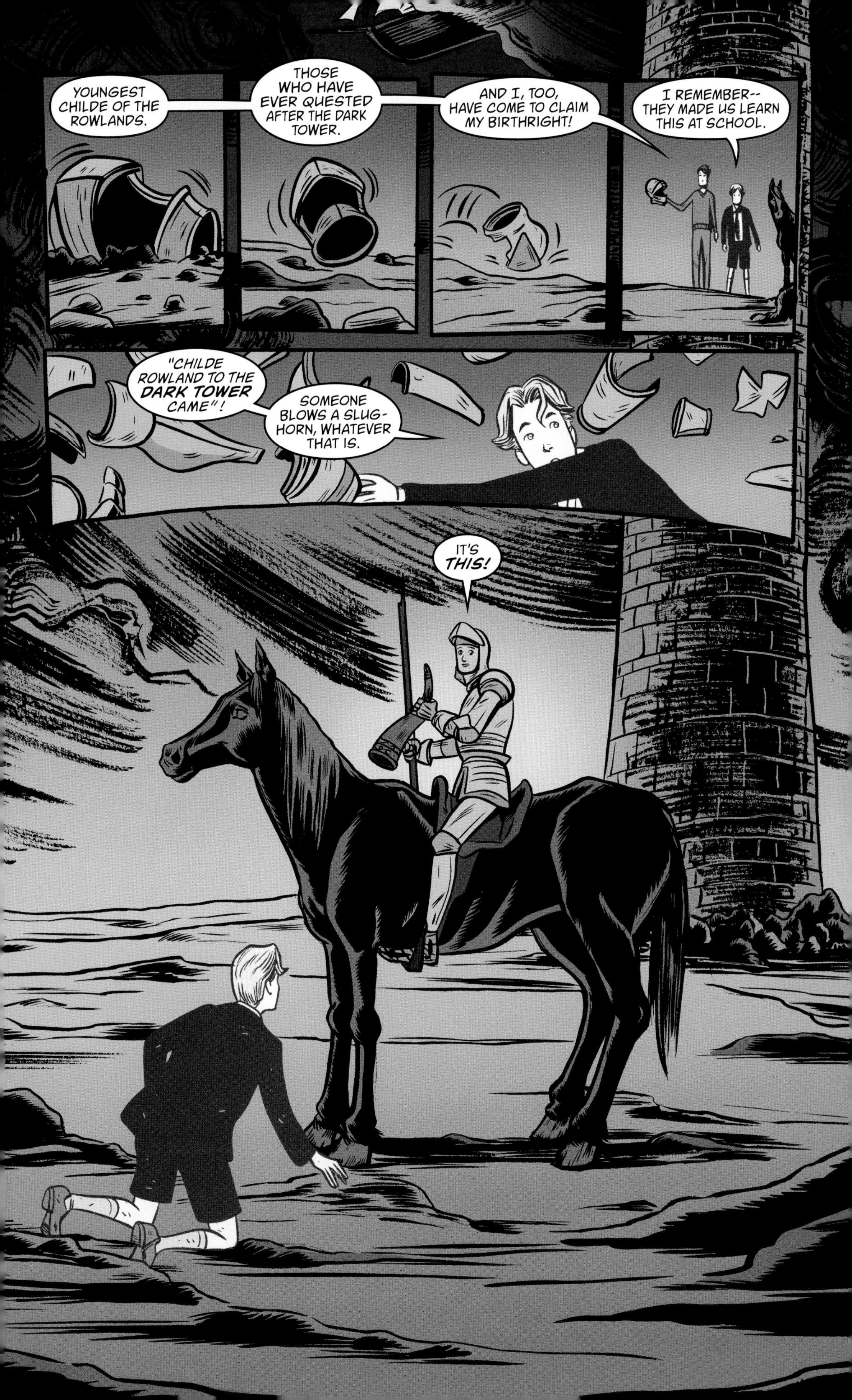
YOUNGEST CHILDE OF THE ROWLANDS.
THOSE WHO HAVE EVER QUESTED AFTER THE DARK TOWER.
AND I, TOO, HAVE COME TO CLAIM MY BIRTHRIGHT!
I REMEMBER-- THEY MADE US LEARN THIS AT SCHOOL.
"CHILDE ROWLAND TO THE **DARK TOWER** CAME"!
SOMEONE BLOWS A SLUG-HORN, WHATEVER THAT IS.
IT'S **THIS!**

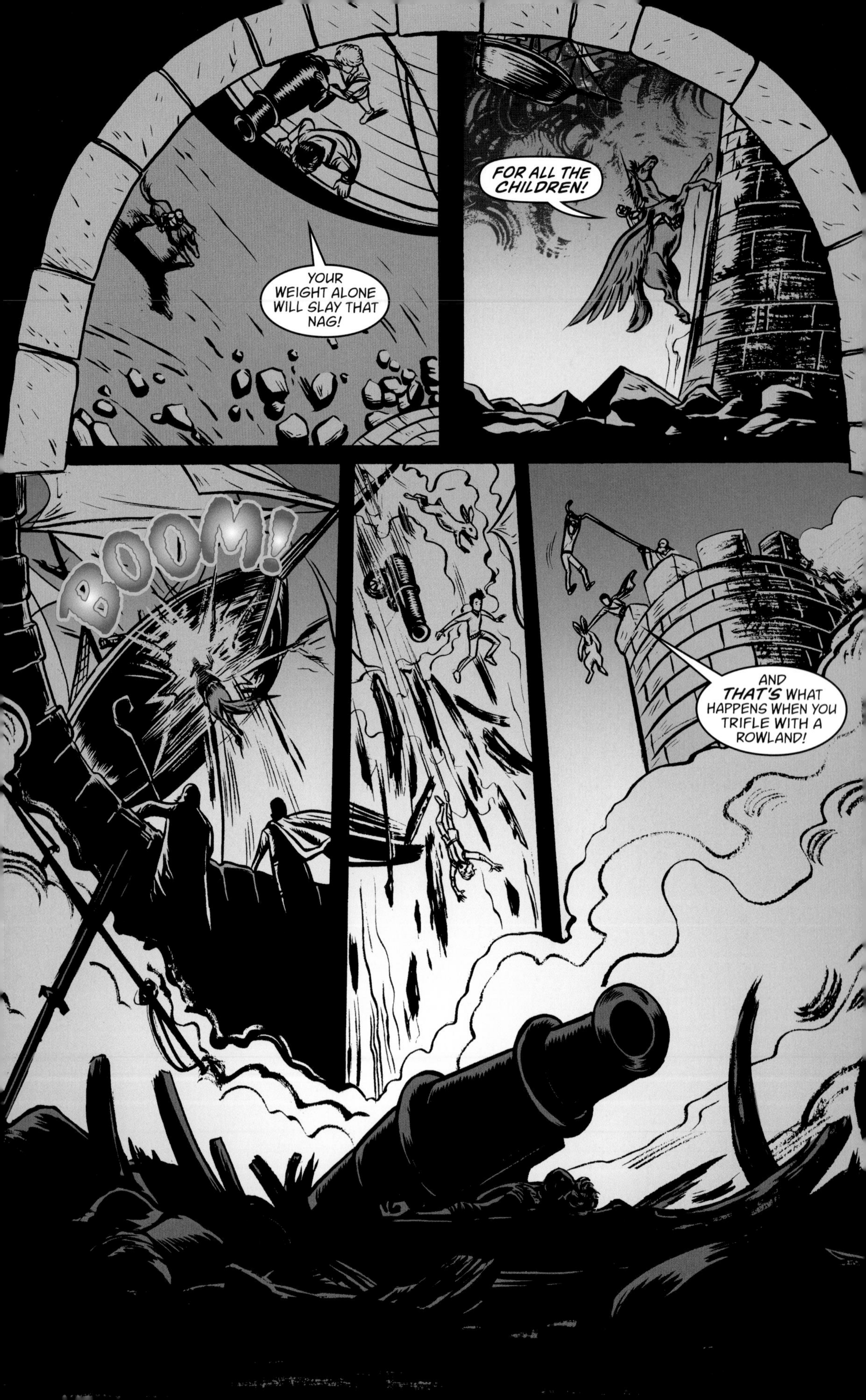
YOUR WEIGHT ALONE WILL SLAY THAT NAG!
FOR ALL THE CHILDREN!
BOOM!
AND THAT'S WHAT HAPPENS WHEN YOU TRIFLE WITH A ROWLAND!

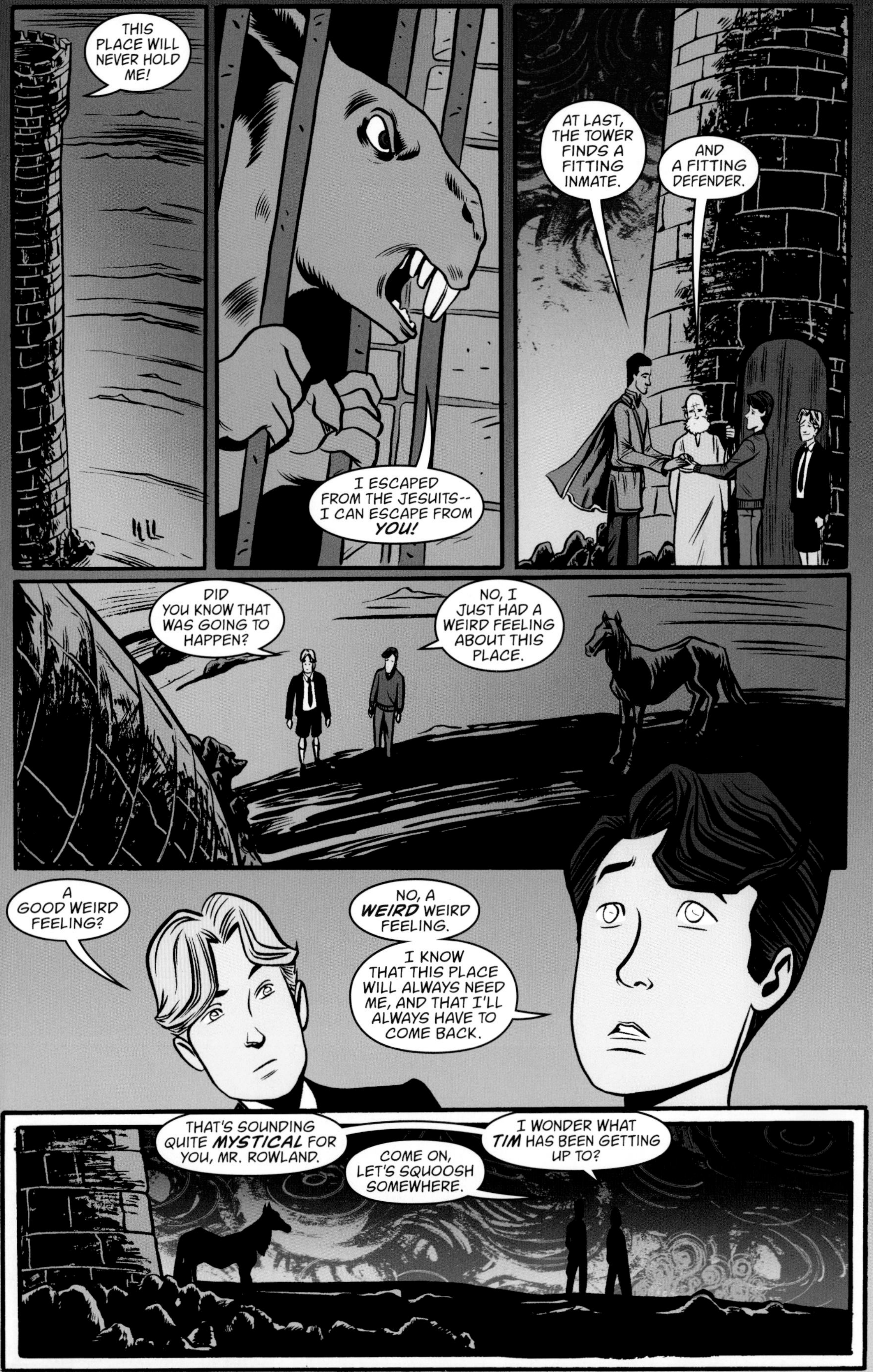

THIS PLACE WILL NEVER HOLD ME!
I ESCAPED FROM THE JESUITS-- I CAN ESCAPE FROM YOU!
AT LAST, THE TOWER FINDS A FITTING INMATE.
AND A FITTING DEFENDER.
DID YOU KNOW THAT WAS GOING TO HAPPEN?
NO, I JUST HAD A WEIRD FEELING ABOUT THIS PLACE.
A GOOD WEIRD FEELING?
NO, A WEIRD WEIRD FEELING.
I KNOW THAT THIS PLACE WILL ALWAYS NEED ME, AND THAT I'LL ALWAYS HAVE TO COME BACK.
THAT'S SOUNDING QUITE MYSTICAL FOR YOU, MR. ROWLAND.
COME ON, LET'S SQUOOSH SOMEWHERE.
I WONDER WHAT TIM HAS BEEN GETTING UP TO?

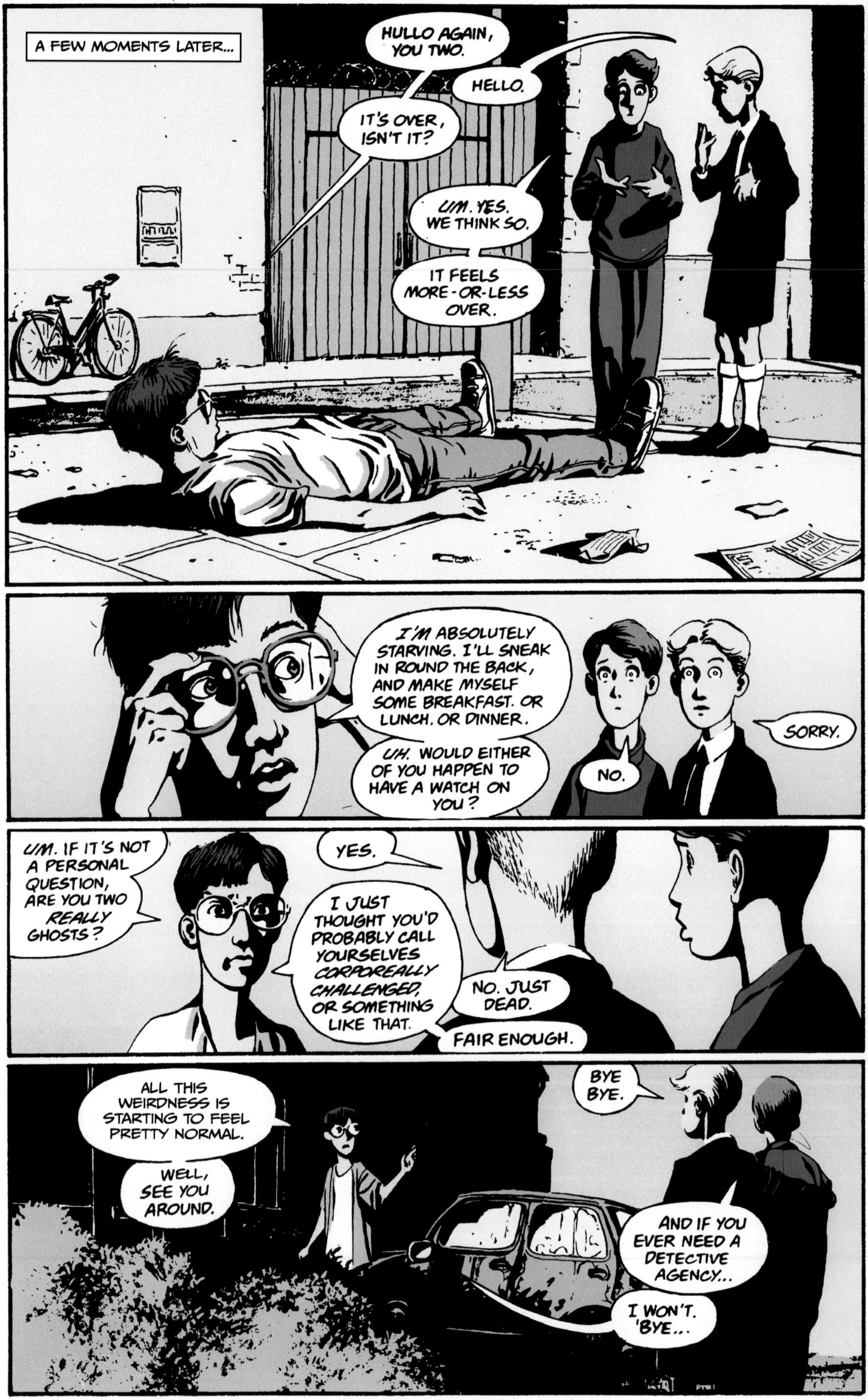
A FEW MOMENTS LATER...
HULLO AGAIN, YOU TWO.
HELLO.
IT'S OVER, ISN'T IT?
UM. YES. WE THINK SO.
IT FEELS MORE-OR-LESS OVER.
I'M ABSOLUTELY STARVING. I'LL SNEAK IN ROUND THE BACK, AND MAKE MYSELF SOME BREAKFAST. OR LUNCH. OR DINNER.
UH. WOULD EITHER OF YOU HAPPEN TO HAVE A WATCH ON YOU?
NO.
SORRY.
UM. IF IT'S NOT A PERSONAL QUESTION, ARE YOU TWO REALLY GHOSTS?
YES.
I JUST THOUGHT YOU'D PROBABLY CALL YOURSELVES CORPOREALLY CHALLENGED, OR SOMETHING LIKE THAT.
NO. JUST DEAD.
FAIR ENOUGH.
ALL THIS WEIRDNESS IS STARTING TO FEEL PRETTY NORMAL.
WELL, SEE YOU AROUND.
BYE BYE.
AND IF YOU EVER NEED A DETECTIVE AGENCY...
I WON'T. 'BYE...

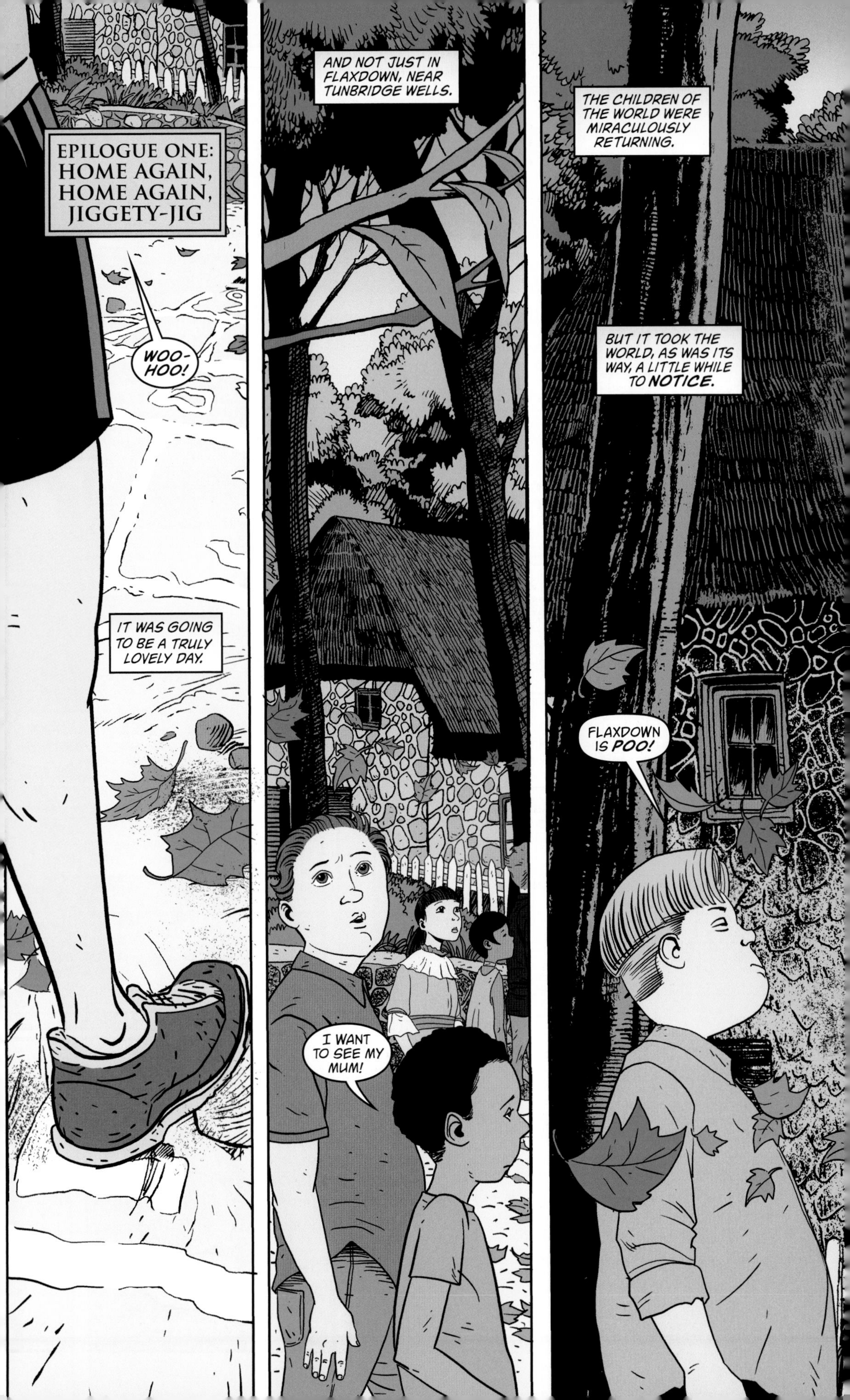
EPILOGUE ONE: HOME AGAIN, HOME AGAIN, JIGGETY-JIG
WOO-HOO!
IT WAS GOING TO BE A TRULY LOVELY DAY.
AND NOT JUST IN FLAXDOWN, NEAR TUNBRIDGE WELLS.
I WANT TO SEE MY MUM!
THE CHILDREN OF THE WORLD WERE MIRACULOUSLY RETURNING.
BUT IT TOOK THE WORLD, AS WAS ITS WAY, A LITTLE WHILE TO NOTICE.
FLAXDOWN IS POO!

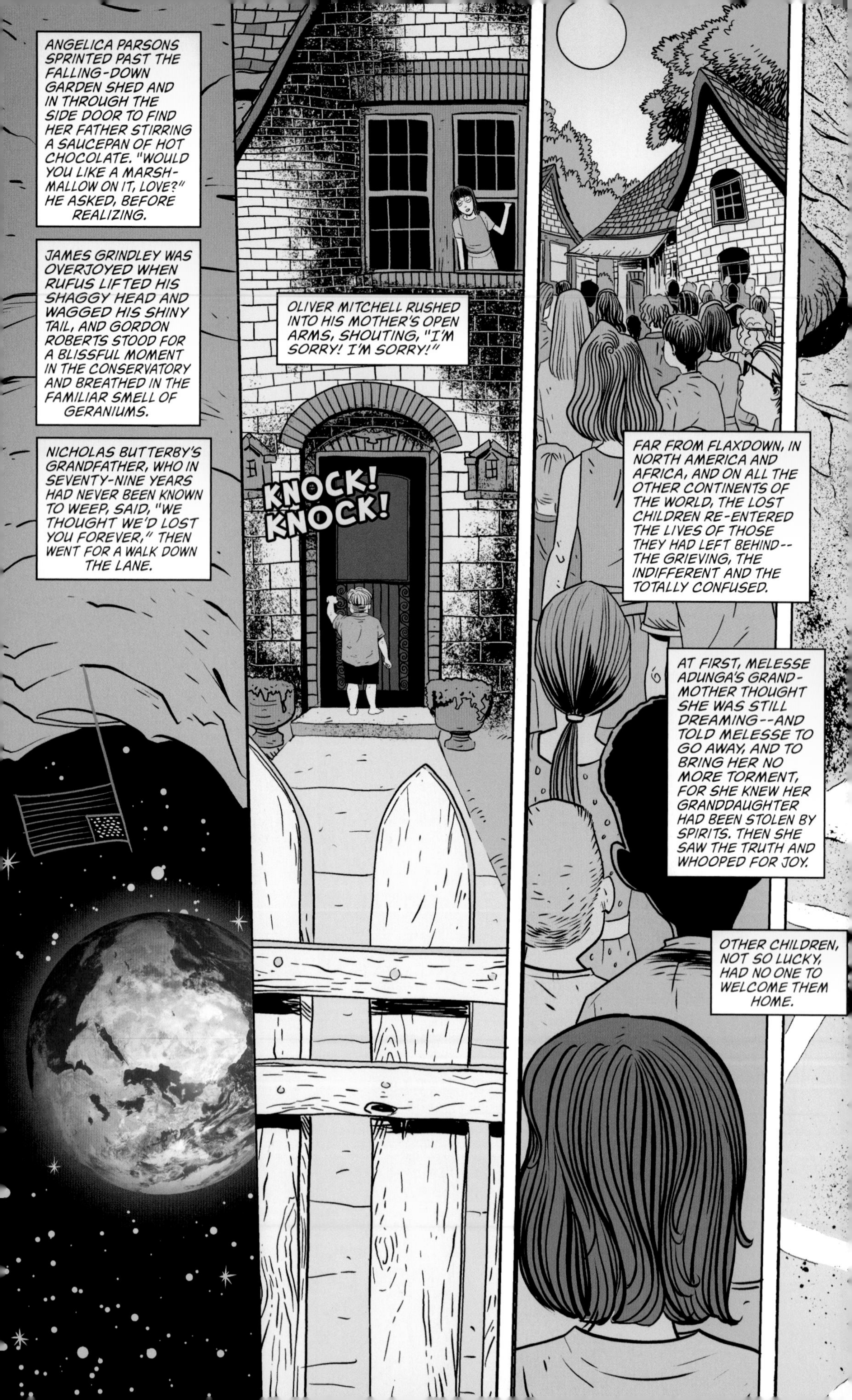
ANGELICA PARSONS SPRINTED PAST THE FALLING-DOWN GARDEN SHED AND IN THROUGH THE SIDE DOOR TO FIND HER FATHER STIRRING A SAUCEPAN OF HOT CHOCOLATE. "WOULD YOU LIKE A MARSH-MALLOW ON IT, LOVE?" HE ASKED, BEFORE REALIZING.
JAMES GRINDLEY WAS OVERJOYED WHEN RUFUS LIFTED HIS SHAGGY HEAD AND WAGGED HIS SHINY TAIL, AND GORDON ROBERTS STOOD FOR A BLISSFUL MOMENT IN THE CONSERVATORY AND BREATHED IN THE FAMILIAR SMELL OF GERANIUMS.
NICHOLAS BUTTERBY'S GRANDFATHER, WHO IN SEVENTY-NINE YEARS HAD NEVER BEEN KNOWN TO WEEP, SAID, "WE THOUGHT WE'D LOST YOU FOREVER," THEN WENT FOR A WALK DOWN THE LANE.
OLIVER MITCHELL RUSHED INTO HIS MOTHER'S OPEN ARMS, SHOUTING, "I'M SORRY! I'M SORRY!"
KNOCK! KNOCK!
FAR FROM FLAXDOWN, IN NORTH AMERICA AND AFRICA, AND ON ALL THE OTHER CONTINENTS OF THE WORLD, THE LOST CHILDREN RE-ENTERED THE LIVES OF THOSE THEY HAD LEFT BEHIND-- THE GRIEVING, THE INDIFFERENT AND THE TOTALLY CONFUSED.
AT FIRST, MELESSE ADUNGA'S GRAND-MOTHER THOUGHT SHE WAS STILL DREAMING--AND TOLD MELESSE TO GO AWAY, AND TO BRING HER NO MORE TORMENT, FOR SHE KNEW HER GRANDDAUGHTER HAD BEEN STOLEN BY SPIRITS. THEN SHE SAW THE TRUTH AND WHOOPED FOR JOY.
OTHER CHILDREN, NOT SO LUCKY, HAD NO ONE TO WELCOME THEM HOME.

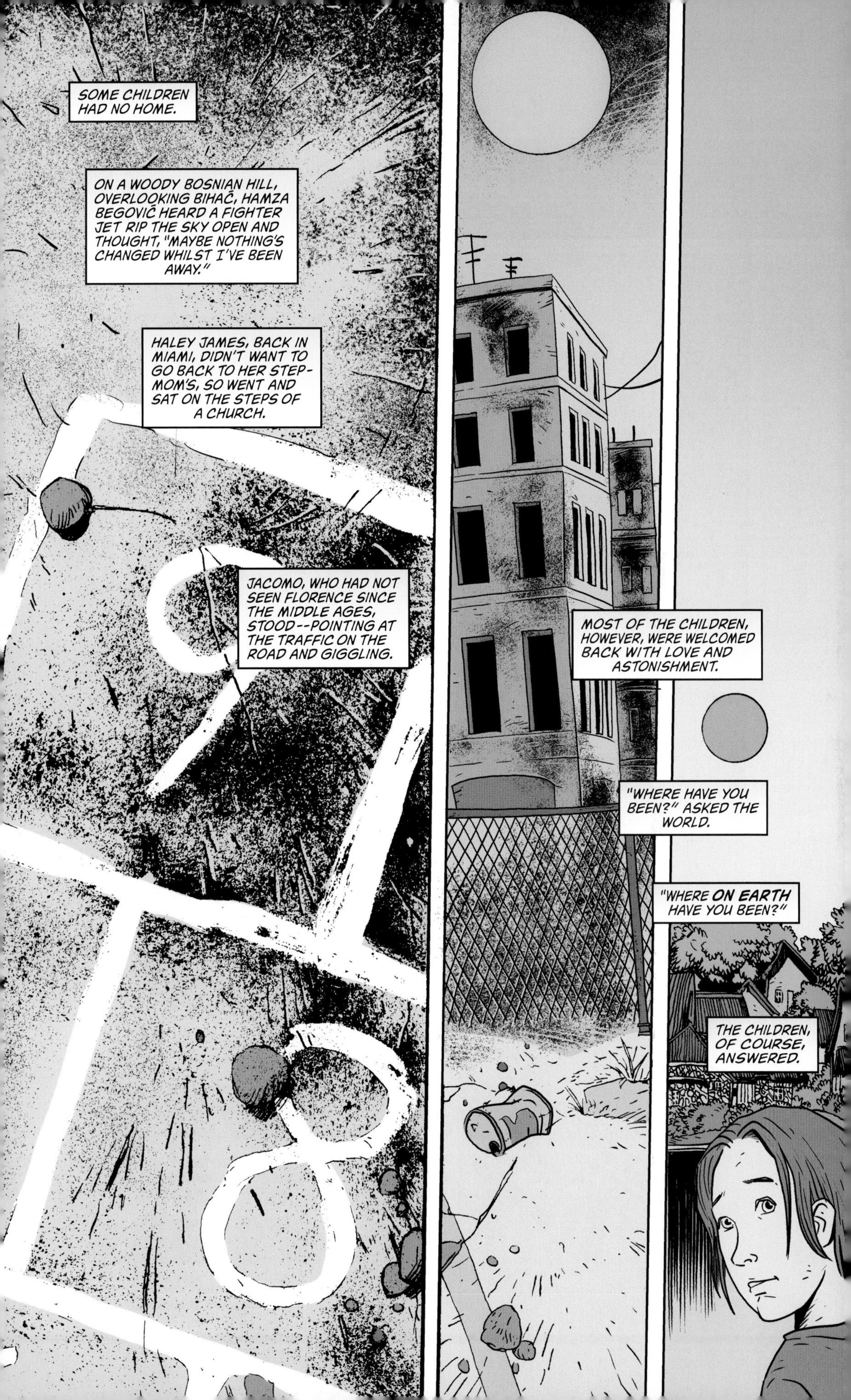

SOME CHILDREN HAD NO HOME.
ON A WOODY BOSNIAN HILL, OVERLOOKING BIHAČ, HAMZA BEGOVIČ HEARD A FIGHTER JET RIP THE SKY OPEN AND THOUGHT, "MAYBE NOTHING'S CHANGED WHILST I'VE BEEN AWAY."
HALEY JAMES, BACK IN MIAMI, DIDN'T WANT TO GO BACK TO HER STEP-MOM'S, SO WENT AND SAT ON THE STEPS OF A CHURCH.
JACOMO, WHO HAD NOT SEEN FLORENCE SINCE THE MIDDLE AGES, STOOD--POINTING AT THE TRAFFIC ON THE ROAD AND GIGGLING.
MOST OF THE CHILDREN, HOWEVER, WERE WELCOMED BACK WITH LOVE AND ASTONISHMENT.
"WHERE HAVE YOU BEEN?" ASKED THE WORLD.
"WHERE **ON EARTH** HAVE YOU BEEN?"
THE CHILDREN, OF COURSE, ANSWERED.

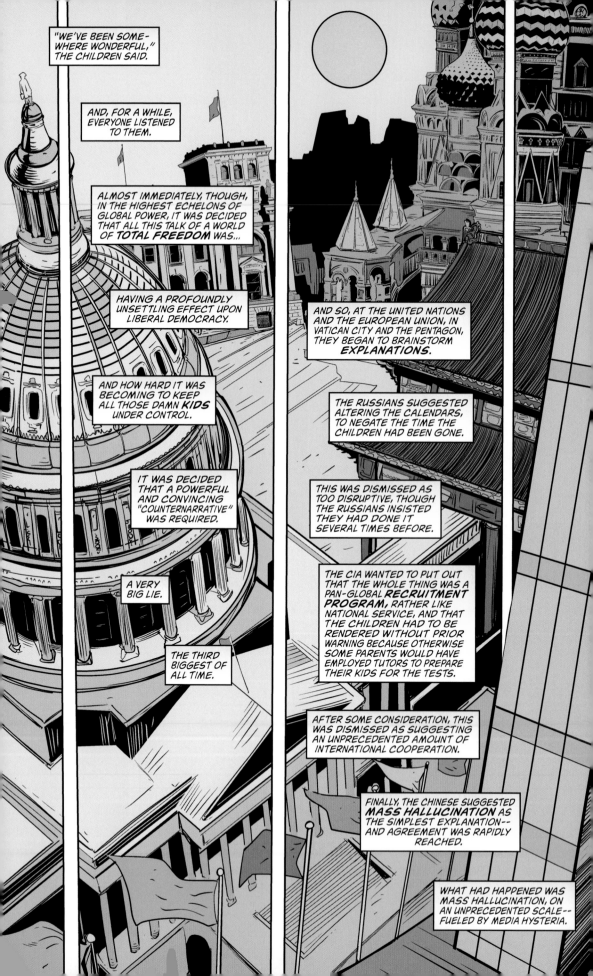

"WE'VE BEEN SOME-WHERE WONDERFUL," THE CHILDREN SAID.

AND, FOR A WHILE, EVERYONE LISTENED TO THEM.

ALMOST IMMEDIATELY, THOUGH, IN THE HIGHEST ECHELONS OF GLOBAL POWER, IT WAS DECIDED THAT ALL THIS TALK OF A WORLD OF **TOTAL FREEDOM** WAS...

HAVING A PROFOUNDLY UNSETTLING EFFECT UPON LIBERAL DEMOCRACY.

AND HOW HARD IT WAS BECOMING TO **KEEP** ALL THOSE DAMN **KIDS** UNDER CONTROL.

IT WAS DECIDED THAT A POWERFUL AND CONVINCING "COUNTERNARRATIVE" WAS REQUIRED.

A VERY BIG LIE.

THE THIRD BIGGEST OF ALL TIME.

AND SO, AT THE UNITED NATIONS AND THE EUROPEAN UNION, IN VATICAN CITY AND THE PENTAGON, THEY BEGAN TO BRAINSTORM **EXPLANATIONS**.

THE RUSSIANS SUGGESTED ALTERING THE CALENDARS, TO NEGATE THE TIME THE CHILDREN HAD BEEN GONE.

THIS WAS DISMISSED AS TOO DISRUPTIVE, THOUGH THE RUSSIANS INSISTED THEY HAD DONE IT SEVERAL TIMES BEFORE.

THE CIA WANTED TO PUT OUT THAT THE WHOLE THING WAS A PAN-GLOBAL **RECRUITMENT PROGRAM,** RATHER LIKE NATIONAL SERVICE, AND THAT THE CHILDREN HAD TO BE RENDERED WITHOUT PRIOR WARNING BECAUSE OTHERWISE SOME PARENTS WOULD HAVE EMPLOYED TUTORS TO PREPARE THEIR KIDS FOR THE TESTS.

AFTER SOME CONSIDERATION, THIS WAS DISMISSED AS SUGGESTING AN UNPRECEDENTED AMOUNT OF INTERNATIONAL COOPERATION.

FINALLY, THE CHINESE SUGGESTED **MASS HALLUCINATION** AS THE SIMPLEST EXPLANATION-- AND AGREEMENT WAS RAPIDLY REACHED.

WHAT HAD HAPPENED WAS MASS HALLUCINATION, ON AN UNPRECEDENTED SCALE-- FUELED BY MEDIA HYSTERIA.

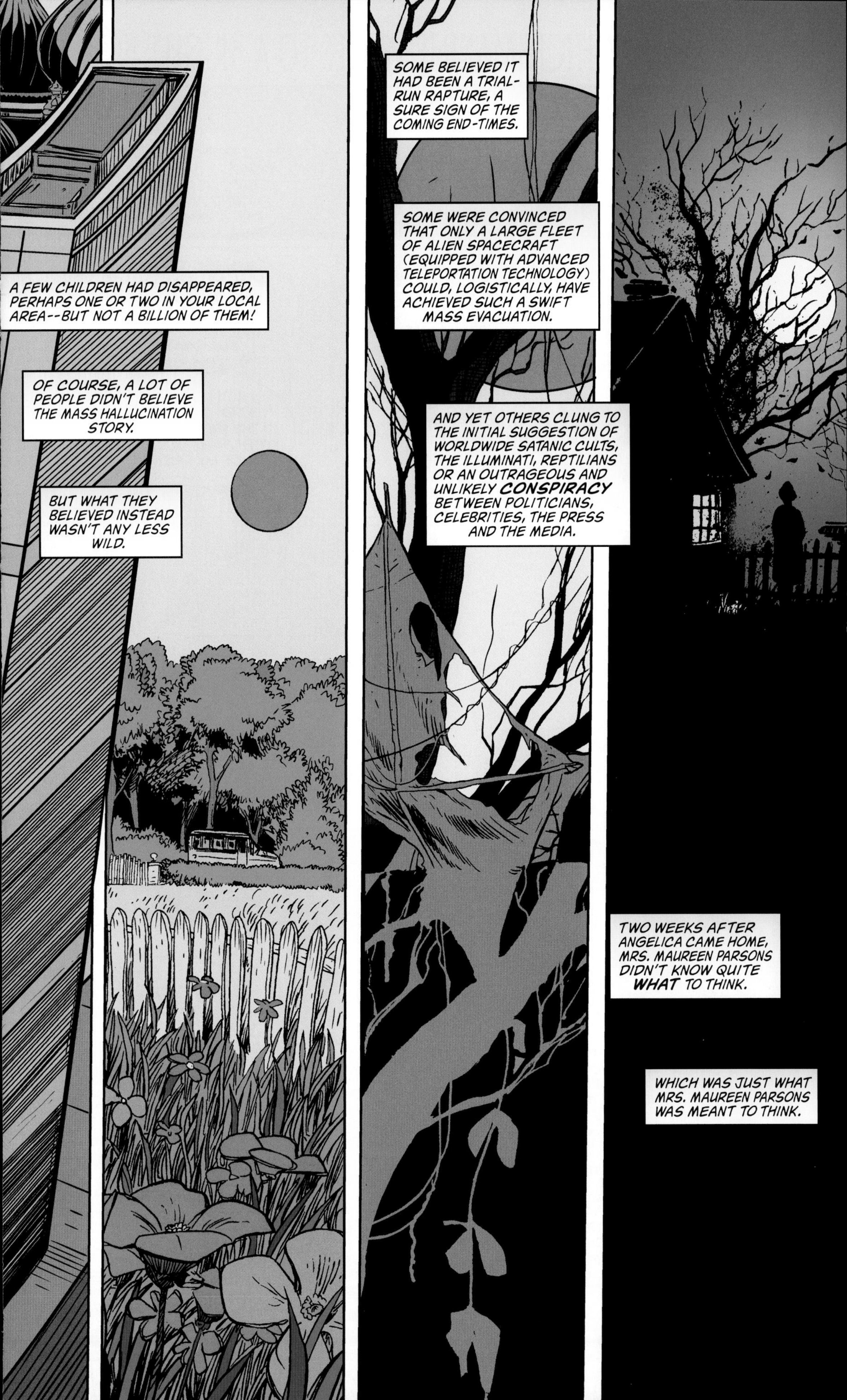
A FEW CHILDREN HAD DISAPPEARED, PERHAPS ONE OR TWO IN YOUR LOCAL AREA--BUT NOT A BILLION OF THEM!
OF COURSE, A LOT OF PEOPLE DIDN'T BELIEVE THE MASS HALLUCINATION STORY.
BUT WHAT THEY BELIEVED INSTEAD WASN'T ANY LESS WILD.
SOME BELIEVED IT HAD BEEN A TRIAL-RUN RAPTURE, A SURE SIGN OF THE COMING END-TIMES.
SOME WERE CONVINCED THAT ONLY A LARGE FLEET OF ALIEN SPACECRAFT (EQUIPPED WITH ADVANCED TELEPORTATION TECHNOLOGY) COULD, LOGISTICALLY, HAVE ACHIEVED SUCH A SWIFT MASS EVACUATION.
AND YET OTHERS CLUNG TO THE INITIAL SUGGESTION OF WORLDWIDE SATANIC CULTS, THE ILLUMINATI, REPTILIANS OR AN OUTRAGEOUS AND UNLIKELY CONSPIRACY BETWEEN POLITICIANS, CELEBRITIES, THE PRESS AND THE MEDIA.
TWO WEEKS AFTER ANGELICA CAME HOME, MRS. MAUREEN PARSONS DIDN'T KNOW QUITE WHAT TO THINK.
WHICH WAS JUST WHAT MRS. MAUREEN PARSONS WAS MEANT TO THINK.

EPILOGUE TWO: IN WHICH MAXINE WAKES TO A BRIGHT NEW DAY

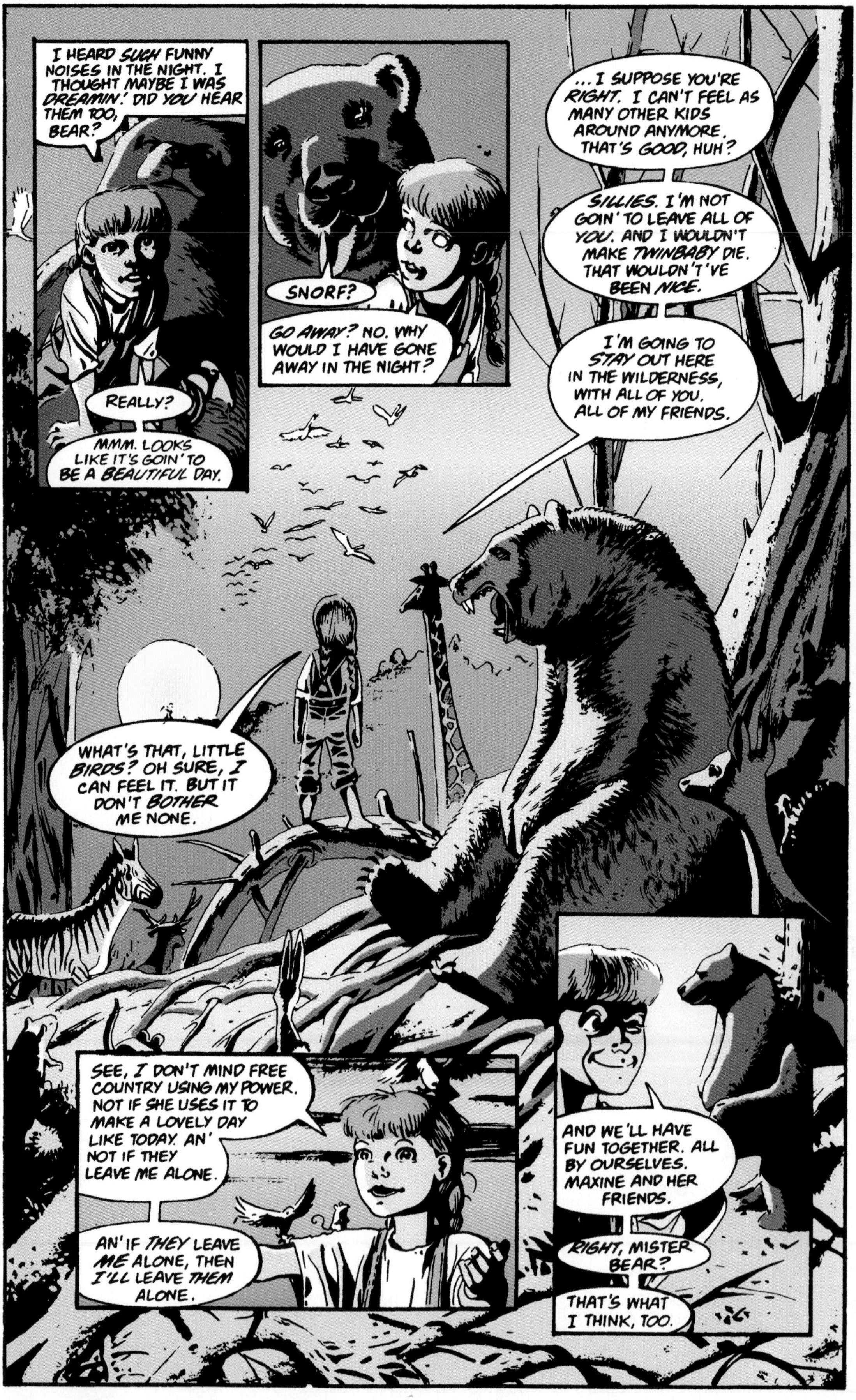

I HEARD SUCH FUNNY NOISES IN THE NIGHT. I THOUGHT MAYBE I WAS DREAMIN.' DID YOU HEAR THEM TOO, BEAR?
REALLY?
MMM. LOOKS LIKE IT'S GOIN' TO BE A BEAUTIFUL DAY.
SNORF?
GO AWAY? NO. WHY WOULD I HAVE GONE AWAY IN THE NIGHT?
...I SUPPOSE YOU'RE RIGHT. I CAN'T FEEL AS MANY OTHER KIDS AROUND ANYMORE. THAT'S GOOD, HUH?
SILLIES. I'M NOT GOIN' TO LEAVE ALL OF YOU. AND I WOULDN'T MAKE TWINBABY DIE. THAT WOULDN'T'VE BEEN NICE.
I'M GOING TO STAY OUT HERE IN THE WILDERNESS, WITH ALL OF YOU. ALL OF MY FRIENDS.
WHAT'S THAT, LITTLE BIRDS? OH SURE, I CAN FEEL IT. BUT IT DON'T BOTHER ME NONE.
SEE, I DON'T MIND FREE COUNTRY USING MY POWER. NOT IF SHE USES IT TO MAKE A LOVELY DAY LIKE TODAY. AN' NOT IF THEY LEAVE ME ALONE.
AN' IF THEY LEAVE ME ALONE, THEN I'LL LEAVE THEM ALONE.
AND WE'LL HAVE FUN TOGETHER. ALL BY OURSELVES. MAXINE AND HER FRIENDS.
RIGHT, MISTER BEAR?
THAT'S WHAT I THINK, TOO.

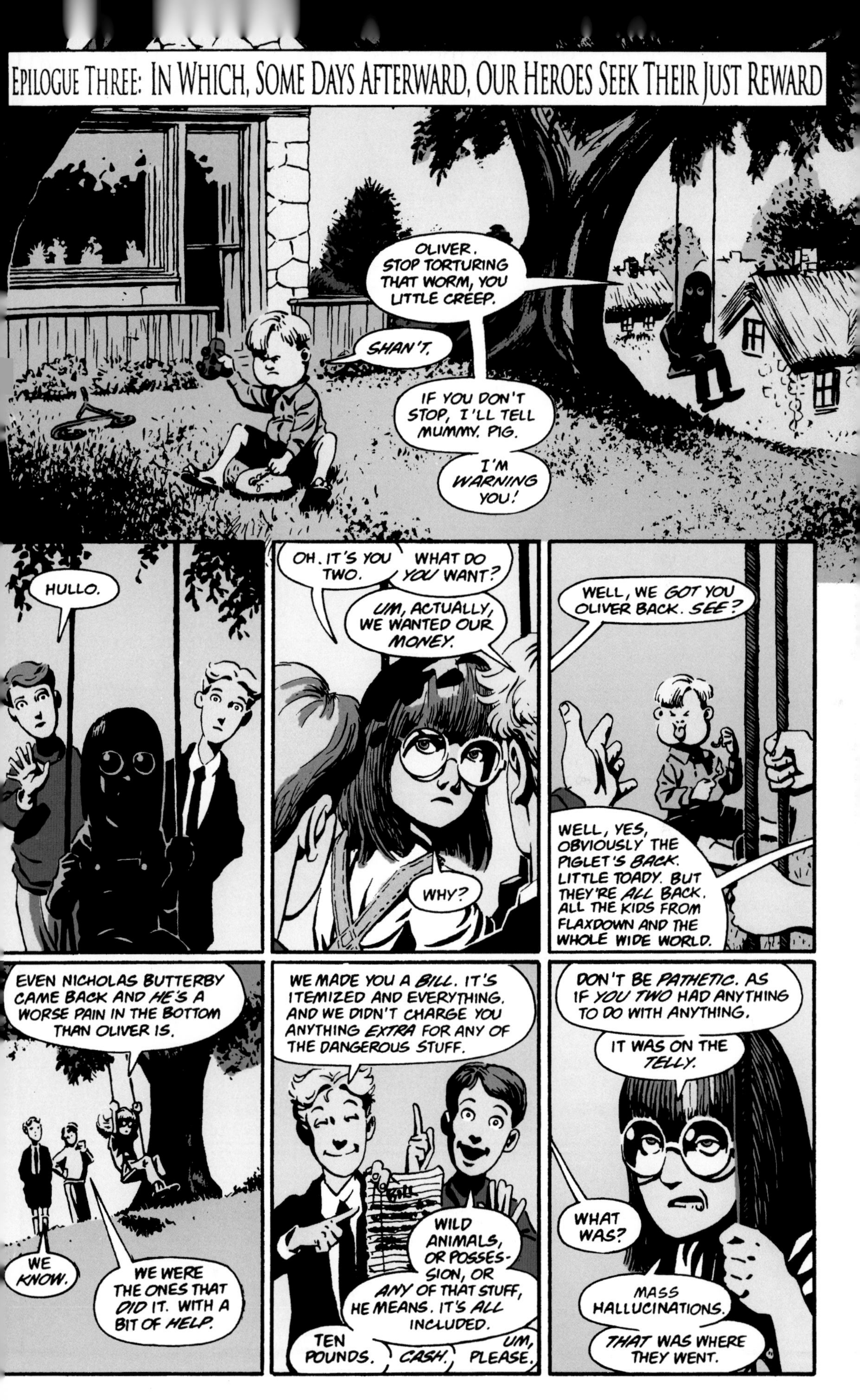
EPILOGUE THREE: IN WHICH, SOME DAYS AFTERWARD, OUR HEROES SEEK THEIR JUST REWARD
OLIVER. STOP TORTURING THAT WORM, YOU LITTLE CREEP.
SHAN'T.
IF YOU DON'T STOP, I'LL TELL MUMMY. PIG.
I'M WARNING YOU!
HULLO.
OH. IT'S YOU TWO.
WHAT DO YOU WANT?
UM, ACTUALLY, WE WANTED OUR MONEY.
WHY?
WELL, WE GOT YOU OLIVER BACK. SEE?
WELL, YES, OBVIOUSLY THE PIGLET'S BACK. LITTLE TOADY. BUT THEY'RE ALL BACK. ALL THE KIDS FROM FLAXDOWN AND THE WHOLE WIDE WORLD.
EVEN NICHOLAS BUTTERBY CAME BACK AND HE'S A WORSE PAIN IN THE BOTTOM THAN OLIVER IS.
WE KNOW.
WE WERE THE ONES THAT DID IT. WITH A BIT OF HELP.
WE MADE YOU A BILL. IT'S ITEMIZED AND EVERYTHING. AND WE DIDN'T CHARGE YOU ANYTHING EXTRA FOR ANY OF THE DANGEROUS STUFF.
WILD ANIMALS, OR POSSES-SION, OR ANY OF THAT STUFF, HE MEANS. IT'S ALL INCLUDED.
TEN POUNDS.
CASH.
UM, PLEASE.
DON'T BE PATHETIC. AS IF YOU TWO HAD ANYTHING TO DO WITH ANYTHING.
IT WAS ON THE TELLY.
WHAT WAS?
MASS HALLUCINATIONS.
THAT WAS WHERE THEY WENT.

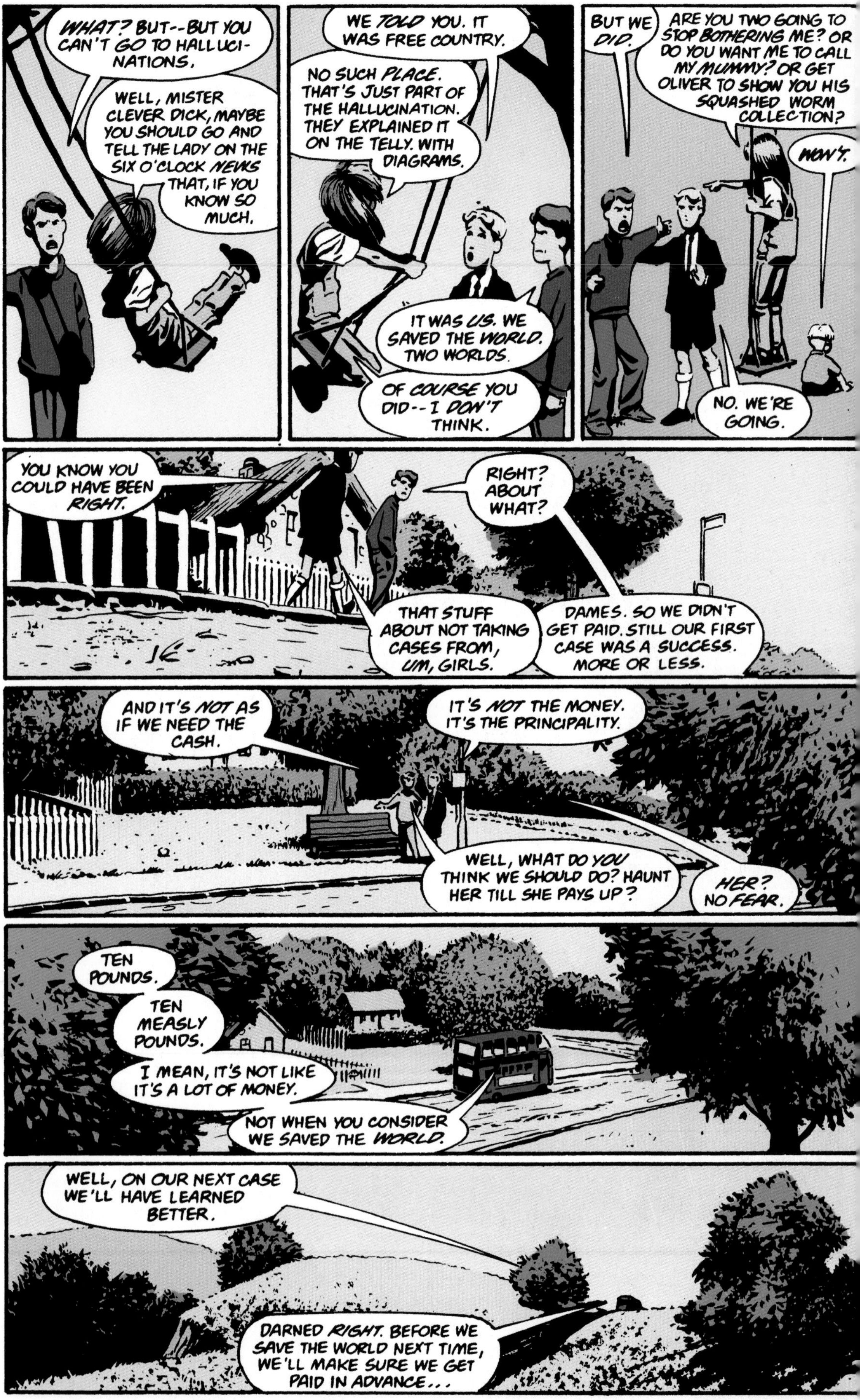
WHAT? BUT--BUT YOU CAN'T GO TO HALLUCINATIONS.
WELL, MISTER CLEVER DICK, MAYBE YOU SHOULD GO AND TELL THE LADY ON THE SIX O'CLOCK NEWS THAT, IF YOU KNOW SO MUCH.
WE TOLD YOU. IT WAS FREE COUNTRY.
NO SUCH PLACE. THAT'S JUST PART OF THE HALLUCINATION. THEY EXPLAINED IT ON THE TELLY. WITH DIAGRAMS.
IT WAS US. WE SAVED THE WORLD. TWO WORLDS.
OF COURSE YOU DID--I DON'T THINK.
BUT WE DID.
ARE YOU TWO GOING TO STOP BOTHERING ME? OR DO YOU WANT ME TO CALL MY MUMMY? OR GET OLIVER TO SHOW YOU HIS SQUASHED WORM COLLECTION?
WON'T.
NO. WE'RE GOING.
YOU KNOW YOU COULD HAVE BEEN RIGHT.
RIGHT? ABOUT WHAT?
THAT STUFF ABOUT NOT TAKING CASES FROM, UM, GIRLS.
DAMES. SO WE DIDN'T GET PAID. STILL OUR FIRST CASE WAS A SUCCESS. MORE OR LESS.
AND IT'S NOT AS IF WE NEED THE CASH.
IT'S NOT THE MONEY. IT'S THE PRINCIPALITY.
WELL, WHAT DO YOU THINK WE SHOULD DO? HAUNT HER TILL SHE PAYS UP?
HER? NO FEAR.
TEN POUNDS.
TEN MEASLY POUNDS.
I MEAN, IT'S NOT LIKE IT'S A LOT OF MONEY.
NOT WHEN YOU CONSIDER WE SAVED THE WORLD.
WELL, ON OUR NEXT CASE WE'LL HAVE LEARNED BETTER.
DARNED RIGHT. BEFORE WE SAVE THE WORLD NEXT TIME, WE'LL MAKE SURE WE GET PAID IN ADVANCE...

The End

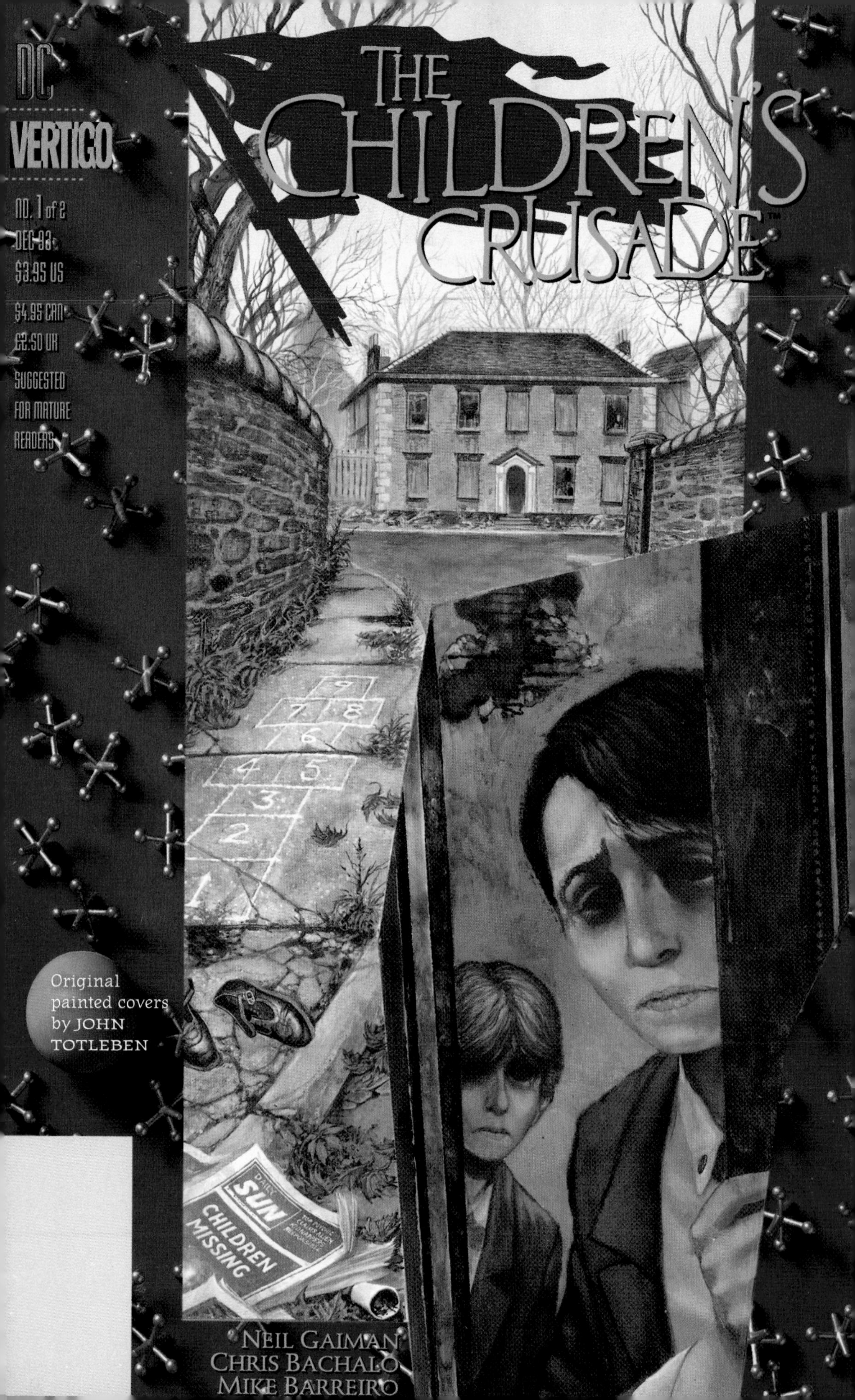
DC
VERTIGO
NO. 1 of 2
DEC 93
$3.95 US
$4.95 CAN
£2.50 UK
SUGGESTED FOR MATURE READERS
THE CHILDREN'S CRUSADE™
Original painted covers by JOHN TOTLEBEN
DAILY SUN
CHILDREN MISSING
NEIL GAIMAN
CHRIS BACHALO
MIKE BARREIRO

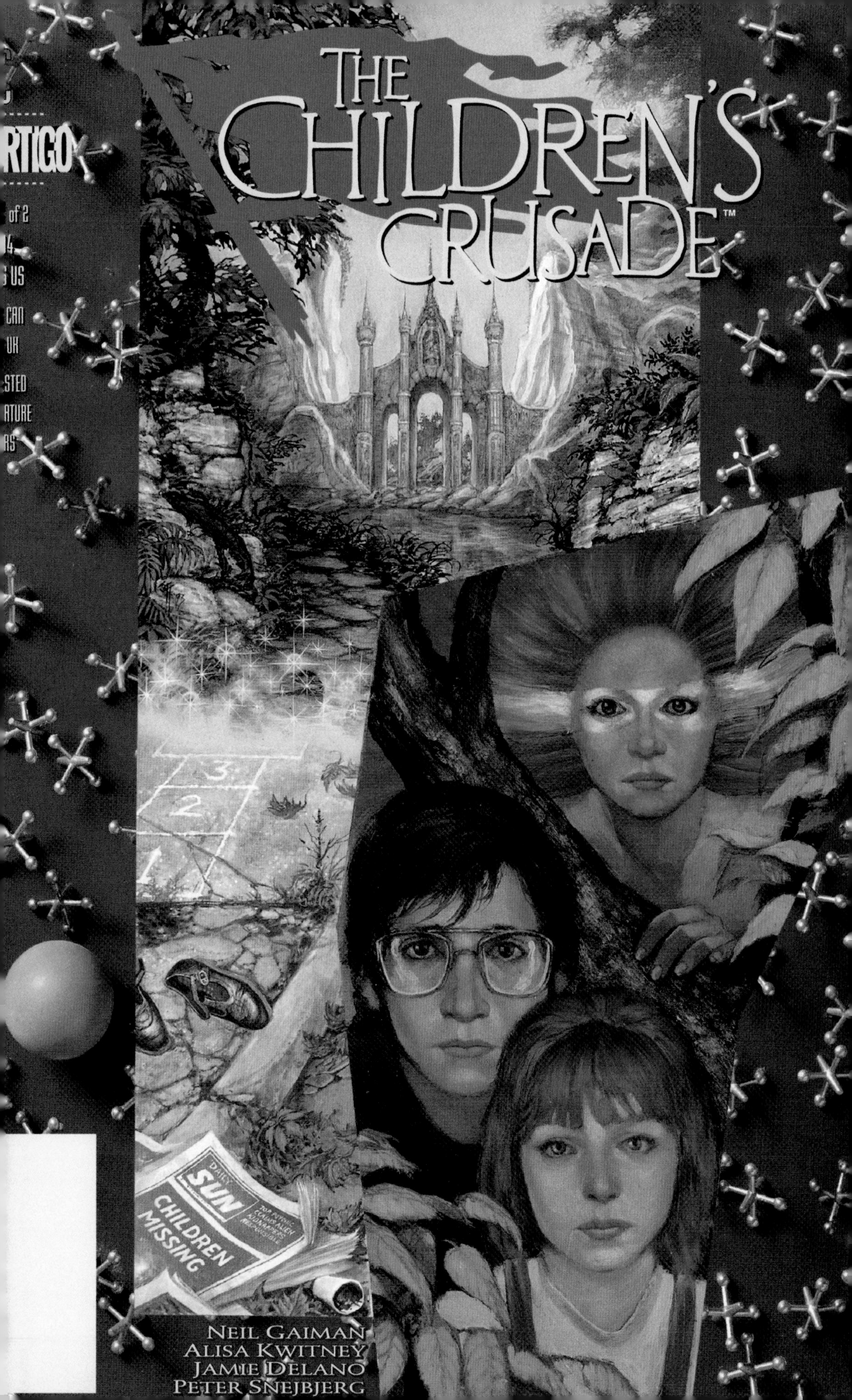

THE CHILDREN'S CRUSADE™
of 2
DAILY SUN
CHILDREN MISSING
NEIL GAIMAN
ALISA KWITNEY
JAMIE DELANO
PETER SNEJBJERG

THE SANDMAN VOL. 4:
SEASON OF MISTS

READ THE COMPLETE
SERIES!

THE SANDMAN VOL. 1:
PRELUDES &
NOCTURNES

THE SANDMAN VOL. 2:
THE DOLL'S HOUSE

THE SANDMAN VOL. 3:
DREAM COUNTRY

THE SANDMAN VOL. 4:
SEASON OF MISTS

THE SANDMAN VOL. 5:
A GAME OF YOU

THE SANDMAN VOL. 6:
FABLES &
REFLECTIONS

THE SANDMAN VOL. 7:
BRIEF LIVES

THE SANDMAN VOL. 8:
WORLDS' END

THE SANDMAN VOL. 9:
THE KINDLY ONES

THE SANDMAN VOL. 10:
THE WAKE

THE SANDMAN:
ENDLESS NIGHTS

THE SANDMAN: THE
DREAM HUNTERS

NOW WITH FULLY
REMASTERED
COLORING

FROM THE *NEW YORK TIMES* # 1 BEST-SELLING AUTHOR

NEIL GAIMAN

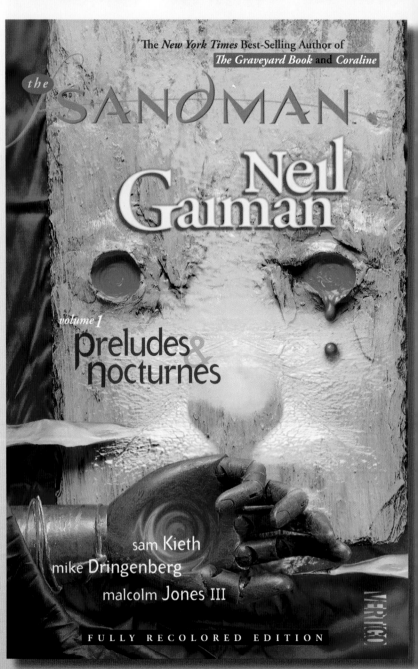

The *New York Times* Best-Selling Author of *The Graveyard Book* and *Coraline*

the SANDMAN

Neil Gaiman

volume 1
preludes &
nocturnes

sam Kieth
mike Dringenberg
malcolm Jones III

FULLY RECOLORED EDITION

VERTIGO

READ THE ENTIRE SERIES!

THE UNWRITTEN VOL. 3:
DEAD MAN'S KNOCK

THE UNWRITTEN
VOL. 4: LEVIATHAN

THE UNWRITTEN VOL. 1:
TOMMY TAYLOR AND
THE BOGUS IDENTITY

THE UNWRITTEN VOL. 2:
INSIDE MAN

THE UNWRITTEN VOL. 3:
DEAD MAN'S KNOCK

THE UNWRITTEN VOL. 4:
LEVIATHAN

THE UNWRITTEN VOL. 5:
ON TO GENESIS

THE UNWRITTEN VOL. 6:
TOMMY TAYLOR AND
THE WAR OF WORDS

THE UNWRITTEN VOL 7:
THE WOUND

THE UNWRITTEN VOL.
8: ORPHEUS IN THE
UNDERWORLD

THE UNWRITTEN:
TOMMY TAYLOR AND
THE SHIP THAT SANK
TWICE

FROM THE WRITER OF *LUCIFER* AND *HELLBLAZER*

MIKE CAREY
with PETER GROSS

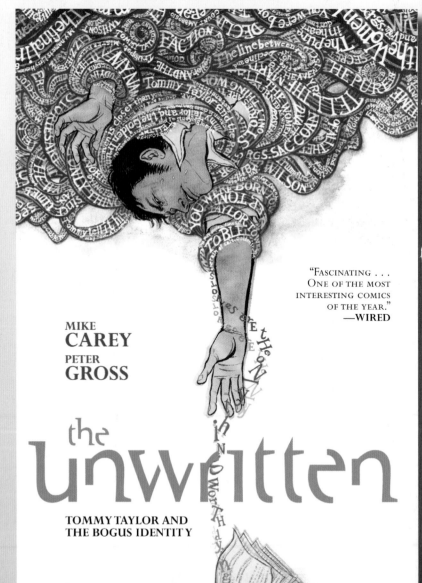

MIKE
CAREY

PETER
GROSS

the
unwritten

TOMMY TAYLOR AND
THE BOGUS IDENTITY

INTRODUCTION BY
BILL WILLINGHAM
CREATOR OF FABLES

*"FASCINATING . . .
ONE OF THE MOST
INTERESTING COMICS
OF THE YEAR."*
—WIRED

VERTIGO